THE CHILD'S CONCEPTION
OF THE WORLD

DIANA

The Child's Conception of the World

By

JEAN PIAGET

Doctor of Science, Professor at the University of Geneva, Director of the International Bureau of Education, Co-Director of the Institut J. J. Rousseau, Geneva; Author of "Language and Thought of the Child," "Judgment and Reasoning in the Child," "The Psychology of Intelligence"

Translated by

JOAN and ANDREW TOMLINSON

LITTLEFIELD ADAMS QUALITY PAPERBACKS

LITTLEFIELD ADAMS QUALITY PAPERBACKS

a division of Rowman & Littlefield Publishers, Inc.
8705 Bollman Place, Savage, Maryland 20763

Reprinted by arrangement with Humanities Press, Inc.

For sale only in the U.S.A., its possessions, and territories.

First published in the English language by Routledge and
Kegan Paul, Ltd., London, in 1929 and reprinted in 1951.

ISBN 0-8226-0213-X

Printed in the United States of America

CONTENTS

INTRODUCTION

PROBLEMS AND METHODS

THE subject of this investigation—one of the most important but also one of the most difficult in child psychology—is as follows: What conceptions of the world does the child naturally form at the different stages of its development? There are two essential standpoints from which the problem must be studied. Firstly, what is the modality of child thought: in other words, what is the scheme of reality which prompts this thought? Does the child, in fact, believe, as we do, in a real world and does he distinguish the belief from the various fictions of play and of imagination? To what extent does he distinguish the external world from an internal or subjective world and what limits does he draw between his self and objective reality? These are the questions which make up the first problem, the child's notion of *reality*.

A second fundamental problem is bound up with that just stated; namely the significance of explanations put forward by the child. What use does he make of the notions of cause and of law? What is the nature of the causality he accepts? Explanation as exercised by savages or in the sciences has been studied, as also the various forms of philosophical explanation. Is the form of explanation presented by the child of a new type? These and like questions form the second problem, the child's notion of *causality*. These two questions of what reality and causality mean to the child are the subject of this book and of its sequel.[1] It is clear from the outset that these problems are distinct from those dealt with in

[1] *La causalité physique chez l'enfant.*

1

a previous work.[1] There the problem was an analysis of the form and functioning of child thought ; here it is an analysis of its content. The two questions though closely related are in their nature distinguishable. The form and functioning of thought are manifested every time the child comes into contact with other children or with an adult and constitute a form of social behaviour, observable from without. The content, on the contrary, may or may not be apparent and varies with the child and the things of which it is speaking. It is a system of intimate beliefs and it requires a special technique to bring them to the light of day. Above all it is a system of mental tendencies and predilections of which the child himself has never been consciously aware and of which he never speaks.

Hence it is not merely useful but essential, first to examine the methods to be employed in studying these beliefs. To judge of the logic of children it is often enough simply to talk with them or to observe them among themselves. To arrive at their beliefs requires a special method which, it must be confessed outright, is not only difficult and tedious, but demands also an outlook, the fruit of at least one or two full years' training. Mental specialists, trained in clinical practice, will immediately appreciate the reason. In order to assess a child's statement at its true worth the most minute precautions are necessary. Some account of these precautions must now be given, since if the reader ignores them he is likely to falsify completely the meaning of the pages which follow and, moreover, to mismanage the experiments should he, as we hope, decide to check them by repeating them himself.

§ 1. METHOD OF TESTS, PURE OBSERVATION AND THE CLINICAL METHOD.—The first method that presents itself as a means of solving the given problem is

[1] J. Piaget, *Studies in Child Logic :*
    Vol. I. *Language and Thought in the Child.* Kegan Paul. 1926.
    Vol. II. *Judgment and Reasoning in the Child.* Kegan Paul. 1928.

that of *tests*; that is to say, the method of posing
questions so arranged as to satisfy the two following
requirements : first, that the question and the conditions in which it is submitted remain the same
for each child, second that each answer be related to
a scale or schedule which serves as a standard of comparison both qualitative and quantitative. The advantages of this method are indisputable in diagnosing
children individually. For general psychology also
the resulting statistics often provide useful information.
But for our particular purpose the test method has two
important defects. Firstly, it does not allow a sufficient
analysis of the results. When working under the stereo-
typed conditions which the test method demands only
rough results can be obtained, which, though interesting
in practice, are too often useless as theory, owing to the
lack of context. This, however, is of slight importance, for
it is obvious that with sufficient ingenuity, the tests can
be so varied as to reveal all the components of a given
psychological reaction. The essential failure of the test
method in the researches with which we are concerned,
is that it falsifies the natural mental inclination of the
subject or at least risks so doing. For example, in trying
to find out how a child conceives the movement of the
sun and moon the question may be asked, " What makes
the sun move ? " The child perhaps answers, " God
makes it move," or " the wind blows it," etc. Such
answers are not to be neglected, even if they be only
the result of " romancing," that is of that peculiar tendency of children to invent when embarrassed by a given
question. However, even had this test been applied to
children of all ages, no real advance would have been made,
since it may well be that a child would never put the
question to itself in such a form or even that it would
never have asked such a question at all. The child may
quite possibly imagine the sun to be a living being moving
of its own accord. In asking " what makes the sun move ? "
the suggestion of an outside agent occurs at once, thus

provoking the creation of a myth. Or in asking the question " How does the sun move ?" one may be suggesting the idea of " how "—perhaps also not previously present— thus stimulating fresh myths such as, " the sun moves by breathing," or " because of the heat," or " it rolls," etc. The only way to avoid such difficulties is to vary the questions, to make counter-suggestions, in short, to give up all idea of a fixed questionnaire.

The same is true in mental pathology. A case of *dementia præcox* may have a sufficient gleam of memory to state correctly who his father was, though habitually he believes himself to be of illustrious parentage. But the real problem is to know how he frames the question to himself or if he frames it at all. The skill of the practitioner consists not in making him answer questions but in making him talk freely and thus encouraging the flow of his spontaneous tendencies instead of diverting it into the artificial channels of set question and answer. It consists n placing every symptom in its mental context rather than in abstracting it from its context.

In short, the test method has its uses, but for the present problem it tends to falsify the perspective by diverting the child from his natural inclination. It tends to neglect the spontaneous interests and primitive re- actions of the child as well as other essential problems.

The question of pure observation next arises. Obser- vation must be at once the starting point of all research dealing with child thought and also the final control on the experiments it has inspired. In the case of the present research it is the observation of the spontaneous questions of children which furnishes data of the highest importance. The detailed study of the contents of these questions reveals the interests of children at different ages and reveals to us those questions which the child is revolving in its own mind and which might never have occurred to us, or which we should never have framed in such terms. Further, a study of the exact form of the questions in- dicates the child's implicit solutions, for almost every question contains its solution in the manner in which it is asked. For example, when a child asks " who made the sun ? " it is clear he thinks of the sun as the product of an act of creation. Or again, when a child asks why there are two Mount Salèves, the big Salève and the little Salève, when there are not two Matterhorns, he evidently imagines mountains as arranged according to a plan which excludes all chance.

We may thus state the first rule of our method. When a particular group of explanations by children is to be investigated, the questions we shall ask them will be determined in matter and in form, by the spontaneous questions actually asked by children of the same age or younger. It is also important, before drawing conclusions from the results of an investigation, to seek corroboration in a study of the spontaneous questions of children. It can then be seen whether the notions ascribed to them do or do not correspond with the questions they themselves ask and the manner in which they ask them.

For example, we shall study later in this volume the question of animism in children. We shall see that when questioned as to whether the sun, etc., is alive, knows, feels, etc., children at a certain age reply in the affirmative. But is this a spontaneous notion or is it a reply suggested directly or indirectly by the question ? To solve this we must search for an indication among collections of children's questions, where we shall find that a certain child of six and a half, Del (see *Language and Thought*, Chapter I, § 8), on seeing a ball rolling in the direction of the observer asked spontaneously, " Does it know you're there ? " We also see that Del asked a great number of questions in order to find out whether an object, such as a leaf, was inanimate or alive. Further, we see that Del, in answer to the statement that dead leaves are certainly dead, retorted " but they move with the wind ! " (*ibid.*, § 8). Thus some children by the form of their questions show that they connect life with movement. These facts show that an interrogatory on animism, undertaken in such a way (for example by asking in the manner of Del if a moving object " knows " that it is moving), is not artificial and that the connection between life and movement corresponds to something spontaneous in the child.

But if the necessity for direct observation is thus made clear its drawbacks are also obvious. The method of pure observation is not only tedious and seemingly unable to guarantee the quality of the results, except at the expense of their quantity (it is, in fact, impossible to observe a large number of children under similar conditions), but also it seems to contain certain systematic defects the two chief of which are as follows.

In the first place, the child's intellectual egocentricity constitutes a serious obstacle to knowing him by pure observation unaided by questions. We have, in fact, attempted to show elsewhere (*Language and Thought*, Chapters I-II) that the child neither spontaneously seeks nor is able to communicate the whole of his thought. Further, if in the society of other children, the conversation may be associated with his immediate activity or play, thus giving no clue to that essential fragment of his thought which is not concerned with action and which develops by being in touch with various adult activities or with nature. In this case conceptions of the world and of physical causality will appear not to interest him at all. Or again, if in the society of adults, he may ask questions interminably but without ever seeking explanations of his own. These he withholds at first because he feels they must be known to every one, then, later, from shame, from fear of being wrong and from fear of disillusion. He is silent about them especially because he regards these explanations, being his own, as not only the most natural but also as the only ones possible. In short, even that which could be explained in words, ordinarily remains implicit, simply because the child's thought is not so socialised as our own. But alongside of those thoughts which can be expressed, at least internally, how many inexpressible thoughts must remain unknown so long as we restrict ourselves to observing the child without talking to him ? By inexpressible thoughts are meant tendencies of mind, syncretic schemas, both visual and motor, in short, all those primitive associations whose existence one feels directly one starts talking with a child. These primitive associations are of the greatest importance, and to bring them to light special methods must be employed.

The second drawback to the method of pure observation is the difficulty of distinguishing a child's play from his beliefs. Take the example of a child, who, imagining himself to be alone, says to the roller : " Have you flattened out all those big stones ? " Is he playing or does he really personify the machine ? In a particular case it is impossible to judge with conviction. Pure observation is inadequate for distinguishing belief from romancing. The only valid criteria, as we shall see later, are based on multiplicity of results and on the comparison of individual reactions.

It is therefore essential to go beyond the method of pure observation and without falling into the pitfalls of the test method, to take full advantage of what may be gained from experiment. With this in view we shall use a third method which claims to unite what is most expedient in the methods of test and of direct observation, whilst avoiding their respective disadvantages : this is the method of clinical examination, used by psychiatrists as a means of diagnosis. For example, one may for months examine certain cases of paranœa without once seeing the idea of grandeur assert itself, though the impression of it is behind every unusual reaction. Moreover, though there are not differentiated tests for every type of morbid condition, yet the practitioner is able both to talk freely with the patient whilst watching carefully for evidences of morbid obsession, and furthermore to lead him gently towards the critical zones (birth, race, fortune, military rank or political standing, mystic life, etc.) naturally without knowing exactly where the obsession may suddenly crop up, but constantly maintaining the conversation on fertile soil. The clinical examination is thus experimental in the sense that the practitioner sets himself a problem, makes hypotheses, adapts the conditions to them and finally controls each hypothesis by testing it against the reactions he stimulates in conversation. But the clinical examination is also dependent on direct observation, in the sense that the good practitioner lets himself be led, though always in control, and takes account of the whole of the mental context, instead of being the victim of " systematic error " as so often happens to the pure experimenter.

Since the clinical method has rendered such important service in a domain where formerly all was disorder and confusion, child psychology would make a great mistake to neglect it. There is in fact no reason, à priori, why children should not be questioned on those points where pure observation leaves the research in doubt. The recognition by the psychologist of mythomania and of suggestibility in the child, and of the fallacies these bring in their train, affords no ground why he should not question the child for the purpose of determining precisely, by clinical examination, the exact part which suggestion and romancing play in the answers.

It is unnecessary to quote examples here, since the following work is principally a collection of clinical observations. It is true that in the nature of things we shall be compelled to schematise our cases, not by summarising them (which would be to misrepresent them), but by taking from reports of conversation only those passages which have a direct interest. From many pages of notes taken in every case we shall thus record only a few lines. It has also not been thought useful to give here complete examples of examinations, since the clinical method can only be learned by long practice. Moreover, it is our opinion that in child psychology as in pathological psychology, at least a year of daily practice is necessary before passing beyond the inevitable fumbling

stage of the beginner. It is so hard not to talk too much
when questioning a child, especially for a pedagogue ! It
is so hard not to be suggestive ! And above all, it is so
hard to find the middle course between systematisation due
to preconceived ideas and incoherence due to the absence
of any directing hypothesis ! The good experimenter
must, in fact, unite two often incompatible qualities ; he
must know how to observe, that is to say, to let the child
talk freely, without ever checking or side-tracking his
utterance, and at the same time he must constantly be
alert for something definitive, at every moment he must
have some working hypothesis, some theory, true or false,
which he is seeking to check. To appreciate the real
difficulty of the clinical method one must have taught it.
When students begin they either suggest to the child all
they hope to find, or they suggest nothing at all, because
they are not on the look-out for anything, in which case,
to be sure, they will never find anything.

In short, it is no simple task, and the material it yields
needs subjecting to the strictest criticism. The psychologist must in fact make up for the uncertainties in the
method of interrogation by sharpening the subtleties of
his interpretation. But, here again, the beginner is
threatened by two opposing dangers, those of attributing
either its *maximum* or its *minimum* value to everything
the child says. The greatest enemies of the clinical
method are those who unduly simplify the results of an
interrogatory, those who either accept every answer the
child makes as pure gold or those on the other hand who
class all as dross. The first, naturally, are the more
dangerous, but both fall into the same error, that is, of
supposing that everything a child may say, during a
quarter, half or three-quarters of an hour of conversation,
lies on the same psychological level—that of considered
belief, for example, or of romancing, etc.

The essence of the critical method is, on the contrary,
to separate the wheat from the tares and to keep every
answer in its mental context. For the context may be

one of reflection or of spontaneous belief, of play or of prattle, of effort and interest or of fatigue ; and above all there are certain subjects who inspire confidence right from the beginning, who can be seen to reflect and consider, and there are others of whom one feels equally certain that they pay no heed to the questions and only talk rubbish in their replies.

It is impossible to state here the precise rules for the diagnosis of these individual reactions, this must be the result of practice. But to render more intelligible the way in which the following observations were chosen from amongst all those at our disposal (for this volume more than 600 observations were collected by the author and on many special points our collaborators further examined a large number of subjects), we shall attempt to classify in certain broad categories the various possible types of answer. As these types are of very unequal value it is important to bear in mind a clear outline of this classification, so as to be able to assign due value to the interpretations.

§ 2. THE FIVE TYPES OF REACTION REVEALED BY CLINICAL EXAMINATION.—When the child appears uninterested in the question and is not stimulated to any effort of adaptation, it replies at random and whatever first comes into its head, without so much as trying to find fun in it or to invent an answer. We shall speak of this reaction as the *answer at random* (called by Binet and Simon " *le n'importequisme* "). When the child, without further reflection, replies to the question by inventing an answer in which he does not really believe, or in which he believes merely by force of saying it, we shall speak of *romancing*. When the child makes an effort to reply to the question but either the question is suggestive or the child is simply trying to satisfy the examiner without attempting to think for himself, we shall use the term *suggested conviction*. We shall include perseveration under this head when it is the result of the questions being in a suggestive series. In other cases perseveration must be regarded as a form of the " answer at random." When the child replies after reflection, drawing the answer from the stores of his own mind, without suggestion, although the question is new to him, we shall say there is *liberated conviction*. The liberated conviction is necessarily influenced by the examination, since the particular way in which the question is worded and presented to the child forces it to reason along a certain line and to systematise its knowledge in a particular manner, but none the less it is an original product of the child's thought, since neither the reasoning it performs in order to answer the question nor the sum total of the previous knowledge on which it draws during its reflection are directly influenced by the experimenter. The liberated conviction is thus, strictly speaking, neither spontaneous nor suggested; it is the result of reasoning, performed to order, but by means of original material (previous knowledge, mental images, motor schemas, syncretic associations, etc.) and original logical instruments (method of reasoning, natural tendencies of mind, intellectual habits, etc.). Finally, when the child has no need of reasoning to answer the question, but can give an answer forthwith because already formulated or capable of being formulated, there is *spontaneous conviction*. There is thus spontaneous conviction when the problem is not new to the child and when the reply is the result of a previous original reflection. We shall naturally exclude from this type of reaction, as from the preceding, answers influenced by teaching received previous to the examination. This involves a separate and naturally very complex problem, which consists in distinguishing from among the answers received those that are the child's own and those that are drawn from its adult environment. We shall reconsider this question later. For the moment we are concerned with more clearly distinguishing the five types of reaction just enumerated, and shall start with the last.

That the clinical examination reveals the existence of spontaneous convictions and aids the child in formulating them for himself is incontestable. These convictions are rare, in the sense that they are the hardest to arrive at, but they nevertheless exist. We shall see, for example, that boys of an average age of 8 can give a correct description in words and a complete diagram of the mechanism of a bicycle. It is evident that such a result and such a synchronism in individual answers point to reflection previous to the examination, even were there no evidence of children asking questions concerning the details of a bicycle. We shall also see that it is enough to ask children of 6-8, " What is the sun doing while you are walking ? " to be told without more ado that the sun and moon follow them, moving and stopping when they do. The constancy of these answers and the spontaneity of the statement compared with the vague nature of the question undoubtedly mark the spontaneous conviction, that is to say a conviction established before the question was asked.

But it is not so much the existence of the spontaneous conviction that the reader will feel inclined to dispute as the boundary line to be distinguished between the spontaneous and the liberated conviction. It is true that one frequently experiences the impression that a question set to a child is one that it has never yet given a thought to, and yet the unexpected originality of the reply seems to indicate previous reflection. How is the line of demarcation to be fixed ? For instance we may ask a child, " Where does night come from ? " In such a form, the question contains no suggestion. The child hesitates, tries to avoid the question and finally replies that it is big black clouds which make night. Is this a spontaneous conviction or is it rather that the child, having never considered such a question, seeks an answer in the simplest hypothesis, and one making the least demand on the imagination ? Either interpretation can be advanced. Both are probably true. Certain children on being asked why the clouds appear, answer, " to make it night." In such cases the explanation of the clouds by the night is clearly spontaneous. In other cases one has the impression that the child is inventing his explanation on the spot ?

It is interesting to observe that in such a case the spontaneous conviction coincides with the liberated conviction, but it is obvious that in general and even in this particular case they have not the same value for the psychologist.

It is naturally quite useless to ask children if they have ever thought about the question asked. Either from lack of memory or of introspection, they are quite unable to say.

But the question whether it is possible in every case to distinguish the spontaneous conviction from the liberated conviction is not very important. The study of the *liberated conviction* is however of the greatest interest. It is important to insist on this, since it is essential to our scheme. It is a question of fact beyond challenge by any theoretical argument that the liberated conviction shows the same uniformity as the spontaneous conviction.

For example, we made the following simple experiment: a stone was dropped into a glass half full of water placed in front of a child who was asked why the level of the water rose. The answers given expressed a liberated conviction in the majority of cases, that is to say in those cases where the child was not already aware that the level of the water would rise when the stone was dropped in. All the children under 9 declared that the water rose because the stone was "heavy," and the rest of the experiment showed that they did not consider the volume of the object but only its weight. Here then is a solution arrived at on the spot but showing a remarkable uniformity amongst different children. In this work will be found a multitude of other examples showing the uniformity of the liberated conviction.

We thus see that even when the solution is invented by the child during the experiment itself, it is not invented from nothing. It implies previously formed schemas, tendencies of mind, intellectual habits, etc. The golden rule is to avoid suggestion, that is to say to avoid dictating a particular answer among all the possible answers. But on the assumption that the liberated conviction can be distinguished from the spontaneous conviction the former are worth serious study, for they reveal, if nothing more, the child's mental predilections.

Let us take another example. A child asked us, " Who made the sun ? " We took this question and put it to a number of little children in the non-suggestive form : " How did the sun begin ? " All the children declared that men had made it. Let us suppose this to be a mere invention of the moment and that the children had never before thought of such a question. There is here a solution which, in the first place, every child chose in preference to a number of others, and in the second place which they refused to set aside even under the pressure of our counter-suggestions. It seems then probable that this artificialist answer, even if of the liberated type, is connected with a latent artificialism, an artificialist tendency of mind natural to children. Naturally this remains to be proved but good grounds are afforded for stating the problem thus. Moreover, the child would not abandon his hypothesis during the remainder of the examination notwithstanding our attempts to make him. This gives a second indication showing that natural tendencies at variance with this artificialist attitude are slight. Otherwise it would be easy to make the child alter his view, to make him invent something else, etc.

In short, the study of the liberated conviction is certainly a justifiable one. The method consists of questioning the child on all his surroundings. The hypothesis is the assertion that the child invents his explanations in such a way as to reveal something of the spontaneous tendencies of his mind. In order to obtain any results by this method it must naturally be checked by a rigorous control, both as regards the manner of asking the questions and the interpretation of the answers. These rules we shall presently seek to formulate.

If the line of demarcation between the liberated and the spontaneous conviction is of only relative importance it is on the contrary absolutely necessary clearly to distinguish the liberated conviction from the *suggested conviction*. It must not be thought that suggestion is easily avoided. A long apprenticeship is necessary before one can learn to recognise and avoid the numerous forms of suggestion possible. Two varieties are particularly dangerous, *verbal suggestion* and *suggestion by perseveration*.

The former is easily distinguished in general but is very difficult to detect in detail. The only means of avoiding it is to learn children's talk and to frame the questions in this language. It is thus necessary when beginning an inquiry on a new topic to make the children talk first, simply as a means of acquiring a vocabulary that avoids all suggestion. Without so doing it is impossible to foresee the far-reaching effects that some apparently inoffensive word may occasion. For example, such words as " going along," " walking," " moving " (" avancer," " marcher," " bouger ") are certainly not synonyms to a child. The sun goes along but it does not move, etc. If one carelessly uses a particular word that is unexpected to the child, one risks stimulating, simply by suggestion, animistic or anthropomorphic reactions which might then be mistaken for spontaneous.

Suggestion due to perseveration is still harder to avoid, for the simple fact of continuing the conversation after the child's first answer tends to make him perseverate along the line he has already adopted. Further, any set examination arranged in series tends to cause perseveration. For example, to ask a child if a fish, a bird, the sun, the moon, the clouds, the wind, etc., are alive is to urge him to say " Yes " to all, simply by force of example. In such a case the answers are evidently " suggested " and certainly not " liberated " in the sense in which we are using the term.

The suggested conviction is of no interest to the psychologist. Whilst the liberated conviction reveals habits of mind formed previous to the examination although systematised under its influence, the suggested conviction reveals nothing beyond the child's suggestibility, which has no bearing on the conceptions it forms of the world.

One would like to be able to rule out *romancing* with the same severity. But the question of romancing is one of the most delicate raised by the clinical study of the child. When the questions are set to children, especially to those of less than 7 or 8 years, it often happens that, looking perfectly candid and serious the while, they merely make fun of the question and invent an answer simply because they like the sound of it. The solution, in this case, is not suggested, since it is completely free and unexpected, and yet it is not to be classed with the liberated conviction for the simple reason that it is not a conviction. The child is simply playing and if he comes to believe what he says it is merely by force of saying it and in the same way as he believes in his games, for the sole reason that he wants to believe in them. But the exact significance of this romancing is a very delicate question. There are three possible solutions. The first consists in comparing the romancing to what in a normal adult one would call "*rotting*." The child makes up the answer to make fun of the psychologist and principally to avoid having to think more about a question which he finds both dull and tiring. This is certainly the correct interpretation in the majority of the cases—which are however more or less rare—found after the age of 8. But it does not explain all the cases before the age of 7 or 8 and there are two other possible solutions.

The second solution compares romancing with the mythomania of the hysteric. The child thus invents, not so much to laugh at the world as because this is a natural process of his thought, and in the case of problems he finds tiresome, the most useful one. According to this second solution the child is partly taken in by it himself, and romances on his own account, as for instance when he resolves for himself some private problem of his own. This is certainly often the case with small children of about 4 or 5. Every one is familiar with the rhetorical questions small children ask aloud and to which they immediately supply the answer themselves. Nagy[1] quotes the following question, " Why have bears got four feet ? " to which the child at once replied : " Because they've been naughty and God has punished them." This is both pure monologue and romance.

Seen in this light romancing has some interest. It explains the solutions a child will give when it can find no better, and thus serves as an indication, negative it is true, but none the less often useful. It is in this sense that romancing answers from children of 4-6 will sometimes be quoted in the course of this work. But it is obvious that care must be taken not to draw from such facts more than a negative indication. The study of romancing as such yields nothing like the wealth of material to be found in the study of the liberated conviction.

Finally, according to the third solution, it is possible that romancing contains traces of earlier convictions or more rarely anticipations of a future one. When we are in the process of relinquishing a cherished conviction by progressive stages we often as it were still play with it, sympathetically, yet without any longer believing in it. So, allowing for the different circumstances, the child's romancing sometimes plays a similar rôle. In discussing artificialism (Chapter XI, § 4), we shall see the half mythical romance of a mentally deficient who imagines his parents to have been present at the beginning of the world. This myth embodies the remains of the small child's belief in the omnipotence of its parents.

The problem is exceedingly complex and from the beginning of our research we must be especially careful not to prejudge the nature of romancing. It is interesting in so far as it does not for the child bear the same relation to conviction as it does for us. We must therefore study it. But it is necessary, whatever our aim in studying it, to distinguish it carefully from the liberated conviction.

[1] Nagy, " Die Entwicklung des Interesses," *Zeitschrift f. exp. Päd.* Vol. V, 1907.

In the following section an attempt will be made to give certain criteria by which this may be done.

The *answer at random* still remains to be dealt with. If the question " What do 3 and 3 make ? " be asked a deficient or a child not yet old enough to know, the answer given is a blind shot such as 4 or 10 or 100. In fact the child seldom makes no answer and prefers inventing one to remaining silent. This is not romancing for there is no systematisation in the invention nor does the child take any interest in it. The child romances to amuse itself ; the " answer at random " on the other hand arises from lack of interest.

From the above classification of the different types of possible answer we may remark the following. The spontaneous convictions, that is to say those formed previous to the examination, are the most interesting. The liberated conviction is instructive in so far as it reveals the child's natural trend of mind. Romancing sometimes gives indications—though principally negative —and provided it is interpreted with the necessary prudence. Finally, suggested conviction and the answer at random are to be severely rejected, the former since they only show what the experimenter wanted the child to express and the latter since they merely reveal the subject's lack of comprehension.

§ 3. Rules and Criteria for the Diagnosis of the Preceding Types of Reaction.—Having made clear the object of our research, we shall now attempt to frame certain rules as guides in the selection of the most interesting answers. In other words we shall try and elucidate the practical means of distinguishing the five types of reaction characterised *in abstracto* in the preceding section.

In the first place, how is the suggested conviction to be distinguished from the answer at random ? The suggested conviction is essentially momentary. A counter-suggestion made not necessarily at once but after a short lapse is sufficient to destroy it ; or it is enough merely to let the child talk for a few minutes and then to question it again indirectly on the same subject : the suggested conviction is like a parasite in the child's mind, which tends naturally to rid itself of the foreign matter.

But this first criterion is not enough. Certain children are particularly susceptible and change their opinions so readily on every subject that it is impossible to rely on these oscillations as a guide. The method is then to pursue the examination more closely. The characteristic of suggested convictions is their lack of connection with the subject's other convictions, and also their dissimilarity with the convictions of other children of the same age and class. This yields two supplementary rules. In the first place, to probe all around the suspect answer to see whether or not its roots are solid, and then to ask the question under as many different guises as possible. Suggestion may thus be avoided by means of patience and analysis.

These three criteria will *à fortiori* serve to exclude the answer at random, which is much more unstable even than the suggested conviction. As regards the answer at random and romancing, they are easily distinguished even independently of the context : romancing is much richer and more systematised, the answer at random being more in the nature of a blind alley.

The suggested answer and the answer at random being now recognisable we must next define the criteria for romancing. Of the three preceding rules, two are useless for its detection. Firstly, counter-suggestion is no weapon against it because the romancer resists the contradictor and romances all the harder the more pressing the objections by which he is opposed. Secondly, the analysis of the roots of the given answer is difficult, precisely because romancing is always so rich in its ramifications that it can appear under the deceptive guise of being solidly ensconced in a setting of systematic convictions. Unlike suggestion, romancing is very difficult to recognise in an isolated case. The only method of tracking it down is to multiply cases. In dealing with a large number of subjects, romancing may be distinguished from the liberated and the spontaneous convictions by means of the three following criteria.

By questioning a large number of children of the same age one finds either that the suspected answer is very general or else that it is peculiar to one or two given children. In the first case the chances are against the likelihood of romancing. In fact, since it is both a free and an individual form of invention it is most improbable that all the children would invent in the same way when answering the same question. But this first criterion is not enough because it is quite possible that a certain question is completely incomprehensible at a given age and can only give rise to romancing. Further, in such a case, romancing may tend to move along an obvious line, thus giving rise to uniformity. This interpretation is particularly applicable where artificialism is concerned. For example, children of 4 to 6 are questioned as to how the moon began. Suppose them to find the question incomprehensible, they will then invent a myth and as the simplest is to have recourse to man they will all say " a man made it." We clearly need a more subtle criterion.

There seems to be a second one at hand. Where a large number of children of different ages are questioned it may be that the suspected answer (which is by hypothesis generally in the lowest ages) will disappear entirely at a certain age level and give place to quite another type of answer. The children in this case could be divided into two stages, without an intermediary stage. On the contrary, it may be that the particular answer disappears progressively and gives place to a maturer type of answer only as the climax of a continuous development. Then the children must be divided into three divisions, two extreme stages and an intermediary stage. It is clear that in the latter case the chances of romancing are much less than in the former. For suppose that on a certain question children start with systematic opinions or a strong natural tendency and this opinion is subsequently brought into conflict with experience or teaching then it is evident that adaptation to the new point of view will not be instantaneous but progressive. On the contrary, the absence of intermediaries between two successive groups of answers would certainly seem to indicate that the first group had no value in the eyes of the child and would thus seem to favour a hypothesis of the general existence of romancing during the first stage.

Finally, a third criterion may profitably be studied : the method of arriving at the right answer. In fact if the answers given by the youngest children examined are not romancing, not only ought the disappearance of these answers to be progressive and not sudden, where the children are classified in groups according to their average ages, but also it should be possible to observe the primitive conceptions still clinging to the first correct answers themselves. In other words, if in a given process three stages can be distinguished one of which is intermediary, the type of answer of the first stage ought to be still traceable, not only during the second stage, but right to the beginning of the third. In such a case, it is practically certain that the answers belonging to the first stage do not result from romancing.

Let us take an example. Children in the first stage maintain that the Lake of Geneva was dug by workmen who filled it with water. Children in the second stage still maintain that the lake was dug, but the water has come from the mountains, and originates from rain itself. Finally, in a third stage the child admits that the lake was made according to a natural law, the rivers hollowed it out and feed it with water. We can conclude that the artificialist answers of the first stage are not romancing, for not only are they general, and not only does the existence of the second stage show that the artificialism does not disappear immediately, but also children are found at the beginning of the third stage who still believe that Geneva existed before the lake and that the lake is beside the town " because you must have the town before the lake." The beginning of the third stage thus still shows the persistence of the artificialist trend of mind.

In conclusion, it is clear that it is comparatively easy to distinguish genuine conviction from romancing. The astonishing resemblance of children amongst one another —at any rate of civilised children, of whatever social class, country or language—makes it possible to see fairly rapidly whether a particular conviction is general, lasting, and even capable of resisting the first adult lessons.

On the contrary, it is difficult—and, curiously, this is the only real difficulty we encountered in applying the method—to distinguish the spontaneous conviction from the liberated conviction amongst the answers obtained. As has already been pointed out : (1) Both resist suggestion ; (2) the roots of both lie buried deep in the thought of the subject under examination ; (3) in both a wide generality of ideas occurs in children of the same age ; (4) both last several years, decreasing progressively rather than being suddenly abandoned ; and finally traces of both are still to be found interwoven with the first correct answers, that is to say with answers depending on the pressure of adult environment.

Are all answers then which satisfy these five conditions to be regarded as due to the child's spontaneous convictions ? In other words, shall we admit that everything the child says which passes these tests has been formulated in its thought, previous to the examination ? It goes without saying that this is not the case. The only means of distinguishing the spontaneous from the liberated is by having recourse to pure observation. It is here that every inquiry must end, just as observation must be the inspiration from which every research starts. The study of questions asked by children themselves is in this respect of the greatest help.

But this method is, as we have already shown, very limited in its use. On many points where the answers obtained by the clinical method seem to be highly systematised, children ask few if any questions. This is often precisely because the convictions disclosed by the clinical examinations have never previously been doubted and have thus never provided matter for question. But in such a case, it is not so much a matter of convictions as of tendencies, implicit in the child's natural trend of mind rather than explicitly formulated. They are points of view that remain subconscious, and undefined motive influences rather than conceptions. How then is the spontaneous conviction or tendency to be distinguished from the liberated conviction ? The rules for the clinical examination cannot furnish the solution. It is to be sought rather in the rules for interpretation in general and it is to these we must now turn.

§ 4. RULES FOR THE INTERPRETATION OF THE RESULTS.—In psychology as in physics there are no pure " facts," if by " facts " are meant phenomena presented nakedly to the mind by nature itself, independent respec-. tively of hypotheses by means of which the mind examines them, of principles governing the interpretation of experience, and of the systematic framework of existing judgments into which the observer pigeon-holes every new observation. We must therefore define at least the general principles which are to guide us in interpreting the children's answers to our questions. Otherwise the reader will be raising mistaken difficulties from the outset—such for example as, What natural trend of mind leads the child to certain replies rather than to others when the reaction is of the liberated type ? What part does the adult play in the child's convictions, etc.?

But the contrary danger of prejudging the nature of the results before they have themselves been analysed, must also be avoided. The important thing is to find a number of rules of interpretation which will unite the maximum of flexibility with the maximum of strictness, in so far as these two requisites can be reconciled. Put more simply, we must find out what rules must be followed to avoid the dangers of premature judgment.

In this connection two points are of especial importance. The first concerns the relation between the verbal formula or conscious systematisation the child gives to its beliefs at the moment of the examination, and the preconscious trend of mind which has urged the child to invent, in whole or in part, a particular solution. For example a child gives an answer which is clearly liberated, that is to say, that we can as it were see the conviction forming under our eyes. Is this answer to be treated as if it was of the " spontaneous " type, or should we rather interpret it by taking account not so much of the actual answer as it stands, as of the tendencies which guided the child in its search ? But in this case how is the choice to be made and how are these tendencies of the child to be interpreted without distorting them ? The question is of extreme importance, in fact the whole value of the clinical method depends on its solution.

There are two conflicting alternatives. The first is that of certain child psychologists who reject, as devoid of significance, all results determined strictly by question and answer (though naturally only so far as such an examination aims at revealing the child's convictions and conceptions and not simply subjecting it to scholastic or mental tests). For these authors every examination tends to falsify perspective and pure observation alone provides an objective standpoint. But to so reserved a view the fact may always be opposed that the results of examinations are constant, at least on an average. When children are questioned as to the meaning of thinking or of names, all the youngest (or at least a sufficiently high number to warrant the word " all ") reply that thinking is with the mouth and that words or names reside in the things, etc. Such uniformity confronts the detractors of the method of examination and justifies, without further grounds, the continuation of this means of research.

The alternative solution is that of those psychologists who regard every answer, or at any rate every " liberated " answer (in opposition to those which come from suggestion, romancing, or want of reflection), as being the expression

of the child's spontaneous thought. This is what certain
contributors to the *Pedagogical Seminary* seem to hold for
example. If these authors are to be believed it is enough
to set a number of questions to children and to collect
their answers to obtain " children's ideas " or " child
theories," etc. Without wishing in the least to misrepresent the value and interest of many of these inquiries,
we think none the less that this value is often something
quite other than what the authors suppose. In other words
we regard as very doubtful the principle according to
which no matter what answer, so long as it be neither
suggested nor the fruit of romancing, possesses the same
coefficient of spontaneity as the answer of a normal adult,
given in the course of an examination, or as a child's
original conviction observed without interference or
examination. It is true that such a principle may give
rise to certain accurate conclusions, but only by chance,
just as truth may often issue from what is false. As a
general principle it is altogether erroneous, and it is
alarming to think of the exaggerations that would result
from questioning children on a number of subjects and
regarding the answers thus obtained as being all of
equal value, and as revealing equally the child's
mentality.

These considerations point the way to the rule of the
just mean : to regard every liberated conviction as an
index, and to seek by means of this index the trend of
mind that is thus revealed. This research itself may be
guided by the following principle. Observation shows
that the child's thought has little systematisation, little
coherence, is not in general deductive, is for the most part
untroubled by the need of avoiding contradiction, juxta-
poses statements rather than synthesises them and accepts
syncretic schemas without feeling the need to analyse. In
other words, the child's thought more nearly resembles
a sum total of inclinations resulting from both action and
reverie (play combining these two processes, which are
the simplest to yield organic satisfaction) than it resembles

the self-conscious and systematic thought of the adult. Therefore, to arrive at the trend of mind by a liberated conviction, the principle is to strip this conviction of every systematic element.

To achieve this, the influence of the question set must first be discounted, that is to say one must abstract from the child's answer the fact that it is an answer. For example, if one asks " how did the sun begin ? " and the child replies " men made it " the only indication to be retained is that there exists for the child a vague connection between the sun and men, or that men count for something in the nature of the sun. If to the questions " how did the names of things begin ? " and " where are the names ? " the child answers that the names come from the things themselves and are in things, all we may conclude is that for the child names belong more to objects than to the subject who thinks of them and that the child is realist from its natural trend of mind. Care must be taken in these two examples not to claim for the child a spontaneous inclination to state the origin of the sun and moon (unless pure observation shows such) nor a concern as to the place of names. The only information that the answer yields is so to speak the direction towards which it points, an artificialist direction as regards the first example, and a realist direction as regards the second.

Next the answers obtained must be stripped of all logical character and care taken not to introduce an artificial coherence where coherence is of an organic rather than a logical character. Thus children will answer that the sun, the moon, the sky, the night are made of clouds and that the clouds are of smoke. The lightning and the stars are of fire which comes from the smoke, etc. A delightful system, according to which the smoke from the chimney is the principle of meteorology and astronomy! Only it does not happen to be a system. The connecting links are only partly realised, half formulated and sketched in the rough rather than clearly outlined. Further, these associations do not exclude others, and others that seem to us to contradict them—thus the child may conceive these same objects as living and conscious, etc.

Finally, an attempt must be made to strip the answers of their verbal element. There is certainly present to the child a whole world of thought, incapable of formulation and made up of images and motor schemas combined. Out of it issue, at least partially, ideas of force, life, weight, etc., and the relations of objects amongst themselves are penetrated with these indefinable associations. When the child is questioned he translates his thought into words, but these words are necessarily inadequate. Thus the child says it is the sun which " makes " the clouds move. Is this to be taken as meaning that the sun attracts or repels the clouds, or that it chases them as a policeman chases a thief and thus " makes " them run away ? Either is possible. But, here again, the important thing is the attitude rather than the formula, the direction of the thought rather than the answer given.

Briefly, the principle for the interpretation of the liberated answer, and also in part for the spontaneous answer, is to regard these answers as symptoms rather than as realities. But where draw the line in this critical elimination ? Pure observation must decide. If a large number of children's questions are examined and the answers obtained by clinical examination compared with these spontaneous questions, it will be seen in what measure a certain trend of thought corresponds with questions systematically asked. Thus, as regards artificialism, but little observation will show that the connection between men and things often assumes spontaneously in the child the relation of maker to thing made : the child spontaneously asks certain questions concerning origin and asks them in such a way as to imply from the start the notion that it is men who have made or contributed towards making the things.

But the above rules will not suffice to resolve all the problems involved in the interpretation of the answers. Unfortunately the study of the child raises a much more

serious difficulty, that of distinguishing from among the
results of the examination the part to be regarded as the
child's original contribution and that due to previous
adult influences.

Put in this form the problem is insoluble.   It involves,
in fact, two quite distinct questions.   The history of the
child's intellectual development is largely the history of
the progressive socialisation of its individual thought, at
first resisting adaptation to social conditions, then becoming increasingly penetrated by surrounding adult
influences.   In this respect all the child's thought is
destined, from the commencement of language, to be
absorbed progressively in adult thought.   Here arises the
first problem.   What is the evolution of this socialisation ?
From the fact that there is progressive socialisation it
follows that throughout the whole course of the child's
development, the contents of its thought fall into two
categories :   one due to adult influence and the other to
the child's original reactions.   In other words, the child's
convictions are the product of a reaction influenced but
not dictated by the adult.   This reaction certainly merits
a study and will be treated during the course of this work.
For the present it is enough to realise that there are three
factors in the problem ;   namely, the world to which the
child adapts itself, the child's own world of thought and
the adult society which influences this thought.   But, on
the other hand there are two very different types of conviction among children which need to be distinguished.
Some are, as we have just seen, influenced but not dictated
by the adult.   Others, on the contrary, are simply
swallowed whole, either at school, or from the family, or
from adult conversations which the child overhears, etc.
These naturally have not the slightest interest.   And this
forms the matter of the second problem, the more important from the point of view of methodology, namely,
how to distinguish those beliefs imposed by the adult and
those showing an original reaction on the part of the child
(a reaction influenced, but not dictated by the adult) ?—

It is evident that these two problems need distinguishing. We must now examine them separately.

As regards the first, two conflicting solutions can be put forward. According to one, there are no such things as convictions strictly the child's own ; nothing can be discerned save traces of stray and incomplete information, received from without, and to know children's own real thoughts one would have to bring up orphans on a desert island. This at heart is the solution implicit in the work of many sociologists. The idea that savages can teach us more than children as to the genesis of human thought, although the savages are known only at second or third hand by those qualified to study them scientifically, rests largely on the tendency to regard the child as entirely moulded by the surrounding social forces. But it may well be that the child's originality has been singularly misunderstood, simply because being egocentric it seeks neither to convince us of the correctness of its mental judgments nor above all to become sufficiently conscious of them to expose them to us. It may well be that we only see in the child his groping uncertainties precisely because he does not bother to speak of or even notice matters which are obvious to him. It is therefore legitimate to refuse to admit *à priori* the absolute conformity of the child's conceptions with those of the world surrounding him. Further, if the logical structure of child thought differs from our adult logic, as we have sought to show elsewhere, it seems probable that the content of child thought is itself partly original.

Must we then adopt the other extreme solution and make the child a sort of schizoid living entirely in its own automatism, although in appearance sharing in the life of the social body ? This would be to misrepresent the fact that the child is a being whose principal activity is adaptation and who is seeking to adapt itself not only to the adult who surrounds it but to nature itself.

The truth lies surely between the two. Stern, in his study of child language, has followed a guiding principle that we may well adopt, whilst enlarging it in favour of the originality of child thought. For with children thought is indeed much more original in its character than is language. At any rate what Stern says of language is *à fortiori* equally true of thought.

Let us admit, says Stern, that in his language the child limits himself altogether to copying the adult slavishly. It yet occurs that this copy contains a number of elements of spontaneity. For, in point of fact, the child does not copy everything. Its imitation is selective ; certain features are copied outright, others eliminated after a period of years. Moreover, the order in which these imitations are made is practically constant. The grammatical categories, for example, are acquired in a fixed order, etc. But what does imitation, made selectively and in a fixed order, signify if not a measure of spontaneous reaction. At any rate such facts point emphatically to the existence of a structure more or less independent of external pressure.

But there is yet more. Even that which seems copied is in reality deformed and recreated. The words the child uses, for example, are the same as we use, but they have a different meaning, either wider or narrower as the case may be. Associations are different ; syntax and style are original.

Stern thus puts forward on good grounds the hypothesis that the child digests what it borrows and digests it according to a mental chemistry of its own. Yet how much more valid are these considerations when applied to the domain of thought itself, where the rôle of imitation, as a formative factor, is evidently much smaller. In fact when dealing with conceptions we are continually meeting what one rarely finds in regard to language—a real clash between the child's thought and its adult surroundings, resulting in systematic distortion by the child of the information imparted to it by adults. To appreciate the extent of this phenomenon one must actually have seen how far children fail to understand even the best lessons.

It may indeed be urged that every language contains both logic and cosmology and that since the child learns to speak at the same time or before it learns to think, its thought will be in terms of the adult social medium. This is partly true. But from the very fact that, for the child, adult language is not what a foreign language is to us (that is to say a system of signs corresponding point for point with already acquired notions), it is possible to distinguish between child notions and adult notions simply by examining the use the child makes of our words and notions. It will then be seen that adult language constitutes for the child a reality which is often hazy in its outlines and that one of the activities of his thought is to adapt himself to this reality, just as he must adapt himself to physical reality itself. But this adaptation which characterises the child's verbal thought is original and presupposes *sui generis* schemas of mental digestion. Thus even when a child constructs a particular notion to correspond to a word of adult language, this notion may be entirely the child's, in the sense that the word was originally as hazy to his intelligence as a certain physical phenomenon might be, and to understand it he had to deform and assimilate it according to a mental structure of his own. We shall find an excellent illustration of this law when studying the child's notion of " life." The notion of " living " has been constructed by the child to correspond to an adult word. But it embraces something quite other than the adult notion of " life " and testifies to an entirely original conception of the world.

The principle to which we are referring consists then in regarding the child, not as a being of pure imitation, but as an organism which assimilates things to itself, selects them and digests them according to its own structure. In this way even what is influenced by the adult may still be original.

It goes without saying that pure imitations and pure reproductions frequently occur. A child's conviction is often simply the passive replica of a conversation it has heard. Moreover, as the child develops, its comprehension of the adult increases, and it becomes capable of assimilating the convictions of its associates without deforming them. How then shall we distinguish in the results of the clinical examination the part due to the child itself and that due to adult conversation which the child has absorbed ? All the rules already prescribed (§ 3) for distinguishing the spontaneous and liberated answers from those due to suggestion during the experiment hold for the solution of this new problem.

First comes the uniformity of the answers of the same average age. In fact, if all the children of the same mental age arrive at the same conception of a given phenomenon, in defiance of the variations in their personal circumstances, their experience and the conversation they have overheard, etc., this may be regarded as a prime guarantee of the originality of the conviction.

Secondly, in so far as the child's convictions follow with increasing age a continuous evolution, there is fresh presumption in favour of the originality of the conviction.

Thirdly, if a particular conviction is really the product of the child's mind, its disappearance will not be sudden and it should be possible to establish a number of combinations or compromises between it and the new conviction which is tending to supplant it.

Fourthly, a conviction having real solidarity with a given mental structure will resist suggestion ; and fifthly, this conviction will present a multitude of proliferations and will react on a number of neighbouring conceptions.

These five criteria, jointly applied, will suffice to show whether a particular conviction has been simply borrowed by the child from adults by passive imitation, or whether it is in part the product of the child's mental structure. Manifestly these criteria will no longer reveal the product of adult teaching at the age when the child can comprehend all that he is told (after the age of 11 or 12). But by then the child is no longer a child and his mental structure is becoming that of the adult.

PART I

REALISM

IN estimating the child's conceptions of the world the first question, obviously, is to decide whether external reality is as external and objective for the child as it is for us. In other words, can the child distinguish the self from the external world ? In an earlier study of child logic [1] we also met at the outset the problem of the self and reached the conclusion that logic develops as thought becomes socialised. So long as the child supposes that every one necessarily thinks like himself, he will not spontaneously seek to convince others, nor to accept common truths, nor, above all, to prove or test his opinions. If his logic lacks exactitude and objectivity it is because the social impulses of maturer years are counteracted by an innate egocentricity. In studying the child's thought, not in this case in relation to others but to things, we are faced at the outset with the analogous problem of the child's capacity to dissociate thought from self in order to form an objective conception of reality.

At first sight the question seems futile. The child, like the uncultured adult, appears exclusively concerned with things. He is indifferent to the life of thought and the originality of individual points of view escapes him. His earliest interests, his first games, his drawings are all concerned solely with the imitation of what is. In short, the child's thought has every appearance of being exclusively realistic.

J. Piaget, *Language and Thought of the Child*. Kegan Paul, 1926.

33

But realism is of two types, or rather, objectivity must be distinguished from realism. Objectivity consists in so fully realising the countless intrusions of the self in everyday thought and the countless illusions which result—illusions of sense, language, point of view, value, etc.—that the preliminary step to every judgment is the effort to exclude the intrusive self. Realism, on the contrary, consists in ignoring the existence of self and thence regarding one's own perspective as immediately objective and absolute. Realism is thus anthropocentric illusion, finality—in short, all those illusions which teem in the history of science. So long as thought has not become conscious of self, it is a prey to perpetual confusions between objective and subjective, between the real and the ostensible ; it values the entire content of consciousness on a single plane in which ostensible realities and the unconscious interventions of the self are inextricably mixed.

It is thus not futile, but, on the contrary, indispensable to establish clearly and before all else the boundary the child draws between the self and the external world. Nor is the method new. The work of Mach and Baldwin has long since made it familiar to psychology. Mach showed that the distinction between the internal or psychic world and the external or physical world is far from innate. It arises from action, which, engendered in a reality, of itself undifferentiated, comes little by little to group images about one or other of these two poles, round which two intercorresponding systems are built up.

Baldwin uses the term *projective* for that primitive state in which images are simply " presented " to consciousness, without there being any distinction between the self and the not-self. This projective stage is characterised by what he terms " adualisms " : the dualisms between internal and external, and between thought and things, in particular, being at this stage entirely absent and only subsequently being gradually constructed by logical development.[1]

[1] J. M. Baldwin, *Thoughts and Things.*

But these views are still theoretical. Mach's hypothesis is not based on a true genetic psychology and "the genetic logic" of Baldwin is constructive rather than experimental. Whence any attempt to pursue more closely his ingenious developments reveals, if not their precarious structure, at least their complexity.

What, for example, does "projection" really mean? The difficulty of distinguishing "projection" from "ejection" renders three interpretations possible. Sometimes there is simply a failure to differentiate between the self and the external world, that is, absence of consciousness of self. Thus it is claimed that when a child speaks of himself in the third person, it is because he sees himself not in the rôle of subject but as if from without. In this case "projection" signifies that the child in question recounts, and perhaps imagines, his own actions as belonging to an external order of things.

In other cases, there is "projection" when we attribute to things characteristics belonging to the self or to thought. Thus the child who places the "name of the sun" in the sun, "projects" an internal reality into the external world.

Finally, it is difficult to distinguish "projection" from those cases in which we endow things not only with our own characteristics but also with such conscious motives as might occasion the sensation we experience in observing them; thus a child, frightened by the sight of fire, endows the fire with malicious designs. It is not the feeling of fear which is attributed to the fire, rather the child projects into the fire the reciprocal sentiment of maliciousness.

It is in this third sense that psycho-analysts have used the word "projection." It is a different sense from the two former but it is obvious that there is a relationship between all three and probably complete continuity. At any rate in all three cases there is "adualism" between the internal and the external.

What then is the mechanism of projection? Does it imply simply failure to classify the contents of consciousness ? This is the impression given by reading Baldwin. He explains clearly enough the process by which the contents are differentiated and the nature of the " dualisms " so formed, but the construction of the primitive and adualistic states is not made clear. This is due, no doubt, to Mr. Baldwin's method. In his later writings his genetic logic is built up with great analytic subtlety, but as if it was dependent on psychological introspection alone, that is to say as if he regarded consciousness as an ultimate datum and took no account either of the unconscious or of the biological factor. But it is questionable whether genetic psychology must not necessarily suppose biological data, and particularly whether " projection " does not result from an unconscious process of assimilation, previously conditioned by the objective world and the self, irrespective of consciousness. If such is the case, the various types of projection are dependent on the various possible combinations of assimilation and adaptation.

But to reveal these processes and to trace their evolution, a minute study of the facts is absolutely essential. Since the field of study is obviously so vast, we shall limit ourselves to the analysis of such clearly defined facts as will throw most light on these difficult questions. We shall adopt a method of regression. Starting from a description of the conceptions children form as to the nature of thought (dualism between thought and things), we shall thence pass to a study of the boundaries children draw, in the matter of words, names and dreams, between the external and internal worlds, concluding with a brief analysis of certain kindred phenomena. The advantage of this regressive method is that in starting with the phenomena that are easiest to interpret we shall be able to disentangle certain guiding threads which we should miss in following a chronological method.

CHAPTER I

THE NOTION OF THOUGHT

LET us imagine a being, knowing nothing of the distinction between mind and body. Such a being would be aware of his desires and feelings but his notions of self would undoubtedly be much less clear than ours. Compared with us he would experience much less the sensation of the thinking self within him, the feeling of a being independent of the external world. The knowledge that we are thinking of things severs us in fact from the actual things. But, above all, the psychological perceptions of such a being would be entirely different from our own. Dreams, for example, would appear to him as a disturbance breaking in from without. Words would be bound up with things and to speak would mean to act directly on these things. Inversely, external things would be less material and would be endowed with intentions and will.

We shall try to prove that such is the case with the child. The child knows nothing of the nature of thought, even at the stage when he is being influenced by adult talk concerning " mind," " brain," " intelligence."

The technique is briefly as follows. The child is asked : " Do you know what it means to think of something ? When you are here and you think of your house, or when you think of the holidays, or of your mother, you are thinking of something." And then when the child has understood : " Well then, what is it you think with ? " If, as seldom happens, he has not grasped the idea, the matter must be further explained : " When you walk, you walk with the feet ; well then, when you think, what

37

do you think with ? " Whatever the answer may be, the meaning behind the words is what matters. Finally comes the question, supposing it were possible to open a person's head without his dying, could you see a thought, or touch it, or feel it with the finger, etc. Naturally, these last questions, which are suggestive, must be kept to the end, that is to say till the moment when the child cannot be made to say anything more of itself.

Moreover, when, as sometimes happens, the child makes use of words he has learnt, such as " brain," " mind," etc., he must be questioned further on the words until it is clear how he came to assimilate them. They may be merely empty phrases, or, on the contrary, they may be exceedingly suggestive deformations of true conceptions.

In this way we have traced three distinct stages, the first of which is easily distinguishable from the other two and appears to contain a purely spontaneous element. During this stage children believe that thinking is " with the mouth." Thought is identified with the voice. Nothing takes place either in the head or in the body. Naturally, thought is confused with the things themselves, in the sense that the word is a part of the thing. There is nothing subjective in the act of thinking. The average age for children of this stage is 6.

The second stage is marked by adult influences. The child has learnt that we think with the head, sometimes it even alludes to the " brain." Three circumstances, however, indicate a certain degree of spontaneity in the child's convictions. The first is the age : this type of answer is always found about the age of 8. But more important is the continuity existing between the first and second stages. Indeed, thought is often looked on as a voice inside the head, or in the neck, which shows the persistence of the influence of the child's previous convictions. Finally, there is the way in which the child materialises thought : thought is made of air, or of blood, or it is a ball, etc.

The third stage, the average age of which is 11-12, shows thought no longer materialised. It is no doubt difficult to distinguish clearly the third stage from the second. But the essential for us is to distinguish the second from the first, that is to say the adult's contribution from the child's conviction.

§ 1. THE FIRST STAGE : THOUGHT IS WITH THE MOUTH. —Stern's daughter,[1] Hilda, thought that we speak with the tongue and animals with the mouth. She further admitted that people think when they talk and stop thinking when their mouths are shut. According to the material we have collected such convictions are very general among children.

MONT. (7 ; 0)[2]: " You know what it means to think? —*Yes.*—Then think of your house. What do you think with ?—*The mouth.*—Can you think with the mouth shut ?—*No.*—With the eyes shut ?—*Yes.*—With the ears stopped up ?—*Yes.*—Now shut your mouth and think of your house. Are you thinking ?—*Yes.*—What did you think with ?—*The mouth.*"

PIG (9 ; 6, backward) : " You know the word ' think ' ? —*Yes.*—What does it mean, to think ?—*When someone is dead and you think of them.*—Do you sometimes think ?— *Yes, of my brother.*—Do you think at school ?—*No.*—And here ? (we were in the school office).—*Yes, I think because you have asked me things.*—What do you think with ?— *The mouth and ears.*—And do babies think ?—*No.*—Does a baby think when its mother talks to it ?—*Yes.*—What with ?—*With the mouth.*"

ACKER (7 ; 7) : " What do you think with ?—*The mouth.*" This statement was reiterated four times in

---

[1] *Die Kindersprache*, p. 210. Leipzig, 1907. See also Sully, *Studies of Childhood*.

[2] 7 ; 0 = 7 years, 0 months. The words of the child are in italics and those of the examiner in Roman lettering. All the words quoted are exactly as they were spoken. Inverted commas mark the beginning and end of a conversation in which no omission has been made. All the subjects were boys unless otherwise stated.

[Translator's note.] French-speaking children generally have a wider vocabulary than English children of the same age, and where on account of an unnatural ring in the English equivalent, any modification has been made, the French phrase is inserted in brackets.

the course of an examination on dreams which appears later. After the questions on animism we added : " Can a dog think ?—*Yes, it listens.*—Can a bird think ?—*No, it hasn't any ears.*—What does a dog think with ?—*Its ears.*—Does a fish think ?—*No.*—A snail ?—*No.*—A horse ? —*Yes, with its ears.*—A hen ?—*Yes, with its mouth.*"

SCHMI (5½) : " What do people think with ?—*The mouth.*"

MUY (6) : " What do you think with ?—*With something, with my mouth.*"

Sometimes, as we have just seen, thinking is not only with the mouth but with the ears.

BARB (5½) : " You know what it means to think ?— *When you can't remember something, you think.*—What do you think with ?—*The ears.*—If you were to stop them up, could you think ?—*Yes . . . no. . . .*"

REHM (5 ; 11) : " You know what it means to think of something ?—*Yes.*—Think of your house.—*Yes.*—What do you think with ?—*With the ears.*—When you think of your house, you think with the ears ?—*Yes.*"

Barb's formula is interesting : to think is to recall a voice or a forgotten sound. The above cases lead directly to the following. These foreshadow the second stage, for the children already say we think with the head, but the thought is not yet internal for it is still associated with the mouth. We shall reserve for the second stage the children who no longer speak of the mouth and who regard thought as a little voice situated in the head. Between the two groups there are innumerable transitions, but in any attempt at classification a line must be drawn somewhere. We shall, therefore, keep for the first stage those children who explicitly use the word " mouth."

CERES (7) : " What do we think with ?—*I don't know.* —Where do we think ?—*In the head.*—Where ?—*In the mouth, inside the head.*"

RATT (8 ; 10) : " When you think of your house, where is what you think ?—*In the head.*—What is there inside your head ?—*Nothing.*—How can you think of your house then ?—*With the mouth.*" " Are there words inside your head ?—*No.*—Is there a voice ?—*Yes.*—Are the voice and thinking the same thing ?—*Yes."*

KENN (7½) : " What do you think with ?—*Inside my head.*—Is the head empty or full ?—*Full.*—If someone opened your head, would they see when you were thinking ?—*No, because they couldn't see.*—If they could look inside your head without ⸍your dying, would they see your thought ?—*You can't hear it when you speak gently.*— What do you think with ?—*The head.*—With what part of the head ?—*The mouth.*—What is inside the head ? Is thought inside ?—*Yes, when you are thinking of something.* —What is inside the head ?—*When you speak.*—Can you think when your mouth is shut ?—*Yes, without speaking.* —What do you think with when you don't speak ?—*The mouth.*—What is there inside the head when you think ? —*Nothing.*—Can you see thought ?—*No.*—Could I hear it ? —*No.*—Could I feel it if I put my finger there ?—*Yes."*

This is an excellent example. The resistance and the spontaneity of the child's conviction are clearly seen ; without any suggestion he starts saying that you can't hear the thought when you speak gently and only then realises that thinking is with the mouth. Thought is thus a silent voice inside the head. Note, however, that you can feel this voice with the finger : Kenn here forestalls those cases in which thought is explicitly assimilated to air (the breath expelled from the mouth in speaking).

In all the above children there is a spontaneous conviction at the root of the answers given. In others there is at first nothing, but during the course of the examination a conviction is " liberated " though it has not been suggested by it, and here is the interesting point, this conviction resembles the former spontaneous one.

METR (5 ; 9) : " When you think, what do you think with ?—*I don't know.*—With your hands ?—*No.*—With your head ?—*No. You can't ever see thinking.*—What do you read with ?—*The eyes.*—Can you think with your eyes shut ?—*Yes.*—With your mouth shut ?—*No, I can't.* —With your ears stopped up ?—*Yes.*—Do babies think ? —*No, they don't know how. They are too little.*—What do we think with ?—*I don't know. I've never seen thinking.*—

Do we think with the head ?—*No.*—What then ?—*With the mouth."*

Here is an excellent example of the liberated conviction. The conviction can be seen gradually emerging, without direct intervention from us, but also without the child immediately finding a solution.

Sometimes varieties are found, but they are rare. Only one child (Go, 5 ; 9) said that thinking was *with the heart.* But this must have been a word he had been taught, for during the course of the questions, Go changed, and stated that thinking was with the ears. With this exception, all the subjects that could not be classified as belonging either to the second or the third stage, stated thinking to be either with the mouth or with the ears. The children being either of a visual or an auditory type, it might have been supposed that their answers would correspond and that all the former would claim to think with the eyes. But this was not found, and the question of imagery seems to play no part. At any rate the only two children who said they thought with the eyes, gave this answer after being questioned on the subject of dreams, which reduces the value of their statements.

How is this assimilation of thought to language to be interpreted ? In the first place, it must be realised that to children the word " thinking " has a restricted meaning ; for them, to think means to reflect, that is, to think with an effort. They have no idea of any other manifestation of thought, excepting the dream of which we shall speak later. The word " memory " is generally unknown to them, and when asked with what they " remember," they either fail to understand or they again give the answer that it is with the mouth. But if the term thought has a restricted sense for them, it is none the less the only word which signifies to children a purely mental act. And as we have just seen, they regard the mouth as the only seat of this mental activity. What follows ?

There is one essential distinction that must be introduced here. Stern [1] claimed that from about the age of 3, a differentiation is made between the psychical and the physical, in the sense that from this time the child uses certain words meaning " to believe," " to appear," etc., as in the sentence, " I think (je crois) she has a headache." [2]   The child, he claims, thus distinguishes between the real it perceives from the interpretation or hypothesis, that is to say between things and thought. But we must guard against the fallacy of accepting that which is only implicitly expressed as being comprehended and for that reason the sphere of action must not be confounded with that of reflection. In the sphere of action, in the actual flow of thought, it is certainly true that the children of whom Stern speaks begin to distinguish immediate perception from suppositions and inferences. This is a notable advance, but it is not a reason for supposing that such children are themselves conscious of the duality (that is to say, have realised what is implied in this action). Above all, it is no reason for assuming that they have deduced from this duality the idea of a reality that is perceived and a thought that interprets it.

In short, there is no ground for supposing they have made any general distinction between the psychical and the physical. The only discovery which these children have made is that they no longer regard reality as being entirely in accordance with their wants and their assertions (see *Language and Thought*, pp. 232, 233). But physical reality at this stage may well be so fully endowed with intentions and with psychical characteristics, etc., that the child can easily fail to recognise the thought as his own or conceive it as a material voice.

In treating of the development of the notion of thought, we may thus regard as primitive the child's conviction

---

[1] *Die Kindersprache.* Leipzig, 1907
[2] The French child distinguishes between " I think " (je pense) and ' I believe " (je crois), where the English child will normally use ' I think " for both. [Translator's note.]

that it thinks with the mouth. The notion of thinking, as soon as it appears, becomes confused with that of voice, that is to say with words, either spoken or heard.

It would certainly be expected that since speech is an activity of the self, some distinction between psychical and physical would already be present at this stage. But there are two fundamental objections to this view : firstly, words are, for the child, a part of material reality ; and secondly, the subjective activity involved in speech is either unnoticed by the child or is assimilated to a material process, such as breathing or blowing. Thought thus consists either of " word-things " or, more rarely, of air.

In fact, to children words convey nothing internal or psychical. We shall try to prove this subsequently by a direct analysis, when we shall find that words are regarded as a part of things and are situated within the things. The function of the ears and mouth is thus limited to collaborating with the things, to receiving words and to sending them forth. So, too, we shall see that at a certain stage the dream is " in the room," in the same way that thought is both outside and inside the mouth. There is no clear distinction between the psychical and internal and the material and external.

For the moment then we must accept a first approximation. When children are questioned " where does thought come from ? " whilst stating that they think with the mouth they will still not hesitate to give an external origin to thought. This is shown in the two following examples :—

ACKER (7 ; 7) told us four times, as we have already seen, that thinking is with the mouth. " When you think with the mouth, where does the thought come from ?— *From the eyes, from outside. You see, then you think.*— Then when you don't speak, are you thinking ?—*Yes.* —What with ?—*The mouth.*"—A moment later : " When you don't say anything what do you think with ?—*The stomach.*" As he said this Acker pointed to the larynx in explanation, showing that he was thinking all the time of voice.

RATT (8 ; 10) told us, as we saw, that there is nothing in the head, when we think. " Can one see the voice ?— *No.*—Can one feel it ?—*Yes.*—Have words got strength ? —*Yes.*—Tell me a word which has strength ?—*The wind.* —Why has the word ' wind ' got strength ?—*Because it goes quickly.*—Is it the word or the wind which goes quickly ?—*The wind.*—Tell me a word which has strength. —*When you give something a kick.*—Is that a word ?— *No.*—Tell me a word which has strength—. . .—What do you think with ?—*With the mouth.*—What is inside the head when you think ?—*Nothing.*—What does the voice do ?—*It speaks.*—You know what words are ?— *When you speak.*—Where is the word ' house ' ?—*In the mouth.*—Is it in the head ?—*No.*"

The value of these examples will perhaps be questioned before our results as to words have been seen (§ 4 and Chapter II). But in the light of these results, the two cases above are quite clear. Neither of the children distinguished words from the things named. Acker thus believed that to see a house was enough to make one instantly think of the word, as if the name was inscribed on the thing. Ratt was unable to understand that it is things and not words that have strength. The word is thus perceived in the thing. Just as to the sensationalists thought was a series of images imprinted on the brain by the stimulus of things, so to the child it is the uttering of words which are placed in the mouth by the agency of the same stimulus.

Here is the case of a child who has his own conception of memory, characteristic of the realism of which we are speaking.

SCHI (6) gave the word " memory " spontaneously. " What is memory ?—*When you remember something.*— How do you remember ?—*It suddenly comes into the mind* (*revient dans notre âme*). *When you've been told something it comes into your mind, then it goes out and then it comes back.*—It goes out ? Where does it go to ?—*Into the sky.* —Do you really believe that ?—*Yes, I don't know, but it's what I think* (*ce que je crois*)."

The flight of the memory to the sky is undoubtedly

made up. But to " go out " and to " come back " are
significant expressions. They must be interpreted literally,
for, as we shall see later, Schi also describes dreams as
" coming out " when he is asleep (see Chapter III, § 3 :
" *When you are not asleep it is inside the head. When you
are asleep it comes out* " . . . " *it goes against the wall* ").
Schi must be credited with no exact idea as to the " how "
of these phenomena, his words simply mean that he has
not yet come to regard memories, words heard, or dreams
as " internal." In dealing with names we shall come on
similar examples of children stating that the name is
" in the room " (see the case of Roc, Chapter II, § 2).

In short, in so far as thought is assimilated to voice it
becomes actually a part of the objects thought of. To
convince the reader of the truth of this conclusion we
must simply refer him to the results of Chapter II. As
to the internal aspect of thought which for the child
consists essentially in the articulation of words, we shall
now try to show that this also is material, and, what is
especially curious, that it also is regarded as actually a
part of the external world.

As a matter of fact, the majority of children are not
aware of this internal activity. To think is to speak and
speaking just happens, but some children do note the
existence of the voice and then, during the first stage,
they assimilate this voice to " the air," the air being both
internal and external, manifest both in breathing and in
the atmosphere.

RON ($7\frac{1}{2}$) : " Can one see thought ?—*Yes.*—How ?—
In front of you.—Where ? There (50 cms away) or right
over there ?—*It doesn't make any difference. The wind
makes the grass move and you see it moving. That is thinking.*
—Is it in front of you or in the brain ?—*Both, you can
think anyhow.*—Can one touch thought ?—*Sometimes,
when the thoughts are real.*"
BRUNN (11 ; 11, backward and slow) : " Has thought
any strength ?—*No, because it is not alive.*—Why is it not
alive ?—*It is air.*—Where is the thought ?—*In the air,
outside.*" But Brunn also states that the thought is in

ourselves ; memory, according to him, " *is a thought.—* Where is it ?—*In the head."*

RIS (8½ ; a girl), whom we shall again meet with in connection with dreams (Chapter III, § 1) stated, without having been previously questioned about thought, that the dream is " *in words.—*And what are the words in ? —*The voice*—Where does the voice come from ?—*The air."*

We shall find similar cases in the second stage (§ 3).

In connection with dreams we shall also frequently find thought assimilated to the air, or the wind, or even " la fumée qui sort du ventre " (breathing). How are these facts to be interpreted ? At first sight one might attribute them to adult influence ; these children have been told of a soul or a mind which is invisible like the air, and they have concluded that thinking is by means of the air. We shall find cases in the second stage which must probably be so regarded. But the above cases seem to resist this interpretation, for these children will not admit that thought is internal ; it is outside as well as inside. Ron, an intelligent child, is particularly clear on this ; he confuses the thinking with the thing thought of. This is what makes him say that when you think of " things which are real " you can touch the thought. Moreover, a systematic adult influence cannot account for the many varieties of answer all relating to voice or breathing (the air, the wind, " la fumée du ventre," etc.).

In short, thought when it consists of words is a part of the things named, and when it consists of voice it is assimilated to air, which is both internal and external. Thus in neither case is there a clear boundary between the self and the external world.

§ 2. LOOKING AND SEEING.—Before proceeding further with the notion of thought, it may be useful to consider briefly what seems to be a confirmation of the above interpretations. Does the same confusion between internal and external exist in children's conceptions of vision ? The subject has not yet been investigated, but in the course of this research we have come by chance on certain facts worth mentioning here, because in themselves very significant. First comes a question quoted by Stanley Hall,[1] coupled with an adult recollection of childhood.

From a boy of 5 years old : " *Papa, why don't our looks mix when they meet.*"

From one of our collaborators: " *When I was a little girl I used to wonder how it was that when two looks met they did not somewhere hit one another. I used to imagine the point to be half-way between the two people. I used also to wonder why it was one did not feel someone else's look, on the cheek for instance if they were looking at one's cheek.*"

Next are three entirely spontaneous cases of confusion between vision and light, which were observed in answer to questions concerning the subject either of shadows or of dreams :—

PAT (10) stated that a box makes a shadow " *because the clouds* (Pat believes it to be the clouds which give light when there is no sun) *can't pass through it* " (*i.e.* because the light cannot pass through the box).

But immediately after Pat said of a portfolio that it made a shadow " *because the clouds can't see that side.*— Are to see and to give light the same thing ?—*Yes.*—Tell me the things which give light ?—*The sun, the moon, the stars, the clouds and God.*—Can you give light ?—*No . . . Yes.*—How ?—*With the eyes.*—Why ?—*Because if you hadn't eyes you wouldn't see properly.*"

DUC (6½) also stated that the light cannot see through a hand, alike confusing " seeing " with " giving light."

SCI (6) said that dreams come " *with the light.*"—" How ? —*You are in the street. The lights* (street-lamps) *can see there . . . they see on the ground.*" " Tell me some things that give light.—*Lights, candles, matches, thunder, fire, cigarettes.*—Do eyes give light or not ?—*Yes, they give light.*—Do they give light at night ?—*No* ?—Why not ? *Because they are shut.*—When they are open do they give light ?—*Yes.*—Do they give light like lamps ?—*Yes, a little bit.*"

These last cases are interesting from their analogy with the theory of perception of Empedocles, who, as is well

[1] Stanley Hall, *Pedagogical Seminary*, Vol. X (1903), p. 346.

known, explained vision as due to the light given out by an object meeting the light that emanates from the eye.[1]

The five cases point to the same conclusion : seeing is for these children partly outside the eye. It comes from the eye, it gives light and they are puzzled why they don't feel it. We do not know whether these beliefs are general or not, but independently they point to the possibility of a thought which is at the same time both internal and external and thus confirm the interpretation given in the previous section.

§ 3. THE SECOND AND THIRD STAGES : THINKING IS WITH THE HEAD.—The convictions of the first stage may be regarded as spontaneous since they are general and, in so far as this is so, cannot be due to adult suggestion. The convictions which characterise the second stage seem, on the other hand, to have been in part assimilated. It is hard to see how children quite alone could have discovered thinking to be with the head. However, it is interesting to note that only after the age of 7 or 8 (in a few cases 6) does the child ask questions of his own accord and assimilate what he is told.

The characteristic of the second stage as opposed to the third is that thought, although situated in the head, remains material. Either the child continues simply to believe that it is voice or breath (first type) or it attempts to understand the words " brain," " intelligence," etc., and imagines balls, tubes, winds, etc. (second type).

The following cases of the first type are of special interest in showing the persistence of phenomena of the first stage, despite progressive pressure from the adult.

FALQ (7 ; 3) : " You know what it means to think ?— *You think of things you want to do.*—What do you think with ?—*With something.*—What with ?—*A little voice.*— Where is it ?—*There* (he points to the forehead)." " Where does the little voice come from ?—*The head.*—How does it happen.—*By itself.*—Does a horse think ?—*Yes.*—What

[1] See Arn. Raymond, *Histoire des Sciences exactes et naturelles dans l'antiquité greco-romaine*, p. 43. Blanchard, 1924.

with ?—*A little voice in the head.*—And dogs ?—*Yes.*—
Does the little voice say words ?—*Yes.*—Why ? Dogs
can't talk.—*They talk, then they listen.*—Where ?—*There*
(pointing to the forehead).—Why ?—*There is something
there.*—What ?—*A little ball."* In the head is also *" a
little mouth.*—Is it there now ?—*Yes.*—You really believe
that ?—*Yes."*—A few moments later Falq speaks of
memory. " Where is it ?—*Inside there* (showing his forehead).—What is there ?—*A little ball.*—What is inside
it ?—*Thoughts.*—What would one see inside if one looked ?
Smoke.—Where does it come from ?—*From the head."*
" Where does the smoke come from ?—*From the thoughts.*
—Is thought smoke ?—*Yes."* " Why is thought inside the
ball ?—*It is a little air and smoke that has come.*—Where
from ?—*From outside.*—Where ?—*The air outside and the
smoke from the chimney.*—Is the air alive ?—*No, it is
because it is the air, and when you think of something it
comes into the ball. When you've thought of something the
thought comes with the air and the smoke."* " How ?—*The
thought makes the air and the smoke come in and they mix."*
" What is the smoke ?—*Breath.*—And the air ?—*The
same."* " Is there breath in you ?—*No . . . yes, when we
breathe.*—When you breathe what comes in and goes
out ?—*Wind.*—Does breathing make air ?—*Yes.*—And
smoke ?—*No . . . yes, steam."*

This case resembles those of Ron, Ris and Brunn (§ 1) ;
particularly in the details concerning " the little ball,"
etc. Falq shows exceedingly clearly how the air, smoke,
breathing and voice are all regarded as of the same nature
and interchangeable. Thus his spontaneous convictions
continue directly in the line of the first stage, but in
addition he has acquired certain notions, such as the
ball in his forehead. The " little mouth " inside the head
recalls the child mentioned by Mlle Malan who said, " it
is the mouth behind there (inside the head) which talks
to my mouth in front."

REYB (8 ; 7) : " What is thought ?—*When you think of
something.*—What does that mean ?—*You want to have it.*
—What do we think with ?—*Our brains.*—Who told you
that ?—*No one. . . .*—Where did you learn the word ?—
I've always known it.—What is the brain ?—*The tubes in
the head.*—What happens in these tubes ?—*Something.*—

What ?—*What you think.*—Can one see thought ?—*No.*— And touch it ?—*No.*—What is it like ?—*What you hear.* —Can you think with the ears stopped up ?—*No.*—With the eyes shut ?—*No.*—With the mouth shut ?—*No.*— Where do the tubes go and where do they start ?—*From the ears.*—And where do they go ?—*To the mouth.*—Who told you about the tubes in the head ?—*No one.*—Have you heard people speak of them ?—*No.*"

The adult influence is clearly marked. But there seems to be a spontaneous reaction when Reyb says that thought is " what you hear."

GRAND (8) stated when questioned on animism that the moon doesn't know anything because " *it hasn't any ears.*" This gives an indication. Later : " You know what it is to think ?—*Yes.*—What do you think with ?—*The head.*—What is thought ?—*It's white inside the head.*— What do you think with ?—*A little voice.*"

MENN (12) also supposes one thinks " *with the head.*— Could one see thought, if one opened the head ?—*No, it doesn't stay inside.*—Could I see it ?—*No.*—Could I touch it ?—*No, it is what talks.*—Could one feel it ?—*No.*—Why not ? What is thought ?—*Yes* (you could feel it). *It's our voice.*"

The last case is striking, showing how the child, although placing thought in the head, has not yet solved the question of internal and external ; thought is " our voice," and the voice " doesn't stay inside."

Similar cases were found in other districts of Switzer-land where Mlle Perret continued the same research.

NIC (10 ; 3, a girl) supposes one could not see thought because, " *I should have to speak to it.*"

E. KUN (7 ; 4) and his sister M. KUN (8 ; 4) were questioned one after the other without being given time to compare. Both stated that thought is in the head and that it is " *white* " and " *round.*" M. Kun said it was " *as big as a large apple* " ; E. Kun that it was " *little.*" This would seem to suggest traces of adult teaching on the brain. However, E. Kun at other times maintained that one thinks " *with the mouth.*—Where is the thought ?— *In the middle of the mouth.*—Can one see it ?—*Yes.*— Touch it ?—*No.*—Why not ?—*Because it is too far away.*

—Where ?—*In the neck."* The combination of spontaneous convictions with instruction received is evident.

In short, the value of these answers is proved by the
continuity they all show between the first and second
stages. At first we had the impression that the " voice "
was a recollection of religious teaching (" the voice of
conscience," etc.), but we gave up this interpretation in
face of the generality of the cases.

None of the above children conceive thought as distinct
from matter. This materialism is also characteristic of the
following children, who under the pressure of adult conceptions no longer identify thought with voice, and we shall
see what strange deformations these conceptions undergo.
In a certain sense these deformations are quite as interesting as the spontaneous reactions of the former children.

IM (6) : Thought is *" my intelligence."* It is *" what makes
us think and try and find out.*—Who told you that ?—*I
wasn't told, but I know."* This *" intelligence "* cannot be
touched *" because it is full of blood."*

Duss (9) identified thought with the *" brain,"* which
is as big *" as a marble."* Duss thought, however, that we
dreamed *" with the mouth."*

ZIMM (8 ; 1) thinks with his " intelligence," but supposes
that if the head was opened one could see and touch this
intelligence.

KAUF (8 ; 8, a girl) thinks with her memory. *" Memory
is something in the head which makes us think.*—What do
you think this memory is like.—*It is a little square of skin,
rather oval, and inside there are stories (les histoires).—*
What are they like ?—*They are written on the flesh.—*
What with ?—*Pencil.*—Who wrote them ?—*God, before I
was born, he put them there."*

Evidently Kauf has made up the details. The tendency
to believe " stories " to be innate may be regarded, however, as spontaneous. This belief rests on the fact we
have frequently observed that children have a complete
amnesia as to the origins of their knowledge, however
recent. For example, Im, as we have just seen, is convinced of having always known of " intelligence." Reyb

has always known he had a brain, etc. (see on this subject *Judgment and Reason*, Chapter IV, § 1). It is, therefore, quite natural that when children come to consider the origin of their knowledge, they believe, like Kauf, that it is innate. We shall find the same thing with the origin of names. It has been suggested that this tendency of children to consider all they have been taught as originating in themselves had probably some influence on the psychical genesis of the Platonic doctrine of memory and similar theories.

The following are cases of children who identify thought with the air, but evidently as the result of a more or less direct adult influence.

TANN (8) thinks with his "*mind.*" "What is the mind?—*It is someone who isn't like we are, who hasn't skin and hasn't bones, and who is like air which we can't see. After we're dead it goes away from our body.*—Goes away?—*It goes away but it stays, when it goes away it still stays.*—What stays?—*It stays, but all the same it's in Heaven.*" Tann has not yet accepted as irresistible the dualism between internal and external. . . .

PERET (11 ; 7) : We think "*with the forehead.*—What is inside it?—*Our mind.*" "Can one touch the mind?—*No.*—Why not?—*You can't touch it. You can't because you can't see it.*—Why not?—*It's air.*—Why do you think it is air?—*Because you can't touch it.*"

The difference is evident between these children and those at the end of § 1 (Ron, Brunn, and Ris, and also Falq § 3) who also confused thought with air, but whose reflections were original and showed no trace of words which they had learnt, whilst Tann and Peret, on the contrary, distort conceptions acquired from their environment. These distortions are, however, always interesting since they show to what extent thought still remains material for children in the second stage.

It cannot, therefore, be asserted that in the second stage thought has yet been distinguished from things. For the child either simply prolongs the first stage by identifying thought and voice or else he is more or less befogged by the mere words to which he clings persistently. In neither case is thought differentiated from the things thought of, nor are words from the things named. There is simply conflict between the child's earlier convictions and the pressure of adult teaching, and this crisis is the only mark of progress in the second stage which otherwise brings the child no new solution.

When is the point at which the child definitely distinguishes thought from things, that is to say the point which marks the beginning of the " third stage " ? The technique we have followed so far cannot alone reveal so subtle a distinction. But used in conjunction with an examination on names and on dreams it provides very useful information. We therefore propose to use simultaneously three tests as a means of revealing whether the third stage has yet been reached.

Before concluding that a child distinguishes thought from things it must be proved, (1) that the child is able to situate thought in the head and to declare it invisible, intangible, etc., in short, immaterial and distinct from the " air " and " voice " ; (2) that the child is able to distinguish words and names from the things themselves ; (3) that the child is able to situate dreams in the head and to realise that if one opened the head the dreams could not be seen. (For points 2 and 3 see the technique outlined later). No one of these tests is alone sufficient, but their simultaneous use we consider adequate to prove the arrival of the third stage.

The following example bears on points 1 and 3 :—

VISC (11 ; 1) : " Where is thought ?—*In the head.*—If someone opened your head, would he see your thought ? —*No.*—Could he touch it ?—*No.*—Feel it as if it was air ? —*No* . . . etc." Then : " What is a dream ?—*It's a thought.*—What do you dream with ?—*With the head.*— Are the eyes open or shut ?—*Shut.*—Where is the dream whilst you are dreaming ?—*In the head.*—Not in front of you ?—*It's as if (!) you could see it.*—Is there anything in front of you when you dream ?—*No, nothing.*—What is inside the head ?—*Thoughts.*—Is it the eyes which see something inside the head ?—*No.*"

The beginnings of the third stage may be placed approximately at the age of 11, though some cases are found at 10, and even at 9. But on the average the essential discoveries that thought is not matter and that it is distinct from the phenomena it deals with, are not made before the age of 11.

§ 4. WORDS AND THINGS.—The first two stages we have just studied are characterised by two confusions, quite distinct from each other though mutually contributory. First, there is the confusion between thought and body ; thought for the child, is an activity of the organism—the voice—it is thus a thing among things and its essential characteristic is material action, either on things or on persons in whom it is interested. Secondly, there is confusion between the sign and the thing signified, the thought and the thing thought of. From this point of view the child cannot distinguish a real house, for example, from the concept or mental image or name of the house. This point remains to be studied.

In what way does this all-important differentiation reveal itself ? Which does the child first conceive as belonging to the thinking subject : the concept, the image or the word ? Certainly not the concept, and we cannot say at what age the notion of " idea " appears. It would make an interesting research to determine at what point such expressions as " a wrong idea," " to have an idea," etc., arise. From the preceding material all we may say is that thing and concept are still confused at the age of 7 by Ron (§ 1), who maintains that we may " touch thought " when it is of " things that are real." It may, indeed, be observed that such a belief involves '' things that are not real," that is to say mental objects— what children name " stories " or things " said for fun." But the study of children's explanations on the subject of dreams shows that these mental objects are not regarded as images but as things, as made of air, or words, etc. The study of dreams will also furnish material as to when the child conceives the existence of mental images and the question can, therefore, be better studied later.

Concerning words, the theories of Sully, Compayré, and many others are well known, according to which it is maintained with much justice that to a child's eye every object seems to possess a necessary and absolute name, that is to say, one which is a part of the object's very nature.   M. Luquet has shown that many children's drawings bear a title simply because of this peculiarity : " The addition of a title has we consider no other meaning than that of expressing the name of the object, which is regarded by the designer as a property as inherent in its essence and as worthy of being reproduced as its visual characteristics." [1]

It will, therefore, be interesting to see at what age children can distinguish the word which designates it from the thing itself.   To solve this problem we used two different techniques.   The most important will be discussed in the course of the next chapter, it deals with the origin and place of the names of things.   The more direct, with which we shall deal now, is also the more questionable.   It consists simply in asking a child if words " have strength," and if he falls into the trap to make him see his own fallacy.   The disadvantage lies in the fact that there is a trap, and, if used alone, we should not have dared to draw any conclusions from this method.   But it becomes interesting when combined with the methods of Chapter II.   Three types of answer, corresponding to three successive stages, were found.   In the first stage (up to the age of 7–8), the children made no distinctions between the word and the thing, and failed to understand the problem.   In the second stage (7–11) the children understood the problem, but were unable to solve it systematically.   During the third stage (after 10 or 11) the correct solution is given.

The following examples illustrate the first stage :—

---

[1] *Journal de Psychologie*, 1922, p. 207.

BOURG (6) : " Can a word have strength ?—*No . . . yes.*—Tell me a word which has strength.—*Daddy, because he's a daddy and he's strong.*—When I say ' cloud,' is the word ' cloud ' strong ?—*Yes, because it gives light at night* (the idea that clouds give light when there is no sun appears to be fairly general).—The word ' umbrella ' only the word, not the ' umbrella ' itself, is that strong ?—*A bit, because someone might poke it in your eyes and that would kill you.*"

Bow (6 ; 5) : " When I say ' umbrella ' I'm saying a word, or ' drawer ' that's another word, there isn't really a drawer, they are just words. If I didn't say words to you, you wouldn't know what I wanted to say. Say a word. . . ."

" The word ' sun ' is it strong ?—*No, because it doesn't weigh much* (the sun).—Is the word ' hit ' strong ?—*No, fairly strong.*—Why ?—*Because sometimes it hurts.*—Is it the word ' hit ' which is strong ? When I say the word ' hit ' with the mouth, only the word, is it strong ?—*No, because the mouth can't shout it.*—Tell me a word which is strong.—*When a horse runs away.*"

CAM (6) : " If I say the word ' run,' I don't run. I say the word with the mouth. Is a word strong ?—*Yes.*— Why ?—*Because you say it.*—If I say the word ' jump ' is it strong ?—*Yes, because children jump with a skipping-rope.*"

The examples of the first stage obviously prove nothing by themselves. It may be that these children realise what a word is, but have no means of expressing the idea, for the word " word " implies for them the presence of the thing itself, in which case the experiment is of no value. It may also be that we were unable to make ourselves understood. In fact, the only means of proving that these children really confuse the word and the thing named is to show that older children manage to understand the problem, though without being able to solve it. This is proved by the examples of the second stage.

The second stage is, therefore, paradoxical. On one hand, the child understands the problem and so distinguishes the word from the thing named ; but, on the other, the distinction is not clear enough to save the child from the trap, into which he continually falls.

The following illustrate this stage :—

KRUG (6) : " Is a word strong ?—*No, it can't do any-thing at all.*—Are any words strong ?—*Some words are strong.*—Which ?—*The word ' strong ' because you are say-ing it's strong.*—Is the word 'elephant' strong ?—*Yes, because an elephant can carry people.*—An elephant can, but simply the word ?—*No, it isn't strong.*—Why not ?—*Because it doesn't do anything.*—What ?—*The word.*—Is the word ' sleep ' strong ?—*It is weak, because when you sleep, you're tired.*—Is the word ' run ' strong ?—*Yes, if the person's strong . . . it is strong the word ' run.' ''*

AUD (8 ; 8) : " Are words strong ?—*No, words are nothing at all. They aren't strong, you can't put anything on them.*—Tell me a word.—*' Curtains.' It isn't strong, because if you put anything on it, it tears. A word isn't strong because you can't build up anything on top of it.— The word is when you speak. If you put anything on ' paper ' (the word) it would break.*—Are there any words that are strong ?—*No.*—Tell me another word.—*' Um-brella-stand.' It is strong because you can put umbrellas in it.* (Like ' curtains,' Aud chose this word because he could see it in the room.)—Is it in the word you put umbrellas ?—*No.*—Is the word strong ?—*No.*—And why isn't the word ' curtains ' strong ?—*Because it tears so easily.*—Is it the word which tears ?—(laughing) *No, the curtains.*—Is the word ' motor ' strong ?—*The word isn't strong but the motor is* (!)—Good, you've got it. Tell me another word that isn't strong ?—*A cobweb because you'd have to put ever such light things not to break it.*—Would the word break ?—*No* (laughing).—Scatter-brains, caught again !—(laughing) *Yes.*—Tell me a word which isn't strong.—*Trees.*—Is that a word that isn't strong ?—*Yes, because you couldn't put anything on it.*—On what ?—*On the trees.*''

These cases are particulary striking since Krug and still more Aud fully realise the problem. Aud, for instance, says at the beginning that a word is " when you speak." He adds, however, spontaneously that the word " paper " is not strong, because paper tears. Clearly in such a case the confusion is more than verbal, and pertains to the systematic difficulty of distinguishing the sign from the thing signified, or thought from the thing thought of.

The following is an example of the third stage, where a child gradually comes to realise the catch in the question, passing from the second to the following stage before our eyes. The answers it will be seen are entirely spontaneous, and it was they which led us to undertake this rapid survey. The child himself spoke of " thought " as of something immaterial and so suggested the idea of asking by way of control if thought had strength. The child's clear and entirely original reaction then gave the idea of setting the same question with regard to words and testing other younger children.

TIE (10 ; 10) : " Has thought got strength ?—*No, it has and then it hasn't.*—Why hasn't it ?—*It depends on what you are thinking of.*—When has it strength ?—*When you think of something strong.*—If you think of this table, has it ?—*Yes.*—If you think of the lake, has it ?—*No.*—If you think of the wind, has it ?—*Yes.*" (Tie had said a few minutes before that the water of the lake had no strength " because it was still," that the wind has strength, " because it can blow down houses," and that the table had, " because things can stand on it.") " Have words got strength ?—*It depends on the word.*—Which ones have strength ?—*The word ' boxing '* . . . *oh, no they haven't any strength* (laughing).—Why did you think they had first ?—*I was wrong. I was thinking it was the word that hit.*"

This example is suggestive in itself. Tie's confusion between the word and the thing is, in fact, accompanied by an explicit and entirely spontaneous confusion between the thought and the objects thought of. The fact that Tie rid himself of the fallacy whilst being questioned only adds further value to the case, since it shows the difficulty which so keen and thoughtful a boy found in answering correctly.

It is unnecessary to continue the inquiry, for the systematic study of " nominal realism " to be undertaken in the next chapter will supply the further information lacking. These cases of which the most characteristic have been quoted, may in the meanwhile be taken to prove that up to the age of 10–11 there is confusion between the sign and the thing signified, and as we saw earlier, it is at about the age of 11 that the idea of thought is dissociated from the idea of physical substance. We thus see that it is between 10 and 11 that the child becomes aware of thoughts or of words as distinct from the things of which he thinks. The two discoveries contribute to one another.

In conclusion, until about 11, to think is to speak—either with the mouth or with a little voice situated in the head—and speaking consists in acting on things themselves by means of words, the words sharing the nature of the things named as well as of the voice producing them.

All this involves as yet only matter and material action and the resulting realism is due to a perpetual confusion between subject and object, between internal and external.

CHAPTER II

NOMINAL REALISM

THE problem of names involves the same difficulties which came to light in studying the dualism that exists in the child's mind between internal and external. Are names in the subject or the object ? Are they signs or things ? Have they been discovered by observation or chosen without any objective reason ? The child's answers to these questions will reveal the extent and the exact significance of the realism which was foreshadowed in the previous chapter.

The problem of names probes to the very heart of the problem of thought, for to the child, to think means to speak. And if " word " is a somewhat vague concept to the younger children (at any rate before the age of 7 or 8 ; that is, during the first stage as distinguished in section 4), what is meant by a " name " is on the contrary quite clear. All the children tested knew the meaning of a " name " ; it was " to call something by" (pour appeler). It is, therefore, perfectly natural to ask how names began, where they are, why they are, what they are, etc. Also in certain cases it may be possible to add to the results thus obtained from conversation with children, confirmatory proof drawn from a study of their spontaneous questions. Indeed, every one must be familiar with the questions on names which characterise the most primitive stages of a child's questioning: What is that ? And a careful examination of these questions shows that in learning the names of things the child at this stage believes it is doing much more. It thinks it is reaching to the essence of the thing and discovering a real explanation. As soon as it knows the name, the problem no longer exists. Later, questions bearing on etymology also furnish useful material and show the same tendency towards a nominal realism.

The following examples of two spontaneous remarks show this interest in names and especially the quasi-magical aspect sometimes taken by nominal realism.

AR (6½) remarked during a building game : " *And when there weren't any names. . . .*"

Bo (6½) replied : " *If there weren't any words it would be very awkward (on serait très ennuyé). You couldn't make anything. How could things have been made* " (if there hadn't been names for them) ? The name thus seems to be a part of the essence of the thing and is even a necessary condition of its being made.

In short, there is nothing artificial about this subject, it is on the contrary a natural centre of interest to children. The only difficulty is to find the right method of setting questions. The criterion will be as usual only to ask questions to which older children can give a correct solution and to which the youngest will give answers that improve progressively with age.

The technique on which we decided after much experimenting is briefly as follows. Eight types of question are asked in the following order : (1) Having made sure that the child knows what a name is, he is asked to give his own name and then " the name of that," " and of that " (as various objects are pointed to). " Very well then, what is a name ? " ; (2) he is next asked, " How did names begin ? How did the name of the sun begin ? " ; (3) the answer having been given he is then asked : " Well, but how did we know that that was what the sun was called ? " (4) " Where are names ? Where is the sun's name ? Where is the name of the lake ? " etc. ; (5) " Do things know their names ? Does the sun know its name ? Do the clouds know they are called clouds or not ? " etc. ; (6) " Has the sun always had its name or was it first without

a name and did it only get its name afterwards?"; (7)
" Why is the sun called ' sun ' ? Why have the Jura and
the Salève got those names " etc. ; and finally (8) " You
are called Henry, your brother is Paul.—You might have
been called Paul and he Henry, mightn't you ?—Well
could the Jura have been called ' Salève ' in the beginning
and the Salève ' Jura ? '—And could the sun have been
called 'moon ' and the moon ' sun ' ? "

These questions will perhaps seem too subtle. But as
all were correctly solved at the age of about 11 or 12 we
are justified in questioning why they are solved no earlier.

§ 1. THE ORIGIN OF NAMES.—In this section we shall
deal with questions 1, 2, 6 and 3. The first question, that
of defining a name, is solved from the earliest age. Question
2 gives rise to 3 groups of answers corresponding to three
stages. During the first stage (5 to 6) children regard
names as belonging to things and emanating from them.
During the second stage (7, 8) names were invented by
the makers of the things—God or the first men. In the
case of the first men, the child generally supposes that the
men who gave the names are those who made the things :
the sun, the clouds, etc. (according to the artificialist
connections to be studied in Part III). During the third
stage, which appears about the age of 9 or 10 the child
regards names as due to men of no particular identity,
whilst the name is no longer identified with the idea of
creation.

The following are answers to question 2, illustrating
the first stage where the name emanates directly from the
thing.

LAV (6½) says that names are "*to call things by*"—
" How did name begin ? How did the sun get its name ?
—*I don't know.*—Where did your name ' Jules ' come from ?
Who gave it you ?—*I don't know.*—Your father ?—*Yes.*
—And where did the name of the sun come from ?—*The
sky.*—Is it the sun or the name of the sun which comes
from the sky ?—*The sun.*—And where does its name come
from ?—*The sky.*—Did someone give the sun its name or
did it get it by itself ?—*Some one gave it.*—Who ?—*The*

sky." " Where did the Arve get its name ?—_From the mountain._—Tell me, did people give it its name ?—_No, etc._"

FERT (7) concerning the name of the Salève : " How did it get its name in the beginning ?—_From a letter._—And where did the letter come from ?—_The name._—And the name ?—_From the mountain._—How did the name come from the mountain ?—_By a letter._—Where did the letter come from ?—_The mountain._—Clouds are called clouds, aren't they ? Where does the name of the clouds come from ?—_The name ? That is the name._—Yes, but where does it come from ?—_The clouds._—What do you mean when you say it comes from the clouds ?—_It's the name they've got._—But how did the name happen ? How did it begin ? —_By itself._—Yes, but where did the name come from ?— _By itself._"

These children evidently distinguish the name from the thing named, but can only conceive the name as coming from the thing itself. The following case is intermediate between this stage and the next :—

STEI (5½) : " Have you a name ?—_Yes, André._—And that ?—_A box._—And that ?—_A pen_, etc.—What are names for ?—_They are what you can see when you look at things_ (Stei thus believes that one has only to look at a thing to ' see ' its name)—Why have you got a name ?— _So as to know what I'm called._—Then what are names for ?— _To know what things are called._—How did the sun get its name in the beginning ?—_I don't know._—What do you think ?—_Because the sun made the name, the sun gave it in the beginning and so the sun is called sun._—And how did you get your name ?—_We have to be christened._—Who christened you ?—_The clergyman._—And did you take your name ?—_The clergyman makes it for us._—How did the moon get its name ?—_The moon ? The moon is called the moon._—How did it start being called moon ?—_God called it that in the beginning._—How did the clouds start being called clouds ?—_God started them by making them._— But are the clouds' names the same thing as the clouds ?— _Yes, the same thing._—How did the Salève first get its name ?—_By itself._—Did the Salève give itself its name or did someone give it its name ?—_It was always called Salève._" Stei thus comes back to the idea that the name emanates from the thing.

During the second stage, this belief suggested in passing

by Stei, becomes more and more pronounced ; the name comes from the person who made the thing and is thus from the beginning intimately connected with the thing itself. The following examples illustrate this :—

FRAN (9) : " You know what a name is ?—*It's to know what the children are called.*—Where do names come from ? How did they begin ?—*Because God said, ' Now it's time to make children and then they must be called by names.'*—What does that mean to ' be called by names ' ?—*So as to know which children.*—How did the table get its name in the beginning ?—*God said, ' Tables must be made to eat from and people must know what they are for.' "*
BAB (8 ; 11) : " How did the sun get its name in the beginning ?—*It was called that.*—Who by ?—*People.*—What people ?—*The first men,* etc."

All the answers are similar. For most of the children the sun, the sky, the mountains, the rivers, etc., were all made by the first men, but as this question is to be studied later (see Part III) it need not concern us here.

Finally, during the third stage, names were not given by the makers of the things but by other men " savants," etc.

CAUD (9½) : *"The sun was first called ' sun ' by a man and afterwards everybody knew.*—Who was the man ?—*A learned man (un savant).*—What is a ' savant ' ?—*A man who knows everything.*—What did he do to find out the names ? What would you do if you were a ' savant ' ? —*I should try and think of a name.*—How ?—*In my head."* Caud then went on to say that God made the sun, fire, etc., and that their names were given them by " savants."

The evolution of the answers given to question 2 thus seems to show a gradual decrease in nominal realism. During the first stage the name is in the thing. During the second it comes from men but was made with the thing. It is thus still, so to speak, consubstantial with the thing and may possibly still be regarded as situated in the thing. During the third stage the name is at last regarded as due to the person who thinks about the thing.

The study of question 6 entirely confirms these views. This question, it will be remembered, consists in asking whether things have always had their names or whether they existed before they had names. This question it will be seen serves principally as a confirmatory proof for question 2. The two questions should therefore not be set immediately after one another or the child will simply draw his conclusions from what he has just said without considering the new problem. If however they are set in the order suggested, the child will treat question 6 as a fresh problem, and his answer will therefore check the value of his answers to question 2.

In the great majority of cases the answers to questions 2 and 6 were in perfect accord, that is to say children of the first and second stages maintained that things did not exist before having names, while the opposite was held by children of the third stage. Question 6, like question 2, is thus not correctly solved before the age of 9 and 10.

The following examples are of children who regard things as having always had names :—

ZWA (9½) : " Which were first, things or names ?— *Things.*—Was the sun there before it had its name ?— *No.*—Why not ?—*Because they didn't know what name to give it* (would not have known ; but the use of the conditional is difficult for children).—But before God gave it its name was there a sun ?—*No, because he wouldn't know where to make it come from.* (The idea of non-existence always causes difficulty).—But it was there already ?— *No.*—And were there clouds before they had names ?— *No, because there wasn't anyone in the world* (!) " We then tried a question outside the scheme, but naturally suggested by Zwa's metaphysics : " If a thing wasn't there could it have a name ?—*No.*—Long ago men used to believe there was a certain fish in the sea which they called a ' chimera ' but there wasn't really any such fish . . . so can't a thing that doesn't exist have a name ?—*No, because when God saw that the things didn't exist he wouldn't have given them names.*—Have fairies got a name ?—*Yes.*—Then there are things that don't exist and have a name ?—*Only fairies.*— Why are there things that don't exist and yet have a name ?—*God made up other names and they don't exist.*"

This inability to dissociate names from things is very curious. The following observation, involving the same idea, we owe to a colleague, Dr Naville. A little girl of 9 asked: " Daddy, is there really God ? " The father answered that it wasn't very certain, to which the child retorted : " There must be really, because he has a name ! "

MART (8 ; 10) : " Has the sun always had its name ?— *Yes, it always had its name when it was born.*—How was the sun born ?—*Like us."* Same answer for the clouds, the Salève, etc.

PAT (10) : " Before the sun had its name was it already there ?—*Yes.*—What was it called ?—*The sun.*—Yes, but before it was called sun was it there ?—*No. "*

BAB (8 ; 11) whose answers to Question 2 have already been quoted : " Has the sun always had its name or was there a sun before it had a name ?—*It's always had its name.*—Who gave it its name ?—*People (des Messieurs).*— And before people gave it its name was it there ?—*Yes.*— What was it called ?—*Sun.*—Who gave it its name ?— *People."*

The following examples are of children who have come to regard things as existing before they had names. These children are 9 or 10 years old and almost all belong to the third stage as previously distinguished.

MEY (10) : " Tell me, did the sun exist before it had a name ?—*Yes, men gave it its name.*—And were there clouds before they had names ?—*Of course."*

VEIL (9½) : " Did the sun exist before it had a name ?— *It was already there.*—What was it called then ?—*It hadn't yet got a name."*

We must now consider question 3. Since nominal realism is so firmly rooted in children's minds up to the age of 9 or 10 that the existence of things before they have names is regarded as impossible, question 3, which concerns how we come to know these names will strike them as perfectly natural. Thanks to the kindness of Mlles Audemars and Lafendel, the heads of the Maison des Petits (the training school attached to the Institut Jean Jacques Rousseau at Geneva), we know that children themselves sometimes ask this question spontaneously concerning the origins of writing, a subject they question with interest. In the cases where the child maintains that the name emanates from the thing or that all objects were christened by God, the question of how we then come to know that such was the name of the sun, etc., follows of necessity. Question 3 need not therefore be regarded as suggestive because it presupposes nominal realism, but rather as being the natural sequence of question 2. Moreover, as with question 2 it is not correctly solved until the age of 9 or 10.

The stages revealed by means of this question are as follows. During a first stage (5–6) the child supposes that we came to know the names of things simply by looking at them. We need only to look at the sun to know it is called " sun." During the second stage (7–8) the child claims that God told us the names of things. During a third stage (after 9–10) the child finally realises that names have been handed down from father to son since the time they were invented.

It will be seen at once that these stages correspond, both logically and chronologically with the three stages distinguished for question 2, though the detail does not necessarily always correspond. The following are examples of the first stage : that is, we know the sun is called " sun " by looking at it.

STEI (5½), it will be remembered, regarded names as coming either from the things themselves or from God : " How did people know what was the sun's name ?—*I don't know, because they saw it.*—How did you know that was its name ?—*I saw it. My mother told me.*—And how did your mother know its name ?—*Because she saw the sun. . . . We learn it at school.*" The name of the Salève comes from the Salève itself according to Stei's account. " How did people know it was called Salève ?—*Because it's a big mountain.*—And is that why it is called Salève ?—*My mother told me its name.*—And how did your mother know ? —*I don't know. At school.*—And how did the masters of the school know it was called Salève ?—*Because they had seen the Salève.*" As to the moon, " *people knew it was called moon because they had seen it.*"

FERT (7), as quoted earlier, said that the name of the Salève came " *from the mountain.*—When the first men

came, how did they know it was called Salève ?—*Because
it slopes.*—How did they know the sun's name ?—*Because
it's bright.*—But where does the name come from ?—
By itself."

FRAN (9) has already said that names come from God:
" Where does the name of the sun come from ?—*From
God.*—And how did we know that the sun is called ' sun ' ?
—*Because it's in the sky. It's not on the earth. It gives us
light in the sky.*—Yes, but how did we know ?—*Because
it's a great ball. It has rays. We knew it was called ' sun.'*
—But how did we know its name was ' sun ' ? We might
have called it something else.—*Because it gives us light.*—
How did the first men know it was called ' sun ' and not
something else ?—*Because the big ball is yellow and the rays
are yellow, and then they just said it was the sun, and it was
the sun.* (This would seen as if Fran was already suggesting the arbitrary character of names but what follows
shows this to be merely appearance or at any rate that
Fran draws no conclusions from the discovery).—Who
gave the sun it's name ?—*God said it was to be the sun.*—
Then how did the first men know it was to be called sun ?
—*Because it's up in the air. It's high up.*—But when I
look at you I can't see what your name is. You've told
me you are called Albert. How did the first men know
the name of the sun ?—*Because they had seen the sun.*—
Did God tell men or did they find it out for themselves ?
—*They found it out.*"

LAV (6½) who, as we saw, believes the name to emanate
from the thing, is convinced of having found out the names
of the sun, etc., by himself, but not difficult names, like
that of the Salève : " You found out the name of the sun
by yourself ?—*Yes.*—And the Salève ? How did you
know it was called Salève ? Did you find that out by
yourself or did somebody tell you ?—*I was told.*—And the
sun ?—*By myself.*—And the name of the Arve ?—*By
myself. . . .*—And the clouds ?—*I was told.*—And the name
of the sky ?—*I was told that too.*—And the name of the
moon ?—*By myself.*—And did your little sister find it out
by herself or was she told ?—*She found it out by herself.*"

These answers are very suggestive, for although they
press nominal realism to its utmost limit they are not
absurd. For indeed, although children may suppose they
need only to look at a thing to know its name, it does not
in the least follow that they regard the name as in some

way written on the thing. It means rather that for these children the name is an essential part of the thing ; the name Salève implies a sloping mountain, the name sun implies a yellow ball that shines and has rays, etc. But it must also be added that for these children the essence of the thing is not a concept but the thing itself. Complete confusion exists between thought and the things thought of. The name is therefore in the object, not as a label, attached to it but as an invisible quality of the object. To be accurate we should not therefore say that the name '' sun '' implies a yellow ball, etc., but that the yellow ball which is the sun really implies and contains the name '' sun.''

This phenomenon is analogous to the '' intellectual realism '' which M. Luquet has so clearly demonstrated in children's drawings. They draw what they know about an object at the expense of what they see, but they think they are drawing exactly what they see.

We must now pass to the second stage (average age 7–8). In this stage the names of things are not to be found merely by looking at them, but have been told us by God.

ZWA (9½) : '' How did the first men know that the sun was called sun ?—*Because God told Noah.*—And how did they know that the Salève was called ' Salève ' ?—*God told Noah and he told it all to the learned men (savants).*—But did Noah live in this country ?—*Yes.*—If a little negro child who had never seen Geneva or the Salève was to come here would he know its name ?—*No.*—Why not ?— *Because he hadn't ever seen Geneva.*—And would he know the name of the sun when he looked at it ?—*Yes.*—Why ? —*Because he had seen it in his own country.*—But would he know it was called ' sun ' ?—*Yes, because he'd remember.*— But would someone who had never seen the sun know its name when he looked at it ?—*No.*''

The child's conviction has only to be shaken and it will revert to the solutions of the first stage. The following is another example of a child hesitating in this way :—

MART (8 ; 10) : '' How do people know what the sun is called ?—*Because they've been told.*—Who by ?—*God tells us.*—Does God tell us things ?—*No.*--How do we know it then ?—*We see it.*—How do we see what the sun is called ?—*We see it.*—What do we see ?—*The sun.*— But how do we know its name ?—*We see it.*—What do we see ?—*Its name.*—Where do we see its name ?—*When it is fine weather.*—How do we know the name for clouds ? —*Because it is bad weather.*—But how do we know that is their name ?—*Because we've seen them.*—What.—*The clouds,* etc."

Finally certain children, to escape from the difficulty, find the solution ready-made in current theology, and then do not hesitate to ascribe the origin of language to literal inspiration, after the manner of de Bonald :—

PAT (10) : " And who gave the sun its name ?—*God.*— And how did we know its name ?—*God put it into men's heads.*—If God had not given it that name could they have given it another ?—*Yes, they could.*—They knew it was called the sun ?—*No.*—And the names of the fishes ?— *God put the names into men's heads.*"

Here is an example of the third stage (9–10) :—

MEY (10) : " And then how did we know the names ?— *They have come down from father to son.*" It will be re-membered that for Mey names were invented by men distinctly after the origin of things.

The study of question 3 has evidently laid bare certain notions ready made or indirectly due to adult influence as well as many spontaneous ideas. The answers of the first stage however are entirely original and the succession of the three stages follows a regular course, showing clearly that it is in part due to the child's own reflection. In fact it is not until the child is sufficiently developed to give up the convictions of the first stage that he seeks anything else and calls in religious ideas he has learned from others. Moreover, the child's rejection of the idea of a language directly due to God in favour of the much simpler solutions found in the third stage is also quite spontaneous.

§ 2. THE PLACE OF NAMES.—The youngest children believed it only necessary to see the sun to know that it

was called " sun." The natural question to ask then is
" where is the name ? " This constitutes question 4. The
correct way to ask it is to remind the child that a thing
and its name are not the same, and then to add, " very
well, where is the name ? "

Coming after question 3, it is not absurd. It may seem
much too difficult, but like the three preceding it is solved
at about the age of 9 or 10 without any suggestion on our
part. Moreover, it is not solved once and for all at a given
age as if it were a question that had long remained unintelligible and then suddenly become clear following on
discoveries which alone had suggested a solution. On the
contrary, from the most primitive to the correct answers
there is a gradual development. This is what really justifies
the question. Further, within each stage there is complete convergence of the individual answers.

Three stages were found. During the first (5–6) the
names of things are in the things ; during the second
(7–8), the names of things are everywhere, or nowhere,
which as we shall see amounts to the same thing ; and
finally, during the third stage (9–10), names are regarded
as in the voice, then in the head and then in thought
itself. This classification involves no false symmetry.
The average age of the children composing each stage
gives the following results : 6 as the age for the first
stage, $7\frac{3}{4}$ for the second, and $9\frac{1}{2}$ for the third.

The following examples are of the first stage. The name
is in the thing. The first case is very subtle and reveals
immediately the nature of the conviction.

FERT (7), as we have seen considers that names come
from the things themselves and that it is only necessary
to see a thing to know its name. After the examination
previously quoted he again maintained that the name of
the sun comes " by itself." " Do you think it made
itself . . .—In the sun."—A moment later : " Where is the
name of the sun ?—Inside.—What ?—Inside the sun.—
Where is the name of the Salève ?—Inside.—What ?—
Inside the Salève.—Where is the name of the clouds ?—
Inside them too.—Where is your name ? . . . . Now look

here, Fert old chap, tell me where your name is ?—*I was given it.*—Yes but where is your name ?—*It's written down.* —Where ?—*In the book.*—Where is the name of the Jura ?—*In the Jura.*—How is the name of the sun inside the sun ? What do you mean ?—*Because it's hot* (!)— If we could open the sun should we see the name ?— *No.*—And why is the name of the Salève inside the Salève ? —*Because there are stones.*—And why is the name of the clouds inside the clouds ?—*Because they are grey.*—And where is the name of the lake ?—*On it.*—Why ?—*Because it isn't in it.*—Why not ?—*Because there's water there.*— Why is the name on the lake ?—*Because it can't go in, it doesn't go into it.*—But is the word ' lake ' on it ? What does that mean ? Is it written ?—*No.*—Why is it on it ? —*Because it can't go into it.*—Is it on top of it then ?— *No.*—Where is it ?—*It isn't anywhere.*"

It is quite clear what Fert wanted to say. The word is in the thing, because it is part of the essence of the thing. It is not written ; it is in the sun, because the sun is hot, in the Salève because the Salève is stony, etc. There is thus nominal realism in the sense defined in the preceding paragraph, namely that the thing includes its name in its intrinsic character although it is invisible. But when he comes to the lake Fert slips into a more material realism : he shrinks from placing the name in the lake. This hesitation is extremely suggestive and shows better than anything else the strength of the child's realism. But under the sway of the absurdities into which he was led, Fert ends by having recourse to the hypothesis which marks the second stage and declares that the name is not in the thing. But it was only our questions that liberated this conviction and it is still so unstable that Fert will be seen to reject it directly after. Just as Fert's last words were spoken the bell for recreation rang and he went out to play for 20 minutes, after which the examination was continued as follows :—

" Where is the word ' lake ' ?—*It is inside it because of the water* " (!) Fert thus assimilates the case of the lake to that of the sun, the clouds, etc. . . . We therefore tried a contrary suggestion : " How is it that people give

the sun a name and then the name goes into the sun ?—
(Laughing) *No, it's only we who know it.*—Then where is
the name of the sun ?—*It isn't anywhere.*—Where would
it be if it had a place ?—*It's we who know it.*—Where is
the name when we think of it ?—*In the sun, when we think
of the sun.*—But where is the name when we think of it ?
—*In the sun.*—Where is the thought when we think ?—
It's what we think.—Where is what we think ?—*It doesn't
matter what* (he confuses the object and the thought).—
What do we think with ?—*When we remember. . . . With
the memory.*—Where is the memory ?—. . .—In the feet ?
—*No.*—Where ?—. . .—In the head ? . . .—*Yes* (very hesitating).—And where are names ? When you think of the
name of the sun, where is the name of the sun ?—*It's we
who know it.*—Yes, but where is it ?—*It isn't anywhere.*—
Is it in the head ?—*No.*—Why not ?—*Because it's we who
are thinking* (fresh confusion between object and thought :
the moment we think of the sun, it is no longer in our head).
—But if the name was in the head, couldn't we think of
it ?—*Yes* (hesitation).—Then the name is in the head ?—
In the head (without any conviction).—Aren't you sure ?—
No.—Why do you think it is not in the head ?—*Because
it is in the sun.*"

The interest of this quotation is in Fert's determined
resistance to our increasingly pressing suggestions and
his final confession of a realism that is still as strong as
ever : for us to think of the sun means that the name of
the sun must be " in the sun."

The other examples are all of the same type :—

HORN (5 ; 3) says that a name is " *what we use. When
we want to say something, or call someone.*—Where is the
name of the sun ?—*High up in the sky.*—Where ?—*In the
sun.*—Where is your name ?—*There* (indicating the
thorax)." Horn then goes on to say that the name of
the Salève is in the Salève " *because you can't walk on it.*—
On what ?—*On the name.*" After which Horn passes to
answers of a later stage.

MART (8 ; 10) : "" Where is the name of the sun ?—*In
the sky.*—Is it the sun or the name of the sun that is in the
sky ?—*The name.*—Why in the sky ?—*Because it is in the
sky. . . .*"

PAT (10) is on the borderline between this stage and
the next : " Where are names ?—*In the head.*—Where is

the name of the sun ?—*In its head.*" Pat had already stated a few moments earlier that the sun knew its name. We attempted to undeceive him : " It doesn't itself know its name ?—*No, the sun doesn't know.*—Then where is it's name ?—*In my head* (third stage).—And where is the name of the moon ?—*In its head.*—And the name of the sun ?—*In its head.*" (!)

In short, the study of the first stage fully bears out what was stated in the preceding section, that in the primitive stage the name of a thing is a part of the thing. But this does not mean that it is inscribed on or materially represented in the thing. It is part of the essence of the thing. It is a characteristic of the thing, though not a psychic one, for the child does not regard the voice as immaterial, although it is invisible.

During the second stage (7–8) the name becomes dissociated from the thing, but is not yet localised in the thinking subject. It is strictly speaking everywhere or rather wherever it has been spoken. It is " in the air." It surrounds whoever uses it. Other children speak of it as " nowhere," as Fert suggested for a brief moment. This statement does not however mean that the name is immaterial and localised in the mind, for the children who reach this conclusion (third stage) start by saying that the name is in the head or in the voice. Thus " nowhere " simply means that the name is no longer localised in the thing. It is still a primitive answer and only found amongst children still to some extent in the first stage.

Roc (6½, a girl) is a typical case of this second stage : "Now tell me, where is the name of the sun ?—*In the sky.*—The sun is in the sky. But where is the name ?—*In the sky.*—Where ?—*Everywhere.*—Where ?—*In all the houses.*—Is the name of the sun here ?—*Yes.*—Where ?—*In schools and in the class-rooms.*—Whereabouts in the class-rooms ?—*Everywhere.*—Is it in this room ?—*Yes.*—Where else ?—*In the corners.*—Where else ?—*In all the little corners* (pointing to the surrounding air).—Where is the name of the Salève ?—*In the houses.*—Where is it in this house ?—*In the class-rooms.*—Is it here ?—*Yes.*—Where ? —*There* (looking up at the ceiling).—Where ?—*In the*

empty space (dans l'espace).—What is the empty space?
—*It's made up of little paths* (des petits chemins pour
passer[1]).—Can you see the name of the Salève?—*No.*—
Can you touch it?—*No.*—Hear it?—*No."* Same answers
for the Rhône, an exercise-book, etc. "And where is
your name?—*In the house.*—Which house?—*In all the
houses which know it.*—Is it here in this house?—*Yes.*—
Why?—*Because we say it.*—Then where is it?—*In the
school.*—Where?—*In the corners.*—You see that house
over there (pointing out of the window) is your name
there?—*No.*—Why not?—*Because the people there don't
know it.*—If someone were to come in here, would they
know that your name was here?—*No.*—Could they
know?—*If someone said it.*—Since when has your name
been in this room?—*To-day, just now.*—How long will
it stay here?—*Till this evening.*—Why?—*Because everyone goes away then.*—We shall be going at 4 o'clock. Till
when will it be here?—*Till 4 o'clock.*—Why?—*Because I
shall be here.*—And suppose you go but we stay, will your
name still be here?—*Yes, it'll stay.*—Till when?—*Until
you go.*—Where will your name be when we're gone?—
With other people.—Who?—*People who also know it.*—
How does it get to the other people?—*Through the window.*
—And will your name be in the house I go to?—*Yes.*
Where?—*In the kitchen* (Roc lives in the kitchen at home).
—Where?—*In the little corners.*—Isn't your name in our
heads?—*Yes.*—Why?—*Because I said it* (my name).—
Isn't it in the little corners then?—*Yes, it is."*

Roc's idea is quite clear despite its paradoxical appearance. The name is no longer in the thing but is associated
with the people who know it. This marks a great progress
from the first stage. But it is not yet within us, it is
localised in the voice, wherever it has been spoken it
remains in the air surrounding us. When Roc says that
the name follows us, that it goes out of the window, etc.,
she is probably not stating anything she believes literally.
The reason she cannot imagine any other way in which
verbal knowledge accompanies us is simply that she has
never considered the question. This case thus shows:
(1) that the name is connected with the thinking subject

---

[1] Note in the French the spontaneous etymology in associating
"espace" and "passer."

and not with the object, but (2) that the name is external to the subject and localised in his voice, that is to say both in the surrounding air and in the mouth. The last part of the examination brought this out very clearly ; Roc wanted to admit, in accordance with our suggestion, that her name was in the head but refused as yet to give up the idea that it was " in the little corners."

STEI (5½) told us spontaneously that the name of the moon " *isn't in the moon.*—Where is it ?—*It hasn't got a place.*—What does that mean ?—*It means it isn't in the moon.*—Then where is it ?—*Nowhere.*—But when you say it where is it ?—*With the moon* (return to first stage).—And where is your name ?—*With me.*—And mine ?—*With you.* —But when I know your name where is it ?—*With you when you know it.*—And the name of the moon ?—*With it.*—And when we know it ?—*With us.*—Where is it when it's with us ?—*Everywhere.*—Where's that ?—*In the voice.*"

This second stage is interesting from the point of view of the dualism of internal and external, and strikingly confirms what we already found with regard to thought, that it is both in us and in the surrounding air. It is true that in the case of words and names this is in a sense a legitimate view, since actually a word must cross the air before reaching the hearer's ear.

But a fundamental difference separates our view from that of the child in the second stage ; for though he admits that names are in the air he ignores completely the fact that their origin lies within ourselves. The process is centripetal and not centrifugal. The name comes from the object and appears in the voice ; true it is then driven forth again by the voice but in no case does it spring directly from an internal " thought."

The third stage on the contrary is characterised by this discovery that names are in ourselves and come from within us. The child asserts outright that they are " in the head." This stage occurs at the age of 9 or 10.

It is not however always easy to distinguish the third from the second stage. The following three cases may be regarded as intermediary : names are localised both in the mouth and in the voice.

BAB (8 ; 11) : " Where is the name of the sun ?—*Over there.*—Where ?—*By the mountain.*—Is it the sun or the name of the sun which is there ?—*The sun.*—And where is the name of the sun ?—*I don't know. . . . Nowhere.*— When we speak of it where is the sun's name ?—*Over there by the mountain.*—Is the name or the sun over there ? —*The sun.*—When we speak where is the name of the sun ?—*In the mouth.*—And where is the name of the Salève ?—*In the mouth.*—And the name of the lake ?— *In the mouth.*"

MEY (10) : " Where is the name of the sun ?—*In the voice when you say it.*"

CAUD (9½) : " Where is the word ' Salève ' ?—*Every-where.*—What do you mean ? Is it in this room ?—*Yes.*—Why ?—*Because we speak of it.*—Where is it in the room ? —*In our heads.*—Is it in our heads or in the room ?—*It is in our heads and in the room.*"

The only way to interpret these answers is to refer to the context. As we have already seen (§ 1) Bab regards names as contemporary with things and made with them, whilst the explanations of Caud and Mey are always much more developed. We are therefore justified in placing Mey and Caud in the third stage whilst Bab, for whom names come from the things into the voice, is still in the second stage. Caud however is still very near the second stage and should strictly be regarded as intermediary.

The following case belongs definitely to the third stage :—

BUS (10) : " Where are names ? The name of the sun for instance ?—*In the head.*—Whose head ?—*Ours, every one's except those who don't know it.*"

In short, it is evident that question 4 gives rise to answers which develop steadily with age and which com-pletely confirm the results obtained by the previous questions. Question 5 must next be considered, that is, whether things know their names : Does the sun know it is called sun ? etc. It may certainly be questioned whether there is not an element of animism in the nominal realism of the first stages. In other words is it partly because the thing knows its name that the name is situated in the thing ? The case of Pat is clear on this point : he holds, as we have seen, that names are " in the heads " of the things, that is to say that things know their names. We found however no constant relation between nominal realism and the attribution of consciousness to things. Fert, for example, localises names in things, but holds that they do not know their names, etc.

Question 5, however, yielded some interesting results. Four types of answer were found. First, there are a few children who suppose everything to be aware of its name :—

FRAN (9) : " Does a fish know its name ?—*Yes, because it can be called a salmon or a trout.*—Does a fly know its name ?—*Yes, because we can call it a fly or a bee or a wasp.*" Similar answers for a stone, a table, etc. " Does a pencil know its name ?—*Yes.*—How ?—*Because it is written on it where it is made.*—Does it know it is black ?—*No.*— Does it know it is long ?—*No.*—But it knows it has got a name ?—*Yes, because there were people who said that it should be a pencil.*" Clouds cannot see us, " *because they haven't any eyes,*" but they know their names " *because they know they are called clouds,* etc."

Secondly, there are a much greater and more interesting number of children (more interesting since one is less inclined to think they are romancing) who confine this knowledge solely to bodies that move :—

MART (8 ; 10) : " Does a dog know its name ?—*Yes.*— Does a fish know it is called a fish ?—*Of course.*—Does the sun know its name ?—*Yes, because it knows it's got its name.*—Do clouds know they are called clouds ?—*Yes, because they've got a name and they know their name.*—Do matches know they are called matches ?—*No, Yes.*—Yes or no ?—*No, because they are not alive.*—Does the moon know its name ?—*Yes.*—Why ?—*Because it's alive, it moves* (!)—Does the wind know its name ?—*Yes.*—Why ? —*Because it makes it windy.*—Does the Rhône know its name ?—*Yes, because it is it that is the Rhône* (!).—Is it alive ?—*Yes, because it flows into the Arve.*—Does the lake know its name ?—*Yes, because it moves.*—Does it know it moves ?—*Yes, because it is it that moves* (!)."

Thirdly, there are those children who consider that only animals and plants or animals alone, know their names. Even children of advanced intelligence, like Mey, will maintain that perhaps trees know their names.

MEY (10) : " Does a dog know its name ?—*Yes.*—A fish ?—*Yes, because if we know we belong to the world (i.e.* that we are men) *fish ought to know it too.*—And does the sun know it is called the sun ?—*No.*—Why not ?—*Because it isn't alive.*—Does the wind know its name ?—*No.*—Do the trees know that is what they are called ?—*No, because we couldn't make them know it.*—Why not ?—*They wouldn't understand.*—Then they don't know their name?—*Perhaps they may, perhaps not.*—Why ' perhaps not ' ?—*Trees can't learn things.*—And why ' perhaps they may ' ?—*They see other trees besides themselves and think they are the same thing.*—And what does that do ?—*They know they are oaks but they can't see it.*"

Finally, there are children who refuse a knowledge of names to everything. The average age of this group was 9–10. The children who associated knowledge of name with movement (like Mart) had an average age of 7. This evolution agrees closely with what will be found later (Part II) in the study of children's animism.

§ 3. THE INTRINSIC VALUE OF NAMES.—So far we have stud'ed names under what might be called their ontological aspect, that is, their existence, place, and origin. There remains the logical aspect ; are names merely signs or have they an intrinsic logical value ? The two problems are strictly dependent on one another and it is evident that names so far as they are situated in things must be regarded as absolute. But though the ontological realism and the logical realism of names may have the same roots, their persistence may perhaps differ. This—that logical realism lasts much longer than ontological—is precisely what we shall hope to show. Questions 7 and 8 are not in fact solved before the age of 10 and 11 or 12 and even those children who localise the name in the head and who believe in the recent origin of names, continue to hold that names imply not the thing but the idea of the thing ; for example, the sun is called thus because it is bright and round, etc.

To begin with question 8—could names be changed? Two stages were distinguished. Before the age of 10 the children said not, after an average age of 10 they agreed that they could. Between the two were several intermediate cases. The following examples are of the first stage :—

FERT (7) : " Are you called Albert ?—*Yes.*—Could you have been called Henry? Would it have been just the same ?—*No.*—Could the Salève have been called ' Jura ' and the Jura ' Salève ' ?—*No.*—Why not ?—*Because they are not the same thing.*—And could the moon have been called ' sun ' and the sun ' moon ' ?—*No.*—Why not ?—*Because the sun makes it warm and the moon gives light.*"

ROC (6½) admits that God might have changed the names : " Would they have been right then or wrong ?—*Wrong.*—Why ?—*Because the moon must be the moon and not the sun and the sun must be the sun !* "

FRAN (9) : " Could the sun have been given another name ?—*No.*—Why not ?—*Because it's nothing else but the sun, it couldn't have another name.*"

ZWA (9½) knows some German and might have been expected to understand the relative nature of names. But he did not : " Could names be changed and things given other names? You are called Louis, could you have been called Charles ?—*Yes.*—Could this chair have been called ' Stuhl ' ?—*Yes, because it's a German word.*—Why are there other names in German? Why don't they talk like we do ?—*Because they can speak a different way.*—Have things got more than one name ?—*Yes.*—Who gave them the German names ?—*God and the Germans.*—You say names could be changed. Could the sun have been called ' moon ' and the moon ' sun ' ?—*No.*—Why not ?—*Because the sun shines brighter than the moon.*—Have you a brother ?—*Gilbert.*—Could Gilbert have been called ' Jules ' ?—*Yes.*—Well, couldn't the sun have been called ' moon ' ?—*No.*—Why not ?—*Because the sun can't change, it can't become smaller.*—But if every one had called the sun ' moon,' and the moon ' sun,' would we have known it was wrong ?—*Yes, because the sun is always bigger, it always stays like it is and so does the moon.*—Yes, but the sun isn't changed, only its name. Could it have been called . . . etc. ?—*No.*—How would one know it was wrong ?—*Because the moon rises in the evening, and the sun in the day."*

Bus (10) says that nothing could be changed : " *because they wanted to give the sun the name of sun.*—If in the beginning the first men had given different names, would we have seen by now that they were wrong or would we never have known ?—*We should have seen.*—How ?— *Because the sun is hot and the moon is not hot."*

The following is an intermediate case in which names might have been changed but " it wouldn't have been so good " :—

Dup (7½, a girl, very forward) : " Could the sun have been called ' stoll ' ?—*Yes.*—No one would have noticed anything ?—*No.*—Could the table have been called ' chair ' ?—*Yes, no.*—Could it or not ?—*Yes, it could."* A star was called a " star " " *because people thought that name would go best.*—Why ?—*I don't know.*—Could it have been called ' nail ' ?—*It wouldn't have been so good,* etc."

Dup shows a great advance on the preceding subjects in having partly realised the conventional character of names and above all in having understood that if names had been different no one would have known. None the less she seems to believe in a certain harmony between the name and the idea of the thing (an etymological instinct, of which many examples occur later) without venturing definitely to state its nature.

The following examples of the second ·stage show children who realise that the character of names is not entirely arbitrary—that is a later stage—but conventional.

May (10) : " Could you have been called Henry ?— *Yes.*—Could the Jura have been called ' Salève ' and the Salève ' Jura ' ?—*Yes, because men could have changed names or made them the opposite.*—Could the sun have been called ' moon ' ?—*Why not ?*—Could it have ? Could that (a table) have been called a chair and that (a chair) a table ?—*Yes.*—If the sun had been called ' moon,' would we have known it was wrong ?—*No.*—Why not ? —*We couldn't have known it was wrong.*—Why not ?—

*Because they would have given the name ' moon ' to the sun.
They wouldn't have seen any difference.*

BAB (8 ; 11) after having given a number of primitive
answers suddenly realised his sophistry and replied to the
last question quite correctly : " Could the Salève have
been called ' Jura ' and the Jura ' Salève ' ?—*Yes.*—
Why ?—*Because it's the same thing.*—Could the sun have
been called ' moon ' and the moon ' sun ' ?—*Yes.*—Should
we have known the names were changed ?—*Yes.*—Why ?
—*Because we'd have been told.*—If no one had told us should
we have known ?—*No.*—Why not ?—*Because names
aren't marked on things.*"

Thus at about the age of 9 or 10, that is to say just at
the age when all the preceding questions were solved, the
child admits that names could have been changed and that
no one would have known. But this answer does not alone
prove that the name has no intrinsic value. It simply
proves the decline of ontological realism : names are no
longer tied up to the things they represent.

Indeed, question 7, " Why does a particular object
have a particular name ? " is not solved until after
question 8, and it is in fact the hardest of all the
questions.

Success in answering question 8 simply shows that a
child regards a name as conventional—it was decided to
call the sun ' sun,' yet there is nothing in its nature which
tells us to call it thus. But the name is not yet arbitrary ;
it is not a pure sign. On the contrary it is justified on
etymological grounds. The word ' sun ' involves the idea
of shining, round, etc. It is not before the age of 11 or
12 that the child gives up making such justifications and
that question 7 is really solved.

Question 7 gives rise to the following stages : Until
the age of 10, all names contain the idea of the thing.
During the second stage (10 and 11) there is simply some
sort of harmony between the name and the idea ; the
name ' fits,' goes well, etc. That is to say the idea of the
thing is still present in some measure, but other names
containing the same idea might have been chosen. Finally,

after 11 or 12 the name contains in itself nothing. It is purely a sign.

The following are examples of the first stage :—

HORN (5 ; 3) : "Why is the sun called what it is ?—*Because it behaves as if it was the sun.*"

ROC (6) : "Why was the sun given that name ?—*Because it shines.*—And the Salève ?—*Because it is a mountain.*—Why are mountains called 'mountains' ?—*Because they are all white.*"

BAB (8 ; 11) succeeded with question 8 but not with question 7 : "Why is the sun called what it is ?—*Because it is all red.*—Why is the moon called what it is ?—*Because it is all yellow.*—And the Salève ?—*Because it is called the Salève.*—Why ?—*Because* . . . —For a reason or for no reason ?—*For a reason.*—Why ?—. . .—Why are clouds called like that ?—*Because they are all grey.*—Does 'clouds' mean that they are all grey ?—*Yes.*"

VEIL (9½) also succeeded with question 8. But he believes the sun is so called "*because it heats*" ; a table "*because it is used for writing,*" etc.

BUS (10) : The Salève is so called "*because it rises up*" ; the stars "*because they are that shape*" ; a stick "*because it is thick.*" "Does the stick mean that it is thick ?—*It is long.*"

FRAN (9) : The Salève is called "Salève" "*because it is a mountain which slopes on all sides*" (see Fran's case, § 1).

These examples might be multiplied indefinitely. They are curiously reminiscent of the cases of syncretism already studied (*Language and Thought*, Chapter VI) and in particular of the cases of "justification at all cost." The principle is the same in all : a word is always associated with its context until it comes to be regarded as implying the whole context.

It is clearly in this verbal syncretism and in the nominal realism with which it is connected that the origin will be found for what M. Bally has called the "etymological instinct", that is the tendency to attribute to every name an origin justifying it.

In the second stage may be grouped those children who,

whilst not so boldly affirming the connection between names and their content yet feel that there is none the less a harmony.

DUP (7½, a girl) : " Why are the stars called ' stars ' ? —*Because people thought it the best name.*—Why ?—*I don't know.*—(see earlier Dup's answers to question 8). The sun was given the name ' sun,' " *because the sun gives more light* (than the moon) *and I think too that the name of sun goes best for the sun, because the people who gave it that name thought it suited it best.*"

MEY (10) after having solved question 8 said, however, that the sun was so called : " *because people thought it was a good name and a bright one.*"

Dup and Mey do not say that the name of the sun implies light. They merely say there should be a connection. In principle this is true, but what in fact they maintain is not the result of a historical hypothesis but is simply the last traces of nominal realism.

Among the children who solved question 7, Mey was the only one we have so far found who succeeded before the age of 11 or 12, and he only arrived at the solution at the end of the examination and after first giving the answers quoted above.

MEY (10) . . . " Why is the moon called by that name ?—*Just, because it is, for no reason.*—Why is the Salève so called ?—*It's a name people found for it.*—Could it have been called ' Nitchevo ' ?—*Certainly, because that's a name too.*"

GEN (11) : " Why is the sun called what it is ?—*Not for any reason, it's just a name.*—And the moon ?— *No reason. Anything can be called by any name you like.*"

It is thus not until question 7 is solved that the child can be supposed to have understood the arbitrary nature of names. Nominal realism in its ontological form is discarded after the age of 9 or 10, but the realism of the logical form does not start to disappear before 11 or 12. In short, logical realism arises from ontological realism but lasts longer.

§ 4. CONCLUSIONS.—The relation of this study of nominal realism to our previous research on the notion of thought remains to be shown.

For the child, to think is to deal in words. This belief involves three confusions, and three dualisms arise in the process of their elimination. First, there is the confusion between the sign and the thing : thought is regarded as inseparable from its object.[1] There is the confusion between internal and external : thought is regarded as situated both in the air and in the mouth. Finally, there is the confusion between matter and thought : thought is regarded as a material substance, a voice, a whisper, etc.

Does the study of nominal realism confirm the existence of these confusions and does it reveal how the child becomes aware of the corresponding dualisms ? It seems so.

To begin with, the confusion of sign and thing is so evidently rooted in the very nature of nominal realism that it is unnecessary to pursue the point.

The confusion of internal and external is, on the other hand, less obvious at first glance. However, the existence of the second stage, which relates to the location of names, is clear evidence of this confusion. In fact when the child first distinguishes the name from the thing named he does not directly place the name " in the head " : he starts rather by situating it in the surrounding air, " everywhere " where it is spoken of. In other words, voice is at the same time both within and outside ourselves. This is precisely what we found in regard to thought, which is at the same time both " outside " and in the mouth.

The third confusion is not actually found but is obviously implied in the second.

The ages at which these three corresponding dualisms appear has only to be studied to reveal how the child comes to discover the non-material nature of thought.

Until the age of 6 or 7 names come from the things themselves. They were discovered by looking at the things. They are in the things, etc. This first and crudest form of the confusion between sign and thing disappears some-

---

[1] M. Delacroix in *Le Langage et la Pensée* speaks of " adhérence du signe."

where about the age of 7 or 8. The disappearance of the confusion between internal and external comes at about 9 or 10, when names are first localised " in the head." But as we saw with the notion of thought, it is not before the age of 11 that thought is regarded as immaterial.

It would therefore seem as if the child first realised that signs were distinct from things and was then led by this discovery increasingly to regard thought as internal. This continuous and progressive differentiation of signs and things, together with the growing realisation of the subjectivity of thought, appears gradually to lead him to the notion that thought is immaterial.

What psychological factors are responsible for this progressive distinction between signs and things ? Most probably the child's growing awareness of his own thought, which takes place invariably after the age of 7 or 8. Its manifestations have been studied elsewhere (*Judgment and Reasoning*, Chapter IV, §§ 1 and 2). But this awareness is itself dependent on social factors, as we attempted to show : it is through contact with others and the practice of discussion that the mind is forced to realise its subjective nature and thus to become aware of the process of thought itself.

CHAPTER III

DREAMS

THE child is a realist and a realist because he has not yet grasped the distinction between subject and object and the internal nature of thought. Obviously, therefore, he will be confronted by grave difficulties when he attempts to explain the most subjective of all phenomena—dreams. The study of children's conceptions as to the nature of dreams is thus of great interest and from a twofold point of view, for the explanation of the dream supposes the duality first of the internal and the external, and secondly of thought and matter.

If this research is to be of value we must as before set aside all we have learned from the analysis of primitive mentality and in particular the important work of M· Lévy-Bruhl. We shall no doubt come across analogies between the child and the primitive at every step ; this will be, however, in the course of studying the child himself without any preconceived ideas, rather than because we are deliberately seeking such analogies.

The technique to be followed in determining what genuinely are children's ideas concerning dreams is more delicate than that of the preceding researches. It is probable, in fact, that children ask many questions concerning their dreams and are given the most contradictory explanations, particularly regarding nightmares, so that it is necessary to be constantly on guard and to try to confirm each result by complementary questions.

The procedure we found most satisfactory consisted of an inquiry bearing on four points, which should always be given in a fixed order. The first concerns the origin of the dream. The question is stated thus : " You know what a dream is ? You dream sometimes, at night ? Then tell me where the dreams come from ? " This question is usually sufficient to start the child talking, particularly when it believes dreams to come " from the head." When the origin is held to be external, the question must be pressed further, and an explanation given as to " how," etc. A particularly equivocal answer is : " It's the night that makes dreams." Some children mean by this simply that it is at night that one dreams, while others, on the contrary, mean that a black smoke (see Chapter IX, § 2) causes the formation of dreams, that is to say of deceptive images, in the room (and not in the head). In short, one must always get to the roots, yet without allowing the question itself to be suggestive and without wearying the child and goading him into the " answer at random."

The second point, the place of the dream, completes the first and forms an indispensable check on it. When the child says that dreams come " from the head," two completely different meanings are possible. The child may believe either that the dream is in the head or he may think that the head produces a dream in the room. Dreams may be regarded as either internal or external just as much when they come from God as when they are made by the night. It is, therefore, of primary importance to determine where the child locates dreams. Moreover, this question is the counterpart to those bearing on the place of thought and of names studied earlier. But in the case of dreams the question raises difficulties. If put thus : " While you dream, where is the dream ? " the danger lies naturally in the child knowing the dream to be in the head yet saying " in front," because it thinks it is being asked where the dream *appears* to be. The answer " in front of us " may thus sometimes mean that the dream is conceived as really in front and at other times simply that the dream appears to be in front of us.

This point calls for the closest attention. The questions must then be asked, " Yes, in front of us, but is it really and truly in front of us or does it only seem to be in front of us ? " Or with the very little ones, " But is there really something in front of us or is it only make-believe ? " etc. But the majority of the children who describe the dream as " in front of us " are just those who are unable to make this distinction between " being " and " seeming " and cannot, therefore, understand the controlling question. This must, however, be proved in each case.

Also it is important to start with the first point before asking, " where are dreams." Otherwise there may be suggestion by perseveration, in the sense that the child who describes the dream as " in front of us " may then be tempted to seek the origin of the dream as external also, though he would not have done so if the question of origin had been asked first.

The third point concerns the organ of the dream. " What do you dream with ? " Finally, the fourth point is the " why " of dreams. This question is suggestive in the sense that to ask : " Why did you dream of your mother, of school, etc. . . ." is to suggest a purpose. In fact all the children over the age of 7 or 8 gave a causal explanation (" because I thought of it during the day, etc."), whilst only the youngest gave the " Why " a pre-causal interpretation. This is a question to be gone into.

It may also be mentioned that to avoid the possibility of suggestion by perseveration, with two or three exceptions, none of the children we questioned on the subject of dreams had previously been questioned on names. and only half had already been questioned on thought.

The answers obtained can be classified as belonging to three distinct stages. During the first (approximately 5–6) the child believes the dream to come from outside and to take place within the room and he thus dreams with the eyes. Also, the dream is highly emotional : dreams often come " to pay us out," " because we've done something we ought not to have done," etc. During the second stage (average age 7–8) the child supposes the source of the dream to be in the head, in thought, in the voice, etc., but the dream is in the room, in front of him. Dreaming is with the eyes; it is looking at a picture outside. The fact that it is outside does not mean that it is true : the dream is unreal, but consists in an image existing outside, just as the image of an ogre may exist, without there actually being a real ogre. Finally, during the third stage (about 9–10), the dream is the product of thought, it takes place inside the head (or in the eyes), and dreaming is by means of thought or else with the eyes, used internally.

§ 1. First Stage : The Dream comes from outside and remains External.—It seems most probable that the first time a child dreams it confuses the dream with reality. On waking the dream is still held to be true and objective, and, above all, the memory of the dream becomes confused with ordinary memories. With regard to nightmares this seems quite evident. Every one knows how hard it can be to calm a child who has just woken from a nightmare, and how impossible it is to convince him that the objects he dreamt of did not really exist. To illustrate the confusion which takes place between the dream and the recollection of actual events the author has collected several typical cases from amongst the personal recollections of his collaborators.

Here is an example :—

" All my childhood I believed that a train had really passed over me. I can remember the exact scene of the adventure : a level-crossing which really existed quite near the house where my parents lived. In my false memory, my mother had just crossed the line pushing a baby in a pram when I realised a train was almost upon me. I had barely time to throw myself down on my back and I can still see the carriages passing over my head at top-speed. Afterwards I got up perfectly safe and sound and rejoined my mother. That is the false memory which I believed true all through my childhood. It was not till about the age of 12 that my

*parents undeceived me, when I was boasting one day (for
the first time !) of having been under a train. The exactitude
of the memory convinces me it must be of a dream which had
centred round the image of the level-crossing I knew so well."*

In the same way, another of our collaborators believed
during a great part of her childhood that her parents had
attempted to drown her in the sea. Here again, the visual
exactitude of the memory certainly seems to indicate a
dream.

Mlle Feigin has had the happy idea of studying how
the child gradually comes to distinguish the dream from
reality. She has found that, up till about the age of 9,
it is not the absurdities of the dream which aid the child's
judgment but that on the contrary, contradiction with the
facts of reality as well as opposition to the views of others
are used as criteria at a still earlier age. But in all cases,
the inquiry has shown that the distinction between the
dream and reality is not always easy and that emotional
dreams, in particular, have a tendency to be completely
confused with reality.

How then does the child explain the dream the first
time he is able to distinguish it from reality ? Evidently
he will regard the dream as a sort of deceptive reality—
just as an Epinal picture [1] may be deceptive by representing things which do not exist—but objective since the
picture in the book is made with paper and colours that
really exist. This may easily be observed. Sully quotes
the spontaneous remark of a child who did not want to
go back to a certain room, *" because it is full of dreams."*

BANF (4½) describes the dream as made of " lights "
which are in the room. These lights are " *little lamps, like
bicycles* " (*i.e.* like the lamps on bicycles at night). These
lights come " *from the moon. It breaks up. The lights
come in the night."* In other words Banf attributes the
" lights " which make the dreams to the most striking
source of light—the moon, which divides into quarters.

[1] Coloured illustrations to children's fairy-tales, etc., so-called from
the town where they were first produced during the eighteenth century.
[Translator's note.]

Had (6 ; 6) : " You know what a dream is ?—*When you are asleep and you see something.*—Where does it come from ?—*The sky.*—Can you see it ?—*No*(*!*) . . . *yes, when you're asleep.*—Could I see it if I was there ?—*No.*—Why not ?—*Because you wouldn't be asleep.*—Can you touch it ?—*No.*—Why not ?—*Because it is in front of us."* And later : " *When you are asleep you dream and you see them* (the dreams), *but when you aren't asleep you don't see them."*

Kun (7 ; 4) says that dreams come " *from the night.*—Where do they go ?—*Everywhere.*—What do you dream with ?—*With the mouth.*—Where is the dream ?—*In the night.*—Where does it happen ?—*Everywhere. In rooms, in houses.*—Whereabouts ?—*In the bed.*—Can you see it ?—*No, because it is only at night.*—Would anyone know you were dreaming ?—*No, because it's near us.*—Could you touch it ?—*No, because you're asleep when you dream.*—Is the dream made of thought ?—*No.*—Where is it ?—*In the night.*—Where ?—*Near.*—Is it the thoughts we think with ?—*No."* And later : " Could anyone see it ?—*No, because if you looked at it, it would go."*

Sci (6) : " Where does a dream come from ?—*From the night.*—What is it ?—*It's the evening.*—What is the night like ?—*It is black*—How are dreams made ?—*They come when you shut your eyes.*—How ?—*I don't know.*—Where are the dreams made ?—*Out there* (pointing to the window).—What are dreams made of ?—*Black.*—Yes, but of what ?—*Of light.*—Where do they come from ?—*From the lights outside.*—Where are they ?—*There are some out there* " (pointing to the street-lamps). " Why do dreams come ?—*Because the light makes them."* (On the subject of light, see Sci's remarks on vision, Chapter I, § 2.) Later on Sci remarked that dreams come " *from the sky.*—What sends them ?—*The clouds.*—Why the clouds ?—*They come."* This belief that the night comes from the clouds is in fact frequent (see Chapter IX, § 2). Sci has thus returned to his idea that dreams are due to the night.

Bourg (6) : " When do you dream ?—*At night.*—Where is the dream when you are dreaming ?—*In the sky.*—And then ? . . .—*It comes in the night."* " Can you touch the dream ?—*No, you can't see and besides you're asleep.*— But if you were not asleep ?—*No, you can't see a dream.* —When you are asleep, could another person see your dream ?—*No, because you're asleep.*—Why can't one see it ?—*Because it is night.*—Where do dreams come from ?

—From the sky." To dream, there must thus be something in the room. But one cannot see it clearly because one is asleep and it is night-time. But, strictly, one ought to be able to see it.

BARB (5½) : " Do you ever have dreams ?—*Yes, I dreamt I had a] hole in my hand.*—Are dreams true ?—*No, they are pictures* (images) *we see* (!)—Where do they come from ?—*From God.*—Are your eyes open or shut when you dream ?—*Shut.*—Could I see your dream ?—*No, you would be too far away.*—And your mother ?—*Yes, but she lights the light.*—Is the dream in the room or inside you ?—*It isn't in me or I shouldn't see it* (!)—And could your mother see it ?—*No, she isn't in the bed. Only my little sister sleeps with me."*

ZENG (6) : " Where do dreams come from ?—*They come from the night.*—How ?—*I don't know.*—What do you mean by ' they come from the night ' ?—*The night makes them.*—Does the dream come by itself ?—*No.*—What makes it ?—*The night.*—Where is the dream ?—*It's made in the room.*—Where does the dream come from ?—*From the sky.*—Is the dream made in the sky ?—*No.*—Where is it made ?—*In the room."*

RIS (8½, a girl) : " Where do dreams come from ?—*From the night.*—Where is the dream when you are dreaming ?—*In my bed.*—Where ?—*In the room quite near, beside me.*—Where does the dream come from ?—*From the night.*—Should I see it, if I was near you ?—*No.*—And do you see it ?—*No* (*cp.* Bourg).—Then what is it ?—. . .—Is it made of something or not of anything ?—*Of something.*—Of paper ?—(laughing) *No.*—Of what ?—*Of words.*—And what are words ?—*Talking* (*en voix*). Where does the talking in the dream come from ?—*From the sky.*—Where in the sky?—. . .—How is it made in the sky ? . . . Does the dream come of itself or does something send it.—*It comes by itself.*—Why do we dream ?—*Because we think of something."* Ris's view is evidently advanced ! But she identifies thought with speech (la voix) and continues to believe the dream comes from without : " What is talking (la voix) made of ?—*Air*—Where does it come from ?—*The air.*—And the dream ?—*From the sky."*

MONT (7 ; o) declares that the things he sees in dreams are " *against the wall.*—Should I see them if I was there ? *Yes.*—Where do they come from ?—*From outside.*—What sends them ?—*People* (*des Messieurs*).—What do you dream of ?—*A man being run over.*—Is he in front of you

when you dream or inside you ?—*In front of me.*—Where ?
—*Under my window.*—Should I have seen him if I had
been there ?—*Yes.*—Did you see him in the morning ?—
No.—Why not ?—*Because it was a dream.*—Where did
this dream come from ?—. . .—Did you make it or someone else ?—*Someone else.*—Who ?—*A man my father knows*
(the one who was run over).—Does he make all the dreams ?
—*Only that one.*—And the others ?—*Other men.*"

Engl (8½) : " Where do dreams come from ?—*I don't
know.*—Say what you think.—*From the sky.*—How ?
—. . .—Where do they come ?—*To the house.*—Where is
the dream whilst you are dreaming ?—*Beside me.*—Are
your eyes shut when you dream ?—*Yes.*—Where is the
dream ?—*Over there.*—Can one touch it ?—*No.*—See it ?
—*No.*—Could someone beside you see it ?—*No.*—What
do we dream with ?—*The eyes.*"

We have made a point of multiplying these examples
to show that though the detail of all these answers differs
widely, in their broad lines they are similar. In fact, for
all these children the dream is an image or a voice which
comes from outside and manifests itself in front of their
eyes. This image is not real in the sense of representing
real events, but as an image it does exist objectively. It
is external to the child and is in no sense mental. The
nature of this belief must briefly be made clear.

To begin with, it will have been noticed that emphasis
was put upon the question : " Would someone beside
you have been able to see the dream ? " The most
realistic among the children, like Had and Mont, agreed
that they would, since they regarded the dream as a
ready-made image which comes and takes its place beside
the dreamer and which is derived from the objects which
figure in the dream. Others, like Bourg, Engl, etc., held
the contrary view, but the interesting point here was that
they claimed that neither could they see the dream. This
was because at the moment they were answering the
question, they were thinking not of the actual sensations
which make up what is seen in the dream, but of that
something which, so they say, manufactures the dream
in the room : " You can't see the dream," according to

Bourg, " because it is night." Here the child is less a
realist. What he situates in the room is simply the cause
of the dream. This by no means indicates that he localises
dreams in the head. Although they can answer that their
eyes are shut whilst they dream, these children all believe,
nevertheless, that it is " with the eyes " that they see the
images that the cause of the dream makes outside. It is
as if there was beside them a something impinging on
their eyes but invisible to all. Compared with the group
represented by Mont these children are in the first stage
of subjectivism, but they are still realist. Compared with
the later stages, the children of the first group are still
entirely in the grip of a primitive realism, whilst the
realism of those in the second stage is due to the necessities
of explanation, that is to say is a derivative type of realism.
Moreover, the two types of reply must evidently coexist
in each child.

In the matter of the localising of the dream, these two
groups of answers correspond to two distinct types of
belief. According to one type (that of Mont, etc.) the
dream is located at the actual spot of which one dreams ;
if the dream is of a man in the street, the dream is in the
street " under my window." But yet there is nothing
real there, because it is a dream, in other words an
illusion ; but the image as image does exist materially
" under my window." There is thus primitive realism
or confusion between " being " and " seeming " : the
dream seems to be in the street, therefore it is in the
street. It must, however, be insisted that this confusion
is never complete with those children who realise that
dreams are illusory. In other words, those children who
locate the dream in the street also believe (through
participation, and in defiance of logic) that it is in the
room. This is the case of Mont who regards the dream
as at the same time " against the wall " of his room and
also in the street. We shall meet more cases of this type
presently (see cases of Metr and of Giamb), so that it is
unnecessary to pursue the point now.

The second type of belief consists simply in admitting that the dream is in the room. This is a realism of a much more interesting kind, since it is not directly dependent on the illusions of the dream itself. It would seem as if children ought to regard the dream as either in the things of which they dream, through primitive realism (as Mont does partially) or as in the head. As a matter of fact, however, children place the dream beside them because they are at the same time too advanced to believe any longer in the reality of the dream but also not yet advanced enough to regard images as subjective and internal representations. To place the dream in the room is thus a compromise between a thoroughgoing realism and subjectivism. " Being " is no longer confused with " seeming " ; but the internal nature of images is not yet understood.

Now this belief in the external nature of images is extremely insistent. One is tempted at first to think the children have not understood the question and think they are being asked where the dream seems to be. But this is not the case. Barb, for example, after having defined the dream as " pictures that you see," absolutely refuses, despite our suggestion, to make the dream internal : " It isn't in me or I shouldn't see it." The following is a yet more striking case, because the child is advanced, has almost given up the beliefs of the first stage and almost spontaneously made the suggestion—to reject it, however —that the dream is within himself :—

METR (5 ; 9) : " Where does the dream come from ?— *I think you sleep so well that you dream.*—Does it come from us or from outside ?—*From outside.*—What do we dream with ?—*I don't know.*—With the hands ? . . . With nothing ?—*Yes, with nothing.*—When you are in bed and you dream, where is the dream ?—*In my bed, under the blanket. I don't really know. If it was in my stomach* (!) *the bones would be in the way and I shouldn't see it.*—Is the dream there when you sleep ?—*Yes, it is in my bed beside me.*" We tried suggestion : " Is the dream in your head ?—*It is I that am in the dream : it isn't in my head* (!)—*When you dream, you don't know you are in bed. You know you are walking. You are in the dream. You are in bed, but you don't know you are.*—Can two people have the same dream ?—*There are never two dreams* (alike).—Where do dreams come from ?—*I don't know. They happen.*—Where ?—*In the room and then afterward they come up to the children. They come by themselves.*— You see the dream when you are in the room, but if I were in the room, too, should I see it ?—*No, grown-ups* (*les Messieurs*) *don't ever dream.*—Can two people ever have the same dream ?—*No, never.*—When the dream is in the room, is it near you ?—*Yes, there !* (pointing to 30 cms. in front of his eyes)."

This case is remarkable. It contains the decisive statement : " It is I that am in the dream : it isn't in my head " ; in other words : The dream is something inside which I am shut up and so I can't at the same time have it all inside me. These words and the commentary following them are highly instructive. Firstly, Metr makes very clearly the distinction between " being in bed " and " knowing you are in bed "—" You are in bed, but you don't know you are." Secondly, Metr (who, by the way, appears to have only one word for " knowing " and " believing ") gives as the proof that the dream cannot be in him, the fact that he, Metr, is " in his dream." And to show that he really is in his dream he adds that when he is dreaming he " knows," that is to say he believes, that he is walking, etc. In other words, whilst knowing the dream to be unreal (and admitting that he alone can see his dream), Metr thinks that he is himself represented in his dream, perhaps only as an image, but as an image of which he himself is the source. Like Mont, Metr thus believes that there is participation between the image dreamed and the thing of which it is the image. In his arguments, however, he is exactly on a level with a child of the second stage, Fav, whom we shall study later. From the examples given so far, it may, therefore, be concluded that as regards the localisation of images, the dream is conceived as a picture situated beside the child, but a

picture interacting with the things it represents and consequently coming partly from the places where these
things are situated.

The next point to consider concerns the substance of
the dream. In this respect the answers of children of the
first stage are identical with those of the second, except
in a simple case where the dream is described as being
made " of night " or of " black." This statement is
directly bound up with the belief in the external origin
of the dream ; the dream comes from outside, from the
night (that is to say from a black smoke), it is, therefore, made " of night." In the other cases, the fabric of
the dream consists of that characteristic with which the
dream itself is most highly charged. Those children who
are struck by the visual character of their dreams—much
the greatest number—believe the dream to be made
" of light." Those who have heard voices in their dreams
suppose the dream to be made " of words," that is to say,
ultimately, " of air."

In considering the origin of the dream we found two
types of answer co-existing in the majority of children.
First are those who offer no real explanation or whose
explanations are simply elaborated from their ideas on
the substance of the dream. For example, a child will
say the dream comes " from the sky," " from outside,"
" from the night," " from the room," all of which statements amount to much the same. When the child stresses
the luminous character of the dream he has recourse to
such sources of light as the moon or the street-lamps to
explain its origin.

What is more interesting is that certain children, on
the other hand, seem to believe that it is the people they
dream of who produce the dream. Thus Mont seems to
suggest that it is the man of whom he dreamed (the man
who was run over and who is a friend of his father) who
himself caused the dream. Mlle Rodrigo, who set the
same questions to some hundred Spanish children, obtained
a large number of answers according to which dreams are

sent not only by God or the devil (which proves nothing in itself) but principally by " wolves " (the child having dreamed of wolves), or " the king " (of whom the child had dreamed), or " men " or " the poor " (the child having dreamed of gipsies), etc. There would thus seem to be participation here also between the person dreamed of and the dream itself ; in other words it would seem that the person dreamed of is in part the cause of the dream, although he need not appear in the dream in flesh and blood.

But on this point care must be taken not to endow the child with a systematic theory but rather to unravel the real significance of his answers. The question as to the " Why " of dreams must first be treated. It appears, as we shall attempt to show, that certain children regard dreams as a sort of punishment, and it is this character of retribution which leads these children to suppose that the persons they dream of must be responsible for the origin of the dream.

The following are examples :—

SCI (6), as we have already seen, attributes dreams to the street-lamps, but this does not prevent him from supposing dreams to have a purpose :—" Why do we have dreams ?—*Because the light makes them.*—Why ?—*Because they* (the dreams) *want to come.*—Why ?—*To pay us out (pour nous embêter).*—Why ?—*So that we shall wake up.*"

BAG (7) :—" Where do dreams come from ?—*At night, from God. God sends them.*—How ?—*He makes the night come and he whispers in our ears.*—How is the dream made ? —*It is made with words.* . . .—What is the dream made of ?—*It is made of letters.*" We asked Bag to tell us one of his dreams : he had dreamed of robbers. " Where did this dream come from ?—*From God.*—Why did God send you this dream ?—*To pay me out, because I wasn't good.*" " What had you done to have such a dream ?—*I'd been naughty, I'd made Mother cry. I'd made her run round the table.*" This last was not from the dream Bag told us, but was true ; after behaving stupidly Bag had tried, in order to escape his mother, to " run round the table " !

GIAMB (8½): " Where do dreams come from ?—*They are when you've done something and you know of it lots of times.*—What does that mean ?—*You've done something and you dream of it every day.*" Giamb would thus seem to have reached the second stage, but as we shall see, he is between the two, the origin of the dream he regards as both internal and external. " Where is the dream when you are dreaming ?—*When you've done something ?*— When you dream, where are you ?—*In bed.*—Where is the dream ?—*At home.*—Where ?—*In the house, where the thing is you've done* (!)—Where is the dream ?—*In the room.*—Where ?—*In the bed.*—Where ?—*All over, every- where in the bed.*—Where does the dream come from ?— *Where you've been for a walk.*—When you dream of Miss S. (the teacher) where does the dream come from ?— *From school.*—What made the dream ?—*Perhaps it was in class, you did something, then you dream about it.*—Why do you dream of the boys ? (he had dreamed of his school- fellows)—*Because they did things they ought not to.*— Why did you dream of it ?—*Because they did things they ought not to.*—What makes dreams ?—*It's what you see while you are dreaming.*—What do you dream with ?— *With the eyes.*—Where does the dream come from ?—*From the children who did the things. It's what the children did.*" We try suggestion : " Does the dream come from the head or from outside ?—*From the head.*—Why from the head ? —*Because you've done something you ought not to.*—Who told you you dream of things you ought not to have done ? —*Because sometimes you are afraid* (fear is felt to be a retribution)." A moment later we tried the following suggestive question : " Who sends dreams ?—*The boys who made us dream.*"

It is clear from these examples that for the child the dream is not usually an accidental happening but is rather an emotional resultant. It may be that certain parents are stupid enough to make use of their children's dreams to make them believe in retribution for wrong- doing but in the cases quoted above the child's belief in the purposive character of dreams seems to be quite spontaneous : Sci, for example, does not draw any moral from the dream, but nevertheless regards it as directed towards a definite end ; Giamb connects his dream with faults he has not himself committed and sees in the fear the dream provokes the proof of its moral character. From this purposiveness to the idea that the dream is caused by persons outside the dream is but a step. Giamb takes the step although he has almost arrived at the second stage.

But, in other respects, Giamb's answers bear a singular resemblance to those of Mont and of Metr, quoted earlier. The essence of Giamb's remarks, as of Mont's, is, in fact, a realism of the image, analogous to nominal realism, and such that the image is conceived as necessarily bound up with the thing it represents. Indeed, although Giamb says that the dream comes from " when you've done something and you know of it," and although following our suggestion he admits that the dream comes from the head, he none the less regards the dream as taking place in the room or at the very spot " where the thing is you've done," that is to say at the place where the thing is which the dream is about. Further, he suggests that the persons the dream is about are the cause of the dream, because they have done " things they ought not to." The dream, according to Giamb, comes " from the children who did the things."

In short, treating these answers merely as negative indications and without ascribing any systematic theory to the child the following conclusions may be drawn. Whilst regarding the dream as false, that is to say as an image displayed in front of us in order to deceive us, the child, nevertheless, adheres to the suggestion that the image is a part of the person it represents and is a material emanation of the facts it has observed. Just as the word participates in the object of which it is the name and is situated both in it and close to us at the same time, so the image participates in the object imagined and is situated both in it and in the room at the same time. The sign is confused with the thing signified. It need not, however, be supposed that the child regards the person of whom he dreams as the conscious and only cause of the dream but simply that he has not yet the capacity to regard the image of a person that he has actually seen as something internal that has been produced by thought. The immediate source of this image is regarded as in the person just as the immediate source of names was held to be in the objects named (Chapter II), and in this case all the more so since the emotional and moral aspect of the dream makes the child regard the image as pursuing him not by chance but in order to punish him.

It is this emotional aspect which explains why it is almost always persons and not things that children regard as causing the images which form their dreams. When the child says that the night or the moon have sent the dreams he has not dreamed of the night or the moon, but when he says that a certain person has sent the dream it means he has dreamed of that person. Also it is obviously easier to maintain the realist attitude towards images when these are of persons than when they are of things ; the image of a person is much more charged with emotion than that of a thing and so is much more likely to be conceived as directly inspired by the person it represents than the image of an object as inspired by the object. The attitude of children towards pictures is, in fact, well known :—

DAN, a child of 14, whom we shall quote presently, remembers having believed during his childhood " *that statues and pictures of people were not alive but could think and see. One wasn't alone so long as there was a picture in the room.*"

DEL (6½) (see *Language and Thought*, p. 207) before a statue : " *Is it dead ?* "

DAR (2) cried because a photograph had just fallen from the wall, and said that the ladies had hurt themselves falling.

In short, apart from the emotional aspect we have just considered, the participation between the images and the persons they represent must be regarded as of the same type as that between names and the things named. Seen in this light, the beliefs we have studied seem easy to interpret. Our interpretation is, moreover, made more acceptable by the fact that when they first dream all children regard their dreams as real. It is principally through the agency of its parents and its social environment that the child becomes undeceived. But for this influence the participation between the persons seen in the dream and the real persons would be much keener.

Is it possible, nevertheless, to find children who systematically admit such participations and who thus systematically believe in their dreams, yet place them on a plane other than that of reality? According to Sully this is so (see *Studies of Childhood*, pp. 103, 104). We have only found a single case favouring this view and a doubtful one at that since it is based only on memories. It must, however, be mentioned, since it might be of value if anyone were to have the good fortune to find similar beliefs by direct observation.

DAN (14) knows nothing of the sociology of primitive peoples and comes of a family entirely free from superstition. The bonds of friendship and confidence which exist between us preclude the possiblity of any attempt on his part to deceive us intentionally in relating the memories of his childhood. Dreams he says were for him "*real.*" They were "*like another world.*" "*Every one went to bed* (in reality) *about the same time and then either one was carried off to another world or else everything changed.*" Dan was quite aware that he remained in his bed, "*but all of myself was outside.*" (We shall find the same expressions given by a child of 8, Fav, in the following section.) The world of dreams was arranged in countries and Dan maintained that he could find the same places in one dream as in another. "*I often had the same dream, about cats. There was a wall, a little train and lot of cats on the wall and all the cats chased me.*" This dream of the cats used to frighten Dan, but to return to the real world he had a device which he used in the dream itself : "*I would throw myself on the ground* (in the dream) *and then I would wake up. I was still very frightened* (once awake). *I had the idea that I had been eaten up by the cats.*"

A point of particular interest is that Dan used these ideas to explain the stories he was told and conversely he used the stories to co-ordinate his world of dreams. Thus, like nearly all the children we questioned on the subject, he would explain how fairies, ogres, etc., must at one time have existed since they are still spoken of in stories to-day. But, according to Dan, this fairy world still survived in the world of dreams. In particular, the voyage which took one from one's bed to join the dream, " had something to do with fairy-tales." "The magic voyages" of fairy-tales must once have been real, since they were still possible in the dream.

As a child Dan had also, associated with the feelings of being a stranger to one's self and of loss of personality that so many children experience, the idea that everything must happen of necessity, that everything was decided beforehand, that one was not responsible and that punishments ought not therefore to exist. But he attributed the same qualities to the dream world ; everything happened there of necessity, but without reference to the real world. It was " like a double life," but a life regulated in advance and independent of the will of the dreamer.

Finally, what seems to prove that these statements really correspond to the actual beliefs Dan held as a child (and that they are not merely systematisations made by him in retrospect at the age of 14) is that this belief in the land of dreams disappeared all at once when he first went to school and mixed with other boys. Indeed, he remembers having wondered whether his school-fellows also went to the land of dreams, and having decided it could not be so, his own conviction suffered definitely.

It is impossible to say how much truth is contained in these memories of Dan. But they seem to point to the fact that, but for the adult social environment, children's conceptions of dreams would show even stronger participation than that already analysed. But, whatever the extent of these participations (which in the child can only be arrived at with difficulty, owing to their emotional colouring) the fact is established that during the first stage the images of the dream are regarded as being external to mind and as emanating from external sources either in the persons and the things dreamed of or in such substances as the night, the light, etc.

§ 2. THE SECOND STAGE: THE DREAM ARISES IN US OURSELVES BUT IS EXTERNAL TO US.—The best proof of the truth of the preceding interpretations is the existence of the second stage. This stage is, in certain respects, more interesting than the first, since it reveals the child's realism in its most determined and developed form. The children of this stage have, indeed, discovered or learned that the dream comes from ourselves, or from thought, or from the head, etc. But, since they cannot understand how an image can be " external " at the moment of seeing it they place it, as in the first stage, in the room beside them.

It seems as if in a large number of cases the child comes independently to the conclusion that he dreams with thought or with the head. The contradictions of the dream with reality force him, in fact, gradually to distinguish the image from the thing it represents, and thus to regard the image, if not as a mental object, at least as an object detached from reality and connected with speech, sight, thought, etc. It is the same process we found with names, when the names are first regarded as existing independently of the thing named.

The following examples are of intermediate cases between the first and second stages, in which may be discerned the first spontaneous, though groping efforts to cast off the idea of an external origin for the dream.

HORN (5 ; 3) : " You know what it is to dream ?—*Yes. It's when you see people.*—Where is the dream ?—*In the smoke (la fumée).*—What smoke ?—*The smoke that comes from the bedclothes.*—Where do the dreams come from ? —*From here* (pointing to his stomach).—Then how is it that they are in the bedclothes while you are dreaming ? —*Because you know it's like that.*" Horn adds that the dream comes in front of the eyes, a few centimetres away. He does not believe thought to be with the mouth but

situates thought in the thorax. Is the smoke with which
he associates the dream, therefore, the respiration ? Comparison of Horn's case with those of Ris (§ 1) and Falq
(Chapter I, § 3) would suggest that this is so ; the dream,
in so far as it is thought, being held to consist in speaking,
in air and in the breath from respiration.

DUG (6½) : " What is a dream ?—*You dream at night.
You are thinking of something* (!)—Where does it come
from ?—*I don't know.*—What do you think ?—*That we
make them ourselves* (!)—Where is the dream while you
are dreaming ?—*Outside.*—Where ?—*There* (pointing to
the street, through the window).—Why outside ?—*Because you've got up.*—And then ?—*It goes.*—While you
are dreaming where is it ?—*With us.*—Where ?—*In the
bed.*—Where.—*Near.*—If I was there, should I see it ?—
No . . . Yes, because you'd be near the bed.—Where does
the dream come from ?—*Nowhere* (!)—What does it come
out of ?—*Out of the bed.*—How does it get there ?—
Because you're dreaming.—Where is the dream made ?—
In the bed.—How ?—*From air* (cp. Horn).—Where does
the air come from ?—*From outside.*—Why ?—*Because the
window is open.*—Why do you dream ?—*Because yester-
day we went bathing and were frightened.*—Is there something that sends the dream ?—*Yes, the birds.*—Why ?—
Because they like the air." Dug then told how he had
dreamed of soldiers. " Where did this dream come from ?
—*From outside.*—Where ?—*From far away, over there*
(pointing through the window).—Why ?—*Because there's
a wind.*—What sends the dreams ?—*The air.*—And then ?
—*The birds.*—And then ?—*The pigeons.*—And then ?—
That's all.—Why the pigeons ?—*Because they're happy
when it's windy.*—Do the pigeons send the dreams on
purpose ?—*No.*—Do they know they are sending them ?
—*No.*—Then why do they send them ?—*Because of the
wind.*—Does the pigeon make the dream ?—*Yes.*—How ?
By bringing the wind.—If there wasn't any wind, could we
dream ?—*No, the dream wouldn't be able to come.*"

These curious cases closely recall the explanations of
the phenomenon of thought given by children at the end
of the first and beginning of the second stages : thought
is voice, that is to say is composed of air and smoke, and
it is both external and internal. (See Rou, etc., § 1,
Chapter I, and Falq, § 3). It is interesting to notice that

Dug, like children when they first distinguish the name from the thing and realise it to be a mental object, declares first of all that the dream is " nowhere," to fall back later into the realism of the first stage.

The following two cases are also intermediate between the first and second stages :—

PIG (9½) : " Where do dreams come from ?—*When you are asleep, you think someone is beside you. When you see something in the day, you dream of it at night.*—What is the dream ?—*Oh, anything.*—Where does it come from ?—*I don't know. It comes by itself.*—Where from ?—*Nowhere.* Where is it made ?—*In the room.*—Where ?—*When you are lying down.*—Where is it made, in the room or inside you ?—*In me . . . outside.*—Which, do you think ?— *Outside.*—Where does the dream come from, from the room or from you ?—*From me.*—Where is it, outside or in you ?—*Beside me.*—Where ?—*In my room.*—How far away ? (He points to 30 cms. in front of him.) "

DUS (9) is a similar case. He likewise believes that the self is concerned in the making of the dream : " Where do dreams come from ?—*When you are ill.*" But the origin of the dream is also external : " Where do they come from ?—*They come from outside us.*" Dreaming is " *with the mouth,*" but the dream is " *in the bed.*—Where ? In the head or outside ?—*Outside.*"

In short, the dream is external to the body and its origin is both internal (the mouth) and external. This is the counterpart of what we saw with the children who claimed to think with the mouth whilst regarding thought as identical with the external air. Pig has moved a big step beyond the first stage in admitting that we dream of things we have seen and thus ourselves play a part in making the dream, but he is still far from the idea that the dream comes from within ourselves, that it has, in fact, an internal origin.

The next cases are definitely examples of the second stage, where the dream comes from us but is external whilst we are dreaming.

SCHI (6) is a very intelligent small boy who answered the questions with a lively interest. His answers are,

therefore, especially valuable : " Do you sometimes have
dreams ? What is a dream ?—*You think* (!) *of something
during the night.*—What do you dream with ?—*With the
soul (avec l'âme), with thought.*—Where does the dream
come from ?—*During the night. It's the night that shows
us the dream.*—What does that mean ? Where is the
dream whilst you're dreaming ?—*It is in the*—(he was
about to say " head "), *it is between the night and the head*(!)
—While you are dreaming, are your eyes open or shut ?—
Shut.—Then where is the dream ?—*It's when you see black
that the dream comes.*—Where is it ?—*While you are not
asleep it's in the head. While you are asleep it comes out*(!)
*When it's night, it's night, but while you're asleep it isn't
night any more.*—When the dream comes, where is it ?—*In
front of the eyes and it goes against the wall.*—Could your
father see it ?—*No.*—Only you ?—*Yes, because it's me
that's asleep.*"

Schi's case gives the key to all the phenomena of the
second stage. Schi knows that the dream is made of
" thought," and that it is ourselves who make the dream.
But he has not yet realised that the dream is internal in
relation to the body. In order to see it, even with the
eyes shut, it must be " between the night and us." Schi
is thus led to admit that the dream " comes out " as
soon as one is asleep. We must take care not to attribute
to Schi a theory as to the nature of this process : Schi
limits himself to stating his immediate impression according to which only external objects can be seen. His realism
prevents him making any distinction between " seeming
external " and " being external." If he regarded the
dream as only " seeming external " he would not have
had to situate it " against the wall," but would have
placed it either in the head or in the objects of which he
dreamed (at school, on the lake, etc.). Schi realises, however, that he alone can see his dream. It will be remembered that Schi, too, held a similar view concerning
thought : " when you have been told something, it comes
into your mind, then it goes out and then it comes back
again." (Chapter I, § 1).

The following case was brought to our notice on account

of a drawing that had been made spontaneously and previous to any examination on our part :—

Fav (8) belongs to a class whose teacher follows the excellent practice of giving each child an " observation notebook," in which the child notes down each day, with or without the help of drawings, an event he has personally observed outside school.   One morning Fav noted down, as always, spontaneously : "I dreamt that the devil wanted to boil me," and he accompanied the observation with a drawing, of which we give a reproduction : on the left Fav is seen in bed, in the centre is the devil, and on the right Fav stands, in his nightshirt, in front of the devil who is about to boil him.   Our attention was called to this drawing and we sought out Fav.   His drawing illustrates very clearly the meaning of child realism : the dream is beside the bed, before the eyes of the dreamer who watches it.   Fav, moreover, is in his nightshirt in the dream, as if the devil had pulled him out of bed.

The following are the observations we made : Concerning the origin of dreams, Fav has passed the beliefs of the first stage.   Like Schi he knows that the dream comes from thought : " What is a dream ?—*It is a thought.*— Where does it come from ?—*When you see something and then you think of it.*—Do we make the dream ourselves ?— *Yes.*—Does it come from outside ?—*No.*" Fav also knows that we think " *with the brain, with our intelligence.*" Further, Fav, like Schi and all the children of this stage, knows that he alone can see his dream ; neither we nor anyone else could have seen the dream of the devil in Fav's room.   But what he has not understood is the internal nature of the dream : " Whilst you are dreaming, where is the dream ?—*In front of the eyes.*—Where ?— *When you are in bed, in front of your eyes.*—Where, quite near ?—*No in the room.*"   We pointed to Fav's portrait of himself which we have marked II, " What is that ?— *That's me.*—Which is most real of you, this (I) or that (II) ?—*In the dream* (pointing to II).—Is this one anything (II) ?—*Yes, it's me.   It was specially my eyes which stayed there* (pointing to I), *to see* (!)—How were your eyes there ?—*I was there altogether, but specially my eyes.*— And the rest of you ?—*It was there too* (in the bed).—How could that be ?—*There was two of me.   I was in my bed and I was looking on all the time.*—With the eyes open or shut ?—*Shut, because I was asleep.*"   A moment later it seemed as if Fav had understood the internal nature of the dream : " When you are asleep, is the dream in you or are you in the dream ?—*The dream is in us, because it's we who see the dream.*—Is it inside the head or outside ? —*In the head.*—Just now you said outside, what does that mean ?—*You can't see the dream on the eyes.*—Where is the dream ?—*In front of the eyes.*—Is there really anything in front of the eyes ?—*Yes.*—What ?—*The dream.*" Fav thus realises there is something internal about the

dream, he knows the dream's appearance of externality to be illusion (" you can't see the dream on the eyes "), and yet he admits that for the illusion to be there, there must really be something in front of him : " Were you really there (pointing to II) ?—*Yes, I was there twice over* (I and II).—If I had been there, should I have seen you (II) ?—*No.*—What do you mean by ' I was there twice over ' ?—*When I was in bed I was really there, and then when I was in my dream I was with the devil, and I was really there as well.*"

These answers point to the following conclusions. Fav does not know how to distinguish the dream's appearance of externality from externality itself. He agrees that there must be something in the head since " it's we who see the dream." This marks a great advance on the first stage. He even agrees that to see the dream as external is to suffer an illusion : " You can't see the dream on the eyes," that is to say that in dreaming you see something external and not internal. But for Fav this illusion is certainly not because we deceive ourselves, or think we see something outside which is, in fact, inside us. For him the illusion consists in our being deceived by material images, which exist objectively in front of us, but which we take not for images but for persons. He does not doubt the existence of these external images. We, as adults, say that there is false perception : he says there is a real perception of something deceptive. The dream is thus for Fav like an immaterial projection, like a shadow, or an image in a mirror. Otherwise it would be impossible to explain his spontaneous reflection," it was specially my eyes which stayed there (I) to see." In short, Fav seems to waver between contradictory statements, though perhaps for him they do not appear so. We have only to recall that he regards thought as a material substance, to understand the paradox in his remarks : on the one hand, we project outside something which arises in our head, and on the other, what we project out has a material existence in the room.

These facts throw light on the nature of the participations between the images of the dream and the persons they represent, such as we found, existing in the first stage. Fav, indeed, certainly seems to admit that the image II contains something of himself. This explains why he holds that it was his eyes " especially " which stayed in his bed (cp. Dan's expression in § 1, " but all of myself was outside " ; cp. also Metr's expression in the same section, " it's I that am in the dream, it isn't in my head "). It goes without saying that this remark of Fav's is only an awkward form of expression and that he does not hold that belief in a dual self which ethnologists like to attribute to primitive peoples (only do the primitives reason like Fav or like the ethnologists ?). But how exactly does the difficulty arise ? Simply because the image II is regarded as external to the subject I. The participation of II and I thus comes from Fav's realism. For us there is no participation between the image and the person represented, since the image is nothing but an internal representation, but for a realist mind which regards the image as in the room, the image retains something of the person. It is the exact counterpart of what we saw with names, which, from the fact that they are not conceived as internal and mental objects, participate in the thing named.

In order to show that these interpretations are not fantastic, we quote some further cases, not so rich as those of Schi and Fav but equally clear on the essential question of the externality of the dream.

Mos (11 ; 6) describes the dream as "*something you think when you are asleep and that you see.*—Where does it come from ?—*It is something you've thought during the day.* Where is the dream ?—*In front of you.*—Can one see it ?— *Oh, no!*—Why not ?—*It's invisible* (this statement is very convincing and shows that Mos is not speaking of images one thinks one sees outside, but of something invisible which is projected by thought and which produces the images outside).—Is it in front of the eyes ?— *No.*—Where ?—*A little further away.*—Where ?—*It is things which pass by and which you don't see.*"

Mith (7½) : " You know what it is to dream ?—*Yes.*— What do we dream with ?—*With the eyes.*—Where does it come from ?—*The heart?*—Where is the dream while you are dreaming ?—*In the dream, in the mind (dans notre conscience).*—Is it really and truly there ?—*No.*— Where is it ?—*Outside.*—Where ?—*In the room.*"

Card (9½) : The dream is "*when you think the house is on fire, when you think you are going to be burned.*—Is the dream true ?—*No, because you're asleep.*—What is it ?— *It's fire. It's when you think of something.*—Where does the dream come from ?—*The head.*—What do you dream with ?—*When you think.*—What with ?—*The intelligence.*— Where is the dream ?—*In the bed.*—Is it inside us or in front of us ?—*In the room.*—Where ?—*Quite near.*—Have you just found that out ?—*No, I knew it already.*"

Gren (13 ; 6, backward) : " Where does the dream come from ?—*When you think.*" It comes " from us "

(Gren points to his forehead). "Where is the dream?—
Here (pointing to 30 cms. in front of his eyes)."

KENN (7½) : The dream is when *"you make up things."*
It comes from *" the mouth.—Are* your eyes open or shut
when you dream?—*Shut.*—Should I see the dream if
I were there?—*No. You don't see it because it isn't near
you.*—Why don't you see it?—*Because it isn't near us.*—
Where is it?—*Not near us.*—Where is it?—*Further away.*—
Where do you think? . . .—*It comes towards us."* "Where
do they come from?—*The mouth.*—When you dream of
school, where is the dream?—*At school, because it's as if
you were at school.*—Is the dream really at school or is it
only as if it were at school?—*It is at school.*—Really and
truly?—*No.*—Is it at school or in your mouth?—*In my
mouth.*—You said it was far away. Is that true or not
true?—*It's far away."*

ZIMM (8 ; 1) contrary to Kenn does not believe the
dream to be at school but places it in front of his eyes.
When he dreams of school, Zimm says : " *I think I'm
there.*—When you dream, is the dream at school or inside
you?—*In my room? "*

BAR (7) is a similar case. Dreams " *come from us.*—
When you dream you are at school, where is the dream?
—*In front of me.*—Outside you?—*Yes.*—In the room?—
In front of me."

The above examples show how little the discovery that
the dream is due to thought modifies the phenomena of
localisation observed in the first stage. Thus although
Kenn may say he dreams with the mouth, he gives, as
the proof that another person could not see his dream,
the fact that the dream is situated at the place it is about.
Our counter-suggestions made no difference. Naturally,
Kenn does not suppose that the dream actually takes
the dreamer " to school " ; he simply believes that the
image of the school, the image seen in the dream, is " at
school," just as children of his age think that, when they
speak, the name of the sun is " in the sun." However,
for the majority of children in the second stage the dream
is close to them, usually 30 cms. in front of their eyes.

But before regarding these interpretations as certain,
we must, according to our usual criterion, first question

more advanced children who are on the point of reaching the correct answer, to see if they were really the victims of the illusions we seemed to find among the youngest. The following three cases are of this type :—

DRAP (15, but rather backward) stated spontaneously when answering the question on thought : " Can one see thought ?—*Yes, in dreaming.*—Why ?—*You dream some-thing and you see it in front of you.*" We then continued along the line suggested by Drap : " What do you dream with ?—*With the memory.*—Where is the dream ?—*Not in any place.*—Where is it, in your head or in front of you ? —*In front. You can see it, but you can't touch it.*—Why in front ?—*Because if it was inside you wouldn't see it* (*cp.* the remark of Barb in the first stage)."

Drap seems more advanced than the preceding cases in saying the dream is " not in any place." But he simply means by this that it is immaterial. The context shows clearly that he still believes the dream to be in front of him. The proof lies in what follows :—

We tried to make Drap understand the internal nature of the dream : " Now you see me, and you remember that you saw me last year. You remember my face ?—*Yes.* —Where is what you remember ?—*In front of my eyes.* —Why ?—*Because you can't see inside the head. It is as if (!) it was in front of me.*" After having understood the difference between being and seeming (" as if "), Drap finally agrees that the image is in the head. He says then that he understands for the first time that the dream is in the head.

His surprise at the explanation clearly shows that previously he had not been able to distinguish " being " from " seeming."

PUG (7 ; 2) : The dream is " *when you see things that aren't true.*—Who told you that ?—*No one.*—Where do dreams come from ?—*I don't know.*—From the head or from outside ?—*From the head.*—Where is the dream ?— *In front of you.*—Where ?—*Quite near* (pointing to 30 cms. from his eyes).—Is it really there or does it seem to be there ?—*I don't know.*—Should I see it if I were there ? —*No, because you wouldn't be asleep.*—And could your mother see it ?—*No.*—But then you say it is outside ?—*No, it is not outside.*—Where is it ?—*Nowhere.*—Why ?—*It isn't anything.*—Is it outside or in the head ?—*In the head.*— Then it isn't in front of you.—*Yes, it is in front of me all the same* (!) "—" Is the dream inside your head ?—*Yes.*— Then it isn't in front of you ?—*Yes, it is everywhere."*

This case shows how little effect suggestion has on a child at this stage. Pug is willing to admit that the dream is in the head, but he continues to believe it is outside and everywhere. His case is precisely parallel with that of Roc (Chapter II, § 2) concerning names : Roc is willing to admit that names are in the head, but he none the less believes them to be present in the room.

GRAND (8) : " You know what it is to dream ?—*Once I saw a man who frightened me in the day and I dreamed of it at night.*—Where does a dream come from ? Where is it made ?—*In the head.*—Where is the dream while you are dreaming ?—. . .—In the head or outside ?—*It seems* (!) *as if it's outside."* Grand thus seems to regard the external nature of the dream as an illusion. But we then asked : " Where is the dream ?—*Neither outside nor inside.* —Where then ?—*In the room.*—Where ?—*All round me.* —Far or quite near ?—*Quite near, when my brother dreams he shivers."*

Since the dream made Grand's brother shiver it must be something, immaterial perhaps, but external. The rest of the examination, as we shall see, placed Grand in the third stage, by a sudden break with what had gone before.

These last cases in which the child reasons and seeks, evidently show that it is not simply through lack of verbal capacity that children of the second stage say the dream is in the room. They clearly distinguish " being " from " seeming." They doubt the external nature of the dream yet without it they can find no explanation of how one can " see something " : " you can't see what is inside the head ! "

In short, the realism of the second stage is much subtler than that of the first. It is a more intellectual, less

obvious realism. But, as such, it confirms our interpretations of the phenomena of the first stage. In fact,
if the essential discovery that the dream is due to the
thinking subject be suppressed from the statements of
the second stage, there remain the following : (1) that
the dream is external ; (2) that in so far as the image of
a person is not a subjective representation on the part
of the sleeper, it must be bound up with that person
through participation. This is just what we saw and
what we found traces of right through the second stage.

§ 3. THE THIRD STAGE : THE DREAM IS INTERNAL
AND OF INTERNAL ORIGIN.—There are two problems still
to be discussed : the manner in which images come
increasingly to be regarded as internal and the child's
views on the connection between thought and dreams.

Some intermediate cases between the second and third
stages must first be considered.

GRAND (8) is especially interesting, for after supporting
the external nature of the dream on grounds which we
have already seen, he arrives spontaneously at the following idea : " *When I make my eyes turn* (by rubbing them),
I see a sort of head inside them (phosphene).—Is the dream
inside or outside ?—*I think it's neither beside me nor in
my room.*—Where is it ?—*In my eyes.*"

PASQ (7½) : " Where is the dream when you are dreaming, in the room or in you ?—*In me.*—Did you make it
or does it come from outside ?—*I made it.*—What do you
dream with ?—*The eyes.*—When you dream, where is the
dream ?—*In the eyes.*—Is it in the eye or behind the eye ?
—*In the eye.*"

FALQ (7 ; 3) : " Where do dreams come from ?—*In the
eyes.*—Where is the dream ?—*In the eyes.*—Show me
where ?—*Behind there* (pointing to the eye).—Is a dream
the same as a thought ?—*No, it is something.*—What ?—
A story.—If one could see behind the eyes, would one
see anything ?—*No, it's a little skin.*—What is on this
skin ?—*Little things, little pictures.*"

It is interesting to note that Grand and Falq are amongst
those children who believe thought to be " a voice in the
head." It will be remembered that children at first be-

lieve they think with the mouth and identify thought with words and regard names as bound up with the things themselves. Then, when they realise that thought is internal, they first regard it as a " voice " situated at the back of the mouth, in the head. Exactly the same happens to their conceptions of the dream. The dream is first an external picture, produced by things, then by the head. Later, when the child begins to realise the internal nature of the dream, he regards it as a picture —according to Falq, as a " story," imprinted in the eye or behind the eye—in short, what the eye can " see " internally, just as the ear " hears " the internal voice of thought.

In the case of dreams as in that of speech, the thought is thus still confused with physical matter. Even the most advanced children, that is to say cases definitely belonging to the third stage, who regard the dream simply as thought and as internal thought, still frequently let out remarks betraying the material nature of this thought.

TANN (8) : " Where do dreams come from ?—*When you shut the eyes ; instead of it's being night, you see things.*— Where are they ?—*Nowhere. They aren't real. They're in the eyes.*—Do dreams come from within you or from outside ?—*From outside. When you go for a walk and you see something, it makes a mark on the forehead in little drops of blood.*—What happens when you are asleep ?— *You see it.*—Is the dream inside the head or outside ?— *It comes from outside, and when you dream of it, it comes from the head.*—Where are the images when you are dreaming ?—*From inside the brain they come into the eyes.* —Is there anything in front of the eyes ?—*No.*"

STEP (7½) : The dream is " *in my head.*—In your head or in front of your eyes ?—*In front of my eyes. No, it is in my head.*" But the dream is " *when you talk to yourself quite alone and then you sleep.*—Where does the dream come from ?—*When you speak alone.*"

Tann is evidently full of adult ideas, but the way in which he has absorbed them is none the less interesting.

The following cases are more advanced and have given up trying to materialise thought and internal images.

They must, therefore, be placed in the third stage that we distinguished concerning thought. It may be noted also that these children are about the age of 10 or 11, which confirms the age we found for this stage.

ROSS (9 ; 9) : The dream is *" when you think of something.*—Where is the dream ? Is it in front of you ?—*In my head.*—As if there were pictures in your head ? How does that happen ?—*No, you see a picture of what you've done earlier."*

VISC (11 ; 1) : You dream *" with the head,"* and the dream is *" in the head.*—It isn't in front ?—*It's as if* (!) *you could see.*—Is there anything in front of you ?—*Nothing.*—What is there in your head ?—*Thoughts*—Do the eyes see anything in the head ?—*No."*

BOUCH (11 ; 10) : " If you dream that you are dressed, you see a picture. Where is it ?—*I'm dressed like other people, then it* (the picture) *is in my head, but you'd think* (!) *it was in front of you."*

CELL (10 ; 7) also says : " *It seems as if I see it* (the house) *in front of me, but it's in my head."*

These examples show how differently these children react, when faced by the same or even more suggestive questions, from the children of the earlier stages. Such expressions as " you think that," " it seems as if," " it's as if," to describe the seemingly external nature of the dream, are new and very characteristic of this stage.

§ 4. CONCLUSIONS.—It remains to disentangle the relations existing between the results just analysed, and the results of our study of names and of the notion of thought. The relationship is very close and there is a remarkable parallelism between the two groups of phenomena. Children's ideas on thought and on words seem to be characterised by three varieties of realism—or, if it be preferred, three " adualisms." All three are also present in the case of dreams and gradually disappear in the same order as with names.

Firstly, children confuse the sign with the thing signified, or the mental object and the thing it represents. Concerning thought in general, the idea and the name of the sun, for example, are regarded as a part of the sun and as having their origin in the sun. To touch the name of the sun would be to touch the sun itself. With dreams we found the case very similar; the image dreamed of is felt to come from the thing or person the image represents. The dream of a man who has been run over comes from the man himself, etc. Further, when the dream is of school the dream is " at school," just as when the sun is thought of, the word or name thought are " in the sun." The confusion is thus between the dream and the thing dreamed of.

In both cases, this realism gives rise to feelings of participation. The name of the sun appears to the child to imply the heat, the colour, the shape of the sun. By direct participation the name passes to and fro like a shuttlecock between the sun and us. In like manner the dream of a man who has been run over seems to come from the man himself and above all it comes charged with emotion, " to pay us out," or " because we've done something we ought not to have done," etc.

But the confusion between sign and thing signified disappears earlier in the case of the dream than in the case of names and thoughts, for the simple reason that the dream is deceptive, which forces the sign to cut itself adrift from the things it represents. It is, moreover, this' deceptive and frightening character of dreams which explains why the participations have such a much stronger affective tone in the case of dreams than in that of names.

The second confusion is between internal and external. In the most primitive stage, words are situated in things, then everywhere and particularly in the surrounding air, then in the mouth alone and finally in the head. Dreams follow a precisely similar course: first, they are in the things (but not for long, owing to the circumstances referred to above), then they are situated in the room, even when their origin is known to be the head (just as words are situated in the surrounding air, even when their source is the mouth); finally, dreams are described as in the eyes and ultimately as in the head and in thought itself.

In the case of thought, this confusion between internal and external gives rise, in the primitive stages, to paradoxical beliefs, such as that according to which thought is a whisper situated at the same time in the head and outside. Children's ideas on dreams entirely confirm this interpretation ; for certain of them the dream is a voice or air that is both external and internal.

Finally, the third variety of realism gives rise to a confusion between thought and matter. Thought is, for those children who have set themselves the question, a whisper, if they suppose thought to be with the voice. It can also be a smoke, since sometimes respiration is confused with voice. The dream, for such children as have considered the question, is equally of air or of smoke. For the youngest who have not yet realised the subjective origin of dreams (first stage) it is simply " of night," or " of light."

In studying the child's conceptions of names we arrived at the conclusion that the confusion between sign and thing signified was the first to disappear (about the age of 7-8). This disappearance leads to the distinction between internal and external (about 9-10) and finally from this distinction arises the idea that thought is something other than a material substance. The process is yet clearer as regards conceptions of the dream. The confusion between the image and the corresponding object disappears very early (5–6). As it disappears the dream is no longer situated in things, and the distinction between internal and external is thus already suggested and becomes complete at about the age of 9–10 (beginning of third stage). Finally, it is not till about 11 that this distinction between internal and external leads the child definitely to understand that the dream is not a material image, but simply a thought.

There is thus a complete parallelism between the child's conceptions of names and of thought and its conceptions concerning dreams. But, it goes without saying, that during the primitive stages, the children themselves see no analogy nor connection between the dream and the word. Neither images nor names are regarded as mental objects and they can thus have no relationship in the child's eyes. The similarity of the phenomena observed in the two cases, and of the steps in the evolution of these phenomena is thus a guarantee of the worth of our experiments and their interpretation. These certainly still need confirming by the repetition of the experiments in different countries in order that the part played by adult influences may be more definitely separated from the spontaneous and constant conviction of the child. But such comparisons as we have been able to make from amongst our material at Geneva, and from the answers collected by Mlle Perret at Neufchâtel and in the Bernese Jura, and those obtained at Madrid and at Santander by Mlle Rodrigo lead us to believe that the constancy and spontaneity with which we have credited the child preponderates over the effect of adult influence.

CHAPTER IV

REALISM AND THE ORIGIN OF THE IDEA OF PARTICIPATION

THE aim of this chapter is to trace the consequences of the realism analysed in the preceding chapters. It is first, however, necessary to state definitely the real significance of our researches on the notion of thought, nominal realism and dreams ; since otherwise the interpretation of our material may give rise to the gravest misconceptions. The impression may have been formed that we endow children, if not with actual theories, at any rate with clear and spontaneously formulated ideas, as to the nature of thought and of names and dreams. But nothing has been further from our intention. We readily agree that children have never or hardly ever reflected on the matters on which they were questioned. The experiments aimed, therefore, not at examining ideas the children had already thought out, but at seeing how their ideas are formed in response to certain questions and principally in what direction their spontaneous attitude of mind tends to lead them.

In such circumstances the results can only be negative and not positive. That is to say the explanation a child gives in answer to one of our questions must not be taken as an example of " a child's ideas," but serves simply to show that the child did not seek the solution in the same direction as we should have, but presupposed certain implicit postulates different from those we should suppose.

It is these presuppositions alone that interest us here and we shall henceforth therefore take no account of the detail of the preceding results (since this detail is not necessarily to be accepted at its face value) and retain simply the following conclusion. The child is a realist, since he supposes thought to be inseparable from its object, names from the things named, and dreams to be external. His realism consists in a spontaneous and immediate tendency to confuse the sign and the thing signified, internal and external, and the psychical and the physical.

The results of this realism are twofold. Firstly, the limits the child draws between the self and the external world are much less rigid than our own ; secondly, the realism is further extended by " participations " and spontaneous ideas of a magical nature.

This is the subject of the following sections.

§ 1. REALISM AND THE CONSCIOUSNESS OF SELF.— The problem of the child's consciousness of self is extremely complex and it is not easy to treat it from a general standpoint. To arrive at a synthesis it would be necessary to undertake inquiries similar to those we have just concluded on thought, names and dreams, for all the contents of a child's consciousness. The problem must, however, be faced since the questions of participation and of magical causality are directly dependent on it.

We shall follow a method of regression, and limit ourselves to determining the curve of transformation of the processes studied in the preceding chapters and tracing it back to where we may conjecture what were the original stages. The method, though dangerous, seems the only one possible.

Two conclusions may be drawn from the preceding analyses. The first is that the child is no less conscious of the content of his thought than we are of ours. He has noted the existence of thoughts, of names and of dreams, and a quantity of more or less subtle particularities. One child stated that we dream of what interests us, another that when we think of things, it is because " we want to have them," another that he dreamed of his aunt because he was so glad to see her again. Mostly children think they dream because they have been frightened by something, etc. Further, there is present in the child a whole extremely delicate psychology, often very shrewd and pointing in every case to a keen appreciation of its affective life. In a preceding work (*Judgment and Reason* Chapter IV, § 1) we maintained that the child's efforts at introspection are extremely crude, but this does not in the least contradict the present contention. It is possible to feel acutely the results of a mental process (logical reasoning or affective reasoning) without knowing how such a result came about. This is precisely the case with the child and is what is meant when the child's " intuition " is spoken of ; a true perception of the contents of consciousness but no knowledge of how these contents were acquired, such is the paradox of this " intuition."

This paradox is closely related to the following facts. The child may be aware of the same contents of thought as ourselves but he locates them elsewhere. He situates in the world or in others what we seat within ourselves, and he situates in himself what we place in others. In this problem of the seat of the contents of mind lies the whole problem of the child's consciousness of self, and it is through not stating it clearly that what is in fact exceedingly complex is made to appear simple. It is indeed possible to suppose a mind extremely sensitive to the least stirrings of the affective life, a keen observer of the niceties of language, customs and conduct in general, yet hardly conscious of his own self, since he systematically treats each of his thoughts as objective and every feeling as common to all. The consciousness of self arises in fact from the dissociation of reality as conceived by the primitive mind and not from the association of particular contents. That the child shows a keen interest in himself, a logical, and no doubt a moral, egocentricity, does not prove that he is conscious of his self, but suggests, on the contrary, that he confuses his self with the universe, in other words that he is unconscious of his self. This is what we shall attempt to prove.

In the preceding chapters we dealt only with the instruments of thought (percepts, images, words, etc.) and not with actual conceptions nor above all with the affective life. The child is almost as well aware of these instruments as we are but he gives them an entirely different setting. For us, an idea or a word is in the mind and the thing it represents is in the world of sense perception. Also words and certain ideas are in the mind of everybody, whilst other ideas are peculiar to one's own thought. For the child, thoughts, images and words, though distinguished to a certain degree from things, are none the less situated in the things. The continuous steps of this evolution may be assigned to four phases : (1) a phase of *absolute realism*, during which no attempt is made to distinguish the instruments of thought and where objects alone appear to exist ; (2) a phase of *immediate realism*, during which the instruments of thought are distinguished from the things but are situated in the things ; (3) a phase of *mediate realism*, during which the instruments of thought are still regarded as a kind of things and are situated both in the body and in the surrounding air ; and finally (4), a phase of *subjectivism* or *relativism*, during which the instruments of thought are situated within ourselves. In this sense then, the child begins by confusing his self—or his thought —with the world, and then comes to distinguish the two terms one from each other.

It seems that we might extend this law even to the contents of the conceptions, including the simplest perceptions. During the primitive stage, the child feels every conception to be absolute, as if the mind and the thing were one, and only gradually comes to regard the conception as relative to a given point of view. Thus in a new sense, the child begins by confusing his self and the world—that is to say in this particular case, his subjective point of view and the external data—and only later distinguishes his own personal point of view from other possible points of view. In fact the child always begins by regarding his own point of view as absolute. We shall see numerous examples later : the child thinks the sun follows him, that the clouds follow him, that things are always as he actually sees them and independent of perspective, distance, etc. . . . In so far as he ignores that his own point of view is subjective he believes himself the centre of the world, whence follow a whole group of finalistic, animistic and quasi-magical conceptions, examples of which occur on every page. These conceptions alone point to the child's ignorance of the fact of subjectivity.

But to be aware of the subjectivity of one's own point of view is relatively an insignificant element in the consciousness of self. This is essentially a feeling of the personal quality of one's desires, inclinations, affections, etc. Yet in relation to these does the child feel its first experiences of pleasure and pain, its first desires, as personal or as common to all ? The probability is that the same law holds good here and that the child starts by being convinced for the simple reason that it has never occurred to it to doubt that everything it feels exists by itself, objectively. It is by a series of disillusions and through being contradicted by others that it comes to realise the subjectivity of feeling. Here again the self results from the dissociation of the primitive consciousness ; the primitive consciousness or unconsciousness that a certain state is either pleasurable or painful is directly projected into the surrounding world of reality, first through absolute realism and then through immediate realism, and it is not until this reality becomes broken up that the feeling arises of a given object and a subjective emotion which gives it its personal value.

In short, to make a broad conjecture and without going into any detail owing to lack of direct evidence, it seems that in the primitive stage the whole content of the infant's consciousness is projected into reality (both into things and into others), which amounts to a complete absence of the consciousness of self. Three groups of observations point in this direction.

Firstly, it is not possible to separate the conceptual

from the affective elements. However primitive a feeling may be, it is accompanied by the consciousness of an object or it itself creates an object. But, it has already been asserted as a result of the phenomena observed in the preceding chapters, that in the primitive state every conception is realistic.

Secondly, the work of Baldwin and still more that of Pierre Janet has made it clear that imitation is due to a sort of confusion between the self and others. In other words, the sound a child hears stimulates him to make the necessary movement to continue it, without the child seeing any difference between the sound that is independent of him and the sound he has produced. The same thing constantly happens to us in cases of involuntary imitation when we identify ourselves with what we are imitating without realising how much belonged originally to the thing we are imitating and how much we have ourselves endowed it with. We discussed in Chapter I,)§ 3) the case of children who think they have themselves discovered what they have as a matter of fact been taught by others. Inversely, children always believe that things which they do not know and have never known, they have merely " forgotten." All that a child knows appears to it to be its own discovery and what it does not know it regards as forgotten. It would seem as if these phenomena were due to hypertrophy of the sentiment of self-esteem ; as a matter of fact they are simply signs of the absence of any clear distinction between external and internal. Imitation is impossible without projection, and this being so, the reciprocal must also be true : the aims and desires of the self must be attributed to others just as much as the actions of others are attributed to the self.

Finally and most important, we know that an infant does not spontaneously localise its organic sensations. A pain in the foot does not immediately draw its attention to the foot, etc. It is rather a wandering pain which is not localised and which every one is thought to share. Even when localised the infant no doubt for a long time still regards it as common to all ; it cannot spontaneously realise that it alone is able to feel the pain. In short, for the primitive consciousness and for us the relation between the body viewed from outside and the body felt from inside is entirely different : what we speak of as internal and what we speak of as external are for a long time equally regarded as common to all.

Unfortunately, it is impossible to control these hypotheses by a direct analysis. But if we use the results obtained from between the limits of 4 and 12 years of age as a basis of inference in respect of ages below these limits it seems to show that consciousness of the internal nature of any state does not result from a direct intuition but from an intellectual construction, and this construction is only possible by a dissociation of the contents of the primitive consciousness.

Moreover, though the analysis of the primitive consciousness is impossible without hypothesis, the dissociation just mentioned can be more directly observed. One of Edmund Gosse's memories of childhood is a valuable case in point. As the result of telling a lie which was neither discovered nor punished, Edmund Gosse came to realise that his father did not know everything, and it was this knowledge that certain things were known to him alone which seems to have strengthened in him the consciousness of self.

" In the first place, the theory that my Father was omniscient or infallible was now dead and buried. He probably knew very little ; in this case he had not known a fact of such importance that if you did not know that, it could hardly matter what you knew. . . . But of all the thoughts which rushed upon my savage and undeveloped little brain at this crisis, the most curious was that I had found a companion and a confidant in myself. There was a secret in this world and it belonged to me and to a somebody who lived in the same body with me. There were two of us and we could talk to one another. It is difficult to define impressions so rudimentary, but it is certain that it was in this dual form that the sense of my individuality now suddenly

descended upon me and it is equally certain that it was a great solace to me to find a sympathiser in my own breast."

The quotation is of striking interest. So long as the child believed in his father's omniscience, his own self was non-existent, in the sense that his thoughts and actions seemed to him common to all, or at any rate known to his parents to the smallest detail. The moment he realised that his parents did not know all, he straightway discovered the existence of his subjective self. Certainly the discovery was made late and only concerns the higher plane of personality. But it shows clearly how the consciousness of self results from a dissociation of reality and is not a primitive intuition, and shows also to what extent this dissociation is due to social factors, that is to say to a distinction the child makes between his own point of view and that of others.

In dealing with the relations between the body viewed as external, and felt as internal, it may be of interest to consider again the child's use of the first person. It is well known that children speak of themselves in the third person before they use the pronoun " I." The idiot described by H. Wallon [1] when receiving correction said, " *See what Fernand's getting* " (" Fernand " being himself). So too a little girl observed by the author said at the age of 2 ; 9 : " *T'es une 'moiselle, 'spas, moi ?*"—meaning " I am a girl, aren't I ? " but literally " you are a girl aren't you, me ? " Baldwin and many others regard this as evidence of a projective stage : the child sees itself as outside its thought, as " projected " in a mirror in front of its own eyes and without experiencing any feeling of subjectivity. This interpretation has been much disputed. Rasmussen sees in it merely the child's imitation of those it knows, who obviously use the child's name and not the pronoun " I." M. Delacroix, in his admirable book, *Le Langage et la pensée*, regards the " I " merely as an instrument of grammar.

But it seems that behind the grammatical question there is also a question of the logic of relations. As late as the ages of 8 and 9, a child will say " I've a brother,

[1] *Journal de Psychologie*, Vol. VIII (1911), p. 436.

Paul," and conclude from it that Paul has not a brother (see *Judgment and Reasoning* Chapters II and III), because he fails to distinguish his own point of view from that of others. May not the same be true of the use of the first person? The difficulty the child here experiences affects in fact all the possessive terms. Egger noticed how when he said to a child of 1 ; 6, " show me my nose, my mouth, etc." the child pointed to its own, and to be understood he had to say " show me Daddy's nose," etc.

Viewed in this light the phenomenon is interesting. Naturally the child who speaks of himself in the third person, situates what he speaks of within his body. But he may not have understood that the conception he has of himself is different from that which others may have. When he speaks of himself he certainly makes no attempt to place himself in the position of someone else, but he believes himself to be seeing from the only possible point of view, the absolute point of view. This fact is important. It shows that Fernand's experience of pain and the judgment he makes on it are not for him equally internal. Only the pain is in his own body, whilst his judgment is made from an undifferentiated point of view that is common to all. Fernand does not realise that it is he who is judging of himself. If he had been asked where was his " self," he would have indicated only half of his consciousness, the half which felt the pain, but not the half which watched the other suffer.

In short, the child who speaks of himself in the third person has undoubtedly already in some degree the feeling of " self "—it seems evident that Baldwin has exaggerated here—though he may not yet be aware of the " I," if by " I " we follow William James and mean that element of the self which watches the life of the rest. This fact alone is enough to confirm what we stated previously of the difficulty the child experiences in establishing the limits between his own internal world and the world that is common to all.

§ 2. PARTICIPATION AND MAGICAL PRACTICES.—In the preceding pages we dealt at some length with the particular nature of the child's consciousness of self because we regard the phenomena involved as of primary importance in revealing the origins of causality. The most primitive forms of causality found in the child seem, in fact, due to confusion between reality and thought, or more accurately, to a constant assimilation of external processes to schemas arising from internal experience. This is what the two following sections will attempt to outline, though the idea will be more fully developed in a later work. In the present section we shall restrict ourselves to enumerating certain cases marked by feelings of participation or of magic, and simply to stating the more systematic cases we have been able to observe during the researches of which we shall treat later.

Following the definition of M. Lévy-Bruhl, we shall give the name " participation " to that relation which primitive thought believes to exist between two beings or two phenomena which it regards either as partially identical or as having a direct influence on one another, although there is no spatial contact nor intelligible causal connection between them. The application of this conception to the child's thought may be disputed, but it is merely a question of words. It may be that the child's idea of " participation " differs from that of the primitive, but they resemble one another, and this is sufficient to authorise us in choosing our vocabulary from among the expressions which have been found most adequate in describing primitive thought. There is no intention of suggesting the identity of the different forms of participation that may be distinguished.

We shall use the term " magic " for the use the individual believes he can make of such participation to modify reality. All magic supposes a participation, but the reverse is not true. Here again the use of the term " magic" may be regretted in speaking of the child, but absolutely no identity is implied between the child's magic and the magic of the primitive.

It is further necessary to distinguish participation and magic from the child's animistic beliefs, that is to say from his tendency to endow inanimate things with life and consciousness. The two groups of phenomena are closely related. For example many children believe the sun follows them.   When the emphasis is on the spontaneity of the sun's action, it is a case of animism.   When they believe it is they who make the sun move, it is a question of participation and magic.   Obviously they are very similar beliefs, but it is worth distinguishing them since we shall be led to the conclusion that animism is derived from participation and not vice versa.   At any rate it is just at the time when the feelings of participation arise from the differentation of the self and the external world, that the self assumes magical powers and that in return, beings are endowed with consciousness and life.

The attempt must now be made to classify the different types of participation manifested by the child and the magical practices to which certain of them give rise. From this list must naturally be excluded all that belongs strictly to play.   Play is continuously interwoven with participations, but they are of a type unrelated to conviction and they must therefore be disregarded.

Participations and magical practices may be classified from the point of view of the content and dominating interest or from the point of view of the structure of the causal relationship.   From the point of view of the content, magical relationship may be connected with fear, remorse (*e.g.* in connection with onanism), desire and fourthly with the feelings of order governing nature.   These four interests will be clearly marked in the examples which follow later, but in the present case a classification from the point of view of structure will prove most useful and we shall therefore group the examples we have been able to collect into the following four categories :—

(1) Firstly, there is *magic by participation between actions and things*.   The child performs some action or mental operation (counting, etc.), and believes that this action or operation exercises, through participation, an influence on a particular event he either desires or fears.   These actions tend to become symbolical, in the sense that they become detached from their primitive context, just as conditioned reflexes become detached from their objects

and become mere signs. (2) There is *magic by partici-pation between thought and things,* when the child is under the impression that reality can be modified by a thought, a word, or a look, etc.; or a psychological characteristic, such as laziness, for example, may be materialised, and a lazy person regarded as giving out a substance or force which can act of its own accord. Here again the partici-pation between thought and things gives rise to actions which tend to become symbolical. (3) There is *magic by participation between objects,* when two or more things are regarded as exerting influence on one another, attracting or repulsing one another, etc., by simple participation, and the magic consists in using one of these things to influence the others. (4) Finally, there is *magic by partici-pation* of purpose. In this case objects are regarded as living and purposive. There is animism. The participation consists in believing that the will of one object can act of itself on that of others and the magic lies in making use of this participation. The most common form is *magic by commandment,* *e.g.* ordering the clouds or sun to go away. In the last two cases also, there is sometimes a tendency towards symbolism.

We shall now give some examples of the first group, that of magic produced by action. Naturally, it is only memories of childhood that we have been able to collect, since children are chary of speaking of their magic during the period when they practise it. We shall quote first of all an interesting case which it is true overlaps into both the first and second groups but which shows emphatically to what lengths the child's magic can go.

This is the case of Edmund Gosse. The detailed and moving autobiography of *Father and Son* certainly makes it clear that a leaning towards magic was the last thing to be naturally supposed from this child's education. His parents had strictly forbidden all imaginative life. He was never told stories. His only reading was either pious or scientific. His religion was rigidly moral and devoid of all mysticism. He had no friends. But through lack of poetry or concrete education, the child's intellectual activity broke out between the ages of 5 and 6 with a wealth of magic, which seems to have been singularly rich :—

" *Being as restricted, then, and yet as active my mind took refuge in an infantile species of natural magic. This contended with the definite ideas of religion which my parents were continuing, with too mechanical a persistency, to force into my nature and it ran parallel with them. I formed strange superstitions, which I can only render intelligible by naming some concrete examples. I persuaded myself that if I could only discover the proper words to say or the proper passes to make, I could induce the gorgeous birds and butterflies in my Father's illustrated manuals to come to life and fly out of the book, leaving holes behind them. I believed, that, when at the Chapel, we sang, drearily and slowly, loud hymns of experience and humiliation, I could boom forth with a sound equal to that of dozens of singers, if I could only hit upon the formula. During morning and evening prayers, which were extremely lengthy and fatiguing, I fancied that one of my two selves could flit up, and sit clinging to the cornice, and look down on my other self and the rest of us, if I could only find the key. I laboured for hours in search of these formulas, thinking to compass my ends by means absolutely irrational. For example, I was convinced that if I could only count consecutive numbers long enough, without losing one, I should suddenly, on reaching some far distant figure, find myself in possession of the great secret. I feel quite sure that nothing external suggested these ideas of magic. . . .*
" *All this ferment of mind was entirely unobserved by my parents. But when I formed the belief, that it was necessary for the success of my practical magic, that I should hurt myself, and when, as a matter of fact, I began, in extreme secrecy, to run pins into my flesh and bang my joints with books, no one will be surprised to hear that my Mother's attention was drawn to the fact that I was looking ' delicate.' "*

The examples to be quoted are mostly not so clear as the above, but our aim is to establish precisely all the intermediate stages between the most subtle and the crudest and least " magical " types. In the example of Gosse it is naturally the practices mentioned at the end (the pins and the blows) that fall into the category of magic through action. But under the same heading we may also place magic based on arithmetic : such as counting very fast or without a mistake as a means of securing a particular object. Such magic, based on arithmetical calculation or on counting, is very common. The following are further examples :—

From one of our collaborators : "*To succeed in any of the various things I was keen about (to win in a game, to have fine weather for an excursion, etc.) I used to do as follows : I would hold my breath and if I could count up to ten (or some other number, easier or harder according to the importance of the event) I felt sure of gaining what I wanted.*"

The fact of success in counting whilst holding the breath is thus regarded both as the sign and the cause of success in the event desired.

A boy of about ten, given to masturbation, was in the habit of counting up to a given number (10 or 15) whenever he was questioned or in any other circumstances, to prevent himself saying anything stupid or to obtain something he desired. The origin of the habit in this particular case, seems to have been as follows. In moments of temptation the child used to count up to a certain number and then to succumb or not to the temptation according as he had succeeded or not in reaching the number under certain conditions. The habit had become a means of decision and finally a magical process.

Here again, the operation of counting is at the same time both sign and cause. Naturally the opposite is found also, that is to say the operation serves not only for obtaining something but also for avoiding misfortune. This happens particularly often with those children—a much greater number than would be supposed—who are haunted every night by fears of death, either for themselves or their parents. On this subject one of our collaborators has very clear recollections :—

Every evening, from about the age of 6 to 8, I was terrified by the idea of not waking up in the morning. I used to feel my heart beating and would try, by placing my hand on the chest, to feel if it wasn't stopping. It was undoubtedly in this way that I started counting to reassure myself. I counted very quickly between each beat and if I could succeed in passing a certain number before a particular beat or in making the beats correspond with even or with uneven numbers, etc., I felt reassured. I have forgotten the details, but I can remember the following very clearly. At regular intervals, from the pipes of the radiator in my room, would come a sudden, deep, rattling sound which often used to make me jump. I used to use this as a proof of whether I should die or not; I would count very fast between one rattle and the next, and, if I passed a certain number, I was saved. I used the same method to know whether my father, who slept in the next room, was on the point of death or not."

The relation of this fact to the manias of the insane and their defensive gestures is clearly brought out. But this example is only the negative aspect of the preceding cases of magic.

The following memory dates from between the ages of 9 and 11 :—

" I often accompany my father when he goes to the rifle range. While my father shoots I sit on a bench. He gives me his cigar to hold. I imagine I can influence the accuracy of his shot by the position of the cigar. According as the cigar is almost vertical (the lighted end downwards), or at an angle of 90°, 120° or 180°, the shot will be only fairly good, good or excellent. The shot never entirely misses since my father is a good shot. However, after two or three good shots have been fired, I lower the cigar for a while, with the feeling that he cannot keep this up." The narrator insisted that it was not in the least a game, and that when pointing the cigar in a particular direction he really believed he was influencing his father's shot.

Other operations or magical actions are based on the pleasurable effect of rhythm or some other æsthetic pleasure which gives rise either to positive acts of magic or to obsessions of a negative nature. Such is the well-known sensation of pleasure common to children, of not walking on the lines of the pavement, or of jumping a stone at every step, etc.

The sensation of pleasure may be entirely æsthetic or completely ridiculous in its origin. But the child has only to desire something strongly or fear something and the game becomes a test, and its success or failure are regarded as the sign and cause of the realisation of what is desired or feared, as in the following example given by one of our collaborators :—

" *When I particularly wanted something I often used to step on every other stone as I walked on the pavement. If I succeeded in doing this as far as the end of the pavement it was a sign that what I wanted would happen. Or I would touch the stones of a wall, tapping every third stone and if I thus succeeded in reaching the last stone of the wall, I was certain of my success, etc.*

Another used to feel threatened by danger if he walked on one of the lines between the stones. If he started by walking on one of these lines he kept it up all the way so as to make the danger less.

The following is another example of these rhythmic movements performed to assure the realisation of some event :—

A child, given to masturbation, whom we shall call Clan, was afraid of being overcome by laziness or stupidity ("abêtissement"). His dreams and his plans for the future showed henceforth a compensating tendency and he planned to become " a great man." To bring this about he adopted the following practice, which must have lasted for some time : " *When crossing X   (a public square) I used to tap the hooped railings enclosing the green with my tram season-ticket. To do this I had to stoop down. I used to do it every morning in order to become a great man.*"

The following is, strictly speaking, more nearly a case of obsession than of magic, but it seems to be the negative version of a case of magic given later :—

One of us can remember, in addition to the pavement rite, a feeling of being impelled to replace every stone she involuntarily moved when walking, or if not, whatever desire she had at the moment would not be realised.

The curious recollection of the childhood of Mlle Vé, reported by Flournoy, should probably find a place here :—

" One of my most distant memories relates to my mother. She was very ill and had been in bed several weeks and a servant had told me she would die in a few days. I must have been about 4 or 5 years old. My most treasured possession was a little brown wooden horse, covered with ' real hair '. . . . A curious thought came into my head : I must give up my horse in order to make my mother better. It was more than I could do at once and cost me the greatest pain. I started by throwing the saddle and bridle into the fire, thinking that ' when it's very ugly, I shall be able to keep it.' I can't remember exactly what happened. But I know that in the greatest distress I ended by smashing my horse to bits, and that on seeing my mother up, a few days later, I was convinced that it was my sacrifice that had mysteriously cured her and this conviction lasted for a long while." [1]

This idea of the magical power of sacrifice reappears in a simpler form in the idea of obtaining some desired object by means of a painful or tiresome action. The following is an example :—

In order not to be questioned in class or bothered by his teacher, a boy was in the habit of putting on and taking off his boots several times before going to school in the morning. His idea was that the more annoying the performance of the rite, the greater his chance of being favoured by Fate.

Finally, there are innumerable rites to ward off danger :—

A boy who lived in a somewhat lonely house was always very frightened on the evenings when his parents were out. Before going to bed he used to draw the curtains by unwinding a sort of roller. He had always the idea that if he could succeed in drawing the curtains very quickly the robbers would not come. But if the curtain took some time to unroll then the house was in danger.

This fact, like those which follow, indicates clearly the the origin of these feelings of participation and of magic caused by a particular movement. The majority of little girls experience in bed at night the most violent fears of the dark and of strange sounds. There are various

[1] *Archives de Psychologie*, Vol. XV (1915), pp. 1-224.

measures of precaution to which they usually turn, such as hiding under the clothes, turning the back to the door, drawing the blankets up exactly to the chin, etc. There is here nothing magical since these are simply means of protection. But some of these movements become dissociated from their primitive context and become rites, like the case of the curtain just quoted, and thence acquire an intrinsic value of their own. Then appears the magic :—

One of us remembers always feeling a sense of protection so long as she had her arms pressed against her body.

Another felt protected if on getting into bed, the clothes were completely tucked in all round so that she could slip in without anywhere unmaking the bed. If by chance she found the clothes not tucked in, or that they had come unmade as she got in, she felt herself threatened by danger.

The origin of the movements is obvious ; to draw a curtain, to brace oneself, or make sure that no one has touched the bed ; but according as the movement loses its primary significance and becomes effective in itself, it becomes magical.

Next must be considered the cases of *magic through participation between thought and things*. Between these and the preceding there are any number of intermediate cases as was shown in the examples of magic based on counting. But the cases to be dealt with now concern mental elements much more closely related to thought than numbers, such, for example, as names and words. These cases thus result directly from the child's realism which we attempted to analyse in the preceding chapters. In these chapters we have already seen many cases where participation was believed to exist between things and thought, between names and the things named, dreams and the things dreamed of, etc. The strongest proof that these participations whose significance we have already noted, are spontaneous and not produced by our questions, is that they give rise to the most authentic cases of magic we found among all the memories of childhood we were able to collect, that is to say to cases of magic by means of names. The following are examples :—

CLAN, the child already quoted, first succumbed to onanism at Mayens-de-Sion. When he came home, he tried under the sway of remorse not to suppress the memory but to suppress the fact itself, or its consequences, that is to say the stupidity ("abêtissement") he feared (see above). To bring this about it was against the actual name of Mayens-de-Sion that he set himself : "*I did all I could to break the name of Mayens-de-Sion.*" To break the name he simply distorted it. He repeated the name aloud, pronouncing it in German, *Máyensersêyens* and accentuating the two syllables "may" and "sey."

In the same way, when suffering under the displeasure of a schoolmaster, he would repeat in his room, once back from school, the master's surname, not only to make fun of him but principally (in so far as the recollection is accurate) to be rid of his influence.

A naturalist, whose work is to-day famous, gave us the following recollection of his childhood. Seated a couple of feet away from his cat and staring into the cat's eyes, he would pronounce many times the formula : "*Tin, tin, pin pin de l'o–ü–in, pin, pin, tin, tin, pin pin de l'o–ü–in, pin pin . . . , etc.*" So far as the memory is to be trusted the aim of this formula was to enable the child to project his personality into the cat : while pronouncing it the child felt himself pervading the cat's being and thus dominating it by participation.

One of us used to enjoy playing at schools at home. She would give good marks to her friends and bad ones to the children she didn't like, etc., though all the time, of course, only addressing empty chairs. The next day, at school, she was convinced of having influenced the questions that were actually asked, and of having helped her friends answer well and hindered her enemies.

Other cases of participation between thought and things rest on a sort of confusion or lack of differentiation between psychical and material characteristics :—

CLAN, like all masturbators, was in fear of losing his intellectual faculties and becoming "lazy." Whence the following rite : "*When accompanying a particularly lazy boy I sometimes chanced to walk hand in hand with him. Then when I was home again I would say to myself that to hold hands with a lazy boy will make me lazy too, and I must do something against it."* Clan would then rub his hands vigorously.

So also certain rites consist simply in thinking of something to make a particular event happen or not. (This is Freud's " all powerful nature of thought.")

It often happens that children—for that matter many adults too—think the opposite from what they want, as if reality made a point of intentionally foiling their desires.

In the same way (according to the memories of childhood we have collected), in order to avoid nightmares— and it will be remembered that up to the age of 10 the origin of dreams is thought to be external—children try on purpose to think of frightening things and of the usual subjects of their nightmares so as to make the dream not come.

The two following cases are further examples of feelings of participation allied to the power of thought :—

Clan's first attack of masturbation was brought about by the sight of a little girl he did not know whom he looked at one day with thoughts of desire. Afterwards Clan asked himself " *if the little girl could have a baby."* Clan asked a similar question after having peeped through a keyhole.

The last case is intermediate between this group and the next :—

One of us can remember how, when he used to play at marbles, in order to make certain of winning, he would contrive to play with the marble used by the player who last won. It was as if the player's skill gave the marble permanently good qualities or as if the marble was made particularly good by the player's luck.

All these cases thus consist in regarding a particular mental element, such as names, laziness, thought and dreams, skill, etc. as intimately connected with the things themselves, and as having its own effective power. Between these and the third group, that of magic by *participation between objects*, are any number of intermediate cases, like the example just quoted of the magical marble, whose powers are regarded as due not to the skill of the player, but to something in the marble. What characterises the third group is that the magical action is no longer the direct issue of a movement or thought on the part of the subject, as was the connection in the two preceding groups, but that it arises from an object or a place, etc., which the subject uses to influence another object of an event. The two following are clear examples, in which the choice of the magical body seems to have been determined by its resemblance to the object which the subject seeks to influence :—

One of us relates this recollection, speaking of herself in the third person : " *A little girl of six used to pass often with her governess by a lake where some rare water-lilies grew. Every time she would throw some little stones into the water (always choosing them round and white) and taking care not to be seen by the governess. She thought that the next day water-lilies would appear in the place where the stones had fallen. For this reason, in the hope of thus being able to reach the flowers she always threw the stones quite near the edge.*"

Another of us recalls the following : " *When people plant a flower in a pot they always put a little stone at the bottom of the pot to prevent the soil being washed away. I had noticed this but had misinterpreted the reason. I used to choose my stone with the idea that on its colour and shape depended the life of the plant. It was just as much a question of the influence of the stone on the plant as of a sort of sympathy between the stone and me ; the stone collaborated with me to make the plant grow.*"

The following is another example, the date of which can be fixed with certainty between the ages of 10 and 11 :—

One of us used to collect shells from the lake and the smallest kinds of snails. On his walks he would experience a number of feelings of participation showing the child's tendency both to see signs in everything and to confuse the sign with the cause of an event, the cause being in this case of a magical nature. Thus, when he was seeking a particularly rare specimen, and on the way he found some other interesting specimen he would decide from this whether or not he would find the specimen he was seeking. This was not based in the least on the similar habitat of the specimens, but solely on occult ties ; such an unexpected discovery ought to lead to another discovery during the day. Or again, when from a distance he thought he saw the particular specimen, but on approaching found he was mistaken, he concluded that he would not find the specimen he particularly wanted that day.

Similar to these cases are those where the bond of participation lies in places, either favourable or unfavourable.

One of us gives the following : *" If on my way to the dentist I passed by a particular street and the dentist then hurt me, I took care, the next time, to go a different way, so that he would hurt me less."*

In this group may be placed also the numerous feelings of participation to which beliefs concerning the air and the wind give rise. As will be shown in the subsequent volume (*La Causalité Physique chez l'Enfant*, Chapter I), children between the ages of 4 and 6 and some even older do not think that air is present in a room ; but they have only to shake their hands or wave a fan, etc. to " make air " (" faire de l'air ") and by this means even believe they can draw in the air from outside through closed windows. This is certainly a case of participation, given that the child neither understands nor attempts to understand the reason for such a phenomenon ; in his eyes, it is only necessary to wave the hand to bring the air, and the air produced by the hands has a direct influence on the air outside.

In the same way, if a child of 4 to 6 is shown a small steam-engine he will explain the movement of the outside wheel as directly caused by the fire, even at a distance (as when the fire is put 50 centimetres away). But the child will often admit that the air outside comes to help the fire, and this again is due to a direct and unintelligible attraction (see *La Causalité Physique*, Section IV). There is thus participation between the air produced by the fire and the air outside.

Again the shadow one makes on the table is often explained by little children as due to a participation with the shadow of the night or the shadow under the trees. It is felt that this comes in the moment the hand is placed over the paper and the shadow of the fingers forms (see *La Causalité Physique*, Section III). Here again the child says clearly that the shadow of the trees " comes," but he cannot say " how " it comes : he simply states that the shadow of the hand comes both from the hand and the trees. It is not a logical identity (as if he were to say " the shadow of the hand is of the same nature as that of the trees "), nor is it an intelligible causal relationship, it is simply " participation."

Finally comes an example intermediate between this and the next group. This is the case of a little girl who endowed her marbles with powers of influencing one another, partly from the idea of their possessing a sort of common essence (those of the same kind necessarily attracting one another) and partly from a kind of participation of will similar to the cases of the fourth group :—

" *When I had just won certain marbles* (by taking them from my opponent), *I never used these marbles to play with again, because I thought I was more likely to lose these than the others, since I had the idea that they would be in some way attached to their former surroundings and have a tendency to return to their former owner.*

Finally, there is the fourth group of participations, those *due to a common will* and which give rise to acts of *magic by commandment*. The cases of this group arise as much from the child's magic as from animism. Two fundamental characteristics are at their origin, namely, the child's egocentricity which makes him believe the world to centre in himself, and his respect for his parents which tends always to make him believe that the world is governed by moral rather than physical laws. Animism and artificialism result from this attitude of mind as soon as it becomes crystallised in definite conceptions. But, before there has been any reflection, this attitude already gives rise to feelings of participation between the child and objects. These are of great variety and must be stated now before they are examined in greater detail and in relation to each group of phenomena.

First come participations in connection with the material nature of thought. Thought is identified with voice, and is in some cases held to be of air, the air being regarded as both internal and external. Whence arise the beliefs according to which air and smoke are drawn to us and become one with our breath or our thought (see Chapter I, §§ 1, 2 and 3). The same convictions are found concerning dreams. As we have already seen, all these convictions are due to a comparatively simple realism and result solely from a lack of differentiation between thought and things.

Then there are a more numerous group of participations connected with the idea of the obedience of objects. Objects obey either the child himself or adults. The following are examples of the first type, beginning with two recollections :—

One of our friends, now a teacher, believed during many years of his childhood (though he had never before revealed it) that he was the " ruler " of the world, that is to say that he could make the sun, the moon, the stars and the clouds move as he willed them.

Clan also had the idea that the stars were his " property."

These two examples are quoted because they so closely resemble the convictions we have been able to observe directly. We shall in fact show later (Chapter VII, § 2) that before the age of 8, the majority of children believe that the sun and stars follow them. With many, however, the emphasis is laid less on the spontaneity of the sun than on the power of the child himself. The following examples are very clear in this respect and concern the movements of the clouds as well as those of the sun and stars.

NAIN (4½) : " Can the moon go wherever it wants, or does something make it move ?—*It's me, when I walk*." And again : " *It comes with me, it follows us*."

GIAMB (7) : " Does the moon move or not ?—*It follows us.*—Why ?—*When we go, it goes.*—What makes it move ? —*We do.*—How ?—*When we walk. It goes by itself."* Giamb then invents the explanation that it is the wind that blows the sun and the moon, but he maintains all the while that it is we who control this movement : " If we didn't move, would the moon go on or not ?—*The moon would stop.*—And the sun ?—*It goes with us too."*

TAG (6½) : " Have you seen the clouds moving ?— *Yes.*—Can you make them move yourself ?—*Yes, by walking.*—What happens when you walk ?—*It makes them move.*—What makes them move ?—*We do, because we walk and then they follow us.*—What makes them follow us ?—*Because we walk.*—How do you know that ?— *Because when you look up in the sky, they are moving.*— Could you make them go the other way if you wanted to ?—*By turning round and walking back.*—And what would the clouds do then ?—*They'd go back.*—Can you make anything else move from far away without touching it ?—*The moon.*—How ?—*When you walk, it follows you. The stars too.*—How ?—*When you move they follow too. The ones that are behind follow the moon."*

SALA (8) : " Have you seen the clouds moving ? What makes them move ?—*When you move they move too.*— Can you make them move yourself ?—*Everyone can by walking."*

TULI (10) : " What makes the clouds move ?—*It's when you walk."*

PORT (9) said that the clouds move when God moves, and then added spontaneously : " *Even when people walk in the street, that makes the clouds move.*—Then can you make them move yourself ?—*Yes. Sometimes when I'm walking I look at the sky. I see that the clouds are moving, then I see the moon doing it too when it's there."*

The nature of these participations and magical ideas is clear. There is no direct participation of substance, there is simply participation of action and principally of purpose : we can command the sun and the clouds, since there is " participation " between their will and our will. It may happen, however, that this dynamic participation involves participation of substance, as for example in cases involving the air, shadows, etc. It seems to children that we possess the power of attracting the air or shadows, whilst producing them ourselves at the same time. We have classed these cases in the group of participations between objects (third group) but their origin lies evidently in a simple dynamic participation of the type quoted above. A case, quoted by Sully, and classed with justice as a magical idea by Leuba and by Delacroix[1] shows clearly this relationship between dynamic participation and participation between objects. " A little girl was out for a walk with her mother one very windy day. The buffeting of the wind delighted her at first, but she soon grew tired of it : ' Wind make Mamma's hair untidy ; Babba (her name) make Mamma's hair tidy, so wind not blow again.' Three weeks later the child was out of doors in the rain ; she said to her mother : ' Mamma, dry Babba's hands, so not rain any more.' The child," Sully adds, " is envisaging the wind and the rain as a kind of naughty child who can be got to behave properly by effacing the effects of its naughtiness. In other words they are both to be deterred from repeating what is objectionable by a visible and striking manifestation of somebody's objection or prohibition." [2]

This commentary shows clearly the moral and dynamic origin of these participations. But from the dynamic participation which consists in relating the wind's will to our own will, to material participation which consists in relating the air we make by waving our hands to the atmosphere itself, is surely not far.

The following is a good example of a dynamic participation becoming material and recalling, moreover, the most striking cases of participation among primitives.

James quotes the case of a deaf-mute who became a professor and gave his recollections (in the third person). This is extracted from recollections relating to the moon [3] :

[1] See Delacroix, *La religion et la foi*, pp. 27-42, Alcan, 1924 ; see the relationship established by Delacroix between magic and desire. See also Leuba, *La psychologie des phénomènes religieux*, Chap. VIII. Alcan, 1914,

[2] *Studies of Childhood*, p. 80.

[3] See *Philos. Rev.*, I (1892), pp. 613-24.

He asked himself with astonishment why the moon appeared regularly. He thought it must have come out just in order to see him. He began to speak to it then and imagined he could see it smile or frown. Finally, he made the discovery that he had been beaten much more often when the moon was visible. It was as if it watched him and reported his misdemeanours to his governess (he was an orphan). He often asked himself who it could be. At last he decided that it was his mother, because whilst his mother had been alive he had never seen the moon. He went to church on Sunday imagining that the moon wanted him to go, as he had been accustomed to go with his mother. His conscience developed, thanks above all to the moon's influence (it was a full moon on the evening when he discovered that some money he had pilfered had disappeared from where he had hidden it).

This extract makes clear participation connected with the origin of things, in which magic is attributed to the adult much more than to the child or to the things themselves. In these cases there is equally a transition from dynamic to material participation. In the most primitive states the child has simply the impression that his parents command the world. For example, there is participation between the sun and men in the sense that the sun has no other reason for existing nor any other activity than furthering the interests of man. Thus, when the child asks himself, or when we ask him, how the sun began, he obviously answers that the sun was made by man, that it results from man (est " né " de l'homme) etc. The belief in a common origin results from dynamic participation.

We shall find numerous examples of such feelings of participation, which precede and announce the more strictly artificialist beliefs. They characterise what we shall call the stage of " diffuse artificialism." We mention them now, since they too give rise, if not to actual magical practices at any rate to a predisposition towards magic. Cases have often been quoted of children begging their parents to stop a storm, or making some similar sort of impossible demand, as if their parents had the power of doing all things. Thus Mme Klein has seen her child asking that spinach shall be turned into potatoes by cooking it.[1] M. Oberholzer quotes the case of a little girl who begged her aunt to make the rain come.[2] M. Bovet recalled the amazement and shock it was to Hebbel, as a child, to see his father in despair at the damage caused by a storm : Hebbel thus realised that his father could not be all-powerful.[3] M. Reverdin recounts the following observation : " Whilst walking in a garden with his son aged 3 years 4 months, he noticed about 50 little beads scattered on the path. The child did not see them. To make him find them, M. Reverdin traced a circle on the path round some of the beads, telling the child he would find a bead in the middle of the ring. After a moment or so the child wanted to play the principal rôle and started making circles himself, thinking that the beads would necessarily be found inside them."[4] Such a case may indeed be merely an instance of " false reasoning " ;[5] the appearance of the bead followed the drawing of a circle, therefore it was the drawing that caused the bead to appear. But it certainly seems as if, in the particular case, there is added to this the child's implicit faith in the power of the adult.

§ 3. THE ORIGINS OF PARTICIPATION AND MAGIC AS MANIFESTED IN THE CHILD.—Like animism and artificialism, of which we shall treat later, the participations and magic manifested by the child seem to have a double origin. They can be explained as due to phenomena either of the individual or of the social order : the first is realism, that is, a confusion between thought and things, or between the self and the external world ; the second is the translation into the physical world of the ideas evoked

[1] *Imago*, Vol. VII, p. 265.
[2] Spielrein, *Archives de Psychologie*, XVIII, p. 307.
[3] Bovet, *Revue de theologie et de philosophie*, pp. 172-3. (Lausanne), 1919.
[4] *Archives de Psychologie*, Vol. XVII, p. 137.
[5] See I. Meyerson, *Année psychologique*, XXIII, pp. 214-222.

in the child's mind by his relations with the persons surrounding him.

Let us first examine the part played by realism and consider under this head two of the psychological theories of magic recently put forward.

In the first place, as is well known, Frazer sees in magic simply the application to external causality of those laws of resemblance and contiguity which govern the association of our ideas. It is evident, however, that this conception explains principally the form the magic takes ; it does not account either for the belief in its efficacy, which accompanies the magical action, or for the irrational nature of the associations such a belief supposes.

To explain the belief in its efficacy, Freud has put forward the following theory. The belief results from desire. Underlying all magic is a special affective quality. The same characteristic is found with the insane ; an insane person believes he has only to think of something to make a particular event occur or not. As a patient told Freud, this attitude involves belief in the " all-powerfulness of thought." But what affective conditions give rise to this belief ? By analysing his patients, Freud was led to consider magic as a result of " narcissism." Narcissism is a stage in the affective development, during which the child is only interested in himself, in his own desires and thoughts. This stage precedes the concentration of any permanent interest or desire in the person of others. But, says Freud, the narcissist being, so to speak, in love with himself, his wishes and his own desires appear to him charged with a special value, whence the belief in the necessary efficacy of each of his thoughts.

This theory of Freud is of undoubted interest and the connection it establishes between magic and narcissism appears well founded. Only, the manner in which Freud explains and conceives this connection seems somewhat unintelligible.

In fact it gives to the infant narcissist the qualities of an adult in love with himself and aware of it, as if the infant could clearly distinguish his self from others. And also, it seems to claim that if a desire has an exceptional value, belief in its necessary realisation must follow. There is here a twofold difficulty.

What is it, as a matter of fact, that prevents us believing in the automatic realisation of our desires ? It is that we know them to be subjective and that we distinguish them from the desires of others and from the realities that the world forces us to recognise. Thus if the infant narcissist believes in the all-powerfulness of thought, it is evidently because he does not distinguish his thought from that of others, nor his self from the external world ; in other words he is not aware of his self. If he is in love with himself, it is not because he knows his self, but because he ignores all that is outside his dream and his desires.

Narcissism, that is to say absolute egocentricity, certainly gives rise to magical conviction, but only in so far as it implies absence of consciousness of self. The term " solipsism " has been used in connection with infants : but the real solipsist does not feel that he is alone, and cannot know his self for the simple reason that we only feel ourselves to be alone after others have left us and that he who has never had the idea of a possible plurality cannot have in the least degree the feeling of his individuality. Thus the solipsist probably feels himself identical with the images he perceives ; he has no consciousness of his self, *he is the world*. We may thus speak of narcissism and maintain that the infant regards everything in terms of his own pleasure, but on condition that we remember that narcissism is accompanied by the most complete realism, in the sense that the infant can make no distinction between a self that commands and a not-self that obeys. At the most the infant distinguishes a desire, arising he knows not whence, and events which happen to bring about its fulfilment.

If we admit this assimilation of the world to the self and the self to the world, participation and magical causality become intelligible. On one hand, the movements of the body itself must be confused with any sort of external movement, and on the other, desires, pleasures and pains must be situated, not in the self, but in the absolute, in a world which, from the adult point of view, we should describe as common to all, but which from the infant's point of view is the only possible world. It follows when the infant sees his limbs move at his own will, he must feel that he is commanding the world. Thus on seeing a baby joyfully watching the movements of his feet, one has the impression of the joy felt by a god in directing from a distance the movements of the stars. Inversely, when the baby takes delight in movements situated in the outside world, such as the movement of the ribbons of its cradle, he must feel an immediate bond between these movements and his delight in them. In short, for a mind that cannot distinguish, or does so but dimly, the self from the external world, everything participates in the nature of and can influence everything else. To put it another way, participation results from a lack of differentiation between the consciousness of the action of the self on the self and the consciousness of the action of the self on things.

It is here that the second factor essential to the explanation of participation and magic comes in. This is the part played by social environment, that is, the rôle of the parents. The life of the suckling is not, in fact, distinguishable in its origin from that of the mother. Its desires and most fundamental needs are necessarily met by a reply from the mother or from someone in its immediate surroundings. Every cry of the baby leads to an action on the part of the parents, and even the desires it can least express are always foreseen. In short, if the baby can barely distinguish its own movements from movements outside itself, there must be for it a complete continuity between its parents' activities and its own.

Two consequences follow. Firstly, the feelings of participation must evidently be strengthened by this continual response of the environment. Secondly, the conduct of people towards it gradually gives the baby the habit of command. The parents, like the parts of its own body, like all the objects that can be moved by the parents or by its own actions (food, toys, etc.), make up a class of things obedient to its desires and, since this class is much the most interesting, the whole world is conceived as of this fundamental type. Whence arises the habit of commanding things by magic.

But let us leave this primitive stage, the description of which is naturally to be taken as purely schematic. The later stages, during which the self is gradually distinguished from the external world, provide in fact very full data as to the nature of the processes whose genesis we have so far merely conjectured.

As we have already seen in the preceding chapters, the child does not simultaneously classify as internal or psychic the various contents of its thought and experience. Words and dreams, for example, are comparatively late in being assigned to thought and the self. And since certain contents are projected into things, whilst others are regarded as internal, it follows that the child must necessarily feel all manner of participations between himself and things. Realism, indeed, implies a feeling of participation between the world and the self, for since it consists in regarding as belonging to things and as originating in things what in fact results from the child's own activity, it follows that this activity is conceived in return as something completely immersed in the things and all-powerful over them. This connection between realism and magical participation is shown in three different ways.

The first, that is to say the simplest, to interpret consists in the attachment of thought and its instruments to things themselves—the counterpart in magic being participation between thought and things (the second of the four groups distinguished in § 2). In fact, from the moment the child confuses thought, or names, etc., with things, through not realising the internal and subjective nature of the act of thinking, it becomes natural for him to use these names or thoughts to influence things. Viewed in this light, all the cases of the second group quoted in the preceding section are easily explicable. To distort a name in order to prevent the consequences of some event or as a means of defence against a master follows as a natural result of regarding names as bound up in the nature of actual things and persons. To shake the hands to free them of the contagious effects of laziness follows as a matter of course if the psychical and the physical are confused after the manner of the children studied in Chapter I. It is harder to explain why children should think the opposite from what they want or think of frightening things in order not to dream of them, for this supposes the endowing of fate and dreams with will. The realism in these cases is accompanied by animism. But they are none the less based on a certain realism similar to that which characterises the previous cases ; it lies in the idea that thought can insert itself directly into the real and thus influence events.

The second manner in which the connection between realism and magic appears lies in the attachment of the sign to the reality, which is shown in the magic provoked by action (first of the groups distinguished in § 2). Actions, in fact, are symbols or signs in the same way as are words, names, or images, and as the child regards every sign as participating in the nature of the thing signified or every symbol as adhering to an actual object, so actions are regarded as having the powers attributed to words and names. This realism of action is thus only a particular case of the realism of signs. We must now try to analyse the relationship between magic by action and child realism in general.

Two types of case exist : those in which the magical gesture is the symbolical reproduction of an action in itself reasonable, and those in which the magical gesture is symbolical from the beginning. In both cases the magic arises from a confusion between sign and cause, that is from making the sign realistic.

Examples of the first type are the more rare. But the cases of magic relating to fear given in § 2 may be quoted as instances. The evolution of this type of magic seems to be as follows. The child begins by performing actions which contain no element of magic, but which, in their original context are simply ordinary acts of protection against robbers or other wicked persons ; such as to lower the curtains so as not to be seen, to see that the bed-clothes are tucked in all round so as to make sure no one is hiding either in the bed or under it, to press the arms to the sides, to stiffen one's self or make one's self smaller. But with repetition these actions lose all rational relation to the primitive context and become simply ritual. It is no longer to prove that nobody is hiding in the room that the child makes sure the bed-clothes are tucked in, but simply because it is a habitual action fitting in with a number of circumstances and which it would be foolish not to perform punctually. So too, in moments of anxiety we make a point of observing ritualistically every detail of our habitual routine, since it is impossible to foresee what may not be the effect of their neglect and because fear, depriving us of the power of reflection, makes us all the more conservative (automatic action taking the place of intelligence). For a rational mind—that is to say in this particular case for a subject conscious of his self and more or less clearly distinguishing the part of subjective habits from that of causal sequences bound up with the events in question and with the external world—the adherence to practice involved is destined merely to reassure us, each action being regarded as a proof that we are behaving as normally as usual. But for a realist mind—that is to say a mind which confuses the internal with the external—each of these actions becomes sym- bolical and is then regarded as the psychical cause as well as the sign : the fact that the bed is properly made becomes not merely the sign but actually the cause of security. Or rather the action becomes symbolical in so far as it is ritual, but a cause, in so far as it is regarded as bound up with the events themselves. This process is very clear in the case quoted in § 2, where the rapidity with which the curtain is drawn becomes a magical means of protection, symbolical because withdrawn from its original context but efficacious because the symbol has remained attached to what it represents.

The examples of the second type in which the magical gesture is symbolical from the outset can be similarly explained, except that the action is related to the primitive context by simple association rather than as a part of a whole. Take for example the cases of rhythmic movements (quoted in § 2), since these are the simplest. They start either as a game or as some sort of æsthetic pleasure, such as the fun of walking on the pavement without stepping on the lines of the paving-stones, or of touching all the bars of a railing without missing one, or of replacing every stone kicked out of place, etc. Now suppose that the child, given to one of these habits, experiences one day a particular desire or fear. He will take care to follow his usual habits on that day, feeling in them the same need of adherence to practice [1] that was referred to above and in such a way that the action becomes one with the affective circumstances, the action being related to the whole by a sort of conditioned reflex or simply by syncretism. To a mind both syncretic and realist at the same time, such a bond leads to magic, for the action becomes symbolical and any symbol of success becomes a cause of success. To succeed in walking on a pavement without touching the lines becomes the sign that the thing desired will happen, and then the symbolical action takes on powers of its own, in so far as these signs are all regarded as one with the thing they signify.

[1] For the part played by this need of adhering to practice, *cp.* I. Meyerson, *Année Psychologique*, XXIII, pp. 214-222. The writer desires in justice to attribute to Meyerson all that is sound in the present section. For the errors, if errors there be, he takes full responsibility himself. See Appendix.

In short, cases of magic by participation of action and of things can be explained in the same way as cases of participation between thought and things. They result from the realist attitude, that is to say from the projection of mental relationships into things ; every sign is regarded as a part of an actual thing and tends thus to be taken for its cause.

There is yet a third manner in which realism leads to magical practices ; this is the belief in participation between objects themselves (the third of the groups distinguished in § 2). The position is more complicated in this case ; the subject acts on an object by means of another object and regards the two objects as influencing one another by participation. According to Frazer it is simply a case of making association by resemblance or contiguity objective. But such a solution is too simple, for it remains to be shown how an association of ideas can be so objective as to become a causal relationship. We must say rather that realism implies lack of differentiation between the logical and the causal relationship. As adults we are aware of an external reality made up of causal connections and an internal subject who attempts at first by analogies and then by laws to understand this reality. To a realist mind, all seems equally real and everything has its place in the same external scheme. From this arise the ideas of precausality and of syncretism that we have studied elsewhere (*Language and Thought*, Chapters IV and V) and which consist in situating in things the entirely subjective connections suggested to the child by his egocentric attitude. Magic by participation between objects is but the final stage in this process. It consists in regarding individual objects as materially bound to one another rather than as dependent on laws and conceptions made by mind.

Take for example the case of the child who believed that by making a shadow he could bring on the night. The postulate of this belief lies in supposing that the shadow is made of night, that it participates in the nature

of night. To a non-realist mind the meaning of the proposition is as follows : the shadow is made by the shade
thrown by the hand just as night is due to the shade
thrown by the earth, therefore the shadow and the night
are similar in that they are both due to the same law.
The similarity lies in their dependence on a general law.
But, as we have previously attempted to show (*Judgment
and Reasoning*, Chapter IV) a realist mind, that is to say
a mind unaware of the subjectivity of its point of view,
reasons neither by logical relationships not, therefore, by
generalisation and necessary deductions, but by syncretic
schemas and by " transduction," that is to say by directly
identifying individual cases. Thus for a realist mind to
identify a shadow and the night does not mean that he
establishes between them a similarity resting on a law,
but that he admits an immediate identity in the individual
cases, in other words material participation ; it is thus
that he explains the shadow as " coming from " the night.
The " transduction " or fusion of individual cases is, in
fact, a realist and not a formal argument. When it is
based on causal sequences that may be directly observed
it appears rational because it leads to the same conclusions
as a formal deduction starting from the same premises.
But when it is based on individual cases, separated in
time and space, it leads to syncretism and in extreme
cases, to participation.

It is evident that this explanation of participation
between objects as due to " transduction " and logical
realism involves certain hypotheses, but we shall deal with
this question less summarily in the subsequent work on
the child's ideas of physical causality.

In conclusion, realism—that is to say in its origin,
absence of differentiation between the self (or thought)
and the external world—necessarily develops into ideas
of participation and magic, and in three ways : by
confusion between thought and things, by a realism
which conceives the sign as itself effective and a
part of the thing for which it stands, and finally,

and more generally, by syncretic fusion of individual substances.

But realism cannot alone explain the whole of child magic. A large number of the participations the child conceives suppose animism and if animism results as we shall see, from egocentric realism, it is thus the product of participations which the child feels to exist from the beginning between his parents and himself. In fact, through not being able to distinguish the psychical from the physical, every physical phenomenon appears to the child as endowed with will and also the whole of nature as obedient to the will of man and his parents. Thus the majority of objects or events which the child tries to influence by magic (when he has no other way of acting on them) appear to him to be full of feelings and intentions, either friendly or hostile. From this arise two types of case. Firstly, many of the rites previously described consist in a procedure designed to bring good fortune or to counteract evil. Thus the child who puts on his boots twice so as not to be questioned in class implicitly supposes that fate is moral and will take account of the tiresome exertion involved in putting on one's boots twice. So too, the child who thinks the opposite from what he desires supposes fate to be in the habit of reading his thoughts in order to flout his wishes, etc. Secondly, there are a whole group of participations which are really animist. These are of the fourth group (described in § 2), the group of magical actions through participation of will. But, even in the phenomena of this fourth group, there is also an element of realism, without which there would be no magic.

The cases of the fourth group are, as a matter of fact, easily explained with the help of the two following facts. In all these groups there is absence of differentiation or confusion between the self and the external world, in this particular group between the subject's own point of view and external movements : thus the child imagines that when he moves, the sun and the clouds move too. Secondly, there is the animist explanation : the child says the sun and the clouds are alive because they follow him. There follows, as a consequence, magic by command ; it is only necessary to command things for them to obey, even at a distance.

It is in these cases of the fourth group that the tendency for magical actions or words to become symbolical is naturally weakest, since the magic of this type is exercised by a sort of command which is as real as a command addressed to a living being. But, as has already been shown, these participations of will develop into magic by thought or gesture which tends always to become symbolic.

In conclusion, it would seem that the evolution of magical actions, whatever the origin of the participations on which they are based, follows the law of which M. Delacroix has made such a profound analytical study in connection with language. Signs begin by being part of things or by being suggested by the presence of the things in the manner of simple conditioned reflexes. Later, they end by becoming detached from things and disengaged from them by the exercise of intelligence which uses them as adaptable and infinitely plastic tools. But between the point of origin and that of arrival there is a period during which the signs adhere to the things although already partially detached from them.[1]

But, if all magic leads to symbolism, it is, as M. Delacroix has very justly shown, because all thought is symbolic. What the magical stage itself shows, in opposition to the later stages, is precisely that symbols are still conceived as participating in things. Magic is thus the pre-symbolic stage of thought. From this point of view the child's magic is a phenomenon of exactly the same order as the realism of thought, names and dreams studied in the previous chapters. For us, concepts, words and images seen in a dream are all, in different degrees,

---

[1] H. Delacroix, *Le Langage et la Pensée*. See in particular the " Remarque finale." Delacroix has elsewhere pointed out very clearly the relationship between magic and realism (*La réligion et la foi*, p. 38).

symbols of things. For the child, they actually emanate from the things. The reason is that we distinguish the subjective from the objective, whilst the child situates in things what is due to the activity of his self. In the same way magical actions are, to the observer, symbols, but to the subject they are effective, precisely because they are not yet symbolic and because they participate in things.

§ 4. CORROBORATIVE PROOF : SPONTANEOUS MAGICAL IDEAS IN THE ADULT.—Before concluding this chapter we shall try to see what traces of the magical ideas found in children and studied in the preceding sections are present among normal and civilised adults, and if they are indeed due to the confusions between the self and the external world which sometimes reappear momentarily in phenomena connected with imitation and emotion. Naturally, we shall only consider magic in a strictly individual sense, such as may be found among intellectual people and shall set aside all that is " superstition," that is to say all practices or beliefs that may have been handed down.

Three cases occur in the adult in which the boundary between the self and the external world becomes momentarily vague and uncertain, exclusive of course of dreaming and reverie in which it would be easy enough to find innumerable feelings of participation. These three cases are involuntary imitation, anxiety and the state of " monoïdeic " desire. We shall try to show that in these three cases, the weakening of the sense of personality leads to realism and the realism to more or less clear magical ideas.

Firstly, involuntary imitation consists in an ideo-motor adaptation to movements perceived in such a way that the subject feels to be his own what actually belongs to another or to the material world. It consists, as Janet has said, in a confusion between the self and the external world. Numerous cases are easily found in which the imitative sympathy is accompanied by a complementary attitude which consists in trying to affect the external world by some action on one's own body. This attitude closely resembles that of infantile magic. The following are examples, beginning with the simplest cases :—

Someone has his nose blocked up. A person present instantly feels the need to blow his own nose in order to free the speaker's nose.

The speaker has a husky voice,—one feels the desire to clear one's own throat, again with the feeling of helping the speaker by so doing.

A person's voice has failed him,—one speaks all the louder not to excite him to imitation, but to lend him one's own strength.

These cases are not very clear, since the implicit attitude can always be rationalised, for it is as if the person sympathising is merely trying to set the other an example. As a matter of fact, observation shows that the action does not involve any such reasoning, the one simply tries to be rid of the irritation felt by seeing or hearing the other.

A collaborator states how before going out with his wife he waited till she had finished her cigarette whilst he smoked a pipe. He noticed that he was drawing at his pipe quicker than usual in order that his wife would finish her cigarette quicker. For a brief moment the illusion was complete, that is, until he became aware of it.

In the same way, one often tries to influence objects. For example, when someone is playing bowls or billiards, and is in doubt whether the ball will reach its mark, he will strain his body forward eagerly with a strong feeling of muscular tension, to make the ball roll in the right direction. He has no distinct idea of what he is doing, but it is clear he identifies himself with the ball in so far as he seeks to affect its course by his action. Imitation thus leads to an attitude of participation.

If anyone sees two cyclists about to collide in the street, he will himself make a recoiling movement to prevent the bicycles crashing.

It thus certainly seems as if confusions due to imitation lead towards magical gestures, which are instantly checked by our habits of thinking, but which, with minds less conscious of the self, would develop spontaneously. Undoubtedly these facts may be considered as being very far removed from actual magic. But they make up at any rate and it is this that we are seeking a clear transition stage between a realism resulting from confusion of the self and the external world, and magic or participation.[1]

In moments of anxiety the adult sometimes manifests the processes described in the case of the child, such as the desire to observe even the most insignificant details of the ordinary routine so that the balance of things shall not be upset. Thus, before giving a lecture, one takes one's usual walk, etc. . . . . In states of extreme anxiety there reappears the child's confusion between the action made to reassure himself and that destined to maintain the balance of reality, in other words the magical attitude. The following is a clear example given by the subject to whom the preceding examples are also due :—

Just before giving a lecture, being rather nervous, he took his usual walk. When nearly at the point where he was in the habit of stopping, he was about to turn back before reaching the exact spot, when he felt compelled to go right to the end (50 metres further on) *in order that the lecture should be a success,* as if to cut his walk short was enough to spoil his luck !

In other states of fear, feelings of participation are found mixed with animist ideas, as in states of desire. The study of these shows that it is generally sufficient ardently to desire something outside of our control (such as good weather or anything depending on luck or chance) in order to have the impression of a sort of hostile power seeking to mock us. The desire thus becomes hypostatised in the things and by projection personifies fate and events. This realist tendency is sufficient to cause any number of magical tendencies.

One of us was travelling at night by bicycle. He had already gone many miles and was still far from his journey's end. The wind and the near approach of a storm made

---

[1] See Delacroix, *La réligion et la foi,* p. 141.

him begin to feel nervous and this was increased by the numerous motors he kept meeting which blinded him with their lights. He suddenly had the idea that to make things worse his tires might burst. He then felt distinctly the need of driving away this idea, *in order that the tire should not burst*, with the clear impression that to think of a burst tire was enough to cause the thing actually to happen !

This is an intermediate case between the realism of thought (Freud's " all-powerfulness of ideas ") and magic due to animism.

In the following examples the latter predominates :—

The same subject was looking for mushrooms, and had already several in his hand which he was about to put in his knapsack, when he decided to wait till he had found one or two more and put them all in together. But then he felt compelled immediately to put away the few he had, so as not to seem as if he counted on finding others, as these would certainly never appear if he seemed too sure of finding them. Another time, he said to himself, as he was walking, that he would put his coat in his rucksack as soon as he had found any mushrooms (so as not to waste time undoing the sack twice). But, a moment later, not having found any mushrooms, and feeling his coat too hot he was about to take it off, when he was struck by the idea that it would be better not to take off his coat for fear of not finding any mushrooms.

It should be noted that the subject had never been superstitious and had never been told during his religious education (Protestant) anything suggesting magical rites. The observations noted here are the more or less conscious tendencies that anyone can observe in himself.

A friend, who is a professor of psychology, made the three following observations on himself. When walking after rain, he had the impulse not to take off his waterproof and put it in his rucksack, in order to prevent the rain from starting again. . . .

When going to pay a call on anyone he hoped he would not find at home he was prompted to change his collar and his clothes in order not to meet them. If he went in his usual clothes they would be sure, on the contrary, to be at home !

Before giving a garden-party, he refused to have the garden prepared so that it should not rain, feeling convinced that if it was raked and weeded it would be sure to rain the whole day.

He resumed his observations thus : " *I always tend not to prepare for anything I want, for fear that what I hope to avoid should happen.*"

Magical practices indulged in by card-players are well known.[1]

It is clear enough that all these examples are derived from a confusion between the self and the external world, with the animistic tendency acting, in certain cases, as a secondary factor. All the last examples result from the extension to the external world of experiences that are well known to the self. If an idea is in your mind it acts on you by suggestion, whence the tendency to try and drive it away even if it concerns a bicycle tire. Not to take one's usual walk is enough to put one in bad form, whence comes the idea that it must be continued right to the end, and not cut short even by 50 metres in order to insure that one's lecture shall be received favourably, etc.

In short, these few examples confirm the conclusions we supposed true in the case of the child, namely that all realism tends to lead to magic. With the adult, realism still remains in imitation, in fear and in desire, and this realism, although of infinitely smaller extent than that of the child, is still enough to bring out certain clear cases of participation and even of magic.

§ 5. CONCLUSION : LOGICAL AND ONTOLOGICAL EGO-CENTRICITY.—In the first three chapters we tried to show that the distinction between thought and the external world is not innate in the child but is only gradually evolved and built up by a slow process. One result of this is of primary importance to the study of causality, namely that the child is a realist in its thought and that its progress consists in ridding itself of this initial realism.

[1] See H. Delacroix, *La réligion et la foi*, p. 43 *sq*. Paris, 1924.

In fact, during the primitive stages, since the child is not yet conscious of his subjectivity, all reality appears to be of one unvaried type by reason of the confusion between the data of the external world and those of the internal. Reality is impregnated with self and thought is conceived as belonging to the category of physical matter. From the point of view of causality, all the universe is felt to be in communion with and obedient to the self. There is participation and magic. The desires and the commands of the self are felt to be absolute, since the subject's own point of view is regarded as the only one possible. There is integral egocentricity through lack of consciousness of self.

We are thus drawn to a conclusion parallel to that to which we were led by our earlier studies of child logic. In his manner of reasoning, equally, the child is only concerned with himself, and ignores more or less completely the points of view of others. But, in logic also, if the child sees everything from his own point of view, it is because he believes all the world to think like himself. He has not yet discovered the multiplicity of possible perspectives and remains blind to all but his own as if that were the only one possible. Also he states his views without proof since he feels no need to convince. The results of this are seen in play, make-belief, the tendency to believe without proof, the absence of deductive reasoning; in syncretism also which connects all things in terms of primitive subjective associations; in the absence of all relativity among ideas; and finally in "transductive" reasoning which, through the agency of syncretism, leads from one particular to another, heedless both of logical necessity and of general laws, because lacking in feeling for the reciprocal nature of all relationship.

There are thus two forms of egocentricity, the first logical and the second ontological. Just as the child makes his own truth, so he makes his own reality; he feels the resistance of matter no more than he feels the difficulty of giving proofs. He states without proof and he commands without limit. Magic on the ontological plane, and conviction without proof on the logical ; participation in the domain of being, and " transduction " in that of reasoning are thus the two converging products of the same phenomenon. At the root both of magic and of conviction without proof lie the same egocentric illusions, namely, confusion between one's own thought and that of others and confusion between the self and the external world.

Ontological egocentricity is a principle essential to the comprehension of the child's world. Just as logical egocentricity provided the key to the child's judgment and reasoning, so ontological egocentricity provides that to his conceptions of reality and causality. Precausality and finalism are, in fact, directly derived from this egocentricity, since, in their assumption that man is the centre of the universe, they consist in a confusion of relationships of a causal and physical nature with those of psychological origin. These primitive relationships come to be justified by animism and artificialism and from their lingering traces are finally made up the integral dynamism which impregnates the child's ideas on meteorology and physics.

PART II

ANIMISM

SINCE the child does not distinguish the psychical from the physical world, since in the early stages of his development he does not even recognise any definite limits between his self and the external world, it is to be expected that he will regard as living and conscious a large number of objects which are for us inert. This is the phenomenon we propose to study and we shall describe it by the current word " animism."

We are aware of all that may be said against the employment of this word, but we feel none the less that the two principal objections can be satisfactorily answered.

The first of these is as follows. The term has been used by English anthropologists to describe those beliefs according to which primitive peoples endow nature with " souls," " spirits," etc., in order to explain physical phenomena. They sought to explain the various means by which the primitive thus arrives at the notion of a soul and at the same time they regarded this notion as giving rise to the animist beliefs. It is well known to-day how superficial was this description of primitive mentality. The penetrating criticism of Lévy-Bruhl and the suggestions made by Baldwin have demonstrated to the point of proof that the processes of the primitive mind are the exact opposite from what was supposed. The primitive does not distinguish mind from matter. It is precisely because he has not made this distinction that all things appear to him endowed both with material properties and with will. It is the existence of this *continuum*, both moral and physical at the same time, which explains the occult participations with which their magic teems, and which has created the illusion that primitives believe in a " soul " in the same sense that we do. M. Lévy-Bruhl refuses, therefore, to use the term animism at all and regards it as bound up with the erroneous interpretations to which it first lent itself.

But we shall not mean by it any more than the word implies; we shall use it merely to describe the tendency to regard objects as living and endowed with will. This tendency is a fact and in giving it a name we have no intention of prejudging the issue of its interpretation. Whatever terminology we may decide to adopt, our problem is to examine whether animism in the case of the child depends on the existence of the notion of " mind " or, on the contrary, on the absence of such a notion.

The second objection that may be raised is certainly more serious. The term animism denotes a belief peculiar to primitive peoples. If we use it here in speaking of the child it is as if we were deciding out of hand the question as to whether these similar beliefs were identical for the primitive and the child. But such is not the case. We shall use the word " animism " simply as a generic term, leaving the question open whether the various types of animism have the same or distinct psychological origins.

On these premises, three main problems present themselves in the study of child animism. First, there is the problem of purposiveness : does the child attribute consciousness to the objects which surround him and in what measure ? The second problem is important to the study of causality : what does the concept of " life " imply to the child ? Does life correspond with consciousness or not, etc. ? Finally, there is the third problem : what type of necessity does the child see in natural laws, moral necessity or physical determinism, etc. . . . ?

Each of these problems will be dealt with in a separate chapter, and in considering the problem of necessity the attempt will be made to solve the question as to the genesis of child animism.

CHAPTER V

CONSCIOUSNESS ATTRIBUTED TO THINGS

THE technique used in the two following chapters is certainly open to serious criticism but the results undoubtedly furnish a number of indications, provided certain reservations are made.

We started by asking the following questions : " If I were to prick you with a pin, would you feel it ? " and " If I were to prick the table would the table feel it ? " The same question is then applied to stones, flowers, metal, water, etc., and the child is asked what would happen if one could prick the sun, the moon, the clouds. It is naturally necessary and this is the most important part of the experiment, to ask " Why ? " or " Why not ? " after each answer. The essential is, in fact, to see if the child replies arbitrarily or in accordance with a system, and in the latter case to discover what is the child's latent conception.

The great danger of this technique lies obviously in suggestion, both ordinary suggestion and suggestion by perseveration. To avoid the former the questions must be given in an unbiased form ; thus, instead of asking " does the table feel anything ? " the question must be " does the table feel anything or nothing " ? But according to the writer's observations the real danger lies not in simple suggestion but in perseveration. If the child starts by saying " yes," (that the flower feels the prick, for example), he will tend to continue answering " yes " to all the other questions. If he started by saying " no "

his answers will tend equally to perseverate. Two precautions are, therefore, necessary. The first is to jump
continually from one extreme to another, thus after asking
whether a dog can feel, the question must then be asked
about a stone or a nail (which are usually regarded as
without consciousness) and then for a flower, then for a
wall or a rock, etc. Only after making sure that there is
no perseveration should the more debatable objects, such
as the sun, the stars, the clouds, etc., be broached. And
here again they must not be presented in order and all
continuity must be avoided. The second precaution lies in
constantly observing the child's implicit systematisation.
This is not easy, since the youngest children neither know
how to justify their statements (*Judgment and Reasoning*,
Chapter I, § 4) nor do they understand their own reasoning
or definitions (*Judgment and Reasoning*, Chapter IV, §§ 1
and 2). Moreover, the child can neither multiply nor
summarise his propositions nor avoid contradictions
(*Judgment and Reasoning*, Chapter IV, §§ 2–3), which compels the experimenter to interpret as he proceeds, always
a delicate operation. Nevertheless, with practice it
becomes fairly easy to detect those children who answer
at random and to recognise those who have genuinely
some latent scheme of systematisation. The difference
between the two reactions is often evident from the first
questions. It is a good plan, therefore, to see these children
again a few weeks later to see if the systematisation has
been preserved.

But we were soon forced to regard the question of the
prick as too narrow. Animist as the child is, he is still
not so anthropomorphic as might be supposed. In other
words, he will easily refuse to admit that the sun could
feel a prick, although believing, all the while, that the
sun knows that it is moving, and knows when it is day
and when night. He will not admit that the sun can feel
pain yet believes it to be aware of its own existence. The
questions must, therefore, be varied for each object and
in accordance with its functions. For example, concern-

ing clouds, the question might be, "when it is cold, do they feel cold or don't they feel anything at all ? " " when they are moving, do they know they are moving or not ? " etc. Further, it is often useful to begin the examination by a series of questions on the verb " feel " and then to repeat these, by way of control, concerning the verb " to know."

We have come to the conclusion that if the questions are handled with the necessary care, perseveration can be avoided. But the objection raised to this technique may go yet deeper. Binet's researches on the testimony of children have clearly shown the dangers involved in setting questions in an alternative form, for they force the solution of a problem that would possibly never have been presented spontaneously in such a form. Therefore, the greatest reservation must be made before drawing conclusions from the results. We give the reader this preliminary warning so that reading the experiments he will not criticise us for making premature judgments.

From the results obtained, four groups may reasonably be distinguished, corresponding *grosso modo* to four successive stages. For children of the first stage, everything that is in any way active is conscious, even if it be stationary. In the second stage consciousness is only attributed to things that can move. The sun and a bicycle are conscious, a table and a stone are not. During the third stage an essential distinction is made between movement that is due to the object itself and movement that is introduced by an outside agent. Bodies that can move of their own accord, like the sun, the wind, etc., are henceforth alone held to be conscious, while objects that receive their movement from without, like bicycles, etc., are devoid of consciousness. Finally, in the fourth stage, consciousness is restricted to the animal world.

It must be stated at the outset that in classifying the results obtained we shall regard this outline as true, that is to say as adequately representing the spontaneous development of animism in the child. But owing to the defects in the method of examination we cannot with certainty say of a particular child that it belongs to a particular stage. It is obvious that two distinct questions are involved. The first is in some degree statistical, and its solution is possible despite uncertainties of detail ; the second is a species of individual diagnosis and involves a far subtler technique.

Two more points call for attention. The scheme outlined above allows certain details to escape notice. Many children's conceptions of consciousness embody certain attributes, such as the fact of having blood, of being able to speak, of being visible (for the wind), etc. But as these views are individual and have no generality they may be neglected here.

Secondly, we shall not distinguish children's conceptions concerning the verb " feel " from those concerning the verb " know." Such shades of distinction as we have detected appear to be principally a matter of words. Possibly children attribute " feeling " to things, longer than they do " knowing." But we have not sought to verify this impression as it is of little bearing on the issue.

§ 1. THE FIRST STAGE: ALL THINGS ARE CONSCIOUS.— The child in this stage certainly never says that everything is conscious. He simply says that any object may be the seat of consciousness at a given moment, that is to say when the object displays a particular measure of activity or is the seat of some action. Thus a stone may feel nothing, but if it is moved, it will feel it. The following examples are chosen from amongst the oldest children found in this stage.

VEL (8½) says that only animals could feel a prick, thus showing he is able to differentiate in his answers. What he means, as a matter of fact, is that only animals can feel pain. Clouds, for example, would not feel a prick. " Why not ?—*Because they are only air.*—Can they feel the wind or not ?—*Yes, it drives them.*—Can they feel heat ?—*Yes.*" But as far as mere consciousness is concerned, any object may be conscious at times : " Can the bench feel anything ?—*No.*—If someone burnt it, would it feel that ?—*Yes.*—Why ?—*Because it would get smaller.*—Does a wall feel anything ?—*No.*—Would it feel it if it was knocked down ?—*Yes.*—Why ?—*Because that would break it."* A moment later : " If I pull off this button (a coat button), will it feel it ?—*Yes.*—Why ?— *Because the thread would break.*—Would that hurt it ?— *No, but it would feel that was tearing it."* " Does the moon know it moves or not ?—*Yes.*—Does this bench know it is here ?—*Yes.*—You really think so ? Are you sure or not sure ?—*Not sure.*—What makes you think perhaps it doesn't know ?—*Because it is made of wood.*—And what makes you think it may know ?—*Because it is here."* " When the wind blows against the Salève, does it feel there is a mountain there or not ?—*Yes.*—Why ?— *Because it goes over it."* " Does a bicycle know it goes ? —*Yes.*—Why ?—*Because it goes.*—Does it know when it is made to stop ?—*Yes.*—What does it know with ?— *The pedals.*—Why ?—*Because they stop going.*—You think so really ?—*Yes* (we laugh).—And do you think I think so ?—*No.*—But you think so ? Can the sun see us ? —*Yes.*—Have you thought of that before.—*Yes.*—What does it see us with ?—*With its rays.*—Has it got eyes ? —*I don't know."*

Vel's answers are interesting because he can differentiate. Despite our final counter-suggestion, Vel endows the sun with vision. He refuses to allow pain to the button but thinks it would be aware of being pulled off, etc. Undoubtedly, Vel has never yet asked himself these questions, but it seems to follow from what he says, that if he has not yet asked them it is precisely because he confuses " acting " with " knowing the action is happening " or " being " with " knowing that one is." Even so cautious an interpretation may, however, be doubted. But in the case of Vel we have a further proof to serve as check. More than a year later we saw Vel again to question him on various physical problems. Naturally, we did not recall to him the questions of the previous year which he had completely forgotten. The following is his spontaneous reaction at the age of $9\frac{1}{2}$:—

We hung a metal box from a double string and placed it in front of Vel, in such a way that, on letting go of the box, the string unwound making the box turn round and round. " Why does it turn ?—*Because the string is twisted.* —Why does the string turn too ?—*Because it wants to unwind itself.*—Why ?—*Because it wants to be unwound* (= it wants to resume its original position, in which the string was unwound).—Does the string know it is twisted ? —*Yes.*—Why ?—*Because it wants to untwist itself, it knows it's twisted !*—Does it really know it is twisted ?—*Yes. I am not sure.*—How do you think it knows ?—*Because it feels it is all twisted.*"

The child who speaks thus is neither under the influence of suggestion nor romancing. The following are further examples :—

KENN (7½) : " If you pricked this stone, would it feel it ?—*No.*—Why not ?—*Because it is hard.*—If you put it in the fire, would it feel it ?—*Yes.*—Why ?—*Because it would get burnt.*—Can it feel the cold or not ?—*Yes.*— Can a boat feel it is on the water ?—*Yes.*—Why ?— *Because it is heavy when you are on it* (= it feels the weight of the people on board).—Does water feel if you prick it ? —*No.*—Why not ?—*Because it is thin* (= not solid).— Does it feel the heat of the fire or doesn't it feel anything ? —*Yes* (it feels it).—Would the sun feel it if some one pricked it ?—*Yes, because it is big.*" " Does the grass feel when you prick it ?—*Yes, because you pull it.*" " If this table were carried to the other end of the room, would it feel it ?—*No, because it is light* (= it would offer no resistance, because it weighs so little).—If some one broke it ?—*It would feel that.*"

Kenn clearly supposes that the degree of consciousness a thing possesses is in accordance with the effort it makes ; a boat feels its passengers, but a light table does not feel when it is carried and grass feels when it is picked, etc.

JUILL (7½) : A stone feels neither heat nor cold. " Would it feel if it was dropped on the ground ?—*Yes.*—Why ?— *Because it would break.*" " Can a table feel anything ?— *No.*—Would it feel if it were broken ?—*Oh, yes.*" " Does the wind feel when it blows against a house ?—*Yes.*— Does it feel it or not ?—*It feels it.*—Why ?—*Because it is in its way. It can't pass. It can't go any further.*" " Tell me some things· which don't feel anything. . . . Do walls feel?—*No.*—Why not?—*Because they can't move* (this answer announces the second stage).—Would they feel anything if they were knocked down?—*Yes.*- Does the wall know it is in a house?—*No.*—Does it know it's tall?—*Yes.*—Why?—*Because it goes right up, it knows it goes right up!*"

REYB (8 ; 7) : " Can water feel anything?—*No.*—Why not?—*Because water isn't all one* (is liquid).—If it's put on the stove, does it feel the heat?—*Yes.*—Why?—*Because the water is cold and the fire is hot.*—Does wood feel anything?—*No.*—Does it feel or not when it burns? Yes, because it can't stop it* (!)—Then it feels or not?—*It feels.*"

All these cases are similar and are free from all taint of suggestion. They show, all of them, the exercise of differentiation. The child endows all things with consciousness but not with consciousness of everything. For example, he refuses to admit that a stone can feel a prick, that the sun knows how many people are in the room, that buttons or spectacles know where they are, etc. But on the contrary, as soon as there is any sort of activity or more especially resistance, there is consciousness ; thus for Kenn a boat knows when it carries a cargo but a table does not know it is being carried ; for Juill the wind feels the presence of an obstacle, but a table feels nothing unless it is broken, for Reyb wood feels it is burning " because it can't do anything to stop it," etc. Such cases are easily interpreted. It is wrong to say the child attributes consciousness to things or at any rate such an expression must only be regarded as metaphorical. As a matter of fact, he has never or but very seldom considered the question as to whether things are conscious or not (he may sometimes do so, however ; see *Language and Thought*, p. 202). But having no notion of a possible distinction between thought and physical objects, he does not realise that there can be actions unaccompanied by consciousness. Activity is for him necessarily purposive and conscious. A wall cannot be knocked down without feeling it, a stone cannot be broken without knowing it, a boat cannot carry a cargo without effort, etc. There is here a primitive failure to dissociate between action and conscious effort. The real problem is thus to know how the child comes to conceive an unconsious action and to dissociate the notion of the action from that of consciousness of the action, rather than to know why action and consciousness appear necessarily connected.

If a parallel be sought among the answers and beliefs of primitives, it is not to animism with its highly emotional colouring, such as is manifest in social rites, that we shall turn, but rather to the little that is known of primitive physics. Mach relates in this connection the story of the Indian chief Chuar, who explained why his men could not succeed in throwing a stone across a ravine by saying that the stone was attracted by the ravine, just as we ourselves might be when suffering from giddiness, and it thus lost the strength necessary to make it reach the other side.[1] Mach further remarks that it is a persistent tendency in primitive thought to regard every subjective sensation as universal.

Our interpretation involves, however, yet another difficulty. It may be questioned whether the answers just analysed are really primitive and constitute the first stage in child animism. In fact, between the ages of 5 and 6 we found some exceptional cases who were in the later stages and also we came on children of 4 and 5 who showed hardly any animist tendency.

Gont (4), for example, answered thus : " Does the sun know that you are here ?—*Yes.*—Does it know you are in the room ?—*It doesn't know anything at all.*—Does it know when it's time to set ?—*Oh, of course !*—Does it know when it's night ?—*Oh, no !* " etc.

But in analysing these answers, allowance having been made for the difficulties involved in setting such questions to children of this age (and with the present technique they are certainly considerable), it will be seen that the child's resistance is usually a matter of words. For the

---

[1] Mach, *La Connaissance et l'Erreur*, trad. Dufour, p. 126.

youngest children the terms " knowing " and " feeling "
are not properly understood and have a more restricted
sense than for older children. " Knowing " means something like " having learnt," or " knowing like a grown-
up." For this reason Gont refuses to allow " knowing "
to a bench, because " *the bench isn't a person* "(un monsieur). In the same way " feeling " means " being hurt "
or " crying," etc. Children as young as this have probably no word to express " being aware of." It is thus
that arise the various anomalies which their answers
reveal at this age.

We may, therefore, admit that the answers in the first
category really characterise a first stage. During this
stage all objects may be conscious, even if stationary, but
consciousness is connected with an activity of some kind,
whether this activity arises in the objects themselves or
is imposed on them from without. The stage lasts on an
average until the ages of 6 or 7.

§ 2. THE SECOND STAGE : THINGS THAT CAN MOVE
ARE CONSCIOUS.—Already in the first stage, the child
regarded consciousness as bound up with some movement,
at least in so far as activity involves movement, but there
was no distinction as to what objects could be conscious ;
a wall, a mountain, etc., were all in this respect the same.
The characteristic of the second stage is, on the contrary,
that consciousness is henceforth restricted to things that
can move, that is to say no longer to objects, which can
for the moment become the seat of a particular movement,
but to those ordinarily in motion or whose special function
is to be in motion. Thus the sun and moon, the stars,
clouds, rivers, the wind, carts, fire, etc., are all regarded
as conscious.

MONT (7 ; 0) : " Does the sun know it gives light ?—*Yes.*
—Why ?—*Because it is made of fire.*—Does it know that
we are here ?—*No.*—Does it know it is fine weather ?—
Yes." So, too, the wind, the clouds, the rivers, the rain
are regarded as conscious. " Does the wind feel anything
when it blows against a house ?—*Yes, it feels it can't go*

any further." " Does a bicycle know when it is going ?—
Yes.—Does it know it is going quickly ?—*Yes.*—Can it
go by itself ?—*No,*" etc. On the contrary, benches, walls,
stones, flowers, etc., can neither know nor feel. " Does
this bench know it is in this room ?—*No.*—Why not ?—
It can't speak.—Does it know you are sitting on it ?—
No.—Why not ?—. . .—Would it know if you hit it or
broke it ?—*No,*" etc.

Mont's choice is quite clear, although he himself does
not give the reasons. In the following cases, the children
are more explicit :—

KAE (11) spontaneously unites consciousness with movement : " Does the sun know anything ?—*Yes, it heats.*—
Does it know that it's hidden from us in the evening ?—
*Yes, because it sees the clouds in front of it . . . no, it
doesn't know, because it isn't it that hides. It's the clouds
that go in front of it.*" Thus, if the sun hid itself, it would
know, but since it is hidden without having done anything itself, it doesn't know. " Does a bicycle know when
it goes ?—*Yes, it feels the ground.*" " Does a motor know
it goes ?—*Yes, it feels it isn't still in the same place.*"
VOG (8 ; 6) : " Does the moon know it shines ?—*Yes.*
—Why ?—*Because it shows us the way at night* (the moon
follows us ; see Chapter VII, § 2).—Does the wind know it
blows ?—*Yes, because it makes a lot of wind.*—Does a
bicycle know when it's going ?—*Yes.*—Why ?—*Because
it can go fast.*" But stones, etc., neither know nor feel
anything.
PUG (7 ; 2) : " Does the sun know when it sets ?—
Yes.—Does it know it gives light ?—*No.*—Why not ?—
Because it hasn't any eyes, it can't feel it." " Does a bicycle
know anything ?—*No.*—Why not ?—*I meant it knows
when it goes fast and when it goes slowly.*—Why do you
think it knows ?—*I don't know, but I think it knows.*—
Does a motor know when it's going ?—*Yes.*—Is it alive ?
—*No, but it knows.*—Is it the driver who knows or the
motor ?—*The driver.*—And the motor ?—*It knows too.*"
Benches, tables, stones, walks, etc., neither feel nor know
anything.
SART (12½) : " Can water feel anything ?—*Yes.*—What ?
—*When there's a wind, it makes waves. Because the wind
makes the waves come, then the water feels something like
that.*" Stones, walls, tables, etc., feel nothing at all.

" Does a watch know anything ?—*Yes, because it tells us the time.*—Why does it know ?—*Because it's the hands which show us the time,*" etc. (!)

It is unnecessary to multiply these examples, firstly because they are all alike, but principally because this stage is essentially one of transition. In fact, children either attribute consciousness to everything or they restrict it to things which move, as if all movement implied voluntary effort. But they soon realise that the movement of certain things, such as that of a bicycle, comes entirely from outside, from the man pedalling, for example. As soon as this distinction is made, the child restricts consciousness to things that can move of their own accord, and thus reaches the third stage.

There is thus only a difference of degree between the second and third stages. To express this difference it is wrong, despite appearances, to say that the child begins by attributing consciousness to all things that move (second stage) and then restricts it to those bodies that move of their own accord (third stage). In reality during both stages the child regards consciousness as being a quality of things that move of their own accord, and, when he attributes consciousness to bicycles in the second stage, it is in the majority of cases because he conceives bicycles as endowed with a certain purposive force independent of the cyclist.[1] The difference between the second and third stage is simply this that the child discovers the existence of bodies whose movement is not self-governed. This discovery leads him to distinguish two types of body and thus progressively to reduce the number of bodies that can move of their own accord. Machines are the first objects to be thus differentiated from living and conscious bodies. Then usually follow the clouds, streams, etc.

What has just been stated as following from the results obtained by using the present technique, is confirmed in

---

[1] The reason for this is further dealt with in a special study of explanations concerning the bicycle (*Causalité Physique*, Sect. IV).

the sequel to this work by means of a much surer technique employed to study the cause of movement. We shall see that, in the primitive stages, the child regards all movement as due in part to an external activity but also as necessarily due to an internal activity, that is to say to a spontaneous, purposive force. It is not till late (after the ages of 7 and 8) that this animistic dynamism gives place to a mechanical explanation of movement, even with regard to machines. This inquiry into movement, made on children, other than those whose answers are analysed here, forms the best corroborative proof we have found to check the value of the present results.

Finally, it must be mentioned that the second stage extends on an average from the ages of 6–7 to 8–9 and the third from 8–9 to 11–12.

§ 3. THE THIRD STAGE : THINGS THAT CAN MOVE OF THEIR OWN ACCORD ARE CONSCIOUS.—This stage is the most systematic and the most interesting of the four. In the majority of cases the animism is more reflective and the motive clearer than in the answers of the preceding stages, which, indeed, showed much more a general trend of mind than any systematic beliefs. According to the terminology adopted they were " liberated " rather than " spontaneous " convictions. On the other hand, many children of the third stage (not the majority, but a considerable number) show a more reflective view and together with many " liberated " convictions are a number that are " spontaneous."

Ross (9 ; 9) started by ascribing consciousness to animals but refusing it to the table : " Would a table feel if I were to prick it ?—*No.*—Why not ?—*Because it is not a person.*—Can the fire feel anything ?—*No.*—If someone threw water on it, would it feel that ?—*No.*—Why not ?—*Because it is not a person.*—Does the wind feel anything when the sun is shining ?—*Yes.*—Doesn't it know it is blowing ?—*Yes.*—Does the sun feel anything ? —*Yes.*—What does it feel ?—*It feels it's heating, etc.*" Ross likewise attributes consciousness to the stars, the moon, the rain and streams, but refuses it to bicycles,

motors and boats. " Are you sure of all this or not very ?
—*Not very.*—Have you thought about it before ?—*No.*—
Why aren't you very sure ?—*I haven't learnt it.*—You
say the wind feels something, but you aren't quite sure.
Tell me what you think, what makes you think that
perhaps the wind doesn't feel when it is blowing ?—
Because it is not a person.—And why do you think perhaps
it does feel ?—*Because it is it* (!) *that blows* " (*cp.* this
answer with Mart (8 ; 10) ; see Chapter II, § 2) : " The
lake knows its name ?—*Yes, because it moves.*—It knows
it moves ?—*Yes, because it's it that moves* " (see all Mart's
answers).

These words " it is it that blows," or " it's it that
moves " contain what is most vital in the third stage
and, therefore, the essence of child animism in its purest
form. The first phrase is all the more striking from being
spoken by one who is " not very sure " of what he is
stating and fully realises that the wind is " not a person."
But since no external cause makes the wind blow, therefore it must do so of its own accord and must be aware
of its movement. " Can the wind do what it likes ? " we
then asked Ross : " Can it stop blowing if it wants to ?—
Yes ?—And can it blow whenever it wants to ?—*Yes.*"
Surely then the wind must be conscious ? Ross, it is true,
was not certain, but it is precisely his uncertainty which
is so valuable in laying bare the motives of his thought.

CARD (9½) attributes consciousness to the sun, the moon,
and the clouds, but refuses it to stones, etc., and even
to the wind : " Does the wind know when it blows ?
—*No.*—Why not ?—*Because it is the cloud that makes it
blow.*" This is the spontaneous expression of one of the
numerous explanations children give as to the origin of
the wind, namely, that it is produced by the movement
of the clouds (see *La Causalité Physique*). The theory
does not, however, concern us at present. The point is
simply that since Card does not regard the wind's movements as spontaneous, he does not attribute consciousness
to it.

SCHI (6, advanced) : " Do the clouds feel that they
are moving ?—*They can feel because it's they that make the
wind.*" This is Card's theory again and the same argu

ment. Schi also speaks thus concerning flowers : " Do
they know when you tread on them ?—*They ought to
know,*" and then explains : " *They must be alive, because
they grow.*"

RATT (8 ; 10) resists all suggestion concerning stones,
walls, tables, mountains, machines, etc., but attributes
consciousness to the sun, the wind, etc. : " Does the sun
feel when it's hot ?—*Yes.*—Why ?—*Because it's the sun
that makes it hot.*—Do clouds feel anything ?—*They feel
the sky.*—Why ?—*Because they touch the sky.*—Does the
wind feel cold ?—*Yes, because it's it that makes it cold.*"
Ratt thus distinguishes the spontaneous activity of the
sun and the wind from the non-spontaneous movement
of machines.

TACC (10 ; 6) makes a very clear distinction between
feeling warm and being warm (" avoir chaud " and
être chaud) : " Does the fire feel warm ?—*No.*—Why
not ?—*Because it is already warm.*—Can it ever feel
warmth ?—*No.*—Why not ?—*Because it isn't alive.*—Can
it feel warm ?—*No, because it is already warm.*" But
directly he turns to the sun, the clouds, the streams, the
wind he conceives consciousness as bound up with movement : " Are the clouds warm ?—*When there is sun.*—
Are they warm or do they feel warm ?—*They feel warm.*"
When we undeceived Tacc he replied : " *I thought they
were alive because they move.*" But he does not regard
consciousness and life as entirely coinciding : " Do the
streams feel warm or are they warm when the sun heats
them ?—*They feel warm . . . they don't feel much, because
they aren't alive.*—Why not ?—*They feel a tiny bit because
they are flowing.*"

The connection between consciousness and spontaneous
movement could not be stated more clearly. Tacc, who
is aged 10½ knows exactly what degree of consciousness
to apportion to everything and for what reason. He
refuses consciousness to things that have been made,
to fire and rain, but he allows it to the sun, the wind,
the clouds and the streams.

IMH (6, advanced) attributes consciousness to the sun,
the clouds, etc., but refuses it to water, because water
cannot move of its own accord : " *It can flow faster, but
only when it's sloping.*" Imh thus belongs to an advanced

stage (the third ; see *Causalité Physique*) as regards the explanation of the movement of rivers.

Wirt (8 ; 4) : " Could the fire feel if someone pricked it ?—*Yes.*—Why ?—*Because it is alive.*—Why is it alive ? —*Because it moves.*—Would a cloud feel if someone pricked it ?—*Yes.*—Why ?—*Because it is alive, because it stays still in the air and then moves when it is windy* (the wind does not always exclude the cloud's moving spontaneously; see *Causalité Physique*).—Can the wind feel anything ?—*Yes.*—Why ?—*Because it blows.*—Can the water feel anything ?—*Yes.*—Why ?—*Because it flows.*" So, too, with the sun and the moon. " Would grass feel if it were pricked ?—*Yes.*—Why ?—*Because it's alive, because it grows.*" But machines can neither feel nor know anything : " Does a bicycle know when it goes ?— *No.*—Why not ?—*It isn't alive.*—Why not ?—*Because it has to be made to go.*" So, too, with motors, trains, carts, etc.

All these examples are clearly similar, although some were observed at Geneva, others in the Bernese Jura, etc. Certainly these children differ from one to another as to what they regard as a spontaneous movement. Some consider that fire acts of its own accord, since it burns all alone once it is lit ; others treat it as an induced activity since it has to be lit. For some, streams are free agents, for others the slope plays a purely mechanical part, etc. In studying the cause of movement it will be shown that every movement gives rise to one or more stages during which it is held to be spontaneous, and to several during which it is held to be determined. Furthermore, these differences of opinion among the children questioned contain nothing that is not easily explicable. It is equally interesting to note that all the children agree in restricting consciousness to bodies that can move of themselves. This result is all the more striking since it will be met with again shortly in connection with the concept of life and quite independent of the present results.

§ 4. The Fourth Stage : Consciousness is restricted to Animals.—The best proof that the present technique is sound and that the answers it evokes are not due to suggestion or fabrication is the existence of the fourth stage. That children of 9, 8 and even 7 manage to answer all the questions negatively and to restrict consciousness to animals alone or to plants and animals alone, clearly shows that the questions cannot have been suggestive. Furthermore, it will be seen that there is a gradual and barely perceptible transition from the answers of the earlier stages to those of the final stage which is evidence of the value of the method adopted (see Introduction, § 3).

The fourth stage is not reached on an average before the ages of 11–12, but several children of 6–7 were found to belong to it.

The first examples show the continuity between the third and fourth stages. The following intermediate cases are especially significant ; consciousness of any sort is denied to all sublunary objects, with the exception of animals, but it is still attributed to the sun and the moon because they move of themselves :—

PIG (9) denies consciousness to the clouds, to fire and to a flower " *because it isn't alive.*" But the sun is able to feel : " Why ?—*Because it is alive.*" The stars cannot feel " *because they are just sparks.*—And isn't the sun a spark ?—*No, it is a light.*" The moon also is conscious, but not the clouds, because they are " *made of smoke* " and smoke " *can't move* " (*ne marche pas*). " Can the clouds move by themselves ?—*No.*—And the moon ?— *Yes.*" Fire can't feel anything " *because you have to make it,*" neither can a stream because " *it's the air that makes it move.*"

GOL (6, very advanced) restricts consciousness to animals and the moon " *because, at night, it always goes to the same place.*" Fire, on the other hand, is not conscious " *because it always stays in the same place,*" neither are clouds because " *the wind drives them* " (*les fait pousser*).

REH (6½) resists all suggestion concerning clouds, the wind, water, etc., but claims also that the sun doesn't feel. " Can the sun feel anything ?—*No*—Why not ?— *Because it isn't alive.*" But when the sun's **movements**

are recalled more definitely he shows a latent animism:
" Why does the sun rise ?   *So that the sun will shine (pour
faire du soleil).*—Why ?—*I don't know.*—What does the
sun do when there are clouds and it rains ?—*It goes away
because it's bad weather.*—Why ?—*Because it doesn't want
to be rained on,*" etc.

It is interesting to note that it is nearly always the
sun and the moon which are the longest to be thought
alive.   They are, in fact, the only bodies whose movements seem as spontaneous as those of animals.   Reh's
case shows also how animism, even when on the point of
disappearing, merges into finalism.   Such a fact shows
in itself what a delicate matter it is to form any general
judgment on child animism.   This animism is far from
simple and is as far from common anthropomorphism as
it is from adult mechanism.

The following are genuine examples of the fourth
stage :—

CEL (10 ; 7) denies consciousness even to the sun and
the moon "*because it is not alive.*"   " What things can
know and feel ?—*Plants, animals, people, insects.*—Is
that all ?—*Yes.*—Can the wind feel ?—*No,*" etc.

VISC (11 ; 1) justifies the same standpoint by saying
each time : " *No* (it doesn't feel anything) *because it is a
thing, it isn't alive.*"

FALQ (7 ; 3) gives as proof each time the matter of which
the object is made ; thus fire can't feel " *because it's burnt
wood,*" clouds " *because they're made of rain,*" the sun
" *because it's made of fire,*" the moon " *because it is a
little cloud* " (this is the spontaneous expression of a
conviction to be studied in Chapter IX, § 3), the wind
" *because it hasn't got a head,*" etc.

The concept of " thing " used by Visc is rarely found
before the age of 11, in the sense of an object without
life.   Its appearance marks the decline of child animism.

§ 5. CONCLUSIONS.—Before continuing the study of
child animism, by proceeding to the analysis of the notion
of " life " and that of the moral necessity of natural laws,
the interpretation to be given to the above results must
be stated more definitely.

The answers obtained have been classified into four different stages. It remains now to see whether the systematisation implied by these stages really exists in the child's spontaneous thought, and if the four types of answer distinguished constitute genuine stages, that is to say successive types of answer.

As regards the first point, the degree of systematisation of animist beliefs is evidently much less than a reading of the above might suppose. In the child, animism is much more a general trend of mind, a framework into which explanations are fitted than a consciously systematic belief. Two fundamental reasons compel us to reduce to such proportions the systematisations we have detected.

The first concerns the logical structure of child thought. Firstly, the child's thought is much less self-conscious than ours, so that even such implicit systematisations as were found in the answers of the second stage, for example, are scarcely recognised by the child himself ; they are due to an economy of reactions (an economy enforcing uniformity) much more than to a deliberate effort to be coherent. From this arises his inability to give a motive to his judgments or to justify each individual assertion. Thus the child in the second stage (life = movement) is unaware of the motives which make him answer " yes " or " no " to the various questions. Realisation of the motive and the ability to justify his answers appears during the third stage, but still in a rudimentary form. It is not till the fourth stage that systematisation becomes reflective rather than implicit, and it is just at this time that the child mind discards animism.

It is unnecessary to refer to the contradictions and difficulties experienced in dealing with elementary logical operations (addition and multiplication of classes and of propositions) which go hand in hand with this lack of reflective systematisation. They have already been sufficiently dealt with (see *Judgment and Reasoning*, Chapter II, §§ 2–4). We need only say that these facts alone suffice to show why we should not dream of guaranteeing the soundness of the present technique as a means of individual diagnosis. In fact, it may easily happen that a child who has just attributed consciousness to a particular object denies it directly after ; a new factor need only intervene to upset the earlier view and make the child forget all he has said, contradict himself, change his beliefs, etc. Care must, therefore, be taken not to regard any of the examinations as establishing an absolute individual diagnosis. But this does not prevent the method having a statistical value, for so long as the investigation is limited to studying the general lines along which child thought develops, individual fluctuations compensate each other and the broad lines of the evolutionary process are disclosed.

To these considerations concerning the structure of thought must be added a second reason showing the divergence of the obtained results from the child's spontaneous thought. To form an idea as to the degree of systematisation of a belief it is usually sufficient to consider its function. What needs urge the child to take account of its implicit animism ? There are certainly only two.

First, according as the child attempts to explain the unforeseen resistance of some object he fails to make obey him, he is compelled to regard it as living. Or, more generally, it is when some phenomenon appears doubtful, strange and above all frightening that the child credits it with a purpose. But this need for an explanation which gives rise to animism is but momentary. As M. Delacroix puts it : " The sun and moon exist only when there are eclipses. The universal does not exist for primitive man." [1]

On the other hand, the child believes in the all-powerful nature of man's command over things and animism serves to explain the obedience of things. But this is only an implicit tendency and there can be no question of a reflective belief. Only cases of exceptional obedience (such

[1] H. Delacroix, *La langage et la foi*, p. 40.

as that of the moon which according to Gol "always goes to the same place") or of exceptional disobedience would lead the child to a genuine reflection.

In short, animism must be regarded as resulting either from an implicit tendency in the child or from its reflection on exceptional cases. This assertion may justly awaken doubts firstly as to the stages we have distinguished above and next as to whether the order of succession traced is not as artificial as the systematisations characterising each stage.

Indeed, the scheme we outlined according to which child animism decreases regularly and logically from the first to the fourth stage, is too simple not to put us on our guard. For, why are there no recrudescences of animism causing the curve of development to fluctuate and also why is no pre-animist stage to be found ? As a matter of fact at about the age of 5 children are found who seem to be much less animist than their elders. Moreover when a child can be studied over a period of several months the same contradictions are found. Zim, for example, was in the first stage in March and in the second the following June. But Vel, on the other hand, was in the third stage in December 1922, and in the first in June 1923 ! Also, when the same child is watched continuously and his questions noted and others asked on the subjects in which he seems most interested, it will be seen that the animism is always varying and is sometimes more, sometimes less.

Such contradictions are of as great interest to the analyst as they are the despair of the statistician. But without further evidence it would be wrong to conclude that the above results were valueless, for their internal convergence, as well as their convergence with all the facts to be shown in the subsequent portion of this book, compel us, on the contrary, to accept them in some measure. The anomalies at whose frequency we have hinted must, therefore, be open to some explanation. There are, in fact, three types of factor which tend to upset to a certain extent the order of the stages outlined. These factors are systematisation, conscious awareness and vocabulary.

The factor of systematisation may be taken to account for the following. It is usually just when an implicit conviction is about to be shattered that it is for the first time consciously affirmed. Thus, as John Burnet has very acutely noted, concerning pre-Socratic thought, a proposition is seldom stated unless it has first been denied.[1] The youngest children are thus animistic, without being able consciously to justify the tendency. But, directly the child comes up against a new hypothesis likely to unsettle it, the first time, for example, that it wonders whether a marble moves intentionally or mechanically (*Language and Thought*, p. 202) it probably adopts the animistic solution, for lack of a better, and then by reflection and by systematising extends its meaning beyond the limits which its new and latent tendencies warrant. Thus thought never progresses in straight lines, but, so to speak, spirally ; the implicit motiveless conviction is succeeded by doubt, and the doubt by a reflective reaction, but this reflection is itself prompted by new implicit tendencies, and so on. This is the explanation that must be given as to why so many older children show a more extensive animism than the youngest ; these children have momentarily found need for this animism, because they have encountered some phenomenon which their thought cannot explain mechanically, but it is a secondary systematisation which has led them to these opinions, and the resulting animism is not identical with but only comparable to that of the younger children.

The second factor which makes such distortion of meaning possible is conscious awareness. Since the child has no clear consciousness of the implicit systematisation in his mind, it necessarily happens that at the time when he comes to realise, either as the result of our questions

[1] John Burnet, *The Dawn of Greek Philosophy*.

or of a spontaneous reflection, the existence of certain of his animistic convictions, he will be led to exaggerate their extent. Thus, when discovering that the clouds know they move he will credit all moving bodies with consciousness without realising that he intends only to attribute it to bodies moving spontaneously. This is that same difficulty of exclusion or of logical multiplication, which we have shown elsewhere to be so largely dependent on factors involving conscious awareness (*Judgment and Reasoning*, Chapter IV, § 2). In simpler language, it means that, in speaking, the child does not succeed— any more than we do—in expressing his thought really accurately ; he is continually straining it, through inability to recollect every shade of meaning. This perpetual lack of adjustment between spoken and implicit thought makes the child appear when questioned sometimes more and sometimes less animist than he really is. And the child is himself deceived. This is the second factor which causes irregularity in the succession of the stages we distinguished.

Finally, there is vocabulary, which also plays an important part. The word " to know," for example, certainly has a narrower meaning to a child of 5 than to one of 10. To a small child " to know " means " to know like a grown-up," to an older child it simply means " to be conscious of." In this way words, by altering in meaning, at times impel the child to extend his animism and at others force him to restrict it.

In conclusion, it is clear how these three factors can account for the inconstancy in the general development of child animism. Are we to conclude that the four types of answer do not constitute stages at all, but that, on broad lines all that can be said is that the child passes from an integral animism to one of a more restricted type ? Obviously not. Each of the children, taken alone, might possibly show an implicit systematisation different from that brought out by our questions, each is capable, also of retrogressive movements in the series of stages just as much as of progressing in a straight line, but, on the average, the four types of answer obtained certainly constitute the types of systematisation through which the child's spontaneous thought really passes, and these four types correspond to four stages.

CHAPTER VI

THE CONCEPT OF "LIFE"

It will be of interest to complete the preceding research by a corresponding study of the ideas children understand by the word " life." There is, indeed, nothing to show that the concepts of " life " and of " consciousness " are completely synonymous any more than they are to an adult. But it seems that the idea of " life " is in certain respects more familiar to the child than the ideas understood by the words " knowing " and " feeling." It seems likely, therefore, that a study of it may reveal clearer systematisations than those found in the preceding chapter and that the children's answers will all show a higher development of logical justification and argument. Moreover, if the results of this chapter are found to agree with those of the preceding, there will be a certain guarantee in this resemblance. We must, therefore, beg the reader to excuse the repetitions which a study of the concept of " life " will inevitably involve.

The technique used is very similar to that followed hitherto. It consists in asking whether each of a number of objects enumerated is alive and why. The same precaution must be taken as before to avoid both simple suggestion and perseveration.

The results obtained have again clearly shown the four stages previously defined in connection with the attributing of consciousness to things. During the first stage everything is regarded as living which has activity or a function or a use of any sort. During the second stage, life is defined by movement, all movement being regarded as in a

194

certain degree spontaneous.   During the third stage, the
child distinguishes spontaneous movement from movement imposed by an outside agent and life is identified
with the former.   Finally, in the fourth stage, life is
restricted either to animals or to animals and plants.
Naturally a child who belongs to a particular stage in the
series will not necessarily belong to the same stage in the
series concerning consciousness (excepting those children
of the second stage who have not yet come to distinguish
spontaneous movement from movement in general).   On
the contrary, each child shows a considerable divergence
between the extension it attributes to the two concepts
of life and of consciousness.   We do not, therefore, intend
to suggest a correlation between individual cases but
rather a parallelism between the respective processes by
which the notions of "life" and of "consciousness"
are evolved.   This is, moreover, of a much greater interest,
since what gives the parallelism its value is the fact
that all suggestion of perseveration is excluded.   Such a
parallelism shows how constant and spontaneous the
child's thought remains notwithstanding the influences
due to its adult environment and the clumsiness of
our questions.

From the point of view of our research, the fact that
the child's notion of life is more systematised than its
notion of consciousness, carries also certain disadvantages.   The child will add to its spontaneous ideas various
adventitious definitions (to live is to speak, or to be
warm, or to have blood, etc.).   But all the children who
gave these secondary definitions were also able to give
the usual answers, all being simply juxtaposed together,
so that it was possible to neglect these various secondary
notions, whose completely individual character clearly
showed them to be the result of chance conversations
overheard, etc.

Further, according to the lengths to which the systematisation of the concept has been carried by the individual
child, retrogressive steps in his development from stage

to stage occur, comparable to those described in the study of the notion of consciousness, which make certain cases particularly hard to classify. But, apart from these two disadvantages, the inquiry proved easier to undertake than that described in the last chapter.

§ I. The First Stage: Life is assimilated to Activity in General.—Despite a certain diversity, the answers of the first stage all rested on a common basis, which lay in defining life in terms of activity, and what was especially interesting, in terms of an activity in most cases useful to man and always clearly anthropocentric.

Vel (8½) : " Is the sun alive ?—*Yes.*—Why ?—*It gives light.*—Is a candle alive ?—*No.*—Why not ?—*(Yes) because it gives light. It is alive when it is giving light, but it isn't alive when it is not giving light.*—Is a bicycle alive ?—*No, when it doesn't go it isn't alive. When it goes it is alive.*—Is a mountain alive ?—*No.*—Why not ?—*Because it doesn't do anything* (!)—Is a tree alive ?—*No ; when it has fruit it's alive. When it hasn't any, it isn't alive.*" " Is a watch alive ? — *Yes.* — Why ? — *Because it goes.*—Is a bench alive ? — *No, it's only for sitting on.* — Is an oven alive ?—*Yes, it cooks the dinner and the tea and the supper.* —Is a gun alive ?—*Yes, it shoots.*—Is the play-bell alive ? —*Yes, it rings.*" Vel even goes so far as to say that poison is alive " *because it can kill us.*"

Tann (8) : " Is a window-pane alive ?—*It's as if it was alive, but it's not like us. The pane stops the air coming in, but it can't move.* — Is it alive or not ? — *It's alive . . .*" " Is a stone alive ? . . . (It's alive) *if you throw it, or if you kick it to make it go.*" " Is a cloud alive ?—*Yes, it's living, and when it comes down in rain it goes back again.*" To elucidate Tann's meaning we used the following procedure, which though very artificial is excellent for determining the child's natural trend of mind : " Which is more alive, a stone or a lizard ?—*A lizard, because a stone can't move.*—The sun or a stone ?—*The sun because it does something, but a stone isn't much use.*—A fly or a cloud ?—*A fly because it's an animal, a cloud is a thing.*— What is an animal ?—*Something that's not like us. It's useful. A horse is useful. It can't go to school. It isn't like us.*—Which is more alive, rain or fire ?—*Rain.*—Why ?

—Rain is stronger than fire, because it can put out fire, but fire can't light rain."

REYB (8 ; 7) : " Are you alive ?—*Yes, because I'm not dead.*—Is a fly alive ?—*Yes, because it's not dead.*—Is the sun alive ?—*Yes because it makes it daytime.*—Is a candle alive ?—*Yes, because you can light it.*—Is the wind alive ? *— Yes, because it makes it cold, it makes people cold.* — Are clouds alive ?—*Yes, because they make it rain,"* etc.

PER (11 ; 7) : " Is thunder alive ?—*I don't think so.*— Why not ?—*It isn't like other things, people or trees or things like that.*—Is lightning alive ?—*No.*—Why not ?— *It isn't any use* (!)—What is a living thing ?—*A man who is alive.*—Is the sun alive ?—*Yes.*—Why ?—*It gives us light.*—Is fire alive ?—*Yes, it's used for lots of things,"* etc.

It is evident what meaning these children give to the word " alive." It means " to do something," or for choice " to be able to move " (Vel, Tann ; a mountain can't do anything, a bench is " only for sitting on"), but it also means to act without changing position, the oven, the candle, etc., are alive. Even such an idea as that of the nature of an animal is defined in terms of utility (Tann). At other times to be alive means simply to have force ; thus poison, rain, etc. are alive.

Some of these children give life the same significance as consciousness (thus Vel and Reyb are also in the first stage as regards the attributing of consciousness to things). Others, however, give life a much wider meaning (for example, Tann and Per, who are in the third stage when the questions concern consciousness).

Despite these differences, however, the answers of this first stage have all a common basis which lies in asserting the idea of a fundamental final cause in nature and a *continuum* of forces destined to bring about these ends. This idea is certainly not peculiar to the answers obtained by means of the present technique, but appears to be one of the most fundamental ideas in child thought. This first stage lasts in fact up to the ages of 6 or 7, and it is well known that at this age the nature of children's definitions bears out in a striking manner what we have just found. According to Binet and many others, children of about the age of 6 define an object by " its use " and not by genus and the specific difference between one genus and another. Thus a mountain is " to climb up " or " to shut in " (*i.e.* to limit the horizon), a country is " to travel in," the sun is " to warm us " or " to give us light," etc. (see *Judgment and Reasoning*, Chapter IV, § 2). That this notion of a final cause implies a creator who has fashioned everything for a determined end will be shown in what follows later and does not immediately concern us. But the idea of so complete a determinism implies that every object is endowed with a particular activity and force destined to enable it to fulfil its rôle. That is to say, that if certain objects obstruct the sun on its way (such as the wind, the clouds, the night, etc.) the sun must necessarily be gifted with the necessary qualities to triumph and to succeed notwithstanding in fulfilling its rôle in the required time. Final cause implies an efficient cause in the form of a force immanent in the object and directing it towards its destined end. To the child's mind the idea of " life " fulfils this function.

We shall again find in a new form a conclusion already formed as a result of the study of children's questions (*Language and Thought*, Chapter V). The very way in which a child frames its questions shows that physical causality is for him still undifferentiated from psychological and purposive association. It is a case of " precausality." It will be clearly seen how near this concept approaches the notion of " life " examined above, life being regarded as a force that is both material and purposive. Children's " whys " are, therefore, at bottom a search for a biological explanation : " Why does the Rhône go so fast ? " is in fact the same order of question as " Why does that ant go so fast ? " it being taken for granted that every animal whilst moving of its own accord is, as stated by Tann, " useful " to man.

Is such an idea primitive or derived ? In other words is it already present in children of 3 or 4, that is to say in children too young to be able to answer our questions, since not yet knowing the word " life " ?   It seems that it is.   At least this is what a study of the language and behaviour of children of this age seems to suggest.   At all events, everything appears to suggest that as soon as the appearance of the word " life " gives rise to a systematisation of the corresponding concept, the form of this concept is from the first that which was found in the stage studied above.

§ 2. THE SECOND STAGE : LIFE IS ASSIMILATED TO MOVEMENT.—As was the case for the corresponding stage in the series dealing with consciousness, so this stage is also one of transition above all.   We obtained, however, quite enough clearly-defined examples to shield ourselves from the reproach of adding another stage which, like a false window, serves no purpose but merely lends symmetry to the edifice.

ZIMM (7 ; 9 and 8 ; 1) was questioned in March and June of the same year.   In March he was intermediate between the first and second stages.   In June he clearly defined life in terms of movement in general :—

In March : " You know what it is to ' be alive ' ?— *It's when you can do things* (this definition seems as if belonging to the first stage, but, as we shall see, Zimm is thinking principally of movement).—Is a cat alive ?—*Yes.* —A snail ?—*Yes.*—A table ?—*No.*—Why not ?—*It can't move.*—Is a bicycle alive ?—*Yes.*—Why ?—*It can go.*— Is a cloud alive ?—*Yes.*—Why ?—*It sometimes moves.*— Is water alive ?—*Yes, it moves.*—Is it alive when it doesn't move ?—*Yes.*—Is a bicycle alive when it isn't moving ?— *Yes, it's alive, even when it doesn't move.*—Is a lamp alive ? —*Yes, it shines.*—Is the moon alive?—*Yes, sometimes it hides behind the mountains.*"

In June : " Is a stone alive ?—*It moves (il marche).* — When does it move ? — *Some days, sometimes.*—How does it move ?—*By rolling.*—Is the table alive ?—*No, it can't move.*—Is the Salève alive ?—*No, it can't move.*—Is the Rhône alive ?—*Yes.*—Why ?—*It moves.* — Is the lake alive ? — *Yes, it moves.* — Always ? —*Yes.*—Is a bicycle alive ?—*Yes.*—Why ?—*It goes (elle marche),*" etc.

JUILL (7½) : " Is a lizard alive ?—*Yes.*—A nail ?—*No.*
—A flower ?—*No.*—A tree ?—*No.*—Is the sun alive ?—
Yes.—Why ?—*Because it moves when it has to* (Parceque
quand il faut (!) il marche).—Are clouds alive ?—*Yes,
because they move and then they hit* (ils marchent, puis ils
tapent).—What do they hit ?—*They make the thunder when
it rains.*—Is the moon alive ?—*Yes, because it moves* (elle
marche).—The fire ?—*Yes, because it crackles.*—Is the
wind alive ?—*Yes, because on a windy day it's cold, it's
alive because it moves* (il bouge).—A stream ?—*Yes, because
it's always going faster.*—A mountain ?—*No, because it's
always in the same place* (elle reste toujours debout).—A
motor ?—*Yes, because it moves,"* etc.

KENN (7½) : " Is water alive ?—*Yes.*—Why ?—*It moves*
(elle bouge).—Is fire alive ?—*Yes, it moves* (ça bouge).—
Is the sun alive ?—*Yes, it moves* (il avance)," etc.

VOG (8 : 6) : " Are you alive ?—*Yes.*—Why ?—*I can
walk and I go and play.*—Is a fish alive ?—*Yes, because it
swims." " Is a bicycle alive ?—Yes.*—Why ?—*It can go.*
—Is a cloud alive ?—*Yes.*—Why ?—*Because it can go* (il
peut aller).—Is the moon alive ?—*Yes.*—Why ?—*It guides
us at night."*

CESS (8) : " Is a horse alive ?—*Yes.*—Is a table alive ?
—*No.*—Why not ?—*Because it's been made." " Is the
moon alive ?—No, because it always stays in the same place.*
—Doesn't it ever move ?—*Sometimes.*—When ?—*When you
walk.*—Is it alive or not ?—*Alive.*—Why ?—*When you
walk." " Is the wind alive ?—Yes.*—Why ?—*Because it
goes gently and then fast* (parce qu'il marche et puis il
court)," etc.

KEUT (9 ; 3) answered the question " You know what
it is to be alive ? " straightway by saying, " *Yes to
move* (!) "

GRIES (9 ; 1) answered as follows from the beginning :
" You know what it is to be alive ?—*Yes, to be able to move.*
—Is the lake alive ?—*Not always.*—Why not ?—*Sometimes there are waves and sometimes there aren't any."
" Is a cloud alive ?—Yes, it moves as if it were walking*
(c'est comme s'il marchait).—Is a bicycle alive ?—*Yes, it
goes* (elle roule)."

KAEN (11) : " Is a stream alive ?—*Yes, it goes* (il roule).
—Is the lake alive ?—*Yes, it is always moving a bit.*—Is
a cloud alive ? — *Yes, you can see it moving* (on le voit
marcher).—Grass ?—*Yes, it can grow."*

The impression these children give is that the assimila-

tion of life to movement is evidently simply a matter
of words. That is to say, the word "life" means
simply movement, but this movement has none of
the characteristics with which we should define
life, such as spontaneity, purpose, etc. The child says
that a stream is alive just as a physicist would say that
a movement has been "imparted to it," that it "has
acceleration," etc.

We think, however, the matter goes deeper, and that
movement in general is really thought to possess the
characteristics of life. Three sound reasons' suggest this
interpretation. The first is that the spontaneous questions of children prove that the definition of life is a
problem with which they are really concerned and that
the assimilation of life to movement has a genuine meaning in their eyes. Thus Del at the age of 6½ (see *Language
and Thought*, p. 197) asks concerning some leaves, "Are
they dead ?—Yes.—But they move with the wind."
The second reason is that this second stage is followed by
one in which the child distinguishes spontaneous movement from movement imparted from without (third
stage). The average ages in fact of children in the
stage under consideration are 6–8, whilst the third stage
lasts on an average from the ages of 8–9 to the ages
of 11–12. But, apart from certain exceptions, it is only
during this later stage that the distinction is made between spontaneous and imparted movement ; until then
all movement is regarded as spontaneous and the assimilation of life to movement is thus more than a mere matter
of words. The third and final reason is that the whole
study of the child's view of the physical world, to be
undertaken later (see *La Causalité Physique*), confirms
the reality of this confusion between the mechanical and
the biological.

§ 3. THE THIRD AND FOURTH STAGES : LIFE IS ASSIMI-
LATED TO SPONTANEOUS MOVEMENT, THEN LATER IS
RESTRICTED TO ANIMALS AND PLANTS.—The best proof
of the genuineness of the convictions of the first and

second stages is the systematisation and persistence of the ideas now to be studied as characteristic of the third stage. The assimilation of the idea of life to that of spontaneous movement marks in fact the most important stage in child animism and the richest in its applications. For before arriving at any such systematisation, the child must for a long time have been feeling out in that direction and have already assimilated the idea of life either to that of activity in general or to that of movement of whatever kind.

The following examples are drawn from the most reflective answers obtained from children of this stage :—

SART (12½) : " You know what it means to be alive ? —*Yes.*—Is a fly alive ?—*Yes.*—Why ?—*Because if it wasn't alive it couldn't fly.*" " Is a bicycle alive ?—*No.*— Why not ?—*Because it's we who make it go.*—Is a horse alive ?—*Yes.*—Why ?—*He helps man.*" " Are clouds alive ?—*Yes.*—Why ?—*No, they're not.*—Why not ?— *Clouds aren't alive. If they were alive they could come and go as they wanted* (ils seraient en voyage).—*It's the wind that drives them* (!)—Is the wind alive ?—*Yes.*—Why ?— *It's alive, because it's the wind that drives the clouds.*—Are streams alive ?—*Yes, because the water is flowing all the time.*—Is a motor ?—*No, it's the engine that makes it go.*— Is the engine alive ?—*No, it's man who makes the engine go.*—Is the sun alive ?—*Yes, it makes the sunshine and gives light during the day.*—Is the lake alive ?—*No, because the lake is all alone and it can't ever move by itself* (il bouge jamais)."

FRAN (15 ; 5) : " Is a worm alive ?—*Yes, it can walk.*— Is a cloud alive ?—*No, the wind drives it.*—Is a bicycle alive ?—*No, it's we who make them move.*—Is the wind alive ?—*No, it goes quickly enough, but it's something else that drives it* (!) (il marche bien, mais c'est autre chose qui le pousse).—Is fire alive ?—*Yes, it can move on its own* (il bouge lui-même).—Is a stream ?—*Yes, it flows all alone.*—Is the wind alive ?—*Yes.*—Just now you said it wasn't. Which do you mean ?—*It's alive.*—Why ?—*It can move by itself* (il bouge lui-même).—Why ?—*It drives itself* (!) (il se pousse lui-même).—Is a cloud alive ?—*No, it's the wind that drives it.*"

BARB (6) is exceedingly clear, despite his age : " Tell

me some things that are alive.—*Butterflies, elephants, people, the sun.*—The moon ?—*Yes, also.*—Are stones alive ?—*No.*—Why not ?—*I don't know ?*—Why ?—*Because they aren't alive.*—Are motors alive ?—*No.*—Why not ?—*I don't know.*—What does it mean to be alive ?—*To be able to move all alone* (!)—Is water alive ?—*No.*—Doesn't it move all alone ?—*Yes."* Later on, however, owing to his age, Barb fell back into the second stage : " Are stones alive ?—*No.*—Not when they roll ?—*Yes, when they roll they're alive. When they're still, they're not alive."*

EUG (8½) : " Are clouds alive ?—*No, the wind drives them.*—Is water alive ?—*No, the wind makes it move.*—Is a bicycle ?—*No, what makes it go is when you ride on it.*—Which is more alive, the wind or a bicycle ?—*The wind, it can go for as long as it wants to. You make a bicycle stop sometimes."*

POIS (7 ; 2) : " Are clouds alive ?—*No, because they can't move, it's the wind that makes them go."* The wind, the sun and the earth are alive " *because they move* (parce que ça bouge)."

NIC (10 ; 3) : A cloud is not alive " *because it can't move* (marcher). *It isn't alive. It's the wind that drives it* (qui le pousse)." The wind, on the other hand, is alive " *because it makes the other things move and it moves itself* (il fait avancer les autres choses et il avance lui-même)."

CHANT (8 ; 11) attributes life to the sun and stars, the clouds, the wind and water " *because they can go wherever they want to,"* but denies it to the lake " *because the lake can't go from one lake to another,"* etc.

MOS (11 ; 6) denies life to machines, to water, etc. " *because they can't move* (bouger),"* but he ascribes it to fire, to the sun and stars and the clouds " *because they move."* Evidently, therefore, he means spontaneous movement.

It is obvious that owing to the difficulty children experience in realising what their own thoughts are, the majority of these cases are less clear than those in the preceding sections. We have discussed elsewhere (*Judgment and Reasoning*, Chapter IV, § 2) the cases of Grand, Schnei, Horn, who belong to this stage yet are unable to think of a definition of life corresponding to the examples they give.

It is unnecessary to deal with the fourth stage, during which life is restricted to animals alone, or to plants and animals. It appears that three-quarters of the children do not reach this stage before the ages of 11–12. Until then the sun and stars and the wind are systematically endowed with life and consciousness.

The majority of children, in the two last stages, assign the same meaning to life as to consciousness, but some, like Sart, give consciousness a wider significance. The reason for this will be considered in the following section.

§ 4. CONCLUSION : THE NOTION OF " LIFE."—The reader cannot fail to be struck by the remarkable correspondence between the four stages analysed in this chapter and the four stages into which the answers dealing with consciousness were classified. Although only two-fifths of the children belonged to the same stage in both series, the evolution of the two notions obeys the same laws and follows the same direction. Undoubtedly, as has already been pointed out, certain adventitious ideas arise which unsettle the notions of some of the children ; yet, although a number of children used such ideas as being able to speak or having blood, etc., to define life, not a single case was found (among those who knew the word naturally) of a child who failed to bring in also the idea of activity and movement. The schema outlined may, therefore, be taken as general.

We must now face the problem that confronted us in dealing with consciousness, as to whether there is direct progression from one stage to the next or whether there exist retrogressive movements which set the child back temporarily in an earlier stage. Evidently it will be the same in both cases, and the three apparently regressive factors found in the attributing of consciousness to things will exist equally in the evolution of the notion of " life."

What is of greater interest is to define the exact relationship which connects the notion of life to that of consciousness ? As regards the signification of the two concepts

the results were very clear. Two-fifths of the children
questioned were found to be in the same stage in each
series. These two-fifths were more advanced in their
ideas concerning life, that is to say, they attributed life
to fewer objects than they did consciousness. Finally,
only one-fifth showed the inverse relationship, that is to
say, regarded objects as living to which they denied
consciousness. In conclusion, therefore, the notion of
consciousness seems to have a wider extension for the
child than the notion of life.

This result is particularly striking among the youngest.
That is to say, children who are in the first or second
stage when speaking of consciousness are generally found
to be in a more advanced stage for ideas concerning life.
The elder children, on the contrary, that is to say, those
in the third and fourth stages, are usually in the same
stage in the two parallel series.

Naturally, in arriving at these statistics we took the
necessary precaution of not questioning all the children
in the same order. Some were questioned on life before
being questioned on consciousness, others the reverse ;
some were questioned first on knowing or being aware,
then on life, and lastly feeling, etc. All the answers were
examined to see they were not due to perseveration. We,
therefore, feel justified in regarding the results as free
from " systematic errors."

What may be deduced from these facts ? They seem to
point to the conclusion that the evolution of the notion of
life determines the evolution of the notion of consciousness. In other words, it is the child's classification of
things into living and not-living which guides him in
attributing consciousness to them. There is certainly
no definite reasoning or purpose in this, at any rate so
far as the younger children are concerned, and this explains the lack of correspondence of the stages between
the two evolutions. But his reflections on " life " accustom
the child to regard the movements of nature as of different
kinds, and this consideration of types (*i.e.* the type of

spontaneous movement) comes gradually to influence his ideas on consciousness.

It is evident from this that the explanation of movement is of extreme importance in the thought of the child. The analysis of this explanation will be undertaken in the sequel to this work (*La Causalité Physique*). For the time being, it need only be said that the extension of the notion of " life " seems to indicate the presence in the child's universe of a *continuum* of free forces endowed with activity and purpose. Between magical causality, according to which all things revolve around the self and the dynamism of material forces the notion of life forms an intermediary link. Born of the idea that all things are directed towards an end and that this end supposes a free activity as the means of attaining it, the notion of life gradually becomes reduced to the idea of force or of being the cause of spontaneous movement.

CHAPTER VII

THE ORIGINS OF CHILD ANIMISM, MORAL NECESSITY AND PHYSICAL DETERMINISM

THERE are three preliminary problems which must be discussed before any attempt can be made to trace the origins of child animism. We shall start by grouping in a first section such facts as we have been able to arrive at by pure observation (in opposition to those collected in answer to questions). Secondly, we shall analyse the only conviction, both systematic and entirely spontaneous, revealed by the preceding questions, namely the belief of children that the sun and moon follow them. Thirdly, we must examine the type of necessity (moral necessity and physical determinism) which the child ascribes to regular movements such as the laws of nature. The study of the obedience of the sun and moon will serve as introduction, moreover, to this more general research, which is indispensable to an analysis of the roots of animism. We shall then be in a position to conclude with an explanation of the origins of child animism.

§ I. THE CHILD'S SPONTANEOUS ANIMISM.—Books on psychology and pedagogy abound in examples of traces of animism shown by children. It would be tedious to quote them all, nor is it necessary since they are not all of equal value. Animism during play (such as the endowing of personality to dolls) forms in particular a special problem which we shall not treat here.

We shall start by giving some adult recollections. Those of deaf-mutes are particularly important, since they show the affective tonality which animism may assume among children who have received no trace of religious education.

James [1] quotes the case of a deaf-mute, Thomas d'Estella, who became a professor and left an account of his early recollections. D'Estrella tells how nothing aroused his curiosity so greatly as the moon. He feared it yet always loved to watch it. He noted the impression of a face in the full moon and thence supposed it to be a living Being. He then tried to prove whether or not it was alive. He attempted this in four different ways. The first was to shake his head from right to left with his eyes fixed on the moon. It seemed to him that the moon followed the movements of his head down and up and from side to side. He thought, too, that the lights were alive for he made the same experiments with them. When he went for a walk he would look to see if the moon was following him and it seemed to do so wherever he went. (For his further reasons for believing the moon to be alive see Chapter IV, § 2.)

Another deaf-mute studied by James [2] spoke of regarding the sun and moon " with a sort of reverence " because of their powers of lighting and heating the earth. Later he tells how his mother talked to him of a Being up there, pointing with her finger to the sky with a solemn look, and how in his anxiety to know more he overwhelmed her with questions to know whether she meant the sun, the moon or the stars.[3]

In the memories of normal children, animism has naturally quite a different affective tonality. Cases such as the following, for example, are not at all uncommon :—

One of us recalls having set herself the following obligations as a child. If by chance she displaced a stone that had been partially buried in the ground, she put it back

[1] William James, " Thought before Language," *Philosophical Review I*, (1892), pp. 613-624.

[2] *Principles of Psychology*, I, p. 266.

[3] See also Pratt, *Psychology of Religious Belief*.

In Sintenis' *Pisteron* (Leipzig, 1800) occurs a very curious account of the formation of an animist belief concerning the sun. Bovet gives a summary of it in *Le Sentiment religieux et la psychologie de l'Enfant*, Delachaux et Niestlé, 1925.

in its place so that it should not suffer from having been moved. Or again, if she brought home a flower, or a pebble she always brought several flowers or pebbles at the same time so that they should have company and not feel lonely.

Another felt compelled, on the other hand, to move stones from the path every now and then so that they wouldn't always have exactly the same view to look at.

This last recollection entirely agrees with that of Miss Ingelow related by Sully.[1]

But let us leave these recollections and consider some remarks and questions furnished by direct observation. It has often been noticed how frequently children's questions betray an animistic point of view, and that what usually prompts them to ask such questions is the observation of movement. Stanley Hall, in particular, has confirmed Sully's statement that the child's questions result from his having assimilated life to movement.[2] He also observed that even those children who have acquired the idea of God endow things with intense powers of organisation.[3] For example, Stanley Hall collected the following questions concerning the wind :—

A boy of 6 years asked what made the wind blow. Was somebody pushing it ? He thought it ought to stop when it came up against a house or a big tree. He asked also if it knew that it was making the pages of his book turn over.

This same question is found with other children of the same age concerning moving objects :—

DEL at the age of 6½ saw a marble rolling in the direction of Mlle V. on a sloping surface : " *What makes it go ?*—It's because the ground isn't flat, it slopes, it goes downhill.— *Does it* (the marble) *know that you're there ?* " (*Language and Thought*, p. 202.)

At the same age we collected also conversations of the following type :—

[1] Sully, *Studies of Childhood*, p. 31.   See also pp. 94-96, in which Sully records observations of children attributing life to smoke and fire, to the wind and even to machines.

[2] *Pedagogical Seminary*, 1903, p. 335.   [3] *Ibid.*, p. 333.

LEV. (6) watching what Hei (6) is doing: "*Two moons.* —*No, two suns.*—*Suns aren't like that with a mouth. They are like the real suns up there.*—*They're round.*—*Yes, they're quite round, but they haven't got eyes and a mouth.*— *Yes they have, they can see.*—*No, they can't. It's only God who can see.*" (*Language and Thought*, p. 24.)

Rasmussen (1) noted in his daughter at the age of four the belief that the moon follows us, a conviction we have already noted frequently and which will be studied systematically in the next section :—

R (aged 4) seeing the moon : "*There's the moon, it's round. . . . It goes on when we go on.*" Later, when the moon was hidden behind a cloud : "*Look, now it's been killed.*" R was told that the moon is not really moving at all and that it only seems as if it is. But three days later she said : "*Every now and then the moon disappears ; perhaps it goes to see the rain in the clouds, or perhaps it's cold.*"

Questions of children of the ages of 5, 6 and 7 are also very often concerned with death, and show their attempts to find a definition of life. In Chapter VI (§ 2) we recalled Del's question (*Are those leaves dead ?*—Yes.— *But they move with the wind !*) which points clearly to the assimilation of the ideas of life and movement.

The animism of younger children is much more implicit and unformulated. They do not question whether things know what they are doing, nor whether things are alive or dead, since on no point has their animism yet been shaken. They simply talk about things in the terms used for human beings, thus endowing them with will, desire, and conscious activity. But the important question in each case is to know just up to what point they really believe in these expressions or to what extent they are merely a matter of words. But it is impossible to question them on this. The only method of gaining an insight is careful observation, both of the child's behaviour and of his words. The following, for example, is the case of a little girl who one morning found the eyes of her doll had disappeared (fallen into the inside of the head). Despair and tears ! She was then promised that the doll should

be taken back to the shop to be mended, and for the next
three days she was continually asking with the most
obvious anxiety whether the doll was still bad and if it
hurt her to be mended.

But in the majority of cases, the child's behaviour is
not nearly so instructive. The best method when a particular expression appears to be prompted by animism, is
to study, by comparison with other remarks of the same
child, the exact use it makes of this expression. The
following is an example of the method, applied to the use
of the interrogative " who " (" qui and qui est-ce que ").
This use of the word " who " (" qui ") to describe things
as if they were people is indeed a striking characteristic
of the language of children between the ages of 2 and 3.
Is it a question of animism or of verbal economy ?

NEL (2 ; 9) knows the word " what " (" qu'est-ce que ")
as she uses it in such expressions as " *what's that ? (qu'est-ce
c'est là)* "—pointing to a dustbin ; " *what's that over there,
boxes ?* "—pointing to some cardboard boxes ; " *what are
you doing there ?* " The same form was used also when
referring to a heap of plates, a stone, a rowan-tree, a field,
a dried-up spring, a tree-trunk, moss, blackberries, a
drawing. The objects thus designed are all, it will be
noticed, motionless. Nel uses the word " who " (qui) [1] (1) for
people : " *who is that playing music ?* " " *who gave that ?* "
(a chalk). (2) For animals : cows, dog, etc. She asked
the question " *who is that calling ?* " about hens, thrushes,
starlings, crows, owls, etc., both when they were in full
view and when she could not see them. In front of a
grasshopper she said : " *Hallo, Grasshopper, who are you ?* "
(3) To trains : *Who's that ?* " (4) To boats : " *Who's
that ?* " (this to a large boat she saw on the lake and
which was unlike the steamers she knew). (5) To mechanical noises : " *Who is making that noise ?* " (a motor).
" *Who is making that banging ?* " (a gun). " *Who is making
that sound ?* " (the same). It is true that in the last examples
Nel may perhaps only mean who is shooting or who is

---

[1] In French " qui " is the equivalent of the interrogative " who "
and " qu'est-ce que " of " what " " Who " is therefore more easily
said than " what." The mistake appears to be much less common in
English. [Translator's note.]

driving the motor, etc. But this explanation does not seem to fit all the cases. (6) To water : " *Who has made it dirty ? Is it the rain who's made the fire-place dirty ?* " (7) To some smooth round pebbles : " *Who's that ? Who is it that I've spat on ?* "

It seems, therefore, that Nel uses " who " for all objects that move and that in this she is attributing life to such objects. Moreover we have found " who " used in speaking of the Rhône and the lake up to the age of 7. This use of " who " certainly proves nothing by itself. But, as remains to be shown, moving bodies inspire innumerable animistic expressions in very young children, the cumulative effect of which is certainly to suggest a tendency of mind rather than a mere metaphorical manner of speaking.

CLI (3 ; 9) speaking of a motor in a garage : " *The motor's gone to bye-byes. It doesn't go out because of the rain* (*elle fait dodo, elle sort pas* . . .)."
BAD (3) : " *The bells have woken up, haven't they ?* "
NEL (2 ; 9) seeing a hollow chestnut tree : " *Didn't it cry when the hole was made ?* " To a stone : " *Not to touch my garden!* . . . *My garden would cry.*" Nel, after throwing a stone on to a sloping bank watching the stone rolling down said : " *Look at the stone. It's afraid of the grass.*"
Nel scratched herself against a wall. Looking at her hand : " *Who made that mark ?* . . . *It hurts where the wall hit me.*"
DAR (1 ; 8 to 2 ; 5) bringing his toy motor to the window : " *Motor see the snow.*" One evening a picture (of some people he knew) fell to the ground. Dar stood up in bed, crying and calling out : " *The mummies* (the ladies) *all on the ground, hurt!*" Dar was watching the grey clouds. He was told that it was going to rain : " *Oh, look at the wind !—Naughty wind, smack wind.—*Do you think that would hurt the wind ?—*Yes.*" A few days later : " *Bad wind.—No, not naughty—rain naughty. Wind good.—*Why is the rain naughty ?—*Because Mummy pushes the pram and the pram all wet.*" Dar couldn't go to sleep, so the light was left on at his demand : " *Nice light* " (*gentille*). On a morning in winter when the sun shone into the room : " *Oh, good ! the sun's come to make the radiator warm.*"

These last remarks clearly show the child's tendency,

noted by Sully, to regard natural objects as big children
that are either good or naughty according to their activity.

Each of these examples is obviously debatable. But
the constancy of the style proves at any rate how little
these children are concerned to distinguish things from
living beings. Anything that moves is described as if it
were conscious and every event as if it were purposive.
" The wall who hit me " thus signifies the child's tendency
to regard all resistance as intentional. The difficulties
involved in the direct analysis of such expressions are
evident. Nevertheless, and this seems the most convincing
argument, these expressions do really seem to arise from
a latent animism since it is not until the ages of 5–7 that
children start asking questions as to how far things are
alive and conscious, while before this age they appear
entirely untroubled by such questions as if their solution
was too obvious to present any problem.

To conclude, we noted two periods in the spontaneous
animism of children. The first, lasting until the ages of
4–5, is characterised by an animism which is both integral
and implicit ; anything may be endowed with both
purpose and conscious activity, according to the occasional
effects on the child's mind of such occurrences as a stone
which refuses to be thrown on to a bank, a wall which can
hurt the hand, etc. But this animism sets no problem to
the child. It is taken for granted. After the ages of 4–6,
however, questions are asked on the subject, showing that
this implicit animism is about to disappear and consequently that an intellectual systematisation is about to
take place. It is now that it becomes possible to question
the child, and that the stages whose succession was
studied in the two previous chapters are found for the
first time.

§ 2. THE SUN AND MOON FOLLOW US.—The animism
which is shown in the questions and conversation of
children of 5–7 has its origin essentially in the appearance
of chance phenomena which the child cannot understand
by reason of their unexpectedness. But the very fact

that these phenomena are the only ones to arouse his interest makes his spontaneous animism appear very limited. Such is not, however, the case. We shall show in the following section that he conceives the world as a society of beings obedient to moral and social laws. There is therefore no reason why he should ask many questions revealing animism; in fact, as we have so often seen (*Language and Thought*, Chapter V), it is the exception which strikes him and which offers him a problem.

If such is the case it ought to be possible to find animist beliefs in the child, which are tacit but none the less systematic. This is what we shall now try to show by analysing a belief, the study of which will form a transition between the study of spontaneous animism and the analysis of the type of necessity which is attributed by children to natural laws. This belief is that, according to which the child regards itself as being constantly followed by the sun and the moon. So far as we can judge from the very great number of children we have questioned at Geneva, Paris and elsewhere, this belief appears to be extremely general and also very spontaneous. It will also be remembered that Rasmussen's daughter at the age of 4 and James's deaf-mute both showed it. Numerous spontaneous instances of the idea have also already been found during the course of the questions on animism. The children whose answers are now given had not already been questioned on animism, but are new subjects, questioned specially concerning the sun and the stars, the causes of movement, etc.

The technique to be followed, in order to eliminate the influence of suggestion is extremely simple. The child is questioned as follows: " When you go out for a walk, what does the sun do ? " If the child has the conviction that the sun follows him he will answer straightway " it follows us." If he has not this conviction, the question is too vague to contain any definite suggestion. The child will then answer: " it shines, it warms us, etc." The **question** may also be asked directly, " does the sun move ? "—and this will often be enough to start the child talking spontaneously.

Three stages were observed. During the first, the child believes that the sun and moon follow him, just as a bird might above the roofs. This stage lasts, on an average, up to the age of 8, but examples are still found up to 12. During a second stage he admits at the same time both that the sun does and does not follow. He tries to avoid the contradiction so far as he can ; the sun does not move but its rays follow us, or the sun remains in the same place but turns so that it can always watch us, etc. The average age of these children is from 8 to 10. Finally, after 10–11, on an average, the child knows that the sun and moon only appear to follow us, and that it is really an illusion due to their great distance. From the point of view of animism, which is all that interests us at present, the two first stages are animist, the third usually marks the disappearance of animism concerning the sun. During the first stage, the child completely and unreservedly endows both the sun and moon with consciousness and will.

The following are examples of the first stage :—

JAC (6) " Does the sun move ? (these words mark the beginning of the examination.—We had previously asked no question of Jac beyond his name and age).—*Yes, when one walks, it follows. When one turns round it turns round too. Doesn't it ever follow you too ?*—Why does it move ?—*Because when one walks, it goes too (il marche).* —Why does it go ?—*To hear what we say.*—It is alive ?— *Of course, otherwise it couldn't follow us, it couldn't shine.*" A moment later : " Does the moon move ?—*Yes, when one walks too, more than the sun, because if you run the moon goes as fast as running, but when you run with the sun it only goes as fast as walking (quand on court elle court, et puis le soleil quand on court, il marche). Because the moon is stronger than the sun, it goes faster. The sun can't ever catch it up* (the illusion is in fact much clearer with the moon than the sun).—What happens when you don't walk ?—*The moon stops. But when I stand still someone else starts running.*—If you were to run and one of your friends were to run in the opposite direction at the same time, what would happen ?—*It would go with the other.*" At the end of the examination, which was then directed to the cause of movement in general, we asked : " What is making the sun move to-day ?—*It isn't moving, because no one is walking. Oh, yes ! It must be moving, because I can hear a cart.*"

Bov (6 ; 5) : " When you are out for a walk what does the sun do ?—*It comes with me.*—And when you go home ? —*It goes with someone else.*—In the same direction as before ?—*Or in the opposite direction.*—Can it go in any direction ?—*Yes.*—Can it go wherever it likes ?—*Yes.*— And when two people go in opposite directions ?—*There are lots of suns.*—Have you seen the suns ?—*Yes, the more I walk and the more I see, the more there are.*" A moment later : " Does the moon move ?—*Yes, when I'm out of doors in the evening and I want to go on the lake, the moon comes with me. If I want to go in the boat, the moon comes with me too, like the sun, it comes as well if it is still there.*"

CAM (6) said of the sun : " *It comes with us to look at us.*—Why does it look at us ?—*It looks to see if we are good.*" The moon comes at night " *because there are people who want to work.*—Why does the moon move ?—*It's time to go and work. Then the moon comes.*—Why does it move ?—*Because it's going to work with the men who work.*—Do you believe that ?—*Yes.*—That it works ?— *It looks to see if they work properly.*"

HUB (6½) : " What does the sun do when you are out for a walk ?—*It moves.*—How ?—*It goes with me.*—Why ? —*To make it light, so that you can see clearly.*—How does it go with you ?—*Because I look at it.*—What makes it move when it goes with you ?—*The wind.*—Does the wind know where you are going ?—*Yes.*—When I go for a walk where does the sun go ?—*It goes with you* (we showed Hub two people walking in opposite directions).—You see, if you were to go that way and I this way, what would the sun do ?—*The sun would go with you.*—Why ?— *With me . . . .*"

JAC (6½) : " What does the moon do when you are out for a walk ?—*It goes with us (elle roule avec nous).*—Why ? —*Because the wind makes it go.*—Does the wind know where you are going ?—*Yes.*—And the moon too ?—*Yes.* —Does it move on purpose to go out with you or because it has to go ?—*It comes so as to give us light.*—Where did you go for a walk ?—*On the 'Plaine'* (a public walk).

The moon went too (la lune elle roulait).—Did it see you ?
—*Yes.*—Does it know when you go for a walk on the
' Plaine ' ?—*Yes.*—Does it care ?—*Yes, it does.*—Does it
know your name ?—*No.*—And mine ?—*No.*—Does it
know there are houses ?—*Yes.*—Does it know I wear
glasses ?—*No.*"

SAR (7) : " What does the sun do when you are out for
your walk ?—*It moves, when I don't move it doesn't move
either. And the moon too.*—And if you go backwards ?—
It goes back."

KENN (7) : " You've seen the moon, haven't you ?—
Yes.—What does it do ?—*It follows us.*—Does it follow
us really and truly ?—*Yes.*—But it doesn't move ?—*No.*
—Then it doesn't follow us really and truly ?—*It follows
us.*—Why does it follow us ?—*To show us the road.*—Does
it know the road ?—*Yes.*—Which roads ?—. . .—Does
it know the Geneva roads ?—*Yes.*—And the Salève roads ?
—*No.*—And the roads in France ?—*No.*—Then what
about the people in France ? What does the moon do ?—
It follows them.—Is the moon there as well ?—*Yes.*—Is it
the same moon as here.—*No, another one.*"

We have already given Giamb's answers at the age of
7 concerning magic (Chapter IV, § 2). We were able to
question him again at 8½ : he still believed that the sun
and moon followed him. " When you are out for a walk,
what does the sun do ?—*It follows us.*—And the moon ?—
Yes, like the sun.—If someone were to meet you, which
would it follow ?—*It would follow one until he went home
and then it would follow the other.*"

BLOND (8) : The moon " *goes with us (avance avec nous)
it follows us.*—Does it really follow us or is it only as if it
followed us ?—*It really follows us.*"

SART (12½) : " Can the moon do whatever it likes ?—
Yes. When you are walking, it follows you.—Does it follow
you or does it not really move ?—*It follows me. It stops
if I stop.*—If I were to walk too, which of us would it
follow ?—*Me.*—Which ?—*You.*—Do you think it follows
everybody ?—*Yes.*—Can it be everywhere at the same
time ? . . .*"

The spontaneity of these answers is apparent. Counter-
suggestion makes no difference. The question as to
whether the sun and moon really follow us or only appear
to do so is not understood. The question of the two

people walking in opposite directions puzzles the child but does not disillusion him. The following answers of the second and third stages show clearly enough by comparison how far the preceding answers really point to a fixed and systematic conviction.

The following are examples of the second stage; the sun and the moon follow us though without themselves moving:—

SART (11 ; 5): " Does the moon move ?—*Yes.*—When you are out for a walk what happens ?—*You see it moving forward all the time.*—Does it follow us or not ?—*It follows us because it's big.*—Does it move (avance) or not ?—*Yes.*—When the moon follows us, does it move (bouge) or not ? . . .—*I don't know.*" Sart obviously does not understand ; on the one hand he has the idea that the moon followed us and on the other the idea that it does not move and he is unable to make the synthesis.

LUG (12 ; 3) will not rest content like Sart with two contradictory beliefs at the same time, but attempts to reconcile them : " What does the moon do when you are out walking ?—*It follows us.*—Why ?—*Its rays follow us.*—Does it move ?—*It moves, it follows us.*—Then tell me . . . (example of the two people walking in opposite directions).—*It stays still. It can't follow the two at the same time.*—Has it ever happened to you that it couldn't follow you ?—*Sometimes when one runs.*—Why ?—*One's going too fast.*—Why does it follow us ?—*To see where we are going.*—Can it see us ?—*Yes.*—When there are lots of people in the town what does it do ?—*It follows someone.*—Which person ?—*Several people.*—How does it do that ?—*With its rays.*—Does it follow them really and truly ?—*You'd think it was us and you'd think it was the moon.*—Does it move ?—*Yes, it moves.*—What does it do ?—*It stays still and its rays follow us* (!) "

BRUL (8) : " What does the sun do when you are out for a walk ?—*It follows us.*—Why ?—*To make it light for us.*—Can it see us ?—*Yes.*—Then it moves ?—*No, you'd think it did.*—Then what does follow us ?—*It follows us, but it stays in the same place* (!)—How does it do that ?—*When you are walking if you turn round it still shines on your head.*—How is that ?—*When anyone looks at it they always see it shining on them.*" Brul then explains that it " stays in the same place " but sends out " its rays."

The substance of these beliefs is clear. The child still believes that the sun follows us. But he has found out (as we shall see Mart find out as the result of an experiment) or has learned that the sun does not move. He cannot understand how these two facts are possible at the same time. Therefore, like Sart, he admits the two contradictory statements without attempting to reconcile them ; in the same way we saw how Sart had learned that the sun and moon are " big," but that he had not understood the significance of this was clear from the conclusions he drew. Or else, like Lug and Brul, the child tries to find a solution for himself, and maintains that the sun is stationary but that its rays follow us !

The following two cases are intermediary between the second and third stages :—

MART (9 ; 5) : " What does the moon do whilst you are walking ?—*It follows us and then it stays still. It's we that move and the moon gets nearer us all the time we're moving.* —How does it follow us ?—*It stays still and it's we who come nearer it.*—How did you find that out ?—*When you pass in front of houses you don't see it any more, you only see the wall.*—Then what did you decide ?—*That it hadn't moved.*—Why did you think it followed you ?—*I made a mistake ; when there wasn't a house there it was all the time in front of me.*—Why does it move?—*No one makes it move ! It's in the same place all the time.*"

FALQ (8) also says that the moon " *follows us.*—Why ? —*Because it's high up and every one can see it.*—If you and I were both walking but in opposite directions which of us would it follow ?—*It would follow you because it's nearer you.*—Why ?—*Because you're in front.*—Why is it nearer ?—*It always stays in the same place.*"

Mart and Falq are still in the second stage in believing that we move nearer the moon when we walk and that the illusion has thus a real foundation. But they are already in the third stage in no longer maintaining that the moon changes place in any way (its rays no longer follow us).

The following are examples of the third stage. The illusion is now completely understood :—

PEC (7 ; 3) : " When you are out walking in the evening, does the moon move ?—*It's far away and you'd say it was moving but it's not really.*"

KUF (10 ; 9) : " *When you're walking you'd say that the moon was following you, because it is big.*—Does it follow us ?—*No. I used to believe it followed us and that it ran after us.*"

DUC (7½) : " What does the sun do when you are out for a walk ?—*It shines.*—Does it follow you ?—*No, but you can see it everywhere.*—Why ?—*Because it is very big.*"

The above answers show the development of the belief in the purposive movement of the sun and moon. Their perfect continuity and the richness of the detail in the accounts of even the youngest children show very clearly that we are dealing with a spontaneous belief, arising from direct observation and already formulated by the child before ever we questioned it. The generality of this spontaneous belief is interesting from three points of view.

In the first place, the facts just stated show clearly enough the child's belief in animism and in an animism that is not very theoretical (its object is not to explain natural phenomena), but affective. The sun and moon take an interest in us :—

" *The sun sometimes watches us,*" says Fran (9), " *when we're looking nice he looks at us.*—Do you look nice ?— *Yes, on Sundays, when I'm dressed like a man.*" " *The moon looks at us and watches over us,*" says Ga (8½), " *when I walk, it walks ; when I stand still it stands still. It copies like a parrot.*—Why ?—*It wants to do whatever I do.*—Why ?—*Because it's inquisitive.*"

PUR (8 ; 8) : The sun moves " *to hear what we're saying.*"

JAC (6) : " *It looks to see if we're being good,*" and the moon " *watches to see that people are working properly* " (Cam, 6), etc.

Secondly, these beliefs are extremely interesting from the light they throw on the relationship between magic and animism. The reader will remember that certain children (Chapter IV, § 2) believe that they themselves cause the movement of the sun and moon : " *It's me when I walk* " (who makes them move), said Nain at 4 years old, "*it's us*," said Giamb at 7. The children we have just quoted have, on the contrary, the impression of being followed by spontaneous beings who could if they so wished go elsewhere. There is therefore magic or animism according as the causal emphasis is laid on the self or on the movement. How is this relationship to be regarded ? There is obviously in such a case complete mutual dependence between magic and animism. The starting point is a feeling of participation resulting from egocentricity, that is to say from confusion between the self and the world ; the child, from always seeing the sun and moon either above or beside him, comes also to believe, by reason of the already formed affective associations which produce child egocentricity, that between the movements of the sun and moon and his own movements there is either dynamic participation or a common purpose. In so far as the child accepts and does not reflect on this common purpose and therefore does not question whether the sun and moon are capable of resisting this obligation to follow us, the attitude is one of magic : he has the impression that it is he himself who makes the sun and moon move. On the other hand, in so far as he is surprised at the obedience of the sun and moon and endows them with the power of resisting, he animates them in so doing and attributes to them the will and the desire to follow him. In short, between magic and animism there is only a difference in egocentricity. Absolute egocentricity implies magic ; the feeling that other beings have an independent existence, on the contrary, weakens the primitive participations and emphasises the purposive character of these beings.

Finally, the beliefs analysed in this section are of great importance to the understanding of the child's conception of dynamics, and we shall thus meet with them again in dealing with the explanation of natural movements. It is found in fact that children of the ages of 7–8 generally maintain that the movement of the sun and moon is due to the air, the wind, the clouds, etc. This seems to suggest a mechanical explanation. But, at the same time, the sun and moon are thought to follow us. Thus added to the mechanical forces, there is a magico-animistic factor which points to the real significance of the child's mechanical conception—to say that the way the sun and moon follow us is due to the wind, etc., amounts to the same as saying that the wind, the clouds, etc. are accomplices, and are equally concerned with us and that all things gravitate around man.

We are thus led to study the type of necessity the child attributes to natural laws. Having once examined this question we may then proceed directly to the problem of the origin of child animism.

§ 3. PHYSICAL DETERMINISM AND MORAL NECESSITY. —As we saw in Chapter V, there are two uses to which a child may put an animistic conception of nature. These are to explain the fortuitous and to explain the regularity of things. Now to explain away the chance occurrence means to exclude it and to seek to bring everything within definite laws. But what are these laws ? As Sully has shown and as we have ourselves been able to verify (*Language and Thought*, Chapter V) they are moral and social laws rather than physical laws. They are the *decus est*. The key to child animism is this, that natural beings are conscious according as they have a part to play in the economy of things.

This characteristic explains both the rôle and the limits of child animism. We have already stated many times that the child is not so anthropomorphic as is usually supposed. He only endows things with consciousness when it is strictly necessary in order that they may fulfil their respective functions. Thus a child of 7 will refuse to admit that the sun can see one in a room or that it knows one's name but will maintain that it can go with us when we are walking because it has to accompany us "to make us warm," etc. The water in a river cannot see its banks, it knows nothing of pleasure or pain ; but it knows that it is moving and it knows when it needs to get up speed in order to overcome some obstacle. For the river moves " so as to give us water," etc.

The following conversation is significant in this respect :—

VERN (6) a child we have never questioned on animism and whom we now saw for the first time. We asked him why a boat floats on the water whilst a little stone, which is lighter, sinks immediately. Vern reflected and then said : " *The boat is more intelligent than the stone.*—What does ' to be intelligent ' mean ?—*It doesn't do things it ought not to do.*"—(Note the confusion between the moral and the physical). " And is the table intelligent ?—*It is cut* (= it is made of wood that has been cut), *it can't talk, it can't say anything.*—And is the sun intelligent ?—*Yes, because it wants to make things warm.*—And the house ?— *No, because it's made of stone. The stones are all shut up* (*fermées*) (meaning that they neither speak nor see, but are material).—Are clouds intelligent ?—*No, because they try to fight the sun* (they do the opposite to the sun).— Is the moon intelligent ?—*Yes, because it shines at night. It lights the streets, and hunters too I think in the forests.*— Is the water in streams intelligent ?—*It is rather good too* (*elle est aussi un peu gentille*).''

These remarks are certainly interesting. In analysing the classification one is inevitably reminded of what Aristotle termed " nature " and what he called " violence." For Vern, the heat of the sun is " natural " since the sun is guided by an internal force towards an end that is useful to life, whilst the movements of the clouds are " violent " since they counteract the sun. And further, if one may be allowed to press the parallel, it should be observed that Vern regards natural activity as " intelligent," that is to say compelled not by physical " necessity " (" necessity " being an obstacle to the activity of " nature "), but by moral obligation—not to do " things it ought not to do."

These answers, therefore, confront us with the problem inevitable to the study of child animism—as to what " nature " means to the child. Is it a collection of physical laws ? Or a well-regulated society ? Or a compromise between the two ? This is what must now be considered. We shall work on the hypothesis, based on the facts collected in the previous chapters, that the child endows things with consciousness principally in order to explain their obedience to a hierarchy. It credits things with a moral nature rather than with a psychology.

How can this hypothesis be verified ? The whole study of the child's ideas of dynamics and physics which we have attempted elsewhere, urges us to adopt it. But, in the meanwhile we can simply ask children whether things do what they want and if not, why not.

This procedure furnished us with very clear results. Up to the ages of 7–8, children refused to admit that things could act as they wanted, not because they lacked the will to do so, but because their will is compelled by a moral law, whose purpose is to regulate everything towards the greatest good of man. The few exceptions we found certainly confirm this interpretation ; when a child of this age regards a certain object as lacking in all moral obligation, he regards it therefore as free to act as it wishes and free because no one is compelling it. Will is thus present in things, but in the great majority of cases this will is controlled by duty.

At the ages of about 7–8 on the other hand the first notions of physical determination are to be found ; certain movements, such as the motion of the clouds or of rivers are explained more and more as due, no longer to a moral obligation, nor to a constraint of a moral law but to a purely physical constraint. This new idea is however slow to become systematised, it is only applied to certain phenomena and it is only at about the ages of 11–12 that it can definitely take the place of the idea of a moral law in the child's scheme of physics. Thus between the ages of 7–8 and 11–12 we shall find various combinations of moral necessity and physical determinism without its being possible to subdivide this period strictly into stages. Finally, it should be noticed that before the ages of 7–8, there is already an element of physical compulsion naturally present in the child's conception of the world, but this compulsion is still very different from the determinism which appears after the ages of 7–8 ; it consists rather in what might be called the material compulsion which necessarily accompanies moral necessity in the child's eyes.

We shall now quote some examples taken at random, showing in each case the part played by moral necessity and physical determinism respectively :—

REYB (8 ; 7) : " Can the clouds do as they like ?—*No.*— Can they move more quickly if they want to ?—*No.*— Can they stop if they want to ?—*No.*—Why not ?— *Because they're moving all the time.*—Why ?—*So as to show it's going to rain (Parce que pour annoncer la pluie).*" " Can the sun do what it likes ?—*Yes.*—Can it stop moving if it wants to ?—*No, because if it were to stop it wouldn't shine.*—Can the moon do what it wants ?—*No.*—Can it stay still if it wants to ?—*Yes.*—Why ?—*Because if it wants to it can stop moving.*—Can it set (aller se coucher) when it wants to ?—*No, because it shines at night.*" If the above remarks of Reyb are compared with the following it will be seen that the regularity of the movements of the clouds, the sun and the moon is explained by their function, whilst that of rivers is explained by determinism : " Can rivers do as they like ?—*No.*—Why not ?—*Because they're flowing all the time.*—Why ?—*Because they can't stop.*—Why not ?— *Because they're flowing all the time.*—Why ?—*Because the wind is driving them. It makes the waves come and makes them flow.*"

ZIM (8 ; 1) supposes that the moon can do as it likes. But there are limits to its powers : " Can it not come in the evening if it doesn't want to ?—*No.*—Why not ?— *Because it's not it who gives the orders* (!) " The sun can do as it likes, but this amounts to the same thing : " It knows it's behind the mountain ?—*Yes.*—Did it want to go there or did it have to ?—*It wanted to.*—Why ?—*So as to make it good weather (parce que pour que ça fasse beau temps).*"

RAT (8 ; 10) : " Can the clouds go faster if they want to ?—*Yes.*—Why ?—*Because they go by themselves.*—Can they go away when they want to ?—*Yes.*—Could they go to-day when it's raining ?—*Yes.*—Then why don't they ?

—Because they don't.—Why not ?—*Because it's raining.*—
Is it they who wanted it to rain ?—*No.*—What then ?—
God.—Could the sun stop shining if it wanted to ?—*Yes.*
—Could it come in the middle of the night if it wanted
to ?—*It wouldn't want to. It's night-time, time to go to
bed.*—Could it if it wanted to ?—*Yes.*—Has it ever done
so ?—*No.*—Why not ?—*It likes to go to bed better.*—You
really believe that ?—*Yes.*—Why doesn't it come in
the middle of the night ?—*It can't.*—Why not ?—*If it
doesn't come it isn't light. If it comes it's light.*—Then why
doesn't it come and make it light at night ?—*The moon
makes it a bit light.*—Can't the sun come too ?—*It doesn't
want to.*—Could it come ?—*Yes.*—Then why doesn't it ?
—*People would think it was morning.*—Why doesn't it let
them ?—*It doesn't want to.*" The moon obeys for similar
reasons : " Could the moon stop in the middle of the
night if it wanted to ?—*No, because it has to shine a bit
longer.*"

Ross (9 ; 9) : " Can the sun do what it likes ?—*Yes.*—
Can it go quicker if it wants to ?—*Yes.*—Can it stop ?—
No.—Why not ?—*Because it has to shine for some time.*—
Why ?—*To warm us.*"

Imh (6) : " Can the clouds do what they like ?—*No,
because all they do is to show us the way.*" We here find the
clouds charged with the necessity of following us which
other children attribute only to the sun and moon. This
reply is all the more significant since Imh is well aware of
the part played by determinism in what concerns streams ;
for example : " Can the water in the streams do what it
likes ?—*No, it can flow faster, but only when it slopes.*"

Juill (7½) : " Can the sun do what it likes ?—*Yes.*—
Can it go away in the middle of the day ?—*No.*—Why
not ?—*Because it's already light.*—And so ?—*It can't.*—
Can it go at 12 o'clock ?—*No.*—Why not ?—*Because it's
already day-time.*—What makes it day-time ? *God.*—
Could he make it day without the sun ?—*Yes.*—Must the
sun be there when it's day ?—*Yes, or else it would rain.*"

Schi (6) : " Could the sun go away at 12 o'clock if it
wanted to ?—*No.*—Why not ?—*Because it has to shine the
whole day.*"

Kent (9 ; 3) : The sun cannot do as it likes " *because
it has to go and make it day where it goes every day.*" The
law of its movement is thus a moral law. So too with the
clouds and the wind : " *They always have to go to the same
place.*" The stars " *have to go at night where they were*

the other night." The streams *" have always to go where there's a path in front of them."*

The following two cases are exceptions; the first is that of a child who endows all objects with freedom of movement for the reason that they are " alone," that is to say that no one commands them nor supervises what they do.

HAD (6) : " Can the sun do whatever it likes ?—*Yes, because it's alone with the moon.*—And the clouds ?—*Yes, because they are alone with the other clouds,"* etc. The meaning of these words is sufficiently clear from the following answer : " Can you do whatever you like ?—*Yes, because my mother sometimes lets me."*

The exception is thus only apparent. Again a child may attribute freedom to all objects, but at the same time credits them with " good will " (bonne volonté) which again makes the answers only an apparent exception to the preceding ones :—

MONT (7) : " Can the sun do whatever it likes ?—*Yes.* —Can it stop giving light ?—*Yes.*—Then why doesn't it ? —*It wants it to be fine weather.*—Can streams do as they like ?—*Yes.*—Could they go faster if they wanted to ?— *Yes.*—Could the Rhône stop flowing ?—*Yes.*—And why doesn't it ?—*It wants there to be water,"* etc.

Finally, it should be noted that will is the most persistent form of the animistic powers which the child attributes to things. In fact, children are found at the ages of 10–12 who no longer ascribe consciousness or life to nature yet still endow it with will and effort.

KUF (10 ; 1) : " Are streams alive ?—*No.*—Do they know they are moving ?—*No.*—Can they want things ?— *No.*—Can they want to go faster ?—*Yes.*—And the same with the sun ? Would the sun like to go faster sometimes ?—*Yes.*—Does it feel that it would like to go faster ? —*No.*" And for Kuf the sun can actually go faster or slower according as it wants to.

The importance of these facts for the evolution of the concept of " force " is unmistakably clear. This continuity established between force and animism by reason of the concept of an " unconscious will " should be noted. The question will be taken up later.

For the present we may conclude that the child is led to explain the uniformity of nature by moral much rather than by natural laws. Things are endowed with a will which they make use of to suit their pleasure and nothing is impossible to them. On the one hand, they are concerned with us, and their will is above all a good will, that is to say a will aiming at man's good. On the other hand, however, there are certain limitations. Natural objects are not sovereign forces : " It's not itself that gives the orders," said Zim, speaking of the moon. It is true that after the ages of 7–8 certain movements, such as those of streams or of clouds, are explained, more and more as due to a physical determinism. But until about the ages of 11–12, there remain a great number of objects, particularly the sun, the moon and the wind, which still obey the primitive moral laws.

It would be interesting to determine at each age the exact proportion of explanations due to moral necessity and physical determinism respectively. But the most fruitful method of attaining this is not the one we have used, but one less verbal and artificial, which consists in making the child explain the reason for each natural movement and phenomenon. We shall attempt it later. The foregoing must therefore be regarded as a simple introduction to the child's dynamics, intended above all to determine the meaning of child animism and to show the contact between this animism and the vaster problems involved in conceptions of movement.

§ 4. CONCLUSIONS. THE SIGNIFICANCE OF THE QUESTIONS ON CHILD ANIMISM, AND THE NATURE OF " DIFFUSE ANIMISM."—The results obtained by means of the various procedures described in Chapters V and VI must be interpreted with the greatest caution. They have in fact a common fault ; their dependence on words. The children's answers were not concerned with concrete

objects which were handled so as to make them understand
their mechanism but with things about which we had
merely spoken.   What we obtained is therefore not animism as it actually functions but the definition of the words
" living," " knowing," " feeling," etc. These definitions
certainly contained constant elements and if our ambition
were limited to the study of verbal intelligence we could
treat the results with confidence.   But how far can they
throw light on the question of intelligence in perception ?

To make this matter clear we must retain only what
may be called the negative element in the answers and
not the positive content of each statement. From this
point of view two conclusions may be noted.

The first is that the child's thought begins with a lack
of differentiation between living and inert bodies since
it possesses no criterion by which to make the distinction.
For us, or rather for adult common sense, two types of
criterion aid this distinction.   First, the fact that living
bodies are born, grow and die.   But curiously enough
none of the children we tested ever invoked this criterion.
Sometimes, indeed, the child told us that plants " grow "
(poussent) but this was for him a way of regarding them
as endowed with spontaneous movement, and the movement of growth was thus conceived as of the same order
as the movement of the clouds or of the sun.   Moreover,
we shall see in studying child artificialism that to a child
almost all bodies are born and grow ; the sun and moon
" are born and grow (poussent)," mountains, stones, iron
" grow " etc.   The facts clearly prove that the origin and
growth of things cannot serve the child as criteria for
distinguishing the living from the inert. From this point
of view there is perfect continuity between all natural
objects.

In the second place, in distinguishing living from
inorganic matter, adult common sense also makes use
of the principle of inertia, which, since the development
of industry, has become more and more one of our intellectual habits. An inaminate body only moves in response

to an external influence, whereas, as common sense asserts, a living being creates movements. But this distinction is obviously of recent date, and it is therefore no wonder that the children we found in the third stage, those precisely who define life in terms of spontaneous movement, were still unable to form a distinction between the apparently spontaneous movement of the sun, the moon, the wind, etc., and the movements of animals.

In short, however cautiously one proceeds and whatever pains one takes to avoid interpreting the children's answers too literally, it remains an undoubted fact that child thought starts with the idea of a universal life as its primary assumption. From this point of view, animism is in no sense the product of a structure built up by the child's reflection but is a primitive principle and it is only by a series of progressive differentiations that inert matter comes to be distinguished from that which is living. In this light, activity and passivity, spontaneous and acquired movement, are bracketed ideas that become gradually detached by thought from the primitive *continuum* in which all is regarded as living.

The second conclusion is that if the living and the inert are undifferentiated in the primitive state the same is true *à fortiori* for conscious action and unconscious movement, or let us rather say for purposive actions and mechanical movements. It may be questioned whether the children's statements concerning the consciousness of things were reflective, but it must in any case be admitted that the distinction between purposive actions and mechanical movements is not only not innate but supposes an already very developed state of mind. No positive experience can in fact compel a mind to admit that things work neither for nor against us and that chance and inertia alone count in nature. To arrive at such an objective view of things the mind must free itself from subjectivity and abandon its innate egocentricity. We have already shown what difficulties such an operation involves for the child.

In short, in so far as it is led to endow things with consciousness, child animism is not the result of a structure built up by reflection but results from the primitive property of mind which consists in the complete lack of differentiation between conscious action and mechanical movement. Child animism presupposes a primitive state of belief in a *continuum* of consciousness. Or rather it is not strictly either knowing or feeling that the child attributes to things but a sort of elementary awareness and will, the minimum necessary to accomplish the functions required by nature. This attributing of will and awareness does not mean that the child regards things as persons—actually, his sense of personality is much less strong than ours—but simply that he confuses purpose and activity. There is a Jewish story that tells how two dull-witted fellows were once having a dispute as to when water boils. One maintained that it boils at 100°. " But," objected the other, " how does it know it's reached 100° ? " This story illustrates the true meaning of child animism ; namely in so far as things show an activity which is reliable in its constancy and utility to man, they must possess a psychic life.

Reduced to its just proportions, child animism thus becomes dependent on a number of fundamental peculiarities of child thought which makes it more acceptable in the eyes of the psychologists than if it bore the appearance of a disinterested and merely theoretical systematisation. Three considerable groups of phenomena point, in fact, to the universal purposiveness which children attribute to objects.

Firstly, there is the child's finalistic attitude, the remarkable prevalence of which is well known. In considering the first stage in the evolution of the notion of life (§ 1) we noted the definition of objects according to their utility, characteristic of the child's mentality between the ages of 5 and 8. As to mechanical movements, the research described in § 3 sufficiently showed that natural laws are interpreted by finalism. Our further researches will show that this finalism colours the whole of their physics—the buoyancy of bodies, the movement of the air in a pump, the function of fire and of steam in an engine, etc. This tendency clearly shows to what an extent the child's universe is governed by ideas of purpose, both in its broad aspects and in its smallest details.

A second group of facts pointing to the same conclusions is furnished by the evolution of questions between the ages of 3 and 7. As has already been shown (*Language and Thought*, Chapter V) these " Whys " are not strictly either causal or finalistic. They lie between the two, which means that the real cause that the child tries to connect with the phenomenon is precisely a purpose, which is at the same time both the efficient cause and the justification of the effect with which he is concerned. In other words, the purpose is creative, the physical cause and the logico-moral reason are still confused in a sort of universal psychological motive impulse.

This is the explanation—which brings us to the third group of phenomena—of why the child starts by confusing physical necessity and moral necessity. If the facts quoted in the preceding section, and which will be constantly cropping up again in a much more spontaneous form, cannot be regarded as the proof of a systematic and explicit animism they are at any rate a clear indication in favour of supposing that the child attributes to nature a universal purpose (see *Causalité Physique*).

It may be claimed, it is true, that the three groups of facts just drawn on do not prove that a child locates the purpose he imagines in connection with a thing, within the thing itself. Such a purpose may equally belong to the creator or creators such as the men (" Messieurs ") by whom everything has been made. The following chapters will show precisely that such a child artificialism exists and that it is as systematic as animism and supposes nature to have been " created " (" fabriquée ") by men. But the problem is to determine whether the child begins by con-

ceiving things as created by man and only then seeks for
the purpose which may underlie individual things or
whether on the contrary he is not first led to seek a purpose
in all things and only then to classify these purposes as
belonging to the creator (artificialism) or belonging to
the things themselves (animism).   Now we know that the
" why," whose appearance coincides exactly with the need
to seek for a purpose in everything, begins to arise between
the ages of 2 and 3, that is to say at a time when artificialism is evidently not yet much systematised.   The most
probable course of the child's mind is, therefore, that which
lies in first seeking for purposes and not till then classifying
the subjects to which the purposes are related.   So that
the three groups of facts summoned to support animism,
or the attribution of purpose to things, as it might be
called in the terms of the present thesis, point to artificialism as much as to animism.

Moreover, it will be shown that at first no such conflict
exists between animism and artificialism as might have
been supposed ; that the child regards a body, such as the
sun for example, as having been made by man is no
reason why he should not regard it also as living, and
living in the same way as a child born to its parents.

In conclusion then, the structure of child animism or
rather of its diffuse animism, in opposition to the more
systematic beliefs regarding the sun, moon, etc. (§ 2) may
be characterised as follows.

Nature presents a *continuum* of life, such that every
object possesses activity and awareness in some degree.
This *continuum* is a network of purposive movements,
more or less mutually dependent on one another and all
tending towards the good of humanity.   Gradually the
child picks out certain centres of force within this
continuum as being animated by a more spontaneous
activity than the rest.   But the choice of these centres
does not become fixed for a long while.   For example, the
child first attributes autonomous activity to his own
person, which has the power of making the sun and the

clouds advance, then to the sun and clouds themselves, which move of their own accord, then to the wind which causes the sun and the clouds to move, etc. The centre of force is thus gradually shifted. This is what explains the vague and unsystematic character of the answers obtained. But although the choice of centres may be undecided the reasons which determine it need not be. Activity in general, movement in general, spontaneous movement opposed to imparted movement : these were the three themes that we found continually recurring in the minds of the children tested, introducing a progressive differentiation within the primitive *continuum* of life and purpose.

§ 5. CONCLUSIONS (*continued*) : THE ORIGINS OF CHILD ANIMISM.—Ribot has remarked that [1] : " In consequence of a well-known though inexplicable instinctive tendency, man attributes purposes, will and causality similar to his own to all that acts and reacts around him, to his fellow-men, to living beings and to those things whose movements make them appear as if alive (clouds, rivers, etc.) " This phenomenon may be seen " amongst children, savages, animals (such as the dog who bites the stone that hits him) ; even the reflective man, returning for the moment to his instinctive state, loses his temper with the table into which he bumps." Freud [2] explains animism as due to a " projection " of which he speaks thus : " To project internal perceptions outside is a primitive mechanism, which our sensory perceptions for example undergo in the same way, and which consequently plays a principal part in our representation of the external world." Are this " inexplicable tendency " of Ribot and this " primitive mechanism " of Freud really inexplicable ? Or is the problem only insoluble because badly stated, and this because certain implicit postulates concerning the limits between the self and the external world alone make " projection " of the internal contents necessary ?

[1] *L'évolution des idées générales*, 4th edition, p. 206.
[2] *Totem and Taboo.*

Indeed, for a certain school of psychology, consciousness
of self is due above all to the direct sensation of something
internal :   for Maine de Biran, the feeling of effort ;   for
Ribot, the sum of the kinæsthetic sensations, etc.   Thus
the consciousness of self is developed independently of
consciousness of the external world.   And so in order to
explain that thought endows objects with life, purpose,
forces, it is necessary to speak of " projection." Stated
in these terms the question certainly becomes insoluble.
Why should one project rather than see things as they
are ?   And if one is but the victim of a deceptive analogy
between things and the self, why is this analogy so firmly
fixed that neither experience nor time can undeceive a
mind thus inclined ?

Let us rather return to the hypothesis to which the
study of the relations between the self and the external
world led us.   Going back to the starting point in the life
of thought we find a protoplasmic consciousness unable
to make any distinction between the self and things.   In
the formation of this consciousness two types of factors
combine.   First come the biological or individual factors
which control the relations between the organism and its
environment.   According to all the evidence it is impossible
in any biological reaction whatsoever to separate the
organism from its environment.   The intellectual adaptation and the motor adaptation from which the former is
derived are no exception to this rule.   Reality is a complex
system of exchanges and complementary currents, the
first determined by the assimilation of things to the
organism and the second by the adaptation of the organism
to the facts of the environment.   The most substantial
part of Bergson's *Matter and Memory* is where he demon-
strates that perception is situated in the object as much
as in the brain, since there is a perfect continuity between
the impulse in the brain and the movements of the object.
There is thus in the beginning neither self nor external
world but a *continuum*.   The social factors also tend to
the same result ;   from its earliest activities the baby is

brought up in a social atmosphere, in the sense that its parents, especially the mother, intervene in all its actions (feeding, suckling, gripping objects, language) and in all its affections. Thus according to this point of view every action is part of a context, so that the consciousness of self does not accompany the child's early movements in any innate manner but is only gradually revealed as a function of the contacts experienced with the behaviour of others. Thus both the social and the biological factors combine at the beginning of the mental life to ensure an absence of differentiation between the world and the self, whence arise the feelings of participation and the magical mentality which results.

If such is the starting point for the child's consciousness it is easier to realise the origins of animism. Four groups of causes, in fact, meet in the genesis of animism ; two belong to the individual and two to the social order.

Those belonging to the individual order are as follows : First, there is *indissociation* of the contents of the primitive consciousness ; for, since ideas of action and of purpose, etc. are necessarily bound together until the progressive dissociation of its ideas leads the child to distinguish purposive from non-purposive actions, the world is regarded by the primitive consciousness as a continuous whole that is both psychical and physical at the same time. Secondly, there is *introjection* according to which the child endows objects with feelings equivalent to those he himself experiences in like circumstances.

Before proceeding to analyse these two factors a distinction must be made between two types of animistic tendency found among the children tested. We shall give the name of *diffuse animism* to the general tendency of children to confuse the living and the inert, that is to say the condition described in the preceding section (§ 4). We shall describe as *systematic animism* the sum total of the explicit animistic beliefs held by the child and of which the clearest is that according to which it believes that the sun and moon follow him (§ 2). We shall show

that, broadly speaking, diffuse animism is explained by
indissociation, rather than by introjection which accounts
more for systematic animism. But it goes without saying
that such a schema is too simple and must be complicated
by numerous qualifications.

Having said this, we shall now attempt to formulate
the rôle played by indissociation. The study of child
realism (Chapters I-IV) showed that certain elements,
one subjective and the other objective, cannot be dissociated in the child's thought, although to us they appear
independent. So far, these are names and the things
named, thought and the things thought of, etc. But the
same holds true concerning movement and life ; all
external movement is regarded as necessarily purposive.
So too for activity in general and consciousness ; all
activity is regarded as necessarily conscious. So too, at
least in the primitive state, are being and knowing ; every
object is regarded as knowing what it is, where it is and
what attributes it possesses, etc. In short, the facts of
child realism show that the mind proceeds from indissociation to dissociation and that mental development
does not in any sense consist in successive associations.
Diffuse animism is thus a primary datum in the child's
consciousness.

It is true that there exists the following difference
between realism strictly speaking (such as nominal realism,
etc.) and the indissociation from which animism arises.
Realism constitutes what is, so to speak, a *primary
indissociation ;* that is one which consists simply in
situating in things characteristics which belong in truth
to mind, but which the mind does not yet realise as
belonging to it (names, for example). The indissociation
which characterises animism is on the contrary a *secondary
indissociation,* which consists in attributing to things,
characteristics similar to those which the mind attributes
to itself—such as consciousness, will, etc. Is this a case
of projection ? Certainly not. That which secondary
indissociation adds to primary indissociation is simply the

unifying element in the idea of a particular object ; that is, it associates groups of qualities into individual entities rather than attributing them to reality at large. But it is the distinguishing mark of the realist mind—and herein lies the indissociation—to arrive at the idea of an object by making use of notions and categories which combine an objective term with the subjective term and which regard them as necessarily indissociable ; thus instead of thinking of the sun as an object which shines, is hot and is endowed with movement, the realist mind thinks of it as an object that knows it shines, that intentionally makes us warm and that moves according to the needs of its own life.

The fundamental postulate in all the answers obtained concerning the endowment of consciousness to objects and the concept of " life " is, in fact, the implicit assumption that all activity is conscious and all movement spontaneous. When Schi maintains that the clouds know they are moving " *because it is they that make the wind*," when Ross says the wind is conscious " *because it is it that blows*," etc., there is an implicit identification between " doing " and " knowing what one does." There is animism through lack of dissociation.

Why, however, is this indissociation of ideas so persistent ? We need only note in what manner dissociation works to realise that its operation is neither simple nor spontaneous. No direct experiment can possibly lead the child to the discovery that a movement is not purposive or that an activity is not conscious. The power of dissociating does not arise from a wider knowledge nor from a developed ability to control circumstances nor from experimentation but from a radical change in the habits of mind. Only a qualitative development of the child's mind can lead it to abandon animism.

What is the explanation of this change in the child's trend of mind ? The dissociation of ideas can only result from his becoming progressively aware of his self and his own thought. As regards the realism involved in names, etc., we have already tried to show that it is the discovery of the symbolic and therefore human quality of names which leads the child, first to dissociate the sign from the thing signified, then to distinguish internal from external, and then finally to differentiate the psychic from the physical. The progressive diminution of his animistic beliefs follows a similar course. According as the child becomes clearly aware of personality in himself he refuses to allow a personality to things. According as he realises his own subjective activity and its inexhaustible scope he refuses to allow self-consciousness to things. Tylor has maintained with regard to savages, that it is the discovery of the existence of thought that brings animism into being. Far from its being so with children, it is ignorance of the psychic which makes them attribute life to things and it is the realisation of the fact of a thinking subject which leads them to abandon animism. In short the dissociation of ideas arises from the growth of the consciousness of self.

This interpretation can be justified by facts which are not limited to those we collected on the subject of child realism. As late as the age of 11–12 a phenomenon is still to be found which suggests what has probably been taking place during earlier years ; this is the difficulty experienced in imagining that one can have the slightest illusion concerning one's own self. The fact is that the less a mind is given to introspection the more it is the victim of the illusion that it knows itself perfectly. The following cases illustrate this :—

Among the nonsense sentences proposed by Ballard as tests [1] is one phrased as follows : " I am not proud, since I don't think myself half as clever as I am in reality." We submitted this sentence to a number of particularly intelligent children between the ages of 11 and 13. The answer, where the children had understood the proposition, was always the same, namely, that the absurdity lies in your supposing yourself less clever than you really are.

[1] See *Brit. Journal of Psychology*, October 1921.

If you are clever, the child argues, you know you are ; if you think yourself only half as clever as you really are it is because you are only half as clever, etc.   You know what you are, you must know yourself, etc.   The point of all these answers is, in short, the impossibility of having any illusions respecting one's self.

The above may be an indication only, but it is significant. We all know that we have illusions concerning ourselves and that knowledge of one's self is the hardest of all knowledge.   Of this, a mind uncultivated, like the child's, knows nothing.   It thinks it knows itself and it believes this exactly in proportion to how little it does know itself. But, if this is so at the ages of 11 and 12, one can imagine what the consciousness of self must be in the first years— the child must suppose he is aware of everything that happens to him, and inversely he can have no idea of any unconscious or involuntary action whatsoever.   It is only by a series of experiences of a social or inter-individual type, causing him to realise that other people's behaviour is not always necessarily intelligent or even intentional, and that one may oneself act under the sway of strange illusions, that the mind forms such improbable conceptions as movement without consciousness or existence without awareness. Naturally, we are not suggesting that the disappearance of animism is necessarily connected with the advent of the idea that there are psychologically unconscious states.   We simply maintain that the dissociation of the primitive semi-psychic, semi-physical ideas, in other words the " depersonalisation " of reality is bound up with the growth of self-consciousness.   So long as the child knows nothing of introspection, he supposes he knows himself perfectly and believes other things to be conscious of themselves.   Inversely, according as the child comes to realise his self he builds up a whole scale of differing tpyes of action, from voluntary and reflective action to involuntary and unconscious action.

In short, animism, or at any rate diffuse animism, results from the indissociation of primitive ideas and only the growth of the knowledge of the self (resulting from social intercourse and comparisons with others) can enable these ideas to become dissociated. But to explain animism thus, seems nothing more than to substitute bare assertion for the idea of " projection," an idea which at least provides something resembling an explanation. And so long as psychology is isolated from biology and the world is postulated as independent of the mind which adapts itself to it, this is obviously true. But if we will only seek in biology the roots of mental operations and give thought its true context by starting from the relation of the organism to its environment, we shall see that the obscure notion of " projection," that is to say of the transposition of the internal contents of consciousness into the external world, arises from the illegitimate and ontological use of the ideas of " internal " and " external." The biological reality is the assimilation of the environment by the organism and the transformation of the organism into a function of the environment. It is a continuity of exchanges. These exchanges naturally suppose an internal and an external pole but each term is in a relation of constant equilibrium and natural dependence on the other. Such is the reality from which the intelligence gradually extracts the ideas of a self and an external world. To say that at the beginning the self and the world are confused is to replace the inexplicable " projection " of the self into things by the idea of assimilation of the external world by the self, an assimilation which is undoubtedly continuous with the biological assimilation itself. The remainder of our research and in particular the inquiry into the origins of the idea of force (see *Causalité Physique*) are aimed at developing the implications of this idea, so that it is unnecessary to pursue it further at the moment.

But the indissociation of ideas can account only for diffuse animism. Certain systematic convictions such as that according to which the clouds and the sun follow us and are concerned with our doings, etc., seem to imply the intervention of other factors. It is here that we need to call in *introjection*, that is to say the tendency to situate in others or in things the reciprocal feelings to those we experience from their contact.

The principle of introjection is clear enough. All that either resists or obeys the self is thought to possess an activity as distinct as that of the self which commands or tries to overcome the resistance. Thus the consciousness of effort supposes force in the resisting object, the consciousness of desire supposes that of purpose in the obstacle, the consciousness of pain that of ill will in the object which is causing the pain, etc.

The cause of the introjection evidently lies in egocentricity, namely in the tendency to believe that everything evolves around the self. To win free of egocentricity, that is, to attain an impersonal view of things, is to be rid of introjection. The following cases clearly illustrate the mechanism. "*Who made that scratch ?*" (indicating her own hand), Nel questioned. "*It hurts there ? It was the wall that hit me.*" (Nel was aged 2 ; 9). Or again, the following recollection of his childhood by Michelet :—

"*I had just escaped having my head guillotined by a window sash. I had climbed on to a chair and was looking down when the window fell with a crash. We both remained a moment stupefied. I was fascinated by this window which I had seen moving by itself like a person and even quicker than I could. I was certain it had wanted to do me harm and for a long while I never came near it without experiencing feelings of fear and anger.*" [1]

The above is the simplest type of case ; objects that provoke pain or fear are regarded as doing so from a conscious purpose, because the self is still egocentric and in consequence is unable to give a disinterested or impersonal judgment. Such cases are innumerable and it is unnecessary to enumerate them further.

On the other hand, a particular case to which attention must be drawn is that of the child who attributes to things

[1] Michelet, *Ma jeunesse*, p. 17.

a movement of an anthropocentric character without realising that this involves an illusion. Such is the case when we believe that the sun and the clouds follow us. In these cases not only does the child mistake the apparent movement for the real, through failing to distinguish the personal from the objective point of view, but also he believes forthwith that the pursuit is intentional, and by introjection he attributes all manner of human feelings to the sun and the moon.

The two following observations belong probably to this category :—

One of us can distinctly recollect the curious experience of turning round quickly to see if the things behind him were still there or had disappeared.

A like experience gave rise to the following. Bohn (1) reports this conversation with a boy of 5 ; 1 : "*Daddy is all that really here ?*—What do you mean by all that ?— *All these things. Can I really see them all ?*—You can see them and feel them. They are always there.—*No, they are not always there. When I turn away from them, they aren't there.*—When you turn back they are always in the same place.—*They are all alive. They are always moving and going away. When I go close to them, they come close to me.*—But aren't they always in the same place ?—*No, I only dream them and they come into my dream and go out of it again.*" Then the child walked slowly about the room touching the things and saying : "*Look at them coming and going away again.*" [1]

These two cases are of great interest. In both the child wants to know whether the changes he observes in his visual surroundings are due to his own change of position, and therefore to his own activity, or to the things themselves. In so far as he tends to the second solution he is animist. In so far as he adopts the first, that is to say is aware of his own part in the continued transformation of the perspective of objects he has ceased to be animist. Both cases occurred at a time when the self, half conscious of itself, felt the strangeness of wondering what part in

---

[1] *Pedagogical Seminary*, 1916: " A child's questions."

the structure of the world was played by things and what by his own activity. The second child shows still, in addition, a semi-magic attitude of participating with things; they " are in my dream."

In these last cases, and in numerous others of the same type, animism thus results from egocentricity. The self is sufficiently conscious of its limitations to know that neither the sun nor things depend directly on its own desire or will (which is why these cases show hardly any magic), but this consciousness is not yet sufficiently developed to realise that the apparent movements of things are due to an illusion in his own perspective.

In short, introjection results from the egocentric tendency to believe that everything gravitates around us and it consists in attributing to things such powers as they would need either to obey us, or to resist.

It would seem that we are here falling back on to the solutions of Ribot or of Freud which regard animism as due to a simple projection. But it must be clearly emphasised that introjection is impossible without the indissociation just referred to. It may be described as a tertiary indissociation (by contrast with the secondary indissociation discussed above) which consists, in attributing to things not only what belongs to us (life and consciousness, which the child regards as inseparable from activity or from movement in general) but also characteristics reciprocal to our own—malice when we are afraid, obedience when we command, intentional resistance when we cannot command obedience, etc. Introjection is in fact impossible to a mind that is not realist—the stone that hurts the child can only be regarded as wicked if all activity is regarded as intentional, etc.

The mutual dependence of introjection and indissociation is confirmed in the clearest manner by these circumstances. The primitive indissociation of ideas has its origin, as has been shown, in the child's realism, that is to say in the absence of all knowledge of self or the incapacity to distinguish the activity of the thinking subject. Introjection, on the other hand, is bound up with egocentricity from which it arises and which it in turn fosters. But it is precisely this egocentricity which accounts for realism —it is the fact of being unable to distinguish the part played by one's own perspective in one's conceptions of objects which causes a mind to be realist and unable to distinguish the subjective from the objective.

Primitive consciousness is thus enclosed within a sort of circle ; to separate the tangled ideas which confuse both the objective and the subjective, thought must first become conscious of itself and be distinguished from things, but to be distinguished from things, thought must not introject into them the illusory characteristics due to an egocentric perspective. Moreover, in the degree in which, by reason of exchange and discussions between individuals, the self becomes aware of itself and breaks away from its egocentricity, it ceases to introject feelings into things and by dissociation of the confused primitive ideas is able to escape from animism even in its diffuse form.

It remains now to discuss the social factors which favour the persistence of animism in children. Here, too, two complementary groups may be distinguished; first, the feelings of participation that the child's social environment must arouse in him, and secondly, the moral obligation which is forced on him by education.

The first of these factors is all important. As was pointed out when considering magic, the child, whose every activity is linked from the cradle onwards to a complementary activity on the part of his parents, must during his first years live with the impression of being perpetually surrounded by thoughts and actions directed to his wellbeing. It must seem to him as if his every aim and motive were known and shared by those surrounding him. He must suppose himself to be continually seen, understood and forestalled. Later, when the child begins to exchange his thoughts with his brothers or friends he still maintains this tendency to believe that his least syllable is understood—a fact which, as we have seen, lies at the root of his egocentric language (*Language and Thought*, Chapters I, III) ; he supposes, that is, that his thought is common to all since he has not attempted to escape from his own personal point of view.

If this is so, this feeling of communion should colour all his vision of the world. Nature must appear peopled with beings either favourable or disquieting. Animals, as has often been noted, cause feelings of this sort and the child certainly has the impression at times of being understood by them or sometimes of making himself understood.

Thus NEL (2 ; 9), whose remarks were quoted in § 10, has frequent conversations with animals : " *Good-bye, cow*," she said to a cow. " *Come here, cow. Come, cow.*" And to a grasshopper : " *You'll see, Miss Grasshopper*"–- (and as it escapes) " *What are you up to, grasshopper ?* "

PIE (6) in front of an aquarium, looking at a salamander : " *Oh, look how surprised it is by that whopper* (a fish). *Salamander, you ought to eat the fish !* "

This seems like romancing, but it must be remembered that children of 8 years old still do not hesitate to believe that animals know their names (see Chapter II, § 6) : " Does a fish know that it is called a fish ?—*Of course !* " (Mart. 8 ; 10).

The cases quoted by Freud under the title of " infantine returns to totemism " [1] are well known. Whatever be the interpretation given to these facts, they teach two things. First, that the child adopts certain animals into his moral life. Secondly, by so doing, he attributes to them a share in certain of the relations existing between him and his parents, for example, if he has done wrong, he feels that the animal knows all about it, etc. In the examples Freud quotes, the part played by educators in the genesis of the child's beliefs certainly needs questioning : people can always be found stupid enough to threaten their children with the fury of dogs or horses if

[1] Freud, *Totem and Taboo.*

they behave badly etc. But the spontaneous tendency children show, when swayed by fear or remorse, to regard the whole world as aware of their fault, is such a general one that the cases quoted by Freud, Wulf, Ferenczi, etc. certainly seem to contain an element of spontaneous conviction.

It seems extremely probable that these feelings of participation may be finally transferred to the things themselves and that this fact constitutes one of the factors of child animism. We seemed to find at least a trace of this tendency of children to feel they are being seen and even watched in certain answers, quoted in § 2 and relating to the sun and moon. The moon " watches us," said Ga (8½). The sun moves "to hear what we are saying" (Jac. 6). The moon is " curious " (Pur 8 ; 8). The sun " watches us " (Fran 9), etc. It has often been noticed, too, how frightened children are when they see the moon from their bed. " The moon sends our dreams " said Ban at 4½. But most convincing is the case quoted by James (see Chapter IV, § 2) of the deaf-mute who associated the moon with his moral life and regarded it as responsible for the punishments he received and finally came to identify it with his own mother, long since dead.

If this is the natural tendency of the child's mind, the feeling of moral obligation which he acquires in the course of his education must be distinguished as a special factor in animism. As M. Bovet has shown in his admirable study [1] the feeling of obligation results from respect for instruction. But as was shown (*Language and Thought*, Chapter V) a child of 6 may ask many questions concerning rules and inhibitions, whilst with children from 2 to 5 questions are repeatedly asked in the form : " Why must we do that ? "—" Must we do this ? "—" Should it be done like that ? " etc. Concern of this sort is evident throughout the child's whole mentality, although it is well

---

[1] Bovet, " Les conditions de l'obligation de conscience," *Année Psychologique*," Vol. XVIII (1912).

before any need has arisen to explain the " why " of such phenomena. Physical necessity is confused with moral necessity ; natural law has a moral origin, and the power of nature is regarded as of the type of compulsion a chief exerts over his obedient subjects or that adults exert over children. That this is a special factor of animism was sufficiently shown in § 3 of this chapter : it is not because the child believes things to be alive that he regarded them as obedient, but it is because he believes them to be obedient that he regards them as alive.

In short, factors of the individual order and those of the social order (the second being moreover an extension of the first) meet in the formation and development of child animism. To be complete, yet another factor must be mentioned, which although not itself a cause of animism is certainly of great importance in its systematisation : this is the language of the environment.

This is so for two reasons. As M. Bally has put it, language always lags in its aptitude for expression. That is to say, when speaking in images we are always compelled to draw on forms of expression that we have really outgrown. For example, we say " the sun is trying to break through the mist," which is an animistic and dynamic way of speaking, and moreover takes no account of the distance which in reality separates the sun from the mist and suggests they are actually engaged in conflict. It is therefore not to be wondered at that the child takes literally personifications of language (such as the French " le soleil se couche "), finalistic expressions (such as " the river is flowing to get to the lake "), anthropomorphic or artificialist expressions (such as " the heat is making the water boil," " the steam is *trying* to escape ") and even quasi-magical expressions (such as " the clouds *foretell* rain "). Adult language provides the very conditions necessary to foster the child's animism and this the more so, since generally speaking the child takes all metaphors literally —it looks to see " a broken arm " tumble on to the ground, whilst the phrase " go to the devil " constituted, for a child of 9 of our acquaintance, the proof that the devil is not far off.

But it is obvious that in all these cases, language is not the cause of child animism in general. It is simply the cause of animism following one particular line—already determined—rather than another. There is simply, as Stern[1] maintains, "convergence" between the regressive tendencies of language and the child's natural trend of mind. It is not the child which is moulded by language ; it is the language which is already childish.

But this is not all. As was pointed out by W. Jerusalem[2] language itself, apart from this exceptional imagery, "dramatises" the simplest judgments. The fact of separating the subject from the verb and the predicate leads the mind to substantialise the subject and to endow it with an activity of its own and with distinct qualities, as if the subject was something more than the sum of its actions and the sum of its qualities. When, for example, Ross (9 ; 9) says that the wind may not know what it is doing " because it is not a person " but it none the less must know that it is blowing " *because it's it that blows*," he is, in the most interesting way, putting his finger on this very problem. To say of the wind " it's it that blows " is in fact to make the wind into something that is both active, material and permanent. It is to be thrice the victim of words. By tolerating the expression " the wind blows " or simply by speaking of the " wind " as if it were a person, language perpetrates, in fact, the triple absurdity of suggesting that the wind can be independent of the action of blowing, that there can be a wind that does not blow, and that the wind exists apart from its outward manifestations. But it is so natural to us to talk in this way that we regard it almost as correct. When we say " cold fish calls for mayonnaise " we do not suppose that the fish itself actually calls at all, but when we say " the wind blows " we really believe that " it " blows. This is

[1] *Die Kindersprache*, Leipzig, 1907.
[2] *Die Urtheilsfunction*, Vienna and Leipzig, 1895, pp. 109-111.

the explanation of Ross's reasoning. He is a materialist without realising it, as are common sense and language itself.

Such cases certainly favour Max Müller's doctrine that the animism of savages, together also with all religion, is a " disease of language." Again, it is obvious that it is simply a matter of convergence between language and mentality, be it primitive or child. Thought creates language and then passes beyond it, but language turns on thought and seeks to imprison it.

To conclude, we have seen how complex is the genesis of animism. But it will have been noticed that, apart from the verbal factor, the factors conditioning the genesis of the child's animism are approximately those conditioning the formation of feelings, of participation, and of magical causation. Animism and participation are in fact complementary phenomena, or are rather, the independent phases of the same process of naturalising reality. Three stages may be distinguished in the process. During the first stage, the self and things are completely confused : there is participation between all and everything, and desire can exert a magical activity over reality. During the second stage, the self is differentiated from things, but subjective aspects still adhere to things. The self is now felt partially to participate with things and believes itself capable of acting on them from a distance because it regards the various instruments (words, images, gestures, etc.) by means of which it thinks of things, as inseparable from the things. Moreover, things are necessarily animate, because since the self is not yet distinguished from things, psychical and physical ideas are not yet dissociated. During this second stage, magic and animism are therefore complementary. This is the period when the child, believing itself to be followed by the sun and the moon, can interpret the fact equally in terms of magic (" it's I who make them move ") or of animism (" it's they who follow me "). Finally, in a third stage, the self is so far distinguished from things that the instruments of thought can no longer be conceived as adherent in things, words are no longer in things, images and thought are situated in the head. Gestures are no longer effective. Magic is no more. But, as was shown (Chapter II, § 8), the distinction between sign and thing signified appears before that of internal and external and above all before that of psychic and physical. In other words, the distinction between the self and things may be fairly advanced without the dissociation of subjective from objective ideas having reached the point of causing animism to disappear. During this third stage animism therefore remains whilst magic tends to disappear. Feelings of participation tend also to come to an end or at any rate they assume the completely animist form of simple communion between minds—thus according as the child continues to believe the sun to be alive after giving up the idea that it follows us, the sun will perhaps still appear to him as concerned with our doings and desiring our well-being, but this involves merely an intelligible relationship between one person and another. It is no longer participation, strictly speaking, in the sense that material participation is no longer possible. That animism survives magic and in rationalising the primitive participations comes to absorb them, is what will be shown by the cases quoted in the succeeding research on artificialism. We may merely conclude for the moment that during the primitive stage magic and animism are both related and complementary.

PART III

ARTIFICIALISM

WE shall borrow the term artificialism from a study which M. Brunschvicg has devoted to the physics of Aristotle.[1] According to M. Brunschvicg, two tendencies whose real antagonism has been shown by stoic and mediæval physics came to converge in the peripatetic system ; one of these leads Aristotle to regard all things as the product of art, and of an art analogous to human technique; the other urges him to attribute to things, internal forces and appetites similar to those possessed by living beings. " Aristotle," says M. Brunschvicg, " speaks alternately as a *sculptor* and as a *biologist.*"[2] To the first of these tendencies, that which leads to the conception of things as resulting from a transcendent act of " creation," M. Brunschvicg gives the name " artificialism." The artificialism of Aristotle is, to be sure, learned and in keeping with the entire peripatetic philosophy and in particular with the materialism of the logic of classes. Moreover, this artificialism is immanent as much as transcendent : creative activity is attributed to Nature (regarded, it is true, as baleful) just as much as to a divine mover. Child artificialism, on the contrary, is more implicit than systematic and transcendent rather than immanent : it consists in regarding things as the product of human creation, rather than in attributing creative activity to the things themselves.

---

[1] L. Brunschvicg, *L'expérience humaine et la causalité physique,* livres V-VII.
[2] p. 140.

But here also, as in the case of animism, the name matters but little. Provided we note clearly the differences existing between child animism and Greek animism, it is an advantage to use the same word in both cases to signify the same tendency to confuse material causality and human creation.

Still more, the conflict that M. Brunschvicg stresses between the immanent dynamism of biology and the transcendent dynamism of artificialism in the physics of Aristotle, may perhaps correspond, on an obviously lower reflective plane, to the dualism represented in the child by animism and artificialism—which in consequence must correspond to some very general tendency in the history of human thought : things are regarded on one hand as living and on the other as created. The questions now to be considered are whether this dualism in the child's thought is primitive or merely derived, whether it gives rise to contradiction or whether there is a stage which involves both animism and artificialism ?

But child artificialism is much too intricate a phenomenon—both in its manifestations and in the psychological components lying at its root—for it to be possible to give our research a systematic form. The course we are compelled to follow is analytic much more than synthetic, that is to say, that we shall study one after the other the explanations which children give as to the origins of the sun and moon, the sky, rivers, primitive matter, mountains, etc., rather than trace the different stages of artificialism throughout its history. The method we shall follow has, moreover, certain advantages in that it is not based on any prejudice concerning the homogeneity or above all the synchronism of the child's artificialist conceptions.

Further, we must make it clear that we shall deal here only with children's ideas concerning origins and take no account of ideas concerning the activity of things or the cause of their movements. These last questions will form the subject of the sequel to this work (see *Causalité Physique*).

Finally, we must offer Sully a well-earned tribute for having emphasised the existence and importance of child artificialism. According to him, "the one mode of origin which the embryo thinker is really and directly familiar with is the making of things." [1]

---

[1] See Sully, *Studies of Childhood*, pp. 79, 127.

CHAPTER VIII

THE ORIGIN OF THE SUN AND MOON

IT may seem strange to ask children where the sun and the moon and the stars come from. The idea of it did not occur to us for a long while, and when it did we hesitated to apply it for fear the children should think we were making fun of them. As a matter of fact, however, scarcely any question seems absurd to a child. To wonder where the sun comes from is no stranger to him than to speculate about rivers or clouds or smoke. This may suggest that the children, on their part, are trifling with the psychologists and that their replies have no significant correspondence with a real and spontaneous process of thought in their minds. That this is not the case, we think is borne out by the investigations which are now to be recounted and which it is claimed bear evidence of genuine spontaneity. Children's questions indicate a real interest on their part in the sun and the stars, and the very form in which they put the questions points to the nature of the solution which they themselves are inclined to favour. This point must be briefly examined for it is very important not to corrupt the child's natural tendencies by means of inept tests.

It is only necessary to glance through a list of questions put by children of from 3–5, to find examples like this : FRAN (2 ; 5) asks " *Who made the sun ?* " The very form of this question is artificialist. Stanley Hall quotes the following examples : At 5 years of age, " *Why is there a moon ?* " At 3½ years, " *What makes the sun shine ?* " and " *Who is it puts the stars in the sky at night ?* " At 5 years, " *Who is it makes the stars twinkle ?* "

Furthermore, a spontaneous interest in the phases of the moon is to be noticed which we shall see is related to artificialism. At 5 years: " *Why isn't the moon round now when it is sometimes ?* " At 9 years: " *Why isn't the moon always the same shape ? Why is it big sometimes and little at others ?* " and " *What's the moon made of ?* "

It is clear enough from these questions that there is a tendency to consider the sun and moon as being made by somebody and to find an originating cause for their activities. The same thing is apparent in the following instance :—

D'Estrella, one of the deaf-mutes quoted by W. James (Chapter VII, § 10), recounts how he thought that the sun was a ball of fire. At first he thought there were lots of suns, one for each day. He did not understand how they could rise or set. One evening he happened to see some boys who were throwing up and catching string balls which had been dipped in oil and lighted. This made him think of the sun and he decided that it must have been thrown up and caught in the same manner. But by whom ? Then he supposed that there must be a tremendously strong man hidden in some way behind the mountains (the town of San Francisco is surrounded by mountains). The sun was a ball of fire with which he played, throwing it up very high in the sky every morning and catching it again every evening. He supposed that God (*i.e.* the very strong man) lit the stars for his own use just as we light the gas.

When allowance had been made for the logical form which d'Estrella gives his recollections, they correspond in a striking degree to the replies which we are about to analyse. What, in short, we have to do is to make the questions we put to the children correspond to a certain extent with some of the spontaneous questions which they themselves ask. But if the results are to be convincing, we must do still more. We must establish in the replies given to our questions at different ages a continuous development and this development must itself follow a definitely marked curve or gradation. This is precisely what the facts do show.

It is, in fact, possible to distinguish in the development of conceptions relative to the origins of the sun and moon three stages more or less clearly marked. During the first, the child ascribes them to human agency (or divine, but we shall see that this amounts practically to the same thing). During the second stage an origin half natural, half artificial is propounded; they are due, for instance, to the condensation of the clouds, but the clouds themselves come from the roofs of houses or from the smoke which is produced by men. Finally, during the third stage, the child reaches the idea that human activity has nothing to do with the origin of the sun. The child invents a natural origin (condensation of the air, of the clouds, etc.) or, less frequently, refuses to speculate on the matter as being too difficult for him.

§ I. A PRIMITIVE EXAMPLE OF THE FIRST STAGE.—One of the most illuminating cases that we have obtained is that of Roy, in which certain primitive characteristics show well the original connection between animism and artificialism. We quote it almost in its entirety:—

Roy (6; 0): "How did the sun begin?—*It was when life began.*—Has there always been a sun?—*No.*—How did it begin?—*Because it knew that life had begun.*—What is it made of?—*Of fire.*—But how?—*Because there was fire up there.*—Where did the fire come from?—*From the sky.*—How was the fire made in the sky?—*It was lighted with a match.*—Where did it come from, this match? —*God threw it away.*" After a moment's pause: "What is life?—*It is when one is alive.*—What made life begin? —*We did, when we started living.*"

Then after another interval and in connection with the four quarters of the moon, Roy said: "*The moon has become a whole one.*—How?—*Because it's grown.*—How does the moon grow?—*Because it gets bigger.*—How does that come about?—*Because we get bigger* (Parce que nous on grandit).—What makes it get bigger?—*It's the clouds.* (Roy said a little earlier that it is the clouds which cut the moon and make it into a crescent: "*It is the clouds which have cut it.*")—What do they do?—*They help it to grow.*" "How did the moon begin?—*Because we began to be alive.*—What did that do?—*It made the moon get*

bigger.—Is the moon alive ?—*No . . . Yes.*—Why ?—
Because we are alive.—How was it made ?—*Because we
were made.*—And that makes the moon get bigger ?—*Yes.*
—How ? . . . Why ?—*It is the clouds that have made it
get bigger.*—Is the sun alive ?—*Yes.*—Why ?—*Because we
are alive.*—Does it know when it's day ?—*Yes.*—How ?
—*It can see that it's day.*"

Three weeks later we saw Roy again and made sure
that he had forgotten what we had previously talked
about. " How did the sun begin ?—*With fire.*—Where
did it come from ?—*From a match.*—How did the sun
get big ?—*Because we get big.*—Who makes the sun get
big ?—*The clouds.*—And we ?—*It's because we eat.*—Does
the sun eat ?—*No.*—How do the clouds make the sun
bigger ?—*Because the clouds get bigger too.*"[1] " And how
did the moon begin ?—*With fire too.*—How did it get
bigger ?—*Just like we get bigger.*—Why did it get bigger ?
—*Because the clouds made it get bigger.*—How ?—*Because
they get bigger too.*—If there were no clouds would the moon
get bigger then ?—*No . . . Yes. All the same it would be
able to, just like we do.*"

This case is worth studying closely, because it shows
extremely clearly how artificialism and animism arise
simultaneously out of the primitive participations that the
child establishes between things and man.

There are, in fact, three tendencies in Roy's thought :
(1) An artificialist tendency ; the sun and moon have
been made by man. Their origin lies in the flame of a
match. (2) An animist tendency ; the sun and the moon
are alive, they know when it is day-time, and what we are
doing, etc. (3) A tendency to establish participations
between them and ourselves ; they grow because we
grow, they began to live " because we were made "

---

[1] In order to understand Roy's statements it should be noted that
in other conversations Roy has said :—

(a) It is the clouds which make the wind and vice versa (Chap. IX, § 7,
and *Causalité Physique*, Chap. I).

(b) We are ourselves full of wind, which has at the same time something to do with the clouds ; it is this wind which makes us get
bigger (*Causalité Physique*, Chap. II).

(c) In its origin the wind has come from men : it is " *somebody who
blew* " (*Causalité Physique*, Chap. II).

One can distinguish here a system of participations.

("parce que nous, on s'est fait "), etc. Let us try to determine how far these three tendencies are primitive and what are the relations existing between them.

First of all, it is clear that the artificialist myth according to which the sun and moon come from the flame of a match, is not so primitive as the feelings of participation between the sun and moon and human beings ; it is the myth which is derived from these feelings and not the inverse. The myth is, in fact, more or less an effort of invention. Roy made up the myth when pressed to define the origins but his spontaneous thought was satisfied with a much vaguer relation between the sun and man. This relation amounted to no more than this, that man in coming to life thereby provoked the same sort of activity in the sun and moon. This does not constitute an idea that the sun was actually made by man, it simply indicates a participation between them and it was only when Roy was asked to define this participation more exactly that he had recourse to frank artificialism, that is to the myth of their origin in human construction.

The same is true with animism. In Roy's view the sun and moon "grow," they are conscious, alive, etc. But there are no grounds for supposing that this animism is prior to the feelings of participation Roy experiences ; the sun and moon grow because we grow, they are alive because we are alive, etc. The relations between animism and participation have been sufficiently discussed in earlier chapters and it is not necessary to return to them here. The notion of participation leads to that of animism and by nature precedes it, though animism may subsequently react on participation by confirming and consolidating it.

It seems then that the impressions of participation that Roy experiences are at the root of the other manifestations of his thought. But what are these participations ? To say that the moon grows bigger "because we get bigger," that it is alive "because we are alive," is to use formulæ which, in the first instance, express simple images or comparisons, without concern as to a causal

explanation. As far as Roy is concerned it is also a habit
of speech which he used to reply to other questions ; as
for example, the wind goes along " *because we go along,*"
and the sun does not try to go away " *because sometimes
we don't try to.*" But the study we have made of the
belief that the sun and moon follow our movements has
shown clearly enough (Chapter VII, § 2) that a heavenly
body which moves " when we move " moves as a result
of our movement. Still further, when Roy claims that
the moon came into being " because we began to live "
and that " that made the moon grow bigger," or again
when Roy affirms that even without the help of the clouds,
the moon would have grown because of us, it seems that
he has in view not merely analogy but genuine causality.
Analogy may enter into Roy's reasoning, but only inasmuch as analogy and causality are always confused by
children still in the stage of " precausality," that is to
say where the logical or the moral is confused with the
physical.

It may be that the impressions of participation to which
the question of the origins of the sun and moon give rise
are to be explained as follows. When Roy said that they
began to exist " when life began " and " because we
began to be alive " it seems that he might have been
thinking in more or less vague terms of the origin of
babies and that his ideas on the origin of things might be
a function of his ideas on the birth of human beings.
Roy, like many children, has perhaps begun to wonder
where babies come from, and from that to ask himself
questions as to the origins of things, with the implicit
tendency to relate the birth of things to that of men.
We shall see subsequently some examples of artificialist
interests originating and developing along these lines.
We must first inquire what are the ideas of children on
the origin of babies. Their first impression is of a connection between babies and parents : they feel that the
latter play an essential part in the arrival of the baby—
either that they have bought, found or otherwise obtained

it. Finally, they invent an explanation for their conviction, namely, that the parents have made it. In this
case the feeling of a connection precedes the myth and
actually gives rise to it.

Whatever may be thought of this particular proposition,
whose accuracy may be judged by what follows, we can
understand the true relations existing between Roy's
feelings of participation, animism and artificialism ; the
foundation of them is in the feelings of participation, and
it is when the child seeks to systematise these feelings
that he has recourse to animistic and artificialist myths.

Thus, on the one hand, Roy, when urged to define
the contents of his participations which seem to partake
of the character both of analogy and of causality, fell back
on animist explanations. For example, speaking of the
clouds, he replied :—

" Can we make the clouds grow bigger ?—*No.*—Why
do they grow bigger ?—*Because we grow bigger* (Roy
admits thus what he has just denied).—Why do you
grow bigger.?—*Because I eat.*—Does that make the clouds
bigger too ?—*No, they grow because they know that we do."*
And after a moment : " How did the clouds start ?—
Because we were growing.—Is it we who make them grow
bigger ?—*No, it isn't us, but the clouds know we are growing."*

In other words, the universe is a society of like beings
living according to a well-ordered code of rules ; every
analogy is at the same time a logical relationship since
analogy signifies common or interacting purposes and
every purpose is a cause. One even feels that, for Roy,
the members of this universe necessarily imitate each
other so that when we grow the moon and the clouds
are forced to follow suit. Clearly, when Roy is made to
define his ideas his participations develop into animistic
explanations.

But, on the other hand, in this universe consisting of a
society of living beings, Roy gives the first place to man
(or alternatively to God, which amounts to the same
since he conceives God as a " gentleman " who lights

matches and throws them away).   The sun, moon, clouds, etc., were brought into being by the appearance of man. It is man's growth which stimulates growth in things, etc.   Here actually lies the difference between participations of the artificialist type and those of the animist type.   Though they are different they are not contradictory but complementary.   Artificialism is then, in its simplest form, the tendency to believe that human beings control the creation and conduct of other beings which are regarded as being in some degree alive and conscious. But here, as in animism, when the child is invited to be precise, he invents a myth.   In the case of artificialism the myth consists of a fiction whereby man has created matter.   The myth of the match in which the sun originates, marks a pronounced stage in artificialism, inasmuch as Roy now provides the details of the process of creation whereas hitherto he has limited himself to the simple conviction that such a process existed.   But, from the very outset, artificialism is mingled with the feelings of participation which the child experiences, not so much between his self and things, but rather, between his parents or adults in general and the world of matter.

To conclude, Roy's artificialism comes, like his animism, from his feelings of participation and without any contradiction with animism.   They are, considered separately, two complementary systematisations of the same feelings of participation.

§ 2. The First Stage : the Sun and Moon are made Artificially.—Roy's case has led us to certain hypotheses which will serve as the main thread in our research. In the following more developed cases the artificialist myths stand out more clearly from the primitive participations.

Purr (8 ; 8) : " What is a crescent (croissant de lune) ? —*The moon has cut itself up.*—How ?   Does it cut itself up or is it something else that does it ?—*It is the moon that does it.*—On purpose ?—*No, it is when it is born, it is quite small.*—Why ?—*It can't be big at first.   It's like us*

when we are little babies. It does just the same.—When
there's a crescent is it always the same moon?—*Sometimes it's the same, sometimes it's another.*—How many
are there?—*Lots. So many that you can't count them.
The moon is of fire too.*—Why is it cut up?—*So as to be
able to shine in more than one place.* . . . (= it cuts itself
up in order to shine at the same time in different places).
Where does it come from?—*From the sky.*—How did it
begin?—*It came from Heaven. It was born from God* (!)
—And the sun.—*It was born from God too.*

JACOT (6½) believes that the sun is of fire : " How did
it begin?—*It was quite tiny.*—Where does it come from?
—*From Heaven.*—How did it begin in the sky?—*Always
getting bigger.*" Jacot says that the sun is alive and
conscious. It has grown like a living thing. It was made
by human beings.

GAUD (6 ; 8) : " What is the moon like?—*Round.
Sometimes there is only half of it.*—Why is there only half
of it?—*Because that is how it starts.*—Why?—*Because
there is a lot of daylight* (he means that the moon remains
small during the day and only grows at night).—Where
is the other half?—*That's because it's not finished, not
absolutely finished.*—What does it make itself like?—
Round.—How does it begin?—*Quite small ; then it keeps
on getting bigger.*—Where does it come from?—*From
Heaven.*—How does it make itself?—*Quite tiny.*—Does
it make itself all alone?—*No, God does it.*—How?—
With his hands." Gaud adds that the moon is alive and
conscious. It deliberately follows us about, etc. The
sun is equally alive and has been made.

MOC (10 ; 2, backward) is a very curious case because
of his affective reactions. He says about the sun : " *It
used to be quite small, then it got big.*" He assigns life and
consciousness to it. But to the question " where does
it come from? " he is seized with embarrassment, blushes
violently, turns his head away, and finally, in great
discomfort says that the sun comes from " *the person
who has made it come.*—What do you mean?—*From the
person who made it.*—Who was he? A man?—*Yes.*—
Was it really a man or was it God?—*Oh ! God or a
man, or someone.*" The cause for this embarrassment is
certainly not to be found in the difficulty of the problem
for it was clear that Moc had a solution in his mind but
it was one which he shrank from confessing. It was no
sort of religious compunction, for during the whole con-

versation Moc was, without systematic preference, ready to regard God or " man " indifferently as the author of any particular phenomenon. The only explanation of his embarrassment is that he is upset when he is spoken to about birth. He must have been told that everything to do with birth is taboo and the questions concerning the sun seemed to him of a shocking nature. For this reason it was not possible to proceed further with his examination. Such a case shows how intimately animism and artificialism may be connected.

In the foregoing cases one can see that the children identify the advent of the sun and moon with the birth of a living being it being granted, naturally, that the child conceives such a birth as a sort of manufacture whose process is not precisely understood but which is in essence the construction of something living. In any case, the children whose replies are recorded above speak of the growth of the heavenly bodies, as if the sun and moon began by being tiny like babies.

The following children, on the contrary, try to define the manner in which the manufacture took place though sometimes this manufacture is still identified with a birth. Also, as we shall see, the children continue to consider the sun and the moon as being alive and conscious ; animistic and artificialist tendencies are still complementary to each other :—

CAUD (9 ; 4) : " How did the sun start ?—*With heat.*—What heat ?—*From the fire.*—Where is the fire ?—*In Heaven.*—How did it start ?—*God lit it with wood and coal.*—Where did he get the wood and coal ?—*He made it.* —How did the fire make the sun ?—*The fire is the sun.*" Up to now it seems that Caud is no longer animistic but this is not so : " Does the sun see us ?—*No.*—Does it feel the heat ?—*Yes.*—Does it see at night ?—*No.*—Does it see in the day ?—*Yes, of course ! It sees because it makes the light for itself.*"

FRAN (9) : " How did the sun begin ?—*It was a big ball.*—How did it begin ?—*By getting bigger and bigger and then afterwards they told it to go up in the air. It is like a balloon.*—Where did this ball come from ?—*I think it is a great stone. I believe it is made of a great ball of it.*—Are you sure of all that ?—*Yes, sure.*—How did it get made ? —*They made it into a big ball.*—Who did ?—*Some men."* At the same time Fran thinks that the sun sees us and deliberately follows us. On the other hand, the identification of the sun with a stone is not contradictory with the assertion that the sun has grown, for we shall see that a great number of children believe that stones grow in the earth. Here again are artificialism and animism closely related.

As to the moon, Fran, like many other children, believes that it is the same object as the sun but that on account of the night it loses its brightness : the moon " *is the sun. But when it is dark there can't be any sunshine."* It is true that the moon is bigger. But that is " *because it has to brighten up the darkness. It has to be bigger because very often people come home in the dark and then the sun* (= the moon) *shines."*

DEB (9) : " How did the sun start ?—*With matches.*— How did that make the sun ?—*From the flames.*—Where did the matches come from ?—*From home."* None the less he believes the sun to be living and conscious.

GALL (5) was born in 1918, which perhaps has some bearings on his cosmogony : " Where did the sun come from ?—*It came in the war.*—How did it begin ?—*When the war ended.*—Has there always been a sun ?—*No.*— How did it begin ?—*A little ball came.*—And then ?—*It grew big.*—Where did this little ball come from ?—*From the fire."*

Here is a case which is intermediate between the last cases and those of the second stage in the sense that the child begins to perceive the possibility that the sun and moon may have come from the clouds. But, in particular aspects, the idea becomes swamped by considerations like those in the preceding cases :—

HUB (6½) : " Has the sun always been there ?—*No, it began.*—How ?—*With fire. . . .*—How did that start ?— *With a match.*—How ?—*It was lighted.*—How did that happen ?—*By striking the match.*—Who struck it ?—*A man.*—What was his name ?—*I don't know."* The moon was made " *in Heaven* " that is to say " *in the clouds.*— How were the clouds able to make the moon ?—*Because it is lighted.*—What is ?—*The cloud.*—How ?—*With fire.* —Where does this fire come from ?—*From the match."*

" What lit it ?—*A bit of stick with a red thing at the end.*"
Hub is thinking here of the rockets sold on gala nights ;
the moon for him is a cloud set alight by rockets fired
off by people.   The origin of the clouds also is artificial :
" Where do the clouds come from ?—*From the sky.*—
How did they start ?—*In smoke.*—Where does the smoke
come from ?—*From stoves.*—Does smoke make the moons
then ?—*Yes.*"

As regards the stars, the explanations given in the
first stage are the same as those we have just met with in
regard to the sun and moon.

JAC (6½) supposes that the stars are on fire and that
they are made by people.

GIAMB (8½).   The stars are to show what the weather
will be like : " *If there are stars it is going to be fine ;
when there are none it is going to rain.*"   They are " *made
of light.*—Where does this light come from ?—*It is the
lamp-posts outside which light them up, which makes them
come.*"   " How did they start ?—*A man made them.*—Do
they know that they are shining ?—*Yes.*"

FRAN (9) : " *People took little stones and made them into
little stars.* "

GRANG (7½) : What are the stars ?—*Round things.*—
Made of what ?—*Made of fire.*"   It is God who made
them.

The reason for this artificialism lies evidently in the
finalistic attitude which makes all children believe that
the function of the stars is to indicate the weather.   They
serve " *to show if it will be fine to-morrow* " (Caud, 9 ; 4).
" What are the stars ?—*They are to show if the next day
will be fine* " (Cercs, 9).

It is not necessary to multiply examples.   Let us
examine briefly the significance of these facts before
describing the second and third stages.   It is clear that
the detail, that is, the variation between one child and
another can be regarded as romancing.   But the central
idea, that is the belief that the stars are made by man
must be considered as a spontaneous mental impulse on
the part of the child.   For all that, there are two questions
to be asked in connection with the homogeneity of this
first stage.

In the first place, the existence of two groups of children has been observed, namely, those who speak of the " birth " of the sun, without defining the manner of this birth and those who describe with some measure of precision the way in which the sun is made. It would appear that this constitutes two stages. But, on the one hand, there seems to be no dividing line of age between these two groups and, on the other, the children of both groups maintain that the sun and the moon are living and conscious. From the evidence in hand one is justified only in seeing two types of replies characteristic of the one stage and having really the same meaning, it being remembered that the manufacture of the sun with a match or a stone or with smoke is by no means incompatible with the conception which children of this age have of the birth of a living being. Unfortunately, we can only put this forward as an hypothesis without directly verifying it on our children, since it would be most indiscreet and dangerous from the pedagogical standpoint to question these children on the problem of the birth of human beings or even of animals.

A second question may be raised. Sometimes the children attribute the making of the planets to the God of their catechism and sometimes simply to " a man." Does this mean two types or two stages ? We shall see later, when we come to discuss the ideas of M. Bovet on the genesis of religious feeling, that on broad lines one can distinguish the following evolution. The child begins by attributing the distinctive qualities of the divinity— especially omniscience and almightiness—to his parents and thence to men in general. Then, as he discovers the limits of human capacity, he transfers to God, of whom he learns in his religious instruction, the qualities which he learns to deny to men. On broad lines, then, there should be two periods, one of human artificialism and the other of divine artificialism. However, we do not believe that this distinction is a useful one at this juncture and particularly in connection with this question of the origin of the planets. The fact is that too many adult influences supervene likely to upset the spontaneous conceptions of the child and a gradation corresponding clearly to a definite age is not observable.

This last circumstance raises a very serious difficulty, on the solution of which the whole question of child artificialism turns.   Is this artificialism spontaneous or are the child's conception of the origins of things to be attributed to its religious training ?

As far as those phenomena are concerned which we shall study shortly (origins of clouds, rivers, mountains, stones, etc.) the question hardly arises or, at all events, takes another form, for we shall see a native artificialism in play of a kind so evidently spontaneous that the influence of religious instruction clearly counts for little. But where the sun and the moon and the stars are concerned a strong influence may be at work [1] since the planets are much nearer in association to a God living in Heaven than are the material objects located on the earth. But, in our opinion, religious instruction has influenced only a section of the children under our observation and even among those whose artificialism is thus qualified it is limited to intensifying a tendency towards artificialism already pre-existing in the child and not created by it.

On the one hand, our statistics indicate that children of the first stage attribute the making of the planets to man as often as to God. One might comment on this that the religious instruction may have been miscomprehended, that the child has transferred to men that which was averred of God, or that imagination, stirred by teaching, has added to the data. One finds, however, that before any religious teaching has taken place, artificialist questions are being framed by children of 2 to 3 years old. '' Who made the sun ? '' asked Fran at 2 years 9 months. Furthermore, if religious teaching is to be held responsible for the artificialism of children of four to six years of age, it will be agreed that in order to account for the deforma-

[1] See *Genesis* i. 14-18.

tion which has been observed there must be a powerful natural inclination in the child to refer the making of material objects to man. The idea of the " birth " and the growing up of the planets, the belief that the four quarters of the moon are made afresh with each new moon or that they result from some artificial dissection of the moon, the notions concerning matches, flaming stones, rockets which set fire to clouds, etc., are so clearly manifestations of this tendency that they must surely be recognised as spontaneous. Finally, the facts quoted by W. James—notably the recollections of infancy of the deaf-mute, d'Estrella—indicate sufficiently that spontaneous artificialism can exist in the child.

On the other hand, even where we can trace distinctly the influences of religious teaching we can see that it is not positively accepted by the child but is assimilated in an original form. This being the case, there must have pre-existed a spontaneous tendency towards artificialism which is the sole explanation of the distortion which the teaching undergoes. The following is a good example of artificialist belief stimulated by religious teaching, but in which the information imparted to the child has been seriously disfigured by his own contribution to it :—

GAVA (8½) : The sun is alive because " *it keeps coming back.*—Does it know when the weather is fine ?—*Yes, because it can see it.*—Has it eyes ?—*Of course ! When it gets up it looks to see if it is bad weather and if it is it goes off somewhere else where it's fine.*—Does it know that it's called the sun ?—*Yes, it knows that we like it. It is very nice of it to make us warm.*—Does it know its name ?— *I don't know. But sometimes it must hear us talking and then it will hear names and then it will know.*" All this seems to be pure romancing, but as we shall see Gava almost identifies the sun with God : " When your daddy was little was there a sun then ?—*Yes, because the sun was born before people so that people would be able to live.*— How did it start ?—*It was made in Heaven. It was a person who died and then went to Heaven. In Sunday School he is called God.*—Where did this person come from ?—*From inside the earth.*—Where from ?—*I don't know how he was made.*—How did that make the sun ?—*The person was very red and that made the light. Even in the morning before the sun is out, it is light all the same."* In other words this person (Jesus Christ) has set fire to Heaven and this light made the sun. Gava is thinking probably of Christ's halo. He went on to tell us of a picture in which God was like the sun but with arms and legs ! " What is the sun made of ?—*It's a big red ball.*—Made of what ?—*Of cloud . . . I don't know.*—Did it start a long while ago ?—*Since there have been people.*—Not before ?—*No, because there wouldn't have been anything to light.*—Did it start at the same time as people or after ?—*It started as soon as there were little children.*—Why ?—*So that children should have the fresh air.*—If you were to speak to the sun would it hear ?—*Yes, when you say your prayers.*—Do you say your prayers to it ?—*Yes.*—Who told you to do that ?—*At Sunday School I was told always to say my prayers to it."*

This remarkable example throws light on the three following cases :—

Kuf (10 ; 1) said that the sun moves because something pushes it. " Is it in it or outside, this something ?—*Inside.*—What is it ?—*It is God."*

One of our research workers remembers clearly having associated God with the sun for some years, either believing that God lived in or behind the sun, or else conceiving them as participating one with another. Every time she said her prayers in the evening she thought of the sun and in particular of the gap between two of the peaks in the Bernese Alps which were visible from her room and in which the sun used to set in winter.

One of our collaborators remembers taking a walk with his father in the course of which they watched the sun setting. The father observed that it was only through the sun that we were all able to live. The child had a sudden revelation that the sun was something to do with God. He decided finally that though his father did not go to Church, etc., it was because he worshipped the sun or was bound to the sun by ties of reverence more strongly than he was to God.

Such facts are very instructive. They reveal first of all how far adult instruction can be disfigured by the personal manner in which the child assimilates it, and, furthermore, they reveal what are the laws of this assimilation. There are, in fact, three tendencies at the roots of these disfigurations and these three tendencies are complementary. The first is the tendency to consider the planets as participating with mankind and with his will. As examples of participations with human will, or active participations, Gava considers the sun to originate in the need of human beings for light or perhaps in the need for providing fresh air for little children, and our collaborator, mentioned above, considered the sun and his father as being bound together very closely by bonds of submission, commandment or protection. As examples of more material participations there are the three children already quoted who considered the sun as being more or less identical with God, whilst at the same time differing from him, as in the case of the deaf-mute quoted by James, who identified the moon with his own mother. (Chapter III, § 15.) These participations expand, in the first place, into artificialist myths. For example, Gava thinks the sun has come from Christ's halo. Later they expand into animism—as that the sun is living, conscious, and endowed with will. In short, religious instruction is not received passively by the child but is disfigured and assimilated in conformity with three tendencies existing prior to this instruction. These latter are, precisely, the tendency to invent participations, the tendency towards artificialism and the tendency towards animism, whose significance has already been studied.

We may thus conclude our analysis of the first stage by saying that the integral artificialism indicated therein is fundamentally spontaneous, though in certain cases it may be influenced by the education imparted by adults as far as concerns the detail of the child's conceptions. In neither case, however, is there contradiction between this artificialism and animism.

§ 3. THE SECOND AND THE THIRD STAGES: THE ORIGIN OF THE SUN AND MOON IS FIRST PARTLY, THEN COMPLETELY, NATURAL.—The best proofs of the spontaneous nature of the child's artificialist conceptions is their continuity and the gradual manner in which they disappear. Children of 10 to 11 years arrive independently at the idea that the planets have a natural origin, and between this third stage and the first there exists a series of intermediate cases.

The intermediary cases constitute the second stage, the children who belong to this stage attributing to the planets an origin that is half artificial and half natural. In the majority of cases (that is to say, where the beliefs are spontaneous) the planets are held to have been made by a natural process but from substances of artificial origin. Thus, for example, the planets have come naturally from the clouds, but the clouds are made of the smoke from chimneys. In other cases, more or less influenced by adult instruction, planets are said to be the fire of volcanoes or mines, mankind having played some part in their formation. We may commence with these latter explanations which are the least interesting since adult instruction has played some part, even if only indirectly, in their formation.

FONT (6 ; 9) says that the sun is conscious, it is made of fire and it comes " *from the mountain.—Where* from ?— *From the mines.—What* is it ?—*People go looking for coal in the ground.*" As to the moon : " *It was made by the sun.* —How ?—*With the fire from the mountain.—Where* does the moon come from ?—*From the mountain.—What* was there in the mountain ?—*The sun*—Where does the sun come from ?—*From the mountain.—How* did it begin ? —*With fire.*—And how did this fire begin ?—*With matches.* —And how did the mountain begin ?—*With the earth* . . . *It was people who made it.*"

Font illustrated his statement by a drawing showing half a moon coming out of a mountain.

MARSAL (mentally deficient) said: " *I thought perhaps that the sun came out of volcanoes. When they were in eruption it made a ball of fire.*" The original thing about Marsal is that he believed that human help was necessary to send the sun up in the air. It was " our ancestors " who threw the sun up in the air " like a balloon."

The principle of these explanations is quite clear. The child starts with two observed facts, namely, that the planets come from behind the mountain and that they are like fire. The synthesis of making the fire come from the mountain follows. If he has been taught about them the child will think of coal-mines or of volcanoes. He adds to this (and it is here that these examples show themselves to be of the second stage, and not of the third) the idea that men have played a necessary part in the genesis of the planets. It is men who have made the mine or who have sent the sun into the air.

Here are some examples of a type of reply, that is both more ordinary and more interesting, for the influence of instruction is not yet felt :—

GIAMB (8½) is still in the first stage as far as the stars are concerned, but already in the second as far as the sun and the moon are concerned : " How did the sun begin ?—*It was a big cloud that made it.*—Where did this cloud come from ?—*From the smoke.*—And where did the smoke come from ?—*From houses.*—How did this cloud make the sun ?—*They stuck to each other until they became round.*—Are the clouds making the sun now ?—*No, because it's already made.*—How did the clouds make the sun shine ?—*It's a light which makes it shine.*—What light ? —*A big light, it is someone in Heaven who has set fire to it.*" It can be seen how Giamb invokes an artificialist myth as soon as he is embarrassed. What follows will show that he is ready to replace this myth by an explanation according to which the smoke flamed up in order to light the sun. " What is the sun made of ?—*Of stone.*—And the clouds ?—*They are made of stone as well.* —Why doesn't the stone fall down ?—*No, it's the smoke from houses.*—Then the sun is made of stone and smoke at the same time ?—*No, nothing but smoke.*" (One feels that Giamb holds to these two explanations at the same time ; he is about to abandon the one according to which the sun is a stone which somebody has set fire to, and he is on the point of adopting definitely the other according to which the sun is a cloud of flaming smoke.) " How do the clouds make the sun burn ?—*It's the smoke which makes it burn because there is fire in the smoke.*" The sun is conscious and deliberately follows us about. (See

Giamb's case—Chapter VII, § 11.) After an interval he was asked: "What is the moon like?—*Yellow.*—What is it made of?—*Of cloud.*—Where does this cloud come from?—*From the smoke when it gets yellow.*—Where does this smoke come from?—*From the stove, sometimes when it is cold the smoke becomes yellow.*" (This is true that in winter smoke has a yellow-greenish tint.) "How does the smoke make the moon?—*The chimney smokes and it is sometimes yellow, sometimes white.*"

GAVA (8½), who is in the first stage as far as the sun is concerned, belongs to the second stage for his explanation of the quarters of the moon: "*It was made by the air.*—How was that?—*Perhaps it was clouds which had not melted away and then they made a big round thing.*" The air and the clouds are practically the same thing for Gava. A few months later he was asked: "What is the moon made of?—*Perhaps it is clouds, the clouds were small and then they were squeezed together and that made a ball.*—Has there been a moon for a long while? —*Since things began living*" (*cp.* Roy, see § 1). "How did the moon begin?—*First of all it was quite tiny then it grew, it's other clouds which have come.*—Where did they come from?—*It was the steam which went up into the sky when things were being cooked.*—Is the moon alive?—*It must be because it comes back every evening.*"

BRUL (8½): "What is the sun made of?—*Of clouds.* —How did it begin?—*It began by being a ball.*—Where did this ball come from?—*From the clouds.*—What are the clouds made of?—*Of smoke.*—Where does this smoke come from?—*From the houses.*"

LUG (12 ; 3): "How did the sun start?—*It started with fire.*—What fire?—*From the fire in the stove.*—What is there in the stove?—*Smoke.*—Well, how did it happen? —*The smoke went up and then it began, it caught fire.*— Why did it catch fire?—*Because it was very warm.*" When asked if he were sure of all this, he replied: "*Not quite.*—What is the sun?—*A great ball of fire.*—How did it begin?—(After long reflection) *With smoke.*—What smoke?—*From houses.*" He gave the same explanation for the moon.

These explanations are very interesting because of their spontaneous characters, they start from true observation, that is, that the moon by day when it is white and spotted with shadows looks like a little cloud. The resemblance is particularly striking when one only sees a half-moon, that is, when according to a child, the moon is in the act of making itself. Since children of this stage (8 to 9 years on an average) assert that clouds come from smoke, the origin of the sun and moon seems quite clear to them.

As to stars, children of this stage explain them in the same manner or else they suppose them to have come from the sun or the moon as do children of the third stage.

Between the second and the third stage, there is a complete continuity. If that part of the explanation be cancelled according to which the clouds are said to issue from the chimneys, an entirely natural explanation of the origin of the sun and moon is left, and it is this explanation which is given in the third stage. This we find, on the average, after the ages of 9–11, though sometimes earlier. Here are some typical examples. The sun and moon have come from the clouds and the clouds themselves are compressed air or steam:—

Not (10 ; 0): "What is the sun made of?—*Of flames.*—Where do these flames come from?—*From the sun.*—How did they begin, did something make them? —*They made themselves.*—How?—*Because it was warm.*— How did they begin?—*The sun was made of flames of fire.* —How?—*Because it was warm.*—Where?—*In the sky.*— Why was it warm?—*It was the air.*" The sun then is the product of incandescent air, and according to Not, the moon is also made of air.

Re (8½): " How did the sun begin?—*It came.*—How? —*Because it moved.*—Where did it come from?—*From the Jura.*—What is the sun made of?—*There are, lots of little clouds.*—What are clouds made of?—*They are all squeezed together.*—Where did these clouds come from when the sun began?—*From the sky.*—What are the clouds?—*It's when there are lots of red things* (the little red sunset clouds).—Where?—*On the Jura.*" Re claims to have seen these clouds in the evening, and it is true that from Geneva one sees the sunset over the Jura. As to the moon: " How did it begin?—*In a round thing.*— A round thing made of what?—*Of little red clouds.*—Where did the clouds come from?—*From the Jura.*—And before that?—*From the mountain.*" Re does not think that the clouds have anything to do with smoke. They made themselves alone in the sky which itself is made " *of blue clouds.*" He regards the sun and moon as both living and conscious in spite of the quite natural manner of their formation.

CHAL (9 ; 5) : " How did the sun begin ?—(Thoughtfully) *First it was small, then it got big.*—Where did this little sun come from ?—*It must have been made by the clouds.*—What is the sun made of ?—*Of air.*" As to the clouds they also come from the air.

AUD (9 ; 8) : " What is the sun made of ?—*Of clouds.*— How did the sun begin ?—*To begin with, it was a ball and then it caught fire.*" The clouds from which the sun was born also came from the sky, the sun is, therefore, " *a cloud from the sky.*"

ANT (8½) : " How did the moon begin ?—*The stars ran into each other, and that made the moon.*—And where do the stars come from ?—*They are flames which have always been there from the beginning.*"

GERV (11) : " *The sun and the moon are the same thing, when the sun sets it makes the moon which shines during the night.*" The moon seems to Gerv bigger than the sun : " *When the sun sets I've seen it get much bigger* (in order to change itself into the moon).'' Gerv was asked if he had never seen the sun and the moon together during the day, he said he had, but that it was an illusion. What seems to be the moon is just a white shape, and is only the reflection of the sun on the sky. As to the origin of the sun, Gerv said : " *The moon* (= the sun) *is made of rays of light heaped up together and that makes the moon. Sometimes it's big, sometimes it's small, according to the month. It must be made of fire.*"

All these cases reveal a remarkable effort to explain the sun and moon in terms of atmospheric condensation or of clouds, and by the spontaneous combustion of these condensed bodies. Making allowance for circumstances, one can see the likeness between these conceptions and the theories of the pre-Socratic thinkers.

The foregoing cases seem to embrace only information that has been observed and acquired entirely by the child. The following cases, on the other hand, embody information due to contact with adults :—

Mart and Schm have learned that electricity is " a current," and that there is electricity in clouds.

Jean, Ant, etc., have learned that there was fire in the earth and that this fire finds its way out through volcanoes, etc. These children draw from such knowledge their explanations of the origin of the sun and moon, which are consequently partly and indirectly influenced by adults. They must be quoted for they contain elements of original reflection which are of the same type as the explanation in terms of atmospheric condensation and of clouds.

MART (9 ; 5) : " How did the sun begin ?—*I don't know, it's not possible to say.*—You are right there, but we can guess. Has there always been a sun ?—*No. It's the electricity which has always been growing more and more.*— Where does this electricity come from ?—*From under the earth, from water.*—What is electricity ?—*It's the current.*" " Can a current of water make electricity ?—*Yes.*—What is this current made of ?—*It's made of steam.*" (Steam, electricity and current seem to him to be all the same thing.) " How did the electricity make the sun ?—*It is current which has escaped.*—How has it grown ?—*It's the air which has stretched, the electricity has been made bigger by the air.*"

SCHM (8 ; 8) : " How did the sun begin ?—*With fire, it's a ball of fire which gives light.*—Where does the fire come from ?—*From the clouds.*—How does that happen ? —*It's electricity in the clouds.*—Do you think that somebody made the sun ?—*No, it came all alone.*" The sun is alive and conscious.

It will be seen that these cases, apart from the language used are very similar to the preceding ones : for Mart, the sun is burning air, and for Schm it is a glowing cloud.

Two cases follow in which the sun is said to have come out of volcanoes or out of the earth :—

JEAN (8 ; 6) : " How did the sun begin ?—*In a ball of fire.*—Where did it come from ?—*From the earth.*—How did that happen ?—*It went up in steam.*—Where did it come from ?—*Out of the ground.*"

ANT (8½) : " *It* (the sun) *came out of the earth.—*

How did that happen ?—*A flame came out of the earth and that made the sun.*—Are there flames in the earth ?—*Yes.*—Where are they ?—*In volcanoes.*"

In these cases acquired knowledge has been used, but in an original way which at all events shows the tendency of children of this stage to explain the origin of the sun and moon in an entirely natural process.

Let us now pass to explanations of the origin of the stars. Children of the third stage in thinking of the stars instinctively seek similar natural explanations, as a result the stars are said to be emanations of the moon or of lightning, etc.

TACC (9 ; 7) : " What are the stars ?—*They are made of fire.*—How does that happen ?—*They are little sparks which have collected together and made a star.*" These sparks come from a fire in the sky, and the fire " came all by itself."

DEB (9 ; 0) : " What are the stars ?—*Little bits of lightning.*—What is lightning ?—*It comes when there is thunder.*—What makes the lightning ?—*When two clouds meet each other.*"

STOECK (11 ; 0) : " How did the stars begin ?—*With the sun.*"

MARC (9 ; 5) : " Where did the stars come from ?—*From the sun.*"

Of course, a child is not necessarily in the third stage at the same time for the stars, the sun and the moon. In general, it seems that a natural explanation of the stars is the first to appear.

Observation seems to show that the more advanced children are, the less easily they formulate a hypothesis on the origin of the sun and moon. It is only for the little ones that everything is quite simple. Between 11 and 12, a child very often replies " It isn't possible to say," or " I have no idea," etc. Artificialism, even when it has become immanent, as in the third stage where constructive activity is withdrawn from man to be attributed to nature itself, leads thus to a crisis and a tentative agnosticism succeeds an over-audacious cosmogony.

It should be observed that up to the end animism is

intimately connected with artificialism. Children of the third stage are very interesting in this respect. About half of them are no longer animistic at all whereas more than three-quarters of the children of the second stage were still so. Natural explanations have destroyed their belief in the consciousness of the planets. As to the other half of the children they remain animistic but their animism is in some degree submerged. The planets are no longer concerned with us, they no longer follow us, etc., but they remain conscious of their own movements. Finally, in certain cases, one can see the disappearance of an animism which is explicitly bound up with artificialism.

BOUCH (11; 10), for example, is a sceptical child who complains of having been deceived by grown-ups: " They have stuffed me up with stories," he kept on saying, and he is particularly careful as to what he himself admits. He was asked if the sun knew that it went forward, he replied, " *If there is a God, the sun knows it, but if there isn't, it doesn't.*"

This reply is very curious and shows well enough that the consciousness with which things are endowed is part of the belief in a general system. If God controls things they are conscious, otherwise they are acting mechanically.

§ 4. THE QUARTERS OF THE MOON.—It is best to consider separately this problem of the phases of the moon on which we have already touched in dealing with the origin of the sun and moon. It will serve moreover as a control in showing us if the children's explanations correspond by age with the gradations that we have already established. There is no particular reason why it should, and we can consider this new problem as partly independent of the preceding one, that is to say as constituting a genuine control.

In actual fact, three stages emerge analogous to those already established, they are integral artificialism, qualified artificialism, and natural explanation.

During the first stage, the phases of the moon are regarded as being either moons which have been born or moons which have been cut up by people. These are two forms of integral artificialism.

The cases of Roy (6 years), of Gaud (6½ years), and of Purr (8; 8 years) (see §§ 1 and 2) may be recalled first. In these the quarters of the moon were said to be moons which were beginning, that is which had just been made and which were growing just like babies. It [is not necessary to return to these cases.

As to the belief according to which the quarters are moons which have been cut up by people, here are three examples :—

FRAN (9; 0): " What is the moon like ?—*Quite round.—Always ?—No, sometimes it's only a half.—*Why only a half ?—*Because sometimes it has been cut.—*Do you really believe that ?—*Yes I do.—*Why has it been cut ?— *So that it should look prettier.—*Who cut it ?—*People.—* Can the moon come round again ?—*No, afterwards they go and look for the other half of the moon and then they make it whole again.*"

BUL (7½): " *It was cut up by people to make half a moon.*" DOU (5 ; 0) : " *It must have been cut in two.*"

As to the second stage, it shows a mixture of artificialism and natural explanation :—

HUB (6½) : " Is the moon always round ?—*No.—* What's it like ?—*Sometimes a crescent, it is very worn out. —*Why ?—*Because it has done a lot of lighting.—*How does it come round again ?—*Because it is made again.—* How ?—*In the sky.*"

CAUD (9 ; 4) : " Does the moon see you ?—*Yes, some days it is round and sometimes it's only half or quarter.—* Why ?—*God makes it round or half in order to count the days* (notice the way in which the child has disfigured an explanation which obviously was presented quite otherwise).—It has been cut ?—*No, it makes itself round and then afterwards in half.*"

In both cases a union may be seen, which is in no way contradictory in a child, of a natural process which involves being worn out or cut up, and of a controlling or a constructive action which is of a quite human order. In the third stage, this second fact is eliminated and an entirely natural explanation is sought for the phenomenon. This explanation presents itself in two forms, characteristic of two successive sub-stages. At first the moon is regarded as having cut itself in pieces or having been cut up by the wind by a process of dynamism in which are united an artificialism and an animism which have become entirely immanent :—

MART (9 ; 5) : " Why is the moon in quarters ?—*There is only half, the wind has cut it into pieces.*—Why ?—*I don't know.*—Where is the other half ?—*Fallen on the ground.*—Can you see it ?—*No, it makes the rain* (the moon being a cloud there is nothing strange in the fact that it turns into rain).—Is it the same moon which comes round again or is it another ?—*It's the same, it gets big again.*— How ?—*The wind makes it get big again.*"

ACK (8 ; 7) : " *Sometimes there is a full moon, sometimes quarters.*—How does that happen ?—*It divides itself up all alone.*—And then what happens to the rest of the moon ? —*It is hidden by the clouds.*—And when there are no clouds? —*It is hidden in heaven by God.*—Why does it divide itself up ?—*Because it wants to make the weather bad, and when there is a full moon it wants to make good weather.*"

RE (8 ; 0) : " How are the quarters of the moon made ?—*There is nothing but a little bit left of it.*—Where is the rest ?—*On the Jura.*—How does that happen ?— *It gets broken.*—How ?—*It gets unstuck.*—Does it get unstuck by itself, or is there someone who does it ?—*By itself.*—How does it grow again afterwards ?—*It comes together again.*—How ?—*It joins up with the other piece.*— Does it know that it wants to join up with the other piece ?—*Yes.*—Why is it not always round ?—*Because it makes itself small.*—Why ?—*Because it doesn't keep itself big all the time.*—Why ?—*Because it is cold after it rains.*"

NOT (10 ; 0) : " *Half of it goes to one side, and the other to the other side.*—Why ?—*To show what weather it is going to be.*—How does that happen ?—*Because it gets warmer, it means that it will be good weather or bad weather.*" The moon thus acts of its own accord and consciously.

These cases are interesting in several respects. It is clear that they are influenced by adult suggestions, in particular where the child knows that the quarters of the moon show what the weather is going to be. But these adult suggestions have been assimilated in an original manner, and two curious reactions may be noted. First, the confusion between the sign and the cause, the moon both causes the weather and foretells it, causing it because it foretells it. Secondly, there is the finalistic dynamism with which the child endows the moon. The moon, the wind, the sky, and the clouds are each moved by an internal force tending towards a common end, and when they act on each other it is by intelligent collaboration and not in accordance with a mechanical system.

The second type of explanation of the quarters of the moon found during the third stage is more positive. The phenomenon is the result either of the pivotal movement of the moon which gives the illusion of its being cut in pieces or else it is due to the obstruction of a cloud. The moon thus ceases to take part in the process.

LUG (12 ; 3) : " What is the moon like ?—*Round.*— Always ?—*No.*—What else does it look like ?—*It's cut through the middle, in the evening it's round, and in the day it's cut in two.*—Why ?—*Because it's day-time.*—Where is the other half ?—*Gone away.*—Where to ?—*To another country where it's night.*—How does that happen ?—*It has to go to another country.*—How does it happen ?—*Half of it goes away to another country.*—How does that happen ? —*It goes away when it's day-time here.*—Does it cut itself up ? — *No.* — Then what happens ? — *It lights up the countries where it's night whilst it is day here.*—Is it always whole ?—*Yes.*—Is it never in half ?—*Yes, in the day-time because it has turned round* (!)—Why can't you see it round during the day ?—*Because you see it from the side.* (Lug means to say " in profile.")—What does that mean ? —*At night it shines ; and by day it turns away and lights another country."* " Is the moon round like a ball ?— *No, like a cake."* Though he hesitates to admit the hypothesis according to which the moon divides itself up, Lug puts forward this remarkable explanation, which seems entirely spontaneous, that the moon is like a cake changing its shape according to the direction in which it is turned.

SCHM (8 ; 8) : " What is there funny about the moon sometimes ?—*It's round and then it turns into a crescent.*— How does that happen ? *When it gets big it makes it cold.* —Where is the other part ?—*You can't see it, it's hidden by clouds, but it's there all the time.*—And when there are no clouds ?—*There are some really all the time.*—How does the moon get big again ?—*The clouds go away.*—Do they know they've got to go away ?—*The other part of the moon lights up and then it shines through the clouds."*

CARP (8, 7) : " *It's the clouds which hide it.*—And what happens to the other half ?—*It's behind the clouds.*—Is it cut ?—*No, it's behind the clouds."*

It is not possible to say if these last cases (of which we have found many examples) are spontaneous or not. They seem to show a degree of spontaneity. As to the case of Lug, it may be compared with the examples we have seen in Chapter VII, § 2, in which the moon follows us without actual movement by turning and sending its rays after us, etc. (See cases of Sart, Lug and Brul.)

To conclude we can now assume that the explanations of the phases of the moon confirm the scheme which was put forward in connection with the explanations of the origin of the sun and moon. An integral artificialism, derived from primitive participations, gives place to a qualified artificialism, and this is finally replaced by natural explanations at first dynamic and finalist (that is immanent artificialism) which ultimately become more and more mechanical.

CHAPTER IX

METEOROLOGY AND THE ORIGIN
OF WATER

It is obvious that, like the primitive, the child makes no distinction between astronomy and meteorology. The sun and moon are of the same order as the clouds, lightning and the wind. We shall therefore pursue our research by studying explanations concerning the origin of other celestial bodies, and adding to these, explanations of the origin of water.

As was the case with the sun and moon, a large number of spontaneous questions asked by children has convinced us that the problems we are about to set are in no way foreign to the child's natural interests. The following cases prove as much :—

These questions are taken from the collection made by Stanley Hall.[1] At 5 years old : "*Why does it rain ?—Where does it come from ?*" At 6 : "*What is fog ?—Who made it ?*" At 7 : "*Where does snow come from ?*"—*Who makes thunder and lightning ?—What is thunder ?—What is it for ?—Who makes thunder, etc ?*" At 8 : "*Who makes the snow ?* At 11, concerning a river : "*I want to know what has made it so big. It hasn't rained much.*"

From the material collected by Mr Klingebiel (to be published shortly), we quote the following at the age of 3 years 7 months : "*Tell me, Mamma, is it God who turns the tap in the sky so that the water runs through the holes in the floor of the sky ?*" At 3 ; 8 : "*Tell me, Mamma, did God make the sea at X—— and that at Z—— too ? He must have a big watering-can, then.*"

In the questions asked by Del (see *Language and*

[1] *Pedag. Semin.*, 1903 (X).

Thought, Chapter V) at the age of 6½ : " *Why* (doesn't the lake go as far as Berne) ?—*Why isn't there a spring in our garden ?* (p. 226)—*How do you make one* (a spring) ? —*Do you need a spade as well to make a spring ?*—*But how is the rain made in the sky ?*—*Are there pipes or streams for it to run in ?*—*Why* (does thunder happen of its own accord) ? —*Is it true* (that is does it happen of its own accord) ?— *But there are not the things for making fire in the sky.*— *Why do you see lightning better at night ?* (p. 228)—*Who makes the Rhône go so fast ?* " (p. 264) etc., etc.

There is also James's deaf-mute, d'Estrella, already quoted in Chapter VII (par. 10) and in Chapter VIII, Introduction, who provides many interesting recollections :—

When d'Estrella looked at the clouds he imagined them to have been made by God's big pipe (d'Estrella referred to God as the " *great strong man, hidden behind the hills, who used to throw the sun into the air every morning* " ; see Chapter VIII, Introduction).   Why ?—Because he had often noted with childish admiration the eddies of smoke rising from a pipe or cigar.   The fantastic shapes of the clouds as they floated by in the air would often fill him with wonder.   What powerful lungs God must have ! When it was misty the child supposed it must be God's breath in the cold morning.   Why ?—Because he had often observed his own breath in such weather.   When it rained he was quite sure God must have taken a large mouthful of water and spat it out from his huge mouth in the form of a shower.   Why ?—Because he had frequently remarked the skill with which the Chinese of San Francisco thus watered the linen to bleach it.

Such identifications of clouds with smoke and of mist and rain with the breath or the saliva may appear curious. We shall however find many instances.

The above questions and recollections already suggest that we shall find the same explanations given concerning meteorology and water as were found with the sun and the moon.   The questions asked by the youngest children and the recollections of the deaf-mute are frankly artificialist.   To ask " who made " or " what is it for " is in **fact** to suggest the answer in the questions.   On the other hand as the children become older the more their questions show them to be seeking a physical explanation. We may therefore expect to find again the same process of evolution that was found in the explanations concerning the sun and moon : the change from an integral artificialism to a more and more positive explanation.

We shall exclude from this chapter a certain number of questions that will be discussed later in the study of dynamics as it presents itself to the child (see *Causalité Physique*) for they are related rather to the causes of movement than to the origin of objects. Such are for example the question of the waves, of the movement of rivers, the movement of clouds, etc. But it is principally the great question of the origin of the wind and the air— a question that is inseparable from the study of movement —that we prefer to reserve for a special chapter (*Causalité Physique*, Chapters I–II).

§ 1. THE SKY.—Questions concerning the sky, the night and clouds form a whole that can only be broken up artificially. We are forced however to start with the analysis of one of these terms for fear that too much will obscure the research. Moreover, in the continuous series of explanations that lead from integral artificialism to a natural explanation it is equally impossible without arbitrariness to distinguish the three stages that were established in the case of the sun and moon. However it seems useful to maintain the plan, for a landmark of some sort is as indispensable as it is arbitrary. In psychology, as in zoology and botany, classes and species are necessary but they depend as much on the free choice of the classifier as on the data to be classified.

For the youngest children (2–6 years), the sky is situated somewhere near the height of the roofs or mountains. " *Do they go right to the sky ?* " Del asked about some fireworks (*Language and Thought*, p. 209). He also regards the sky as touching the horizon.[1] Thus at 3 years old, An saw a cow in the distance in a field and asked " It's

---

[1] Cf. Sully, *Etudes sur l'enfance* (trad. Monod), p. 14

over there near the sun, isn't it ? " In these circumstances it is natural that the sky at first gives the child the impression of being a ceiling or a solid arch and likewise of having been made either by men or by God.

The following are examples of the first stage during which there is integral artificialism :—

GAL (5) : The sky is " *of stone.*" It isn't flat but is " *round.*" It is God who made it.

GAUD (6 ; 8) : *It's God who made it.*—What of ?—*Earth.* It is blue because God " *made it blue.*"

ACK (8 ; 7) : It is God who made it. " *He took some earth.*"

BAR (9 ; 5, backward) : " *It is made of big stones. Big slabs of stone.*—Why doesn't the sky fall ?—*Because if it fell, it would tumble on the houses and people would be killed.*—What prevents it falling ?—*It is well stuck.*—Why ?—*Because the slabs of stone are fastened to something.*"

But it also happens that the sky is regarded as a crust of hard clouds which prepares the way for the explanations of the second stage.

FRAN (9, backward) : The sky " *is a kind of cloud.*—How did the sky begin ? . . .—*It is they* (= men) *who made the sky.*—How ?—*They found a lot of clouds and then the men* (les Messieurs) *took hold of them to press them hard together, then they said, ' We'll see if they will stick.'*—Is the sky hard ?—*Yes.*" As for these clouds, they come from the smoke of the houses. The " material cause " and the " efficient cause " of the sky are thus both artificial.

BUL (7 ; 6) supposes that the sky is hard. It is made " *of air* " or " *of blue.*" It has been made by men.

The youngest children (3–4) usually say that the sky is made " of blue " ; the blue then later becomes either of stone or earth or glass or of air or clouds. But during the first stage the sky is almost always conceived as solid.

During the second stage the child makes an effort to find a physical explanation for the origin of the sky. The " efficient cause " of the form of the sky thus ceases to be artificialist. But the matter of which the sky is made remains dependent on human activity; the sky is of clouds and the clouds have been produced by the chimneys of houses, boats, etc.

GAVA (8½) : "What is the sky made of ?—*It's a sort of cloud that comes.*—How ?—*The steam from the boats goes up to the sky and then it makes a great blue streak.*—Is the sky hard or not ?—*It's like a kind of earth.*—Made of what ?—*It's like earth which has lots of little holes ; and then there are the clouds, they go through the little holes, then when it rains, the rain falls through the little holes.*—How did it begin ? . . . —*When there was earth, that perhaps made houses, and then there was smoke, and that made the sky.*—Is the sky alive ?—*Yes, because if it were dead, why then it would fall down* (cp. the definition of life in terms of activity).—Does the sky know it holds the sun or not ? —*Yes, because it sees the light too.*—How does it see it ?— *Well it knows when the sun rises and when it sets.*—How ? —*Because since it was born* (= the sky) *it has known when the sun was there and now it can know when the sun rises and when it sets.*" The sky is thus a great living cloud, but a cloud that has been produced by the smoke from houses and boats.

GIAMB (8½) : "What is the sky made of ?—*Of air.*— Why is it that the sky is blue ?—*It's when the trees are swinging they make the air go up high* (we shall frequently meet this belief concerning the origins of wind; see *Causalité Physique*, Chapter II, par. 1)—But why is it blue ?—*Sometimes the smoke is blue and it falls on to trees and that makes the sky blue.*"

GRANG (7 ; 6) : "What is the sky made of ?—*Clouds.* —And when it's blue, is it made of clouds ?—*Yes.*" But the sky is solid : God lives above it. The clouds joined together without being helped by anyone but they came from houses. They are alive.

During the third stage the child succeeds in freeing himself from all artificialism. The sky is made up of air or of clouds. It has come into being of its own accord. The clouds of which it is made are of natural origin. During this stage, moreover, the idea of a solid arch is in course of disappearance.

REY (8) bridges the transition between the second and third stage. The sky is still a solid arch : "*It's hard.*"

But it has been formed of its own accord from materials of natural origin : " *There are a lot of little clouds packed together.*—What are they made of ?—*They are thick.*— What is the sky made of ?—*It is blue.*—And made of what ?—*Of clouds.*—And the clouds ?—*They are blue.*" " *Sometimes there are some that are blue.*" As to the origin of these clouds Rey argues in a circle : the sky makes the clouds and the clouds make the sky. " What are clouds made of ?—*Of sky.*—And the sky ?—*Of clouds.*— . . .*" etc.

TRACC (9) : " What is the sky ?—*It's clouds.*—Clouds of what colour ?—*Blue, black, grey or white.*—Can you touch the sky ?—*No, it's too high.*—If you could go up high, could you touch it ?—*No.*—Why not ?—*Because it's air, it's clouds.*—What are the clouds made of ?—*Dust.* —Where do they come from ?—*From the ground. The dust goes up.*—What holds it together ?—*It's the wind that keeps it together.*"

LUG (12 ; 3) : " What is the sky ?—*It's a cloud.*— What colour ?—*White.*—Is blue sky a cloud ?—*Of course not !*—What is it ?—*It's air.*—How did the sky begin ?— *With air.*—Where did the air come from ?—*From the ground.*—What is there above the sky ?—*It's empty.*"

STOECK (11) : " What is the sky made of ?—*Of clouds, and of water and of air.*—And what makes the blue ?— *Water.*—Why is it blue ?—*It's the water that makes it.*— Where does the water come from ?—*Mist.*"

These conceptions undoubtedly show adult influence. If the children had never asked the question they couldn't at the ages of 10 or 11 know that the sky is made of air or that it is not solid. But the entire interest lies in knowing how the children assimilated what they heard. In this respect a marked evolution can be seen as they grow older : a decrease in artificialism at the expense of a progressive search for explanations which identify elements (air, smoke, clouds, water), such explanations being not unlike those of the pre-Socratics.

The best proof that these results are more or less independent of environment is that they are found elsewhere than at Geneva. Mlle Rodrigo has been kind enough to set the same questions to some hundred Spanish children between the ages of 5 and 11 at Madrid and at Santander. Apart from several vague answers and others due to conceptions that had been taught, the explanations were the same as those found at Geneva. On an average they are somewhat backward in relation to the answers obtained in Switzerland, but the order of succession of the answers is the same. Calculating the average age for each of the three types of explanation, gives 7 years old for explanations according to which the sky is made of stones, earth, bricks, etc., 8½ years old for conceptions according to which it is of cloud, and 10 years old for explanations which embrace air.

§ 2. THE CAUSE AND THE NATURE OF NIGHT.—This group of conceptions and explanations is much more independent of the child's education than has been the case of those considered so far. It is therefore of some interest to see if the process of evolution arrived at in the preceding inquiries still holds for the explanation of night. It will be shown that such is indeed the case. It is possible in fact to distinguish four stages in the evolution of this explanation. During the first stage the child gives a purely artificialist explanation of night, but without stating how it is made. During the second and third stages the explanation is half artificialist and half physical : night is a great black cloud, moved by human powers, and which fills the whole atmosphere (second stage), or which simply blocks out the day (third stage). Finally, in the fourth stage, night explains itself by the disappearance of the sun.

In the first stage the child limits itself essentially to explaining the night by its use, which clearly illustrates the starting-point of all artificialism. If he is pressed to follow up his finalist explanation with a causal explanation, he will then call in men or God, but without stating how such a phenomenon occurs.

MOR (5) : " Why does night come ?—*Because it is dark.* —Why is it dark ?—*Because it is evening. Little children ought to go to bed.*—Where does night come from ?—*The*

sky.—How does the sky make the night ?—*Through God.*
—What makes it dark ?—*I don't know.*"

LEO (7½) : " Where does night come from ?—*The sky.*
—How is the night made in the sky ?—*Because there's a
watch, and in the morning it points right up and in the
evening it's let down.*—Why ?—*It's down because night-time
is coming.*—And what does that do ?—*Because it's night.*
—What does the night do when the hand points down ?
—(The night comes) *because there's the hand pointing
down.*—Have you known that long ? . . . —*Because at
home there's a sort of lamp, then a hand ; when it falls
that makes it night.*" As far as we could understand this
" sort of lamp " was a meter that was turned on at night
when the electricity was used. " How did this watch
begin ?—*God made it.*—What is God ?—*A person.*—What
does he do ?—*He works.*—Why ?—*For children.*" It is
clear that for Leo the movement of the hand of a
meter-clock is both the sign and the cause of the
night. Leo takes no account of the " how " of this
phenomenon.

GILL (7) : It is " *at night that we go to sleep, then it is all
dark.*—Why is it dark ?—*To go to bed.*—Why does it
become dark ?—*It is the sky that becomes dark, that makes
everything dark.*"

DELESD (7 ; 8) : " What is it that makes it all dark at
night ?—*It is because we go to sleep.*—If you go to sleep in
the afternoon, is it dark then ?—*No, sir.*—Then what
will make it dark this evening ? . . .*" Despite this
objection Delesd maintained that it is because we sleep
that it becomes night.

These answers are of great interest. Their common
basis lies in declaring that it is night because we sleep.
In certain cases (Gill, for example) the association appears
to be simply teleological : night comes so that we can go
to bed. But in other cases, and probably in the most
primitive, sleep is both the final and the efficient cause of
night. There is precausality. The child is unconcerned
with the " how " : he simply seeks the purpose which
causes night, and this purpose is evidently the fact that
children sleep. Then, under the influence of the questions,
the child completes this precausal association by an
artificialist myth. Such is the case of Leo, but it is evident

that the myth is nothing but an addition to the precausal association " night is produced by sleep."

During the second stage the precausal connection between night and sleep remains the principal factor in the child's explanation but the " how " as to the formation of night has been found. Night is a great black cloud which comes and fills the atmosphere and is due to the action of men or of God. But it is clear that the pioblem is merely deferred. How does man's need or his desire for sleep succeed in producing the big black cloud. For this the child has no thought.

VAN (6) : " What is night ?—*When we sleep.*—Why is it dark at night ?—*Because we sleep better, and so that it shall be dark in the rooms.*—Where does the darkness come from ?—*Because the sky becomes grey.*—What makes the sky become grey ?—*The clouds become dark.*—How is that ?—*God makes the clouds become dark.*"

Duc (6) : " Why is it dark at night ?—*Because it is time to go to bed.*—What makes it get dark ?—*The clouds make it.*—Did you know that ?—*I've found it out now.*— How do they do it ?—*Because some of them are dark.*— You've already seen the moon and the stars at night. Were there clouds those times ?—*Yes, sir.*—Are there always clouds at night ?—*No.*—And when there aren't any clouds does the night come of its own accord ? . . . —Why is it dark when there aren't any clouds ?—*It's the clouds that make it.*" A few weeks later : " What makes night ?— *Because clouds come that are all black.*—Are there always clouds when it's night ?—*Yes.*—And why is it light when it is light ?—*So that we can see.*"

BOURG (9) : " Where does night come from ?—*It's the air which becomes black.*—Why does the air become black at night ?—. . .—And in the day ?—*Then the air is white.* At night is it black air that comes or does the white air become black ?—*The white air goes away.*—Where does the black air come from ?—*The clouds.*"

MART (8 ; 10) : It's dark at night " *because we sleep at night, you can't see anything.*—Why is it dark ?—*Because the sky becomes dark.*—What makes it ?—*Oh ! I don't know.*—What do you think ?—*Because it's bad weather.*— What makes it get dark ?—*The bad weather.*—Is it always bad weather at night ?—*Not always.*—Then when it's good weather what makes it get dark ?—*Because the clouds catch one another up* (= join together)."

FRAN (9) : " What is night ?—*It's when it's all dark.*— Where does the darkness come from ?—*From the sky.*— How did night begin ?—*Because of the clouds that are all black.*—Where do they come from ?—*From the sky.*—Do they come during the day or the night ?—*The night.*— Why don't they come during the day ?—*Because it's light in the day. At night it's dark. If they came in the day it would make it night!*—But why do they only come at night ? How does it happen ?—*Because it's darker at night.*—Do the clouds know they are moving or not ?— *Yes, when the clouds come, they all go together so that you can't see a single spot of white.*—Do they do it on purpose ? —*Yes.*—Why ?—*Because we ought to go to sleep."*

ZWA (9) : " What is night ? Where does it come from ? —*Because it's as if it's going to rain, it becomes dark.*— What is the darkness ?—*It's the night.*—Where does it come from ?—*It comes from the clouds.*—Why does it come every evening ?—*Because people are tired.*—What makes night come ?—*The sky. It gets dark.*—Why ?—*So that people can go to bed."*

PAT (10) : Night is " *darkness."* " Where does it come from ?—*God.*—How does God make it ?—*I don't know.* —Where does it come from ?—*The clouds.*—How ?— *They get dark."*

For the children of the second stage night is thus big black cloud or black air. This cloud does not block out the day. It is not a screen. It is night itself, either because it is derived from the " black air " (Bourg) or because it produces black reflections.

The answers are interesting from the point of view of artificialism. The cause that moves the cloud is either the will of man or of God and is completely explained by the obligation to make us sleep. On the other hand, the artificialism is combined with an integral animism : the fact of commanding a cloud implies that it consciously obeys. As to the origin of this cloud, whether sent by God or by men, it is the same as that of all clouds in general : it is the smoke from the houses.

The artificialism of the second stage is thus less complete

than that of the first : man is no longer directly the cause
of the formation of night. He is merely the agent of its
movement.

Numerous traces of this practical artificialism are still
to be found in the third stage. But great progress has
been made, in the sense that the night is no longer regarded
as a substance, but simply as the absence of daylight.
The child still calls in the clouds to explain night, but the
night no longer actually consists of " clouds," they merely
" block out " the daylight. Night is thus henceforth
held to be a shadow, in the adult sense of the word.

But it is evident that the passage from the conception
of night-substance to that of night-shadow is not immediate
but insensible. There exist numerous intermediate cases
in which the child wavers between the two conceptions
without succeeding in making up its mind. The following
is an example : on the one hand it is said that the clouds
block out the day (third stage), but on the other hand it
is still believed that the cloud must be black to produce
the night, which comes to the same thing as still assimilating the night to a black substance (second stage).

ROUL (7) : " What is night ?—*Black clouds.*—Where
do they come from ?—*The sky.*—How ?—*They pass in
front of the white clouds.*—Why do they come at night ?—
To hide the white clouds. They come to their place (answer
of the second stage).—How does that happen ?—*They
come by themselves. They move.*—How ?—*God makes them
come.*—Could you make it night in this room ?—*Yes.*—
How ?—*By shutting the shutters.*—What would happen
then ?—*You wouldn't see the daylight any more.*—Then
why would it be dark in the room ?—*Because the shutters
are shut.*—Is that night then ?—*Yes.*—Is there a black
cloud in the room when the shutters are shut ?—*No.*—
Then what is it, this night in the room ?—*You can't see
the day any more.*—And the night outside, what is that ?
—*The sky is blocked out by the great black clouds that come.*
—Must they be black to block out the day ?—*Yes.*—
Could the day be blocked out by white clouds ?—*No,
because they couldn't block it out.*"

Roul thus gives two explanations side by side. On the

one hand, night is made up of black clouds which take the place of " the white clouds " and on the other, night is a shadow produced by a cloud that acts as a screen. The next cases clearly belong to the third stage, that is to say they define the night from the outset and without suggestion as a shadow produced by the clouds blocking the daylight.

MAI (8 ; 7) : " What is night ?—*It is when it is no longer light.*—Why isn't it any longer light ?—*When the clouds are in front of the light.*—Who told you that ?— *No one.*—And the light ?—*When there aren't any clouds.* —What makes the light ?—*The sky. . . .*"

BAB (8 ; 11) : " Why is it dark at night ?—*Because the sky is hidden and the clouds.*" It is the clouds that thus hide the sky : " *The clouds cover the whole sky and you can't see anything.*—Where do the clouds come from ?—*The sky.*—What colour are they ?—*Grey.*—Would white clouds do just as well to make night ?—*Yes.*—Why ?—*Because they all do.*"

It is clear that the clouds no longer play the same part as in the second stage, that is to say the part of producing darkness solely by their presence, whether they fill the atmosphere or cause black reflections. The clouds henceforward act as a screen, whatever their colour. Thus to make it night, it needs merely to " cover the sky " and thus hide the light which comes from the sky.

Finally, during the fourth stage the children realise that night results solely from the sun's disappearance. They do not of course know that the earth revolves round the sun. It is, moreover, completely useless to teach them this too early since they cannot possibly understand it. We have seen children of 9 and 10 years old who had been taught the idea that America is the other side of the globe ; they had concluded that America is like a lower story compared with Europe and that to reach America the sun had to cross the sea by a tunnel which pierced what formed the floor of Europe and the roof of America. But without knowing that the earth is round the child can succeed in understanding that day is caused by the sun and night by its disappearance.

In fact during the preceding stages and even during the third, the sun is not regarded as indispensable to day. Day is caused by white clouds or white air or by the sky :—

Thus Deu (7) told us that the night is "*a black cloud that hides the white sky.*" Although this answer is of the third stage Deu believes it to be the sky that makes it light : "*The sun isn't like the light. The light makes every thing light, but the sun only the place where it is.*"

During the fourth stage, on the contrary, the child finally realises that it is the sun that causes the daylight. This is usually due to adult influences but we believe that certain subjects make this discovery unaided. The following are examples of the fourth stage :—

CAUD (9½) : " Where does night come from ?—*It's when the sun sets that night begins.*—Who told you that ? —*I've seen it.*—Why is it night when the sun sets ?— *Because it isn't day any more.*—Why does the sky become black at night ?—*Because you can't see the daylight at night. You can't see where the sky is.*"

BONN (8½) : " Why is it black at night ?—*When it's time to go to bed.*—Why is it dark at night, what do you think ?—*Because the sun is hidden.*—What makes it day ? —*When there's the sun.*"

The succession of these four stages thus shows a progressive decrease in artificialism at the expense of an attempt to find explanations that shall be more and more adapted to physical reality. The order of succession of these stages, in particular of the first two, clearly indicates one of the roots of the child's artificialism : he begins by being interested in the " why " of things before he has any concern for the " how." In other words he starts from the implicit postulate that everything has some meaning in the order of things : everything is conceived according to a plan and this plan itself is regarded as contributory to the good of human beings. Night is " so that we can sleep." This is the starting point (first stage). Only then is the child concerned to know the author of the phenomenon and how it arises (second stage). The author is naturally man himself for whose sake the night exists. The " how " is the smoke of the chimneys which makes the clouds and the black air that fills the atmosphere. By what means has Providence secured the regular return of night ?—The child does not even ask this. He is so sure that it is moral necessity and not chance or mechanical force that ordains the course of things that he supposes without seeking further, that men's wishes, coupled with the good will of the smoke and the clouds, themselves suffice to secure the constant succession of nights. Such, then, is child artificialism, so long as religious education has not intervened to complicate it by conceptions foreign to his spontaneous thought.

§ 3. THE ORIGIN OF THE CLOUDS.—To the child mind, the sky and the night are essentially made of clouds. We must, therefore, next consider whence the clouds come. This provides a most choice field for the study of artificialism, for here the child may reveal complete spontaneity.

On the subject of the origin of clouds we have statements collected from Paris, Nice, Savoy, the Valais and Geneva. Mlle Margairaz set the same questions at Carouge, Mlle M. Roud in the Vaudois district, and Mlle M. Rodrigo in Spain. The results obtained in these different environments have been found to tally, often with a parallelism so striking that the conclusions which follow may be accepted with confidence.

Three stages may be distinguished in the evolution of explanations concerning the origin of the clouds. During the first stage (average age 5–6 for Geneva), the cloud which is usually regarded as solid (of stone, earth, etc.) is conceived as made entirely by men or by God. During the second stage (average age 6–9 for Geneva and Paris) the child explains the clouds by the smoke from the roofs and maintains that if there were no houses there would be no clouds. The artificialism is thus more indirect than in the first stage but is still very systematic. Finally, during the third stage (from 9–10 on the average), the clouds are of entirely natural origin : the cloud is condensed air or moisture, or steam or heat, etc.

The following are examples of the first stage :—

AUB (7) : " Where do clouds come from ?—*From the mountain. They come down, and then they stay there.*— What do you think they are made of ?—*Earth.*—Where are they ?—*In the sky.*—How do they get up to the sky ?— *It's God who makes them go up, because they couldn't do it alone.*" Nevertheless, the clouds are alive : " *If they move, of course they must know it.*"

GRIL (7) told us concerning rain : " *It's God who makes it come.*—How ?—*He takes some big balls and he throws them up and it rains.*—What are the balls made of ?— *Stone.*—Do we know when God throws these balls ?— *Yes, we hear the thunder.*" And a few minutes later : " Where do the clouds come from ?—*The sky.*—What are they made of ?—*Stone.*" The clouds are alive and know when they move. So too Tac (6 ; 5) believes the clouds to be made by God : " What are they made of ?— *They're made of stone. Then that breaks. It's stuck fast on to the sky.*"

For RAT (8) the clouds have been made of earth, on the mountain and by men " *because they couldn't make themselves all alone.*"

The use of the clouds is variously interpreted :—

For GRIL (7) clouds serve, as has just been seen, to make thunder and thus to bring rain. They come also " *to make it light.*"

For other children, the clouds are made " *to make it night,*" " *to show it's going to rain,*" etc.

The answers of this first stage are thus comparable to the most primitive explanations of the origin of the sun and moon (see Chapter VIII, §§ 1 and 2). In both cases, the integral artificialism implies animism rather than excludes it. The sun and moon are fires lit by man yet none the less they are alive. The clouds are made of stones or of earth dug up by men and yet they are alive and conscious.

Further, in both cases children are found who believe there is an initial participation between the celestial bodies and man, as if the clouds and the sun and moon had been directly produced by man.

ROY (6) told us, it will be remembered (Chapter VIII, § 1), that the sun and moon began " *because of us, we started being alive,*" and they grew " *because we grew.*" He then added that it is the clouds that make the sun and moon grow bigger. This second statement seems to contradict the first. But we shall see that this is not really so. In fact, a month after we had questioned him about the sun and moon we saw Roy again about the clouds : " Where do the clouds come from ?—*The sky.—* How ?—*The sky makes them.*—How ?—*Because it is useful to make them.*—How ?—*Because that makes them cut in two.*—What is cut in two ?—*The sky.*—What is a cloud made of ?—*Air.*—And the sky ?—*Air too.*—What happened the first time there ever was sky ?—*It has always been.*— But the first time ?—*It was because of the wind.*—Where did the wind come from ?—*The sky.*—How did it happen ? —*It was someone who blew.*—Who ?—*Men.*—What men ? —*The men whose business it was.*"

These conversations suggest romancing. But, besides the fact that Roy has always seemed free from all romancing, exactly the same myths are found in the recollections of childhood of the deaf-mute, d'Estrella, recorded by James, and from which we have already made numerous extracts :—

It will be remembered that to explain the origin of the sun and moon, d'Estrella (Chapter VIII, Introduction) supposed a " great strong man " hidden behind the hills of San Francisco. This man whom in his recollections d'Estrella calls " God " also explains the clouds : *When it was windy he regarded this as an indication of God's temper. A cold wind showed his anger whilst a fresh breeze indicated good humour. Why ? Because the child had sometimes felt the breath issue from the mouths of people who were angry or quarrelling. When there were clouds they came from God's great pipe because he had noted with childish admiration whirls of smoke rising from a pipe or cigar. The fantastic shapes of the clouds would often fill him with wonder as they floated by and he would marvel at the thought of what huge lungs God must have. When it was misty he supposed it due to God's breath in the cold morning because he had often noticed his own breath in such weather.*

During the second stage the origin of the cloud is half

artificial, half natural. It is artificial in so far as the cloud is produced by the smoke from the chimneys. It is natural in that the form and the rising of the clouds are independent of man. As is to be expected the clouds continue during this second stage to be regarded as alive and conscious. The following are examples :—

HANS (5) : " Where do the clouds come from ?—*The sky.*—How does that happen ?—*It's the smoke.*—Where does it come from, the smoke of the clouds ?—*The fire.*— What fire ?—*The fire in the stove.*—What stove ?—*When you cook.*—If there weren't any houses, would there still be clouds ?—*Yes.*—Well then where do they come from ? —*No. There wouldn't be any.*"

BOIS (5½) : " Where do the clouds come from ?—*From the sky.*—What are they made of ?—*Like the sky.*—What of ?—*Of clouds.*—What are the clouds made of ?—*Of blue or white.*—How did the clouds start in the beginning ?— *From the chimney.*—How ?—(The chimney) *it's for the smoke to go out.*—And then ?—*It goes up into the sky, that makes the clouds.*"

MOC (8) : " Where do the clouds come from ?—*From the smoke.*—Where is that ?—*From the chimney.*—If there weren't any houses would there still be clouds ?—*No.*"

PORT (9) : " Where do the clouds come from ?—*From the smoke.*—What smoke ?—*The smoke from the chimneys and from the stoves and then from the dust.*—How does this smoke make clouds ?—*It's painted in the sky. It drinks the air, then it is painted, then it goes into the sky.*—Does this smoke of the clouds only come from the chimneys ?— *Yes, and when there's someone who makes a fire in the woods. When I was in Savoy, my uncle made a fire in the woods, that made smoke, it went into the sky, it was quite blue.*— Have you seen it blue ?—*Yes, it is blue, but when it goes into the sky it is black.*—Do the clouds feel heat and cold ? —*Yes, because it's the clouds that make the cold come and then the heat.*"

MAI (9 ; 6) : " What are the clouds ?—*They're smoke.* —Where does the smoke of the clouds come from ?—*From the chimneys, from the gas-works.*"

BOURG (9 ; 6) explains as we saw in § 2 that night is due to the black air coming out of the clouds: " Where does the black air come from ?—*The clouds.*—Where do the clouds come from ? What are they made of ?—*Of smoke.—Where does the smoke come from ?—The chimneys."*

MARG (10) : The clouds are made "from the smoke." " What smoke ?—*White or grey.*—Where does this smoke come from ?—*The chimneys."* On the other hand, the clouds " *are alive.—Why ?—Otherwise they couldn't move. If they weren't alive they couldn't move."* They are also conscious of what they do.

ZUL (10) : " What are clouds ?—*The smoke that gets lost in the air, then it turns into the clouds. When it rains they get quite white, and sometimes red.*—What are they made of ?—*Smoke."* They are alive " *because they move."*

It is interesting from the pedagogical point of view to note that this moderated artificialism of the second stage is so persistent that even the best lessons that can be given on clouds risk being distorted by the pupil and assimilated to the schema outlined above. In fact we have met quite a large number of school children who knew that clouds are " *en vapeur* " and that this " *vapeur* " is produced by heating or boiling water (an illustration in one of the reading books on steam) but they conclude from this that all clouds have been produced from saucepans. These children have evidently retained their spontaneous explanation but have substituted for the idea of " smoke " that of " steam." The following are examples of this artificialism in which the matter has been borrowed from adult conversation only to be mutilated :—

BUL (11 ; 8) : " How are clouds made ?—*They're the mist from the sea (la vapeur de la mer).*—Why ?—*They come from the mist from the sea, from the water that evaporates.*—Why does it evaporate ?—*The water is hot.*—Why is it hot ?—*Because it's been made hot.*—By what ?—*The fire.*—How did that happen ?—*The fire of the boats.*—Do they heat the water in the sea ?—*Yes."* Moreover, the clouds " *are also water that's been heated in the houses, when the windows are open."* This shows how much a child of nearly 12 has understood of lessons on the evaporation of the sea !

DUCR (8½) : The clouds are " *of steam (vapeur). When water is cooked in the saucepans it makes steam and it goes up to the sky."* On the other hand the clouds are alive

" because they fly in the air as if they were birds, but they go very fast."

The following cases are intermediate between the second and third stages : the child mingles with his artificialism what is clearly a natural explanation. Clouds are thus given a double origin : the smoke or steam of which the the cloud is made arises both from the houses and from the lakes or sea.

CEN (8 ; 6) : " Do you know where clouds come from ? —*Steam.*—What is steam ?—*It's like smoke.*—Where does steam come from ?—*From water when it's boiling or nearly boiling."* " Where does the steam of the clouds come from? —*When you cook the soup.*—Does cooking the soup make the clouds ?—*The steam goes out and it takes water with it."* Cen would thus seem in the second stage but he adds : " Without houses would there still be clouds?—*Yes.*— Where would they come from ?—*Other countries.*—If there weren't houses in other countries either would there still be clouds ?—*Yes.*—How ?—*They'd make fires and there would be smoke and then steam."* And if " they " did not make fires there would still be clouds that came *" from the mountains,"* but Cen doesn't know how they would be made. Cen is thus a child who clearly feels that the clouds are in part independent of man, but he does not know how to explain this and so has recourse, when pressed, to artificialist explanations.

CARIL (11 ; 7) : The clouds are " *of steam.*—Where does it come from ?—*It's made by the sun . . . (it comes) from the sea ; it comes when you heat water.*—Where do the clouds come from ?—*The saucepans."*

These examples obviously show the influence of the lessons the children have been given. The following case, on the contrary, seems to be spontaneous : the clouds have an origin that is at first artificialist, but they are made by a natural process :—

VEL (8½) started by saying : " *The clouds are made of air."* But their first origin is artificial : " How are they made ?—*Of smoke.*—Where does this smoke come from ? —*Stoves.*—Are air and smoke the same thing ?—*No, the smoke makes the air and the air makes the clouds."*

Next comes the third stage during which the children attribute to the clouds an entirely natural origin. Unfortunately the majority of the answers now obtained are directly inspired by school lessons (the reverse of what was found with the sun and moon). " It's the sun that makes the water evaporate." The sun turns it into steam by heating it, etc. But, besides these formulæ that have been learned, are found a number of more or less spontaneous explanations, which alone will be mentioned and which are of interest. The principle of these explanations is the same as that of the explanations that were collected on the natural origin of the sun and moon (Chapter VIII § 3) : that is to say identity of substance. Clouds are of condensed air, of smoke, lightning, heat, moisture, etc. ; air, fire, smoke, steam and water being felt to have the power of transforming themselves, from one to the other just as was maintained in the pre-Socratic physics. The first examples identify the cloud with the smoke of lightning :—

BEN (7½) : Clouds are made " *of the smoke* " that comes from the thunder. " *It's the thunder that brings the water.*" Thus the lightning gives off smoke, and the smoke is changed into cloud which turns into water.

FAV (7) : Clouds are " *of fire.*" Thunder comes from the cloud and the cloud is the smoke of the thunder.

LEF (8½) : " Where do clouds come from ?—*They come from the thunder, they're water.*" The water comes from the thunder because the thunder smokes and the smoke becomes water.

GERV. (11) believes that the clouds are made of the smoke from volcanoes. Correspondingly the earth is made of heaped-up clouds (see Chapter XI, § 3).

The next examples reduce the cloud to air or to compressed air :—

CHEV (8 ; 2) : " What are clouds ?—*Air.*—Where do they come from ?—*Behind the mountain. They're made behind the mountain.*—Tell me how ?—*By a lot of air. The air gets together and then it goes up.*—How are they formed, these clouds which are just above us ?—*By the air up there. There's more air up there than down here.*—But you told me they were made behind the mountain.—*That's so as one doesn't see them being made.*—How are they made ? —*By the air.*—And were those ones overhead us made behind the mountain ?—*Yes, because they went up earlier. They went up in the night, while those by the mountain went up in the day.*—Are they only made behind the mountains ? —*No, some are made before, in front of us. My brother told me so. All the air comes and it makes mists.*—You say they are sometimes made in front of us ?—*Ah, that's by the air down here joining together.*—How does that happen ?— *There is a lot of air that comes. It makes a big heap."*

LIDT (9) : " What are the clouds made of ?—*Air.*— What happens to this air in the sky ?—*It turns into a great cloud, then it becomes very heavy and it falls."*

ZWA (9) : " *There is some smoke from the water which goes up to the sky and makes the clouds.*—Where does the smoke from the water come from ?—*The water makes it.* —Where ?—*Inside. It's made at the bottom of the water and it comes to the top.*—How ?—*Because the lake always goes down more. There is a little sand which goes up like smoke and it goes up to the sky.*—What makes the smoke, the water or the sand ?—*The sand.*—Why does the smoke from the water come out of the sand ?—*Sometimes there are little stones which break and smoke comes out.*—Why ?— *Because the water is strong and so they break."* Zwa evidently means by the term " smoke from the water " the air bubbles that can be seen forming on the wet sand on the banks of the Lake of Geneva.

As to the identity of the cloud with heat and moisture examples will be found when studying the explanations concerning the formation of rain (§ 5).

The originality of these few answers of the third stage is clear. The clouds are explained as due to an entirely natural process, and this process consists essentially in the transformation of substances qualitatively heterogeneous. Further, some children arrive at the interesting notion of a condensation of substances. Thus Chev and Lidt speak of the air " which joins together," which " becomes very heavy," etc. Are these ideas spontaneous ? If one only had these examples to go by one might doubt it and see merely the result of lessons on rain or steam that had been badly understood. But these explanations are of the same type as those that children of 9 and 10 give for the origin of the sun and moon (that they are of air or of condensed cloud), and for the origin of stones (pebbles are earth that has been pressed together) and especially differences of specific weight between objects (a heavy object is " fuller " or " more compressed " than a light object of the same volume ; see *Causalité Physique*). In these conditions there is nothing unlikely in supposing the explanations quoted above to be spontaneous.

If we now examine the results obtained elsewhere than at Geneva, we shall find an exactly similar process of evolution, but with differences in the average age of the stages. At Paris, out of some fifty children examined in detail, it was found that the first stage is at an average age of less than 7, the second gives an average age of 8 and the third of 9½. In Spain these stages are found at an average of 7½, 9 and 10½. In the country, artificialist explanations naturally disappear earlier but the same types of explanation are found. We found young country children claiming that the clouds are produced by the chimneys of the houses at Beaulieu-sur-mer as much as in the heart of the Valais, in the Vaudois or in Savoy.

In conclusion, it is clear to what an extent the child's natural trend of mind impels it to artificialism even in regard to things in appearance as independent of man as the clouds. The details of this artificialism are certainly not of great interest. In particular, the dominating idea among children, according to which the clouds are nourished by the chimney smoke, is the idea which is most natural to minds already leaning towards artificialism. But the detail is of small consequence. The interest is in the general tendencies it supposes. If it be remembered that the sky and also the sun and moon are thought of by the child as formed of clouds above all else, and that night itself is due to a regular activity of the clouds which is intentional or at any rate teleological, the significance of the results analysed becomes clear. Nothing is left to hazard in the child's universe. Smoke itself, which would seem to be the type of useless object dependent solely on caprice, is conceived by the children as forming the material of the sky and as essentially the cause of atmospheric fluctuations and of the night. From the point of view of animism, it follows naturally that during the first two stages the smoke and the clouds are conceived as conscious and alive. During the third stage, on the contrary, animism is in abeyance. But many of the children who identify the clouds with air, or, in accordance with the lessons they have been taught, with water vapour, still regard them as conscious. The question will be considered again in dealing with the movement of the clouds (*Causalité Physique*).

§ 4. THUNDER AND LIGHTNING.—Before passing to the study of children's accounts of the formation of rain, their conceptions concerning storms must be examined. All children are interested in the question of storms. Countless questions may be collected on thunder and lightning. Those of the earliest ages, up to about the age of 6, are manifestly artificialist, even in form. Del at 6½ (*Language and Thought*, p. 173) asks, for example, on being told that thunder happens of its own accord : "*Why does it happen by itself? Is it true ?—But aren't there all the things to make fire with in the sky.*"

The answers obtained may be classified into three stages. During the first, thunder and lightning are regarded as made just as they are in the sky, or on the mountains. During the second stage they are produced by natural means by the clouds or the sun which are themselves regarded as having an artificial origin. During the third stage, the origin of storms is entirely natural.

The following are examples of the first stage, which is hardly ever found beyond the age of 6 :—

STEI (5) : "What is thunder ?—*Hitting with hammers.* —Do you really think that, or are you just making it up ? —*I think it.*—Who hammers ?—*God.*—Why ?—*To make it rain.*—What is lightning ? How is it made ?—*I don't*

know,—By itself?—*Yes. Before the thunder.*—What is
it made of?—*Fire.*—Where does lightning come from?—
*From the fire because it's being lit with matches. It lights
and that makes the lightning.*—Who lights it?—*God.*—
Why?—*He lights it so as to make a noise.*—Why?—
Because he wants to.—Why does he want to?—*I can't
remember any more."*

DON (5 ; 5) : " What is lightning?—*It's made by the
thunder.*—How?—*The thunder cracks and then the lightning,
it's the thunder that makes it.*—What is the lightning made
of?—*Fire.*—Where does the fire come from?—*The
thunder.*—Is the thunder made of fire?—*There's fire in
the thunder.*—Where does the thunder come from?—*The
mountain.*—How is it made in the mountain?—*The
builders do it.*—How?—*They take some iron and make the
thunder with it."*

All the myths in this first stage are alike. The second
stage lasts on an average from the ages of 7 to 9. Thunder
is due to an explosion of the clouds and lightning to fire
coming out of the clouds or the sun, or moon. But the
clouds and the sun and moon are thought to be formed
from the smoke from the houses or from air made by men.

ROY (6 ; 5) : " What is thunder?—*It's lightning. Then
that makes fire and then it growls.*—Where does the fire
come from?—*The sun.*—Why does it growl?—*The moon
makes it growl."* It will be remembered that for Roy the
sun results from a match thrown by God, and in any case
the sun grows bigger by virtue of the clouds which are
produced by people breathing.

DUC (6 ; 10) : " What is thunder?—*It's when the
lightnings meet.*—Where does the lightning come from?—
The sky.—What is it?—*Like fire. It's from the stars."*
The stars, however, have been made by man.

BOIS (5½) starts by forming a reciprocal association
between thunder and the stars : " What is thunder?—
Fire.—How is it made?—*With stars and with fire.*—How
are the stars made?—*By it* (the thunder) *making them
catch fire."* But both result from the lightning which is
formed by the clouds : " Where does the lightning come
from?—*The clouds.*—Is there fire in the clouds?—*Yes.*—
How is that?—*From the smoke."* That is to say the
clouds having been made from the smoke from the roofs
(Bois is definite on this point) they can change back **again**

to fire, which gives birth to the lightning and thence to
the thunder and the stars.

The most common explanation found in the second
stage is that the thunder is produced by the collision
of two clouds and the lightning by the conflagration thus
set up, the clouds being made of smoke and the smoke
containing fire !

CESS (8 ; 6) : " What is thunder ?—*Fire.*—Where does
it come from ?—*The clouds hitting one another.*—Why does
that make a noise ?—*Because they hit one another so hard.*
—What is lightning ?—*Fire.*—Where does it come from ?
—*From the clouds because they've hit one another.*—How
does it happen ?—*Because they're made of fire, like the sun
and the moon.*"

MOC (8) : " Where does thunder come from ?—*The
clouds.*—How ?—*When they hit they burst.*—What is
lightning ?—*Fire.*—Why does fire come out ?—*Because it*
(the thunder) *makes the clouds burst.*"

BO (9½) : " What is thunder ?—*The clouds hitting one
another.*—Why ?—*To make the thunder.*—Where does the
noise come from ?—*Their hitting one another.*—Is a cloud
hard ?—*Yes.*—Like the table ?—*No* (Bo had said shortly
before that clouds are the smoke from the stoves).—What
is lightning ?—*The thunder coming out.*" There is fire
" *in the clouds.*—Is there fire in the clouds now ?—*Sometimes.*—What are clouds.—*Fire.*"

The third stage marks the appearance of purely natural
explanations. The majority of these have been learnt
and concern the " electricity " of the clouds. But, as
usual, a good number of original answers are found
showing a relative spontaneity. These alone will be
quoted. They consist essentially in treating the storm
as the clash of two clouds, but of clouds made of air or
steam, etc. As to the lightning, it arises either from the
explosion or from the friction thus produced, or again
from sparks due to the stars.

CHAL (9) identifies, as has been shown (Chapter VIII,
§ 3), the sun with a cloud and both too with the air. We
saw Chal again a month after these answers were obtained
and he recounted the following : " What is thunder ?—

Noise. It's two clouds meeting.—Why does that make a noise ?—*When they meet they hit.*—Are the clouds hard ? —*No.*—How does it make a noise then ?—. . .—What is lightning ?—*Fire.*—Where does it come from ?—*It comes from the clouds ; that makes the fire.*—Why is there fire in the clouds ?—*Because the sun is made of fire. It's a ball* (of fire).—Does the lightning come from the sun ?— *No.*—Does the fire of the lightning come from the sun ?— *Yes.*—Does the sun make the lightning come ?—*No, the clouds.*—Why does the fire of the lightning come from the sun ?—*Because the sun was a ball of fire and it burst."* The sun, or rather the suns are thus lighted clouds which in bursting set light to other clouds. The clouds them-selves are of air and their explosion causes the thunder.

It has been shown elsewhere (Chapter VIII, § 3) how Ant, And and Gerv explain the formation of the sun and moon as due to heaped-up lightning. Chal provides the corresponding explanation in interpreting the lightning as produced by the sun.

HEND (9 ; 8) : " What is thunder ?—*It's two clouds meeting and that makes the lightning. First they touch and they hit one another and that makes the thunder and lightning.* —Why does it make the lightning ?—*Because the two clouds rub against one another and that makes sparks.*— Why ?—*If you rub two bits of stick against one another that makes sparks too.*—Why do they rub one another ?— *They get hot and afterwards the spark comes."* Hend declares that the cloud is not hard and that it is of steam. But in order for the cloud to be able to move, " the steam must be pressed together a lot."

Ross (10 ; 7) : " What is thunder ?—*The clouds jump-ing.*—How ?—*Because they're meeting.*—And then what happens ? — *The lightning.* — What is that ? — *A flash that is made by the clouds.*—Why do they make a flash ?— *Because they meet."*

These explanations are not unlike those of the pre-Socratics : the air enclosed in the clouds makes them burst and this rending produces a flash, etc.

In conclusion, this rapid survey of the explanations concerning the formation of storms confirms what was seen with regard to the clouds : the evolution of the explanations proceeds from an integral artificialism to an attempt at a natural constitution, the principle of which is the identity of heterogeneous substances. The explanation of rain will complete the whole.

§ 5. THE FORMATION OF RAIN.—The problem of the conceptions concerning rain is one of the most interesting connected with the child's artificialism. For since during the first stages the clouds are regarded as made of stones or smoke there is no reason for supposing the rain to come from the clouds, rather than from the sky itself. But experience has shown the connection between clouds and rain : when it rains there are always clouds. The child knows this perfectly well. What sort of connection then does he imagine to exist between them ? Is the cloud the sign of rain or the cause of it, or is there a confusion between sign and cause as is found among primitives ? As a matter of fact all three solutions are found more or less mixed and without any definite relation to age.

For greater clarity, we shall take first the explanations collected on the origin of rain without considering the relation of the rain to the clouds which will be dealt with later as a separate problem.

From the outset numerous spontaneous questions reveal the child's natural trend of mind from the ages of 2 to 7. Del at the age of 6½ (*Language and Thought*, p. 203) still asks : " *But how is the rain made in the sky. Are there pipes or streams it runs along ?* " (For Del the " streams " themselves have been made by man.)

D'Estrella recounts the recollections of childhood quoted in § 7 : " *When it rained, he (d'Estrella himself) never doubted but that God (' the great strong man ') had taken a big mouthful of water and spat it from his huge mouth in the form of a shower. Why ?—Because he had on several occasions observed the skill with which the Chinese thus watered their linen that was hanging up to bleach.*"

We can classify the answers given into three stages, according to whether rain is explained by an integral artificialism, a mitigated artificialism or a natural process.

The following are examples of the first stage, beginning
with a case which recalls the recollections of the deaf-
mute, d'Estrella.

We saw (§ 3) how Roy (6 ; 5) conceives the clouds as
made by the air from human breath : " *It's from someone
breathing.*" Similarly for Roy the rain comes from the
clouds : " *it comes from the sky.—*And the water in the
sky ?—*From the clouds.*—Where did the water come from
the first time ?—*When there were men who spat a lot.*"
This answer was not given soon after the explanation
of the formation of the clouds. There is therefore no
perseveration.

Usually, however, the water of the rain is regarded as
actually made by man, but it may often be questioned how
far, allowing for the reticences and the sniggers which
go with the youngest children's answers, the " taps " or
pipes of which they speak have not in certain cases (we
suppose nothing more) a fairly clear symbolic meaning.
We shall postpone answering this question until § 7
where it arises again in connection with the origin of
streams.

GRIAR (5½) : " What is rain ?—*It's water.*—Where does
it come from ?—*The sky.*—Is there water in the sky ?—
God sends it down.—How ?—*He throws out buckets of water.*
—Who told you that ?—*No one.*—Where does God get
the water from ?—*In his tap.*—Where does the water
come from for the tap ? . . . (he laughs)."

God is naturally regarded as like a man. DON (5½)
said that the rain comes from the sky and that God sends
it, he added further : " Are there fountains in the sky ?—
Sometimes there are streams. There is God.—What does
he do ?—*He is in his house working.*—Why ?—*For his
master.*—Who is God ?—*He's a man (un Monsieur).*"
PAN (5) : " And where does the rain come from ?—
The sky.—How ?—*I don't know. Perhaps there is a hose
like Daddy has to wet the De Dion (i.e. to wash down the
car).*—Do you think it possible ?—*Yes, it's possible,
because it's the same dirt.*—Where ?—*On the pavements, it
makes puddles of water.*—How does it come ?—*There's a
tap and afterwards there's a pipe that turns and then he
sends the rain to water the flowers.*—Who ?—*God.*"

HANS (5½) : " *It's God who makes it.*—How is it made ? —*He takes some water and then he throws it.*—Where does he take the water from ?—*From the sink.*"

GRIL (7) says that the rain and the water come from the sky : " How does this water come ?—*Down.*—Down where ?—*In the fountains.*—How does it get to the sky ? —*By pipes.*—Where are these pipes ?—*In the street.*— Where do they go from ?—*From the fountains or the canal.* —Where do they go to ?—*Up to the sky,*" etc. It is men who make it rain.

RAM (9) thinks also that it is men and not God who make it rain. The rain goes up to the sky " *by taps.*— How ?—*The water flows in the taps.*—And then ?—*It makes little drops and then it goes up to the sky.*—How does it go up ?—*In spouts of water.*—Why don't we see them ? —*Because they're so thin.*"

It is unnecessary to multiply the instances of such myths, the gist of which are moreover well known. It is, as always, open to question exactly how far the children believe what they are saying and at what point they start romancing. But the important thing is to realise that they have nothing with which to replace this artificialism. Whether they make up the details or not they can only explain things by having recourse to human activity and not to the things themselves.

This is why, during the second stage, the child comes to endow things with human activity. In fact, during the second stage direct artificialsim is no longer found in that the rain no longer comes from taps in the sky. But there is indirect artificialism, in that it is an object derived from human activity, like the smoke from the houses, etc. that produces the rain. But then, and this is what marks the continuity of the first and second stages, this thing that produces the rain becomes itself endowed with an immanent artificialism : there is collaboration between us and the things. This collaboration is expressed by the childish phrase : " faire faire " (=get made). Man and God get the rain made (" font faire la pluie "), that is to say they " make " (font) something, but the smoke, the sky or the clouds also " make " (font) something. The two meanings of the word " faire " are thus completely confused.

The following are examples of the second stage :—

BLAS (8 ; 10) : " Where does rain come from ?—*It comes from the clouds.*—How ?—*The smoke goes up and then that makes the clouds.*—What smoke ?—*The smoke from the houses.*—How does this smoke make rain ?—*Because the heat makes the clouds melt.   It* (the smoke) *turns back again and then it becomes water.   Because the smoke melts, it changes shape and then water comes.*"   Moreover, the clouds do this intentionally and consciously : they know they're going forward " *because it moves.   So do we know when we're moving.*"

PORT (9) : The clouds are from the smoke of the houses again, " *then it becomes black and then it turns into water.*" " *It melts just for a minute and then afterwards it becomes water.*"   And the clouds move to our commands : " *When people walk in the street too, that makes the clouds move.*"

MARG (10) : " Where does the rain come from ?—*The sky.*—How ?—*It's the clouds and the smoke.*—Where does the smoke come from ?—*The chimneys.*—How does this smoke cause the rain ?—*Because it melts.*—Does the smoke melt ?—*Yes.*—What makes it melt ?—*The heat.*"   The clouds again are alive and conscious.

MOC (8) : " Where does the rain come from ?—*The sky.*—What is it ?—*Water.*—How is it made ?—*The clouds.* —How ?—*Because they jump.   The clouds jump and then the rain comes.*—What do you mean by saying they jump ? —*I mean that they burst.*—Where do the clouds come from ?—*The smoke.*—Where ?—*From the chimneys.*"

For these children therefore the clouds move about intentionally to wherever rain is necessary and transform themselves into water.   The process of the formation of rain is thus in one sense natural but the clouds are still regarded as produced by the smoke from the houses and above all they obey us either directly (Port) or indirectly. What happens then when these children are taught that the rain results from the evaporation of the sea ?   Their spontaneous idea, which is also artificialist, simply becomes fused with the teaching they have received and they then conclude that the smoke from the houses " goes and

fetches " water from the sea. The following are examples
of this confusion of the child's own idea with the lesson
he has been taught :—

DEM (8) : " *At night, sometimes, not always, the clouds
go down and draw up the water.*" But clouds are made of
smoke. " Are they made of steam ?—*Of smoke, not steam !*
(laughing).—How do they draw up the water ?—*As if
they liked it.*—What would happen if a boat was there?—
It would be such a shock that it would sink."

BONG (9 ; 6) also says that the clouds come from the
chimneys and that the clouds make it rain : " You told
me that the clouds were of smoke. Is there water in
the smoke ?—. . .—Where does the rain come from ?—
Fire.—If a fire were lit in this room would that make it
rain on us ?—*No. Because the clouds go down to the sea
and take the water.*—How ?—*They go on the water and the
water goes into the clouds.*—Do they know they are going
to get water ?—*Yes.*"

CEN (8 ; 6) : The clouds are " *of steam,*" that is to say
they are " *of air that contains water.*" " Where does the
steam of the clouds come from ?—*When the soup is being
cooked.*—Does that make the clouds ?—*The steam goes
outside and it takes water with it.*—Is there air in the clouds ?
—*There is air and there's water on top.*"

This shows how even the best lessons can be distorted
by an artificialist mind ! It is clear too what admirable
organisation the child sees in nature, since the smoke from
the houses itself undertakes to fetch water from the sea,
or the air from the saucepans " takes water with it."

This second stage extends on an average from the age
of 7 or 8 to 9½ or 10. It forms therefore a perfect transition
between the first and the third stages in that it maintains
a part of the artificialism of the first stage whilst already
foreshadowing the natural processes on which the child of
the third stage lays stress. In fact, during the third stage
besides numerous explanations that have been learned
(such as that rain is condensed water vapour) are a great
number of original answers which alone will be quoted.
Different types are found corresponding to the types of
reply given concerning the origin of clouds (3rd stage).

When the cloud is conceived as of the smoke of lightning (Ben, Fau, Lef, etc.) water results simply from the cloud " melting." This is similar to the explanation of the second stage, except that the smoke has here an entirely natural origin. It is therefore unnecessary to deal with it further. When the cloud is conceived as of air, water results from the transformation of the air into water :

TRON (8½) : " What are clouds made of ?—*Rain.*— Where does this rain come from ?—*It's air which is turned into water.*" A moment later: " And what are clouds made of ?—*Air.*"

ANT (8) : " Where does the rain come from ?—*The clouds.*—How ?—*Because the clouds have water.*—Why ?— *It's the air* (le vent) *which changes into water.*" Ant believes that the air is itself derived from the clouds which are made of compressed air.

CHEV (8 ; 2) as has already been seen (§ 3) regards the clouds as air " *which joins together.*" " What makes it rain ?—*Because the clouds are wet. They are full of water.* —Where does it come from ?—*Because of the mist. When there is a lot it makes water. It feels like little drops of water when we have it here.*" The mist itself is of air : " *All the air comes and that makes mist.*" Thus again it is the air which finally changes into water.

Finally, other children seem spontaneously to regard the clouds as " heat " or " wetness " or " perspiration," and the rain explains itself.

SCHI (7 ; 4) said that the clouds come from mist: " What is the mist made of ?—*Water.*—Like the water in the tap ?—*No, it's water like when you perspire. It's not quite water when you perspire, it's like water.*—Where does this water come from ?—*I think it comes from being hot. So that it ought to be heat that makes the clouds come* . . .—How is that ? What heat does it come from ?— *It comes from the sun.*—Where does the water come from that is heated by the sun ?—*From the sun itself.*—What is the sun made of ?—*Fire, I think. When it's too hot, it's like when your hands are too hot, the sun perspires, and that makes the clouds cover it.*"

BAR (9 ; 5) : Water comes " *from the clouds.*—What are the clouds ?—*They're like water.*—Are they water ?—*No. heat.*—How does heat turn into water ?—*It makes it* *perspire.*—What ?—*The clouds. Us too sometimes. It's the sun that makes the clouds perspire to make rain.*—How are the clouds made ?—*By little drops that come together and that makes the clouds.*—Where do the drops come from ?—*The sky.*—Where does the water come from, the sky ?—*It's like over rocks, the water flows over them and comes down."

BOUCH (11 ; 10) : Rain is "wetness." "Where did the wetness come from the first time it rained ?—*From perspiration.*—Of what ?—*The sun, when it's too much, it makes it perspire.*" It is thus the sun itself that perspires.

The process of evolution of these explanations plainly recalls the explanations of storms or of the formation of the clouds—air and smoke change into water as well as into fire. The sun itself perspires (Schi), etc.

It remains to examine the question of the relationship the child supposes between rain and the clouds. As the study of the various stages has shown, he begins by thinking the clouds and the rain to be independent and ends by maintaining between them a relation of cause and effect, rain resulting from the cloud. But between these two extremes lies a critical zone which must now be studied because the child wavers in a most interesting way between the idea that the clouds are the " sign " and the idea that they are the " cause " of rain.

GRIL (7) : " Can we see when it's going to rain ?—*Sometimes it thunders.*" But as was shown in § 3 this sign is also cause since Gril conceives the thunder as a stone that God hurls to set free the rain : " *He takes great balls and he throws them and it rains.*" But this cause is irrational, since the rain is not contained in the balls but is set free by them.

REY (7) thinks that God sends the rain by means of a tube and that the clouds are of " *black chalk.*" There is thus no connection between them. Nevertheless, the clouds are a sign of rain : " Can you see when it's going to rain ? —*No, you can only see the clouds.*" " Why are there clouds when it is going to rain ?—*Because God is cross.*" But the clouds are again partly the cause of the rain : " What are the clouds ?—*They're rain that's going to come.*" This last expression does not mean in the least that Rey identifies the cloud with water. He maintains right to the end that it is " *of black chalk.*" The expression contains simply the idea that the arrival of the cloud sets free the rain.

RAM (9) regards the rain as going up to the sky by means of taps. The clouds, on the other hand, are of smoke from the roofs. There is thus no connection between the two phenomena. Ram, however, states that the rain can only go up to the sky if there are clouds : " When does it go up ?—*When there are clouds in the sky.*—Then do the clouds make it come ?—*Yes.*—How ?—*Because they are black.*" But Ram insists that the clouds are of smoke and contain no water. Again the sign is felt to be a cause although the child is unable to explain how the relation works.

ZWA (9 ; 7) as was quoted in § 3 explains the formation of the clouds as bubbles of air that come out of the water. On the other hand, he explains the rain as coming directly from the sky. Thus he sees no direct connection between the rain and. the clouds : " What are the clouds for ?— *To show it is going to rain.*—Do they make the rain or does it come from the sky ?—*It comes from the sky.*—Do the clouds make the rain ?—*No.*—Why are the clouds to show it is going to rain ?—*Because if there weren't any, it wouldn't rain.*" These last words affirm a causal relationship and yet right to the end of the examination Zwa continues to maintain that the rain does not come from the clouds.

Finally, the following case is the plainest example we found showing differentiation between " sign " and " cause." But, as we shall see, the child still conceives the cloud as partially " cause " at the same time that it is " sign."

BOUCH (11 ; 10) conceives rain as the " perspiration " of the sun. The clouds have a natural origin which Bouch refuses to specify. " What are the clouds ? What are they made of ?—*They show it's going to rain, that it won't be fine weather.*—Why ?—*When you see the clouds in the distance you know it's going to be bad weather.*" " If there weren't any clouds, could it rain just the same ?—*Yes* . . . *(no), you know it's going to be bad weather when there are clouds, and it is bad weather at once.*—Why ?—*Afterwards, when there are clouds, the rain comes at once.*—Do the clouds make it rain ?—*They make the bad weather come and that makes it rain.*—Then is it the clouds that make it rain ?—*No, that isn't what makes it rain.*" " Why does it rain when the clouds come ?—*When the clouds come it makes it night, it makes it dark.*—Then why does the rain come ?—*No, there are times when it isn't because the clouds come that the rain falls.*—Why do the clouds show it is going to rain ?—*Because always when the clouds come it rains.*—Why ?—*The clouds show it is going to be bad weather.*—Why ? . . ." These contradictions of Bouch show plainly how he hesitates between the idea that the clouds are a sign and the idea that they are the cause of rain. And even then Bouch does not believe the rain to come from the clouds !

These cases are very instructive. Between the stage during which the child sees no connection between the rain and the clouds and the stage in which the rain comes from the clouds, there is thus present in many children a period of transition during which the clouds foretell the rain. But as soon as the cloud is conceived as a sign it is also conceived as a cause. What sort of a causality is this ? Not a rational causality, since the clouds neither contain the rain nor set it free by any mechanical process. The cloud is rather a cause in the sense that it is a necessary aspect of the event. As I. Meyerson stated concerning certain explanations given by savages : " The cause becomes one aspect, one side of the event."[1] This formula certainly fits the relationship established by our children between the clouds and the rain.

This idea of the sign being regarded as a necessary part of the event is, moreover, of great importance to our research for it constitutes one of the forms of possible transition between artificialist causality (and especially the " participations " which lie at the root of artificialism) and causality by identification of substances. In fact, at the point of departure of the explanations concerning the clouds and the rain we find various feelings of participation—the clouds move when we move, they obey us, they come to make it night and to make us go to sleep, etc. ; the rain comes to water the plants, to clean the houses (*cp.* Pau), etc. At the other extreme of the series

[1] *Année psychologique*, Vol. XXIII, p. 220.

of these same explanations we find a rational causality—
the air condenses into clouds and the clouds melt into
water, etc. How is the passage between these two types
of explanation to be bridged ? First, the feelings of
participation between the clouds, the rain and ourselves,
give rise to various groupings which further strengthen
the artificialist myths when the child invents them—the
cloud thus serves to warn us that God is going to make
it rain, etc. There is thus built up a schema, in which
the rain, the cloud and we ourselves form an indissociable
whole, and it is this schema which gives rise to the artificialist myths that the children make up in answer to
our questions. Then when the artificialist conviction is
in course of disappearing and the human element is thus
dissociated from things, there remains the feeling of a
relationship between the things themselves—the rain and
the clouds are necessary to one another, etc. It is from
this new—so to speak semi-rational—participation that
arise the identifications of substance we found in the
second and third stages. It is thus once more a case of
a dynamic participation giving rise to an identification of
substance.

§ 6. THE EXPLANATIONS OF SNOW, ICE AND COLD.—
The origin of snow and ice may be treated very briefly,
but their explanations must be noted since they have a
certain interest on account of the connection the child
establishes between freezing and cold.

The explanations of the origin of snow and ice may be
classified into three stages. During the first (up to about
the age of 7) there is artificialism.

BOIS (5½) : " How is snow made ?—*It is made by men*
(des messieurs).—How ?—*They make it right up high.*—
What does that mean ?—*They built it.*—What makes it
fall ?—*They make little holes.*—Where ?—*In the sky.*" Ice
is " *snow that has frozen,*" that is to say that has become
" *hard.*"

STEI (5½) : Snow comes " *from the sky.*—How ?—*From
little blue corks.*—What makes it like that ?—*God.*—Why
is the snow cold ?—*Because it has ice.*—Where does the ice

come from ?—*It comes from the snow which stayed when it was very cold.*"

From about the age of 7 the explanation is natural. But two types of answer are found, each no doubt characteristic of a stage. During the second stage (about 7 to 9) the origin of snow is independent of water.

GUT (8 ; 9) believes, for example, that rain comes from steam. But snow comes from " *the flakes.*—Where do they come from ?—*The sky.* — Whereabouts in the sky ?—*From the air.*" For Bul (11) snow is also of air, etc.

TAU (6) : Snow comes " from the sky, and it's the sky that's turned into flakes." For Tau, snow turns into water and ice by being pressed together, but water doesn't change into ice or snow.

FOR Rat (8) it is a mixture of water and sand.

Finally, during the third stage after 9 on the average snow and ice are of frozen water.

GEN (7) : " And where does snow come from ?—*From water. It's dirty water.*—How did the water turn into snow ?—*From the cold.*"

CHAL (9) : " What is snow ? — *It's rain.* — How ? — *It freezes high up as it comes down.*—What is ice ?—*It's water that has frozen.*"

It should be noted that even in the third stage ice is not always regarded as frozen water, but often as compressed snow ; whether the snow itself is thought of as frozen water or as a substance independent of water makes no difference. This fact is interesting since it shows in the first place that identification of substances proceeds no quicker where the activity seems to come from experience (as with ice and water) than where it comes from imagination (as when the air changes into clouds, rain, the sun, fire, etc.), secondly, it shows a new attempt at explanation by condensation similar to those we have already noted, which consists in combining the clouds and the sun into condensed air, etc. It is true that in the case of ice each child knew by experience that a ball of snow when tightly compressed becomes hard and transparent. It is none the less interesting that he explains all ice as due to a process of condensation of snow.

GUT (8 ; 9), who, as we have just seen, associated snow with air, replied as follows : " What is ice ?—*It is the snow when it breaks up into pieces.*—Why ?—*Then it gets hard.* —Why ?—*Because it comes from the ice.*—How does that happen ?—*It is the snow and it goes into pieces.*"

BUL (11 ; 8) said that ice, like snow, is " *made of air.*" Ice " *is made of snow.*" " What do you have to do to get ice ?—*You must wait till it snows.*—Have you ever seen a frozen fountain ?—*Yes.*—Can water freeze, then ?—*Water and snow.*—Can you make ice with water alone ?—*No.*— Why not ?—*Because there is no snow with it.*" Ice is " *squeezed* " snow.

HEND (9 ; 8) begins by saying that ice is frozen snow : " Must there always be snow before there is ice ?—*Yes, because it gets hard and then it gets icy.*—If I put a glass of water outside will there be ice or not ? (this was in winter) —*Not at once ! There will be water at the bottom and a layer of ice on top.*—Will there be snow in the glass before the ice ? . . .—*It is the snow which makes the ice.*"

It is clear, that the identification of water, snow and ice with each other is only progressive.

BUL (11 ; 8) said that " *when ice melts it is only water,*" but he still refused to admit that snow and ice might be water : " Is it water ?—*There is some water as well*—And what else ?—*It is not only water.*"

How, then, are these substances identified with each other. Can we say here, as in the case of clouds and rain, that there is an active participation preceding the identi- fication of the substances with each other before the child understands the action of cold in freezing water. It will be seen that this is the conclusion formed from a study of the relations of cold and freezing. Anticipating this conclusion let us reconsider those cases examined hitherto.

The child comes very early to wonder if it is the cold which makes water freeze or if it is the snow and ice which bring the cold. But it happens that their explanations pass through two phases. During the first there is dynamic participation and at the same time participation of substance between snow and cold—one attracts the other or one produces the other. Cold, on the other hand, is a substance assimilated to the air. During the second phase, it is the cold which produces freezing and the cold is no longer considered as a substance but as the effect of the absence of heat and the result of the sun being hidden.

The first phase is strongly charged with confusions between the sign and the cause and with artificialist participations which show clearly how the identification of substance grows out of dynamic participation.

Roc (6) : " Why is it cold in winter ?—*Because there is snow.*—What is it that makes the cold ?—*The snow.*— If there were no snow would it be cold ?—*No.*—Is it the snow which makes the cold or the cold which makes the snow ?—*The cold makes the snow.*—And where does the cold come from ?—*From the snow.*"

Lu (5½) : " Why is it cold in winter ?—*Because the snow falls.*—It there were no snow would it be cold ?—*No.*— Why does snow fall in winter ?—*Because it's cold.*—Why is it cold in winter ?—*Because God makes it cold.*--What with ?—*With his hand.*—How ?—*He pushes the cold along.* —Where does the cold come from ?—*From the street.*— What is it ?—*It's the wind.*"

Gen (7) : " Where does the cold come from in winter ? —*From the snow.*—And where does the snow come from ? —*From the water, it's dirty water.*—How does the water become snow ?—*Through the cold.*—What is it which makes the cold ?—*The wind.*"

Pat (9) : " What is the cold ?—*The cold is when the snow wants to fall.*—Where does the cold come from ?— *From the wind.*—Why is it cold in winter and not in summer ?—*Because the snow is cold.*"

Hend (9 ; 8) : " Where does the cold come from ?— *From the wind.*—Why is it cold in winter ?—*Because there is wind.*—And what about those days when there is no wind ?—*Then it's because of the clouds whick break up, that makes snow and that makes it cold.*"

For these children, cold produces snow and snow produces cold. But what is the nature of this production ? Is it primarily a simple process, half moral, half physical, of setting each other free. The snow attracts the cold and the cold attracts the snow, they lend each other a mutual aid. Thus for Pat, " The cold is when the snow wants to fall." Inversely for Pur the snow is to " show that it's winter."

PUR (8 ; 8) : " Why does it snow in winter ?—*It's to show that it's winter.*—Why doesn't it snow in summer ?—*Because of the fruit in summer. If snow fell it would spoil the fruit.*—Why doesn't it snow any more when winter ends ?—*To show that the winter is over.*"

This is not a solitary case, most of the younger children reply in the same way when asked to explain why snow comes—they even put the question to themselves. This fact throws light on the foregoing replies. The snow is a sign of cold, cold is a sign of snow, and each produces the other. This is at any rate the case whilst the child considers snow as having been made by God or by man. " Substantialism " follows, consequently, upon this dynamism. Cold is identified as a substance, as air, and this substance is considered on the one hand to emanate from the snow, and on the other hand to enter into the snow as one of its elements. This second attitude is the distinctive mark of the second of the stages which were referred to above.

In fact the identification of cold as air is quite general amongst the younger children. We shall see many cases of it when studying the notions of children on the atmosphere (see *Causalité Physique*). When the child is asked what the air is, it often replies that " it is the cold " as if the cold was a material substance, and if it is asked where the wind comes from, the reply very often is " it comes from the cold." On the other hand, there are a large number of cases where snow and ice are said to be composed of air (see above the cases of Gut and Bul). Bul reckons that the cold comes from the snow and from the cold at the same time, thus : " *It is the snow which brings the cold and the wind as well.*—Where does the cold come from ?—*From the cold.*—What is it ?—*It's air.*"

In short, the reply in this first phase shows clearly enough how the participation, at first dynamic, between snow and cold gradually gives rise to an identification of substances, the snow and the cold being finally conceived as two bodies which are each the product of the other.

During the second phase, on the other hand, the child discovers that the ice is due to the cold and not the inverse. As to the cold in winter it is still interpreted as being due to the wind and then by degrees the child learns to attribute it to the absence of the sun, etc.

CEIN (10) : " Where does the ice come from ?—*It's the wind which freezes water.*—Why is it cold in winter ?— *Because the wind blows."*

BAUD (13) : " Where does the cold come from in winter ?—*Because of the wind.*—Isn't there a wind as well in summer ?—*It's because the air is cold.*—Why is the air cold in winter ?—*Because there's no sun."*

SCHAW (10 : 8) : " Why does the rain fall like snow ? —*Because it is cold.*—Where does the cold come from ? —*Because there's no sun.*—Isn't there any sun in winter ? —*No.*—Where is it ?—*Behind the clouds."*

To conclude, this study of snow, ice and cold confirms what we have already established in the case of clouds and rain, that is, that the explanation by identifying substances is not primary in the child but is derived. During the early years the child becomes aware of the existence of many material objects which it considers have been formed of three separate substances, namely, snow (and ice), water, cold (and air). Each of these three substances seems to it to have been made independently. The rain is sent by God, the snow is made of blue corks (*bouchons*), the cold is air sent by God or by man, etc. But, thereafter, the child discovers that between these substances there are dynamic participations, snow signifies winter, winter signifies cold, and the snow and the cold are mutually productive, etc. From then onwards, as soon as the child gives up artificialism he supposes that beyond these dynamic participations there are participations of substance, and he seeks to explain the substances one by the other, the snow is derived from the cold and from the air, the cold is derived from the snow, etc. At length the development of his powers of observation shows him what is the actual order. It is the cold which causes freezing and not snow which produces cold. Thus, the three moments of the explanations by identification seem to be artificialism and dynamic participations, then identification of substances, and finally the orderly arrangement of causal relationship.

§ 7. RIVERS, LAKES AND SEA, THE PRIMITIVE ORIGINS OF WATER.—If children really have a tendency to artificialism, this tendency should receive free rein in the explanation of rivers and lakes, and the study of questions asked by children would seem to show it. Many of the questions that have been quoted at the beginning of this chapter imply artificialism without any doubt. To ask, for example, why the lake of Geneva does not go as far as Berne is to suppose that there is a moral reason for that and that in consequence the lake has been planned and built.

Children, when asked questions, give replies which may be classed in three stages. In the first of these stages everything has been artificially made—the bed of rivers and lakes and even water itself. During the second stage the bed has been dug out by man, but the water itself has a natural origin. During the third stage all of it is natural.

Here are some examples of the first stage. Amongst them can be distinguished certain cases, probably of the most primitive children, who define the origins of water and suppose them to be physiological, others who conceive water as being artificially made without any conscious or avowed physiological idea, and others finally, who make no sort of definition. This is probably one of the most primitive cases :—

ROY (6) : " How did the lake begin ?—*There was a hollow and somebody filled up one end.*—How did the hollow begin ?—*It was there, some man made it.*—What is a river ?

—It is a hollow with water in it.—How did this hollow
begin ?—*Some man made it.*—Where does the water come
from ?—*When it's warm the water comes.*—What does that
mean ?—*It's the heat.*—How is that ?—*Because we perspire and then we are wet.*—Where does river water come
from ?—*From a little tunnel.*—Where does the water from
the tunnel come from ?—*From a ditch (canal).*—And the
water from the ditch ?—*Some man took the water from a
fountain and put it in pipes.*—But how did water start on
the earth, has there always been water ?—*No.*—Where
did water come from at first ?—*There were a lot of men who
spat a lot."* And it was here that Roy told us what has
been already related in § 5 about the rain.

The interest of this case lies in the physiological origin
that the child attributes to water. It comes from spitting,
and from what one knows of little boys' interests, it is
probable that this phrase is only a polite way of expressing
ideas still more prosaic. It might seem like a poor joke
to suggest that children think of micturition as the probable origin of rivers. But experience has shown us with
certainty that the image crosses children's minds even
whilst they are being questioned.

Ju (7) states, like Roy, that river-beds have been dug
out by men and that the water comes from fountains and
pipes: "And how did the water begin in the pipes? . . .
(Ju turns very pink.)—Say what you think. It doesn't
matter if you are wrong. . . .—*From the water-closet.*
. . ." (At this point, after he had blushed redder and
redder, Ju's eyes filled with tears, and so we changed the
conversation.)

Her (7): "How did the water in the rivers begin ?—
*It is the water which comes when it rains. . . . Sometimes
it is water from the closet. That goes into the drains and the
drains go into the Arve."* As to the river-bed: *"They dug
a deep hollow."*

But here again the memories of deaf-mutes furnish
decisive evidence :—

D'Estrella in the autobiographical letter sent to William
James and intended to complete the account of his
memories of childhood, adds this as to the origin of the
ocean. He went to the sea one day with his companions.

They bathed and it was the first time he had ever been in the sea. He knew nothing of its saltness nor of the strength of the waves. He was knocked over with his eyes and mouth open and but little short of drowned, having no idea how to swim. He felt himself drifting and instinctively began to crawl on the sand, spitting out the water and wondering what made it so salt. He thought it was the urine of the all-powerful god, the " great strong man " who was hidden behind the hills.

But it is clear that most children have not the capacity to frame these hypotheses whilst they are being questioned. They suppose the water to have been artificially manufactured but they are unable to state how.

REV (6) : " Was the lake there when your father was little ?—*No, not then.*" The lake is a hole which someone made. " Where does the water in the lake come from ?— *From the fountain.*—And the water in the fountain ?— *It comes from a tap, and the water comes out of the hole, and then the boats go on it.*—Who made the water in the tap ?— *A man.*—How ?—*He put it in the tub and then it ran out.*"

GRIM (5½) says the lake is a big hole : " How was the hole made ?—*By digging.*—Who did the digging ?—*Some men.*—What for ?—*To put water in it.*—Or do you think perhaps it came by itself ?—*No.*—Where did they dig the water from ?—*From the fountains.*—Where does the water in the rivers come from ?—*From the ground.*—And the water in the ground ?—*From the fountains.*—And the water in the fountains ?—*From the lake.*—And the water from the lake ?—*They fill up buckets and pour them into the lake.*"

RAT (8) : " Where do the streams come from ?—*From the lake, sometimes from the Arve.*—Where does the Arve come from ?—*I don't know, some people poured water into a big hole.*—And what is the hole ?—*Some people dug it.*— And where does the water come from ?—*From the fountains.*—And where does the water in the fountains come from ?—*I don't know, I think someone made it.*—How, what with ?—*I don't know, with something. I think it was with the earth that they made it.*"

These examples could be multiplied indefinitely, but they are all alike. This first stage on the average continues up to 7 or 8 years. The second stage contains children, who, whilst maintaining that the rivers have been dug out by man, affirm that the water comes perhaps from the rain or perhaps from a spring fed by rain. The second stage continues on the average up to about the ages of 9 or 10. Here are some examples :—

BAB (8 ; 11) : " What is a lake ?—*It's a big round thing, a hollow where there is water.*—Was there already a lake when your father was little ?—*Yes.*—And when your grandfather was little ?—*Yes.*—And when the first man lived in Geneva ?—*No.*—Which is the oldest, the lake or Geneva ?—*The lake.*—How did it begin ?—*It was water, which fell.*—Where from ?—*From the sky.*—And the big round thing ?—*It was dug out.*—By whom ?—*By some men.*—Who were they ?—*Workmen.*" The case is the same for the rivers. " Which were there first, the bridges or the rivers ?—*The bridges.*—The bridges were made first ?—*Yes.*—Why ?—*To cross over.*—Why ?—*Because the holes were there although there was no water in them.*"

GEN (7) : " How did the Arve begin ?—*With the rain.*—And how was the hollow made ?—*With machines.*"

BAR (9½) : " How did the lake begin ?—*With rain*—And the hollow ?—*It was dug by men.*—How ?—*With pickaxes.*—A long while ago ?—*Yes.*—Which was there first, Geneva or the lake ?—*Geneva.*" As to the Arve, " *It was dug by some men.*—Why ?—*To make the river.*—And where does the water come from ?—*From the rain.*—How ? Where did it fall ?—*On the ground.*—Where ?—*On the ground, it soaks into the ground.*—And then ?—*It flows into the river.*"

BUL (11 ; 8) : " How did the lake begin ?—*It was dug out.*—By whom ?—*By some men.*—When ?—*A long time ago.*—Who were they ?—*The people long ago.*—Why ?—*To be able to go by boat to Lausanne* " (!) (This explains the question asked by Dell at the age of 6½ : " Why doesn't the lake go as far as Berne.")—Why ?—*To be able to go for a trip in the boat or to go fishing.*—Why ?—*To catch fish.*—Where do the fish come from ?—*God and some men made the lake and God put the fishes in it.*—Was it God or men who made the lake ?—*No, it was God who made the lake.*—Where did he get the water from ?—*He made the streams, and the rivers met in the lake.*—Which is the older, Geneva or the lake ?—*Geneva . . . No. . . . the lake.*"

These few cases show how spontaneous artificialism is in children because when they are taught, or discover for themselves, that water in the rivers comes from the mountains or the rain, they continue to think of the bed of the river as artificial. Moreover, between the second and the third stage, one finds a series of intermediate cases which show clearly the extent to which artificialism is rooted in their minds, if not as a formulated belief at any rate as a general trend of mind. The following cases show, for example, in the form of natural explanations (characteristic of the third stage), a tendency of mind that is clearly artificialist (and derived from conceptions of the second stage).

CHAL (9) : " How was the lake made ?—*It is water which has collected in a hollow.*—Where does the water come from ?—*From the mountain.*—Where does the water of the Arve come from ?—*From the streams.*—And the water of the streams ?—*From the mountains.*—And how was the valley of the Arve made ?—*It was worn out by the water.*—Which is the older, Geneva or the lake ?— *Geneva.*—Geneva or the Arve ?—*Geneva.*—Why are the lake and the Arve just near Geneva ?—*Because of the streams which run down.*—Why here and not anywhere else ?—*Because a lot of streams made themselves here.*— Why is the lake beside the town ?—*Because it divides it* (Geneva lies in fact on both banks).—Why is the town beside the lake ?—*Because the lake is made beside it.*— Why ?—*The streams come down to the town.*—Could they have made themselves further off ?—*Yes, perhaps men began it and the water of the river flowed into it.*"

Chal's artificialism can still be seen to underlie his thoughts because against all probability he insists that the town is older than the lake.

PAR (9) : " Where does the lake come from ?—*It is water.*" " Where does it come from ?—*From the streams in the mountain.*—Where does that come from ?—*From the sky when it's raining.*—How was the hollow for the river made ?—*It was dug out with pickaxes and also when the water flowed down from the mountain it made a hollow.* —Was it the water or the pickaxes ?—*It was the water.*— Has Geneva always been there ?—*Of course.*—Was Geneva there first or the lake ?—*The town, you must have a town before a lake, or else the water would overflow everywhere.*—

Do you know the Arve ?—*Yes, I know it all.*—Was the town or the Arve there first ?—*The town. They made the town then the bridges, then it began to rain and then there was water and it fell into the Arve and the Rhône.*"

This last case is a remarkable example of the tenacity with which the artificialist tendency asserts itself, even in the midst of natural explanations. These last cases are much more interesting than the primitive cases of the first stage because the tendency of the child's mind is seen more indirectly and, therefore, more reliably.

Two cases follow belonging to the third stage in which the explanation of rivers and lakes becomes entirely natural. In the most primitive of the cases in this stage (for example the first of those to be quoted) it will be seen that the explanation is not mechanistic at the outset but that it passes first of all through a stage of eminent artificialism. A certain finalistic dynamism is attributed to the water which enables it to act for man's greatest good :—

BAR (9 ; 5) : " Where does the lake come from ?—*It comes from the rivers.*—How, was it dug out ?—*The water hollowed it out. When the water was strong and there were big waves it drove back stones.*—Which is the older, Geneva or the lake ?—*Geneva . . . both at the same time.*—How does it happen that Geneva is on the edge of the lake ?—*Because if there had not been a lake they would not have had any water !* " The lake is thus explained by reasons which are at the same time mechanistic and finalist, the mechanism serving as a means to the end.

BUR (12 ; 7) : " Where does the lake come from ?—*From the mountain.*—How ?—*When there is snow on the mountains. It melts.*—How was the lake hollowed out ? —*By water.*—And the rivers ?—*Because the stones rolling along hollow it out.*—Which was there first, Geneva or the lake ?—*The lake.*—Which was there first, the Rhône, the Arve or Geneva ?—*The rivers were first.*"

As regards the animism of children in these different stages, we can assert once more that artificialism and animism far from being mutually exclusive imply each other. In fact nine-tenths of the children of the first stage think of the water of lakes and rivers as being conscious and alive, although they regard it as being artificially made without generally defining how it was made. As to the later stages, eight-tenths of the children of the second stage and a third of those of the third stage still think of water as alive and conscious, so that animism decreases proportionately with artificialism.

We might proceed to examine the replies of children who did not know Geneva, but they are so similar to the foregoing answers that it is unnecessary. We have had the opportunity of speaking to children at Beaulieu-sur-Mer and in the Valais about the origin of the Mediterranean or of the little mountain lakes. Mlle Rodrigo has under-taken the same research in Spain and qualitatively the replies are the same. The sea is " *a big hole and people have put water in it.*"—Where did this water come from ? —*From pipes and taps* " (7 to 8 years), etc. At Paris the problem is a different one for the children have not had the same direct experience of the facts of nature as they have at Geneva. Artificialism here is more extreme, but the stages qualitatively are the same, it is only their duration which varies.

CHAPTER X

THE ORIGIN OF TREES, MOUNTAINS AND OF THE EARTH

WE must now consider how the child explains the origins of raw materials such as wood, stone, stuff, etc. These questions are not raised in any formalist spirit, they are problems which interest at least a large number of children. In fact, all the questions that are considered here have actually been put forward by children. Thus in the collection of questions amassed by Bohn [1] are to be found the following which were all asked by the same child. At 2 ; 6: "*Papa, were there people before us?*—Yes.— *How did they come there?*—They were born like us.— *Was the earth there before there were people on it?*—Yes.— *How did it come there if there was nobody to make it.*" At 3½: "*Who made the earth? Was there ever a time when we were not on the earth.*" At 4 ; 9: "*What are rocks made of?*"

Mme Klein in an interesting study [2] records the following questons between the ages of 4 and 5 : "Wie wird Holz? Wie wird Stein?" ("How is wood made? How is stone made?"). The answer was given that stone had always been there, but the child replied "Aber woraus ist er hergekomnen?" ("but what is it made out of"). Other questions relate to the growth of trees, of flowers, to the origin of dust, etc., in fact, all materials give rise to spontaneous curiosity and the very form in which the question is phrased shows in most cases that the child is expecting an artificialist explanation in return.

[1] *Pedag. Semin.*, 1916.
[2] *Eine Kinderentwicklung, Imago*, Vol. VII, p. 251.

§ 1. The Origin of Wood and of Plants.—We find, as usual, three stages in the evolution of the explanations, namely, integral artificialism, a mixture of artificialism and natural explanation, and finally a purely natural explanation. During the first stage, wood is considered as having been artificially made from broken pieces of furniture or else it comes from trees, but the trees have been made by men, either by putting sticks in the ground or else by sowing seeds made by shopkeepers. During the second stage the child understands that wood comes from trees and the trees from seeds or roots and further, the seeds are understood to come from the trees themselves or from other plants such as wheat, but men must harvest them and labour in sowing them otherwise the trees would not grow. Nature is not yet thought of as being sufficient unto itself. During the third stage there is at length an entirely correct explanation.

Here are some examples of the first stage which continues on an average up to 7 or 8 years of age. There are two types of reply, those of children who have not learned that wood comes from trees and those of children who have. These are examples of the first type :—

DAR (4) : "What do you do to get wood ?—*I don't know.*—What do you think ?—*You buy it.*—Where from ?—*From a woman.*—And what did the woman do to get wood ?—*She made it.*—How ?—*She stuck little bits together and made a big bit.*—And how did she get the little bits ?—*They were made with nails.*—How ?—*By sticking them together. You plant the nails. You plant things in the wood.*—But the little bits, how does one get those ?—*I don't know, whilst they are working, big pieces of wood fall down.*"

POR (4½) says that the wood comes "*from the shopkeeper.*" "And what does the shopkeeper do to get the wood ?—*He takes sacks.*—And when he hasn't any more ?—*He buys some from another man.*" And so on indefinitely.

LUG (7) : "What do you do to get wood ?—*You push it through a machine.*—Do you have to put anything in the machine or not to get wood ?—*Yes, you must put something.*—What ?—*You must put some shavings in.*"

RUD (7) says that the wood comes from the shop-keeper who gets it from another shopkeeper and so on. As to the first origin of wood it comes from "*a man who breaks up cupboards.*"

Let us now consider the cases of children better instructed who know that wood comes from trees and that trees come from seeds. We shall see that their artificialism remains entire even in this second case, because even here the seeds are manufactured:—

TER (6½) : "What do you do to get wood ?—*They make it with things.*—With what things ?—*With wood.*—And where does the wood come from ?—*From the forest.*—How ?—*God helps men to make the wood and then they plant it in the ground.*—Where do they get this wood which they plant ?—*First of all they make wood and then they plant it in the ground.*—Are there sometimes new trees ?—*Yes.*—How are they made ?—*You sow things.*—What ?—*Things that you buy in the shops.*—How do you get seeds ?—*They are made.*—By whom ?—*By people.*—What do you have to do to get seeds ?—*You must have round things.*—Where do you find them ?—*On the ground.*—Where ?—*In the fields, you move away the grass and then you take the seed.*—How did they get there ?—*They were lost whilst they were being sown.*—Where did they come from ? —*From the shopkeeper.*—And what did the shopkeeper do to get them ?—*They were sent to him from the factory.*—You don't find seeds ?—*No, they are made.*"

BLAN (6) : "What do you do to get wood ?—*You cut the trunks of trees.*—What do you do to get trees ?—*You sow seeds.*—And the seeds ?—*You buy them.*—Where ?—*In the shops.*—And the shopkeeper ?—(thinks a little) *He makes them.*—What with ?—*With other seeds.*—When the first man came, were there already trees ?—*No.*—How did they begin ?—*With seeds.*—Where did the seeds come from then ?—*From the shop.*"

It is plain that the origin of the trees remains artificialist. There is certainly no question of a creation *ex nihilo,* a notion which appears neither in infant nor in primitive cosmogonies. In trying to draw out the child, one always ends in working round in a circle. The wood is made of shavings, or the seeds are made of seeds.

During the second stage, the idea appears of the formation of the seeds by a natural process, but artificialism is still vital to it in the sense that man continues to be necessary for the reproduction of the trees. Here are some examples :—

DUC (6 ; 10) says that wood "*comes from trees.*—And the trees?—*You plant seed and make it grow.*—And the seed?—*You have to buy it.*—From whom?—*From a shopkeeper.*—And the shopkeeper, how does he get it?—*He makes it.*—How?—*With a machine.*—How do you make seeds with a machine?—*You put it in the machines.*—What is it you put?—*The stuff that grows on the trees.*—What?—*The fruit.*—What do you have to do to get seeds for fir-trees?—*You take the cones.*—And what then?—*You put them in the machine.*—Can you make seeds without taking anything from the trees?—*No.*—If there is no machine can you make the trees grow? —*No.*"

AH (7½) says that the wood comes "*from the trees and the trees come from the seeds. You get the seeds at the factory.*—Which factory?—*The seed factory.*—What do they do at the factory?—*They make them.*—What with? —*With corn.*—Do you think that they make flowers with corn seeds?—*Yes.*" "If there were no people would there be any flowers?—*No.*"

Naturally those children who know the country better do not introduce the idea of the factory so much, but nevertheless they believe that man is necessary to the culture of plants.

BOUV (8) says that fir-trees grow from seed. As to the seed "*you get it from the cones.*—If there were no people wouldn't the firs grow by themselves in the forest?—*No, because there wouldn't be anybody.*—If there were nobody wouldn't there be any seed?—*There wouldn't be any trees.* —Why?—*Because there would be no seed.*—Why?— *Because there would be nobody to take them.*"

This artificialist tendency is obviously deeply rooted even in well-informed children, and even in the suburbs of Geneva where all the children are familiar with the countryside.

There is another interesting question to ask children, and that is, why the leaves of trees are green. During the first stage the child replies as follows :—

Du (4) : " *Because they have been painted.*"
Frez (4) says that " *it is the men who have made the trees in the mountains.*—How ?—*With wood. They found the wood and they found flowers and then they put them on the trees.*—Why are the leaves of trees green ?—*To make the trees pretty.*"
Blan (6) says " *They have been painted.*"

Children in the second stage reply in this way :—

Ol (6 ; 11) : " *Because they are the new leaves which have just grown.*"
Eyn (6) : " Why are the leaves green ?—*Because some-one has planted the seed.*—Why are they green, and not any other colour ?—*Because it is the spring.*"
Gio (7 ; 2) : " *It's the spring which has made them so green.*"
Iwa (9½) : " *The tree turns them green.*—How can the tree do that ?—*The roots make them green when the leaves come out of the root.*—And where do the roots come from ? —*From the seed.*—What colour is the seed ?—*It's the colour of flowers.*—Have you seen blue seed ?—*No.*—Have you seen blue flowers ?—*Yes.*—Well, how does that happen ?—*There is a little blue in the seed.*—Can you see this blue ?—*No.*"

The (*preformist*) tendency of this last reply should be noted.

The first stage continues on an average up to 6 or 7 years, and the second up to 9 years. The replies of the third stage are correct as far as the origin of the seeds are concerned, but children of this stage refuse to give any judgment on the greenness of the leaves or else they give the same replies as those we have just seen.

§ 2. The Origin of Iron, Glass, Cloth and of Paper.—Since these explanations do not provide much interesting material, we can deal with them very briefly.

Amongst quite little children there is a stage which appears to be pre-artificialist, but in reality it simply denotes a period interior to a need for explanations.

OA (4) said of iron that "*you find it, it makes itself all alone.*" The same answers were given for paper and cloth.

FREZ (4) gives the same replies: "*You find iron.—* Is it made or is it found ?*—It is found.*—Where ?*—We have found it at our aunt's.*"

SALA (4): "*You catch it in water with your hands.*" This reply was given for iron, paper, etc.

Evidently this stage, although coming before the period of explanations, is preparing the way for artificialism, the things being provided already, made in a cosmos organised for the needs of man. In these circumstances the earliest explanations will be entirely artificialist. Here is a clear case of transition in point :—

MASS (6): Iron "*is found in the earth.*—But where does this iron in the ground come from ?*—It has been put there.*"

The early explanations of the origin of matter are of two types. Sometimes materials are manufactured out of each other and sometimes they are made of pieces of themselves. Here are some examples of the first type :—

BLAS (5): Iron is "*made with wire,*" that is to say, "*with quite thin iron wire,*" and this latter is made with "*ordinary wire.*" Cloth is made "*with grass.*" Glass is made "*out of ice.*"

Box (6): Iron is made "*with earth.*" So is glass.

Co (6): Iron is made "*with glass.*"

OL (6) gives the same answer and adds that "*You must heat the glass to turn it into iron.*"

FER (7 ; 9): Iron is made of "*scrap iron,*" and "*scrap iron*" is made of "*solder,*" and solder is made from the "*resin of trees.*"

VAU (6): To make iron you put wood into machines and to make paper you must put in glass. ·

RU (7): Cloth is made with "*cobwebs,*" and paper with "*cock's-foot (Pattes de coq).*" This last explanation comes from the fact that in Geneva rags are known as "Pattes."

In short, machines are magic boxes which turn one thing into another according to those external similarities which seize the child's imagination.

Mme Klein, in an article that will be quoted later, relates that her child at the age of 4 asked one day if the spinach for dinner could be cooked long enough for it to turn into potatoes. This testifies to the belief in the omnipotence of adult technique which we shall find when studying children's notions of machines.

The second type of reply is as follows :—

DAR (4) says that iron comes from shops and that little pieces are stuck together to make a big piece.

BEN (5½) says that glass is made out of broken pieces of glass.

OL (6) : " *You find old bits of glass and stick them together.*"

But these replies are made at the same age as those preceding, and are similar to them.

These facts are only interesting so far as they show the tendency of the infant to believe in adult omnipotence. During this same period everything in nature appears to the child to be artificial or manufactured. Later, when the child discovers by degrees that machines are neither omnipotent nor mysterious, natural phenomena will become more and more difficult for him to explain by artificialism and this will give place to the purely physical explanation.

§ 3. THE ORIGIN OF STONES AND OF EARTH.—The question of the soil is much more interesting than that of the foregoing materials. The child's conceptions are less at the mercy of adult influence and of verbalism.

In raising the general question of the origin of stones, a concrete example was used. The children were shown a round smooth pebble like those that they had all seen on the banks of the lake or of the Arve, and they were asked " Why is it round." When the child did not reply that it was worn by water we added the observation, " I found it on the bank of the Arve. Why do you think it is round."

Three stages were observed in the explanations, namely integral artificialism up to 7 or 8 years, natural explanation from 9 to 10 years onwards and an intermediary stage between the two.

During the first stage the earth and the stones are thought of as having been made one from the other or both out of little pieces of stone. Here are some examples :—

DAR (4) : Stones come from " *a house. They are taken from old houses.*—On the Salève there are stones, where do they come from ?—*They are planted in the ground.*—Where do they come from ?—*It is hard to say ! They are made of marble.*"

SALA (4) : The stones " *have been made.*" As to the earth " *it is inside.*—Inside what ?—*Inside the stones.*"

BLAS (5) : Stones " *have been made* " with " *little bits* " of stone, and the earth " *has been made.*"

ZAL (5) : " *It's the men who build houses who make the earth.*"

COUR (5) : " Where do the stones on the Salève come from ?—*It must be people that plant them.*" " How do the stones begin ?—*You put cement, then after you stick them together, and then you hit them with a hammer and that makes them stick.*—What does it mean that the stones are planted ?—*You plant little pieces and then you put the cement and then you stick them together.*"

BLAU (6) says that there are stones even in the country " *because the seeds were put in the ground.*—What sort of seeds ?—*Seeds of stones.*—Where do they come from ?—*From the men.*—What are they like ?—*They are round.*—What use are they ?—*Because they are planted.*—What do they do when they are planted ?—*That makes the stones.*"

HATT (7) : " *The people took some gravel, sand and pebbles and they made stones.*" The stones in the country are there " *because the men threw them there.*" The earth was made by men.

CUV (6) says that all the stones have been made by builders out of earth, the earth is broken stone.

In the first stage then we find three explanations side by side between which nearly every child wavers. The first one consists in saying that the earth is made of stones, and the stones are made of earth, with the possibility of an intermediate material, such as sand. Secondly, the stones are made of little bits of stone which have been left over. This is just what we have already seen in connection with wood, where it will be remembered that wood was said to be made of shavings. The conclusion to which these two theories of the composition of matter lead becomes clearer as the child's explanations grow free of artificialism. This conclusion is an atomism united with the idea of the condensation or rarefaction of a single substance which is the basis of all kinds of soil. Thirdly, there is in many children, though not in all, the idea that the pieces of stone grow like plants. There are stone seeds and stones grow from them. You plant them and they grow, etc. These expressions do not seem to be merely figures of speech, what follows suggests rather that the child actually attributes life to the stone. But we shall see, as the examples quoted already clearly show, that this notion of life does not exclude that of artificial manufacture. Stones are made, they are planted and they grow.

These interpretations receive their best justification from a study of the replies given by children to the question of the smooth round pebble taken from the Arve. This stone is indeed a concrete object with which the child is perfectly familiar, from having played on the shores of the lake or the Arve, and which it was possible to show him instead of merely describing. Furthermore, the elder children, even though they have just said that stones were made by men, replied at once that the pebble had been worn by the water, thus abandoning, when brought into contact with the actual object, their belief in artificialist myths. The younger children, on the other hand, retained their customary trend of mind. The following replies were obtained during this first stage :—

FREZ (4) : " Do you see this stone, why is it round ?— *It is to put in the earth.*—Do you know where I found it ? On the banks of the Arve. Why is it round ?—*It is to put in the earth.*"

POR (4½) : " *It is because they are made round.*"

BLAS (5) : " Do you see this stone, why is it round ?— *Because it is made of flour.*—Do you know where I found it ? On the banks of the Arve. Why is it round ?— *Because it's made of flour.*" Stones in general are made by people "*with white flour*" (he means cement). The pebble from the Arve is thus made like all the rest.

TUL (5) : " Why is it round ?—*Because it wants to be round.*" ' *It is made quite round.*"

EYN (6) : " Why is it round ?—*Because it's not like the others.*—Why not ?—*Because it wasn't made like the others.* —You told me that you find them, and now you tell me that they are made. Which do you really believe, that they're found or that they're made ?—*They grow in the earth.*—I found this stone on the banks of the Arve. Why is it round ?—*I don't know why, because it was found on the bands of the Arve.*" It is clear that in this stage, the terms " made " and " grown " are not contradictory.

WOL (7) : " *It's round because it was made like that.*"

CUV (6½) : " *Because it was made round.*—What with ? —*With damp earth.*"

BLAU (6½) : " Do you see this round stone, where do you find stones like this ?—*On the banks of the Arve.*— Why is it round ?—*Because there are lots of round stones.* —How was it made ?—*By some men.*—Why is it round ? —*Because they made them round.*"

These facts confirm once again what has already been shown as to the association between artificialism and animism.

Before coming to the purely natural explanations of the third stage, we must distinguish and consider an intermediary stage in which the child is partly artificialist, though at the same time appealing to processes of natural formation other than simply that the stone " lives " or " grows."

The following is an important case intermediate between the first and the second stages :—

ROB (7) : " Where do stones come from ?—*You find them in boxes. You find a big stone. You break it, that makes a little stone, and then you make a big stone with it.* (This is the process of decomposition and re-composition with which we are already familiar)—Do you see this stone ? Do you think you could make a bigger stone with it ?—*Oh, yes, you could take a big stone then you could break it and that would turn it into a bigger stone. Oh, yes, that one would easily make a big stone, it's heavy enough !*—Look at this stone, why is it round ?—*You find them like that and you break them and then you make bigger round ones with them.*—Do you know where I found it ? On the banks of the Arve. Why is it round ?—*You break them and then you make them round."*

This case is very interesting. The weight of the stone is used to prove the fact that you can make a big stone with a little one. There is no question here then of a simple process of manufacture, but of a process which involves the capacity of the stone to be compressed or expanded. The particular pebble referred to is compressed and therefore heavy, and once it is broken in little pieces it can be made up again into a stone which is not so heavy, but bigger. It is clear then that to the process of decomposition and re-composition with which we are familiar from the replies in the first stage, a further conception has been added here, that of condensation and rarefaction. But this idea—in Rob's case still bound up with artificialism, as evidenced by the suggestion of compressing the stone—contains in germ the idea of particles of matter. We shall see later that some of the children of the third stage arrive more or less explicitly at this conception. Rob's case is then intermediary between artificialism and what may boldly be called atomism.

In the course of the replies of the second stage, artificialism can be seen to be progressively transferred to nature itself.

BLASE (6½) : " Why is this stone round ?—*To make fire.*—How ?—*By banging on it.*—What with ?—*With a hammer.*—I found it on the banks of the Arve. Why is it round ?—*Because the Arve made it round with water.*—How did the water do that ?—*It takes up earth and sticks it together."*

OL (6 ; 11) says that men made the earth and the sand and the stones. As to the pebble it is round " *because it was in the water.*—What does that do ?—*It makes it swell."* And Ol adds, " *When one drinks too much that makes one swell."*

DEN (7). The stones are made of " *dry cement."* Den then changes his idea, " *they made themselves all alone. The earth made them. I have never seen it happen."*

HORN (5½, very forward in everything) : In order to make a stone " *you take some clay and make the stone.—* Have you been in the country ?—*Yes.*—Have you seen stones on the ground.   Where did they come from ?— *From the factory.*—Here is a stone that I found on the banks of the Arve.   Why is it round ?—*Because it made it like that.*—What ?—*The water.*—How ?—*By making waves.* —And then ?—*They rolled the stone and it got round."* After this excellent explanation Horn replied in connection with another black-and-white pebble as follows : " Why is this stone white on top and black underneath ?—*Because it is made of sand and of earth.*—Why ?—*Because it is solid.*—Who made it ?—*The factory.*—Do you believe that, but I found it on the banks of the Arve ?—*It is the water.* —What did it do ?—*It turned it like that, it put the earth on top."*

It is quite easy to see the mechanism of these first natural explanations.   The child substitutes quite simply a deliberate and artificial activity of water and earth for human art.   It is true that one could interpret each of the expressions that have been recorded in a mechanical and not an artificialist sense, but taken altogether such an interpretation would not suffice for there is clearly here an artificialism which has become immanent, and which has been attributed to nature itself.   In fact, all the processes which the children refer to (swelling, dilation, concentration, adhesion, etc.) are processes which in the same conversation the children attributed to a human technique, and in addition a systematic finalism is apparent in all these conceptions.   Later we shall see in studying the explanations that children give of natural movements (*Causalité Physique*) that waves and water, currents, etc., are spoken of until a very late stage as being produced by a special dynamism and never as the product of a mechanical process.

Here is an intermediary case between semi-human and semi-immanent artificialism of the second stage and physical explanation of the third stage :—

GERV (11) says that he wondered where the earth came from : " *I thought that it was men who had made it, but then*

I thought that that would have taken too long and would have cost too much and also where would they have found the dirt.—Well how did it begin ?—*It came like that, something fell out of the clouds, the clouds fell down and made the earth, the earth is just heaps of clouds.*—And the trees ? —*When the earth was made they came out from under the ground, there were little roots that came and gradually that made a tree.*" With regard to the clouds, Gerve had said a little earlier that they had come out of volcanoes.

Here are some cases of the third stage, that is to say cases where the child explains the earth by the crushing up of stones and stones by the compression of the earth, but each of these explanations follow along lines which are exclusively natural.

Bouv (9½) : " How did pebbles commence ?—*In the earth.*—How did it become stone ?—*It hardened.*—Why ? —*It stayed there a long time and that made it harder.*— How ?—*In the sun it was the heat that made it harder.*— Why ?—*It dried it up.*—If you break a stone what do you have then ?—*Little chips of stone.*—If you break up these little chips ?—*That makes earth.*—If you go on breaking it what does that make ?—*Tiny little stones.*—And if you break them ?—*It makes dirt.*"

Bouv said that you end up by having " *little crumbs of earth.*"

Stoe (11) : " What do you do to get stones ?—*It's dirt which makes stones.*—How ?—*Because it dries in the earth.* —And then ?—*It makes stones.*—If you take two boxes, the same size, and put stones in one and dirt in the other, which would be the heavier ?—*The one with stones.*—Why does dirt which is lighter make stones which are heavy ? —*The dirt is pressed together until it becomes heavy.*—How does it get pressed together ?—*Because it is warm.*—What is a stone made of ?—*Of dirt.*"

Fal (9) : " How is stone made ?—*It is sand which has got hard.*—And how did the sand begin ?—*As dirt.*—If you break a stone what do you get ?—*Sand.*—And if you break the sand, what do you get ?—*Finer sand.*—And if you go on breaking it what do you get ?—*It gets as small as flour.*"

Weng (9 ; 7) : " How did stones begin ?—*With little bits of metal.*—What is that ?—*You find it in the ground, it's a sort of stone.*—And how were the little bits of metal made ?—*With smaller bits of metal.*—What are they made of ?—*Of dirt.*—And how was the dirt made?—*With pebbles.*—How ?—*By being broken.*—What is earth made of ?—*It is made of little bits of metal.*—What is that ?— *It's little bits of stuff all put together.*—And if you break them ?—*You could not go on because then there would be nothing at all."*

Without falling into the temptation of supposing that these children are putting forward an explicit atomism, we may try to distinguish in these replies how much is spontaneous and how much is suggested by the questions. The spontaneous element is the idea that the stone and the dirt are composed of the same material, but in varying degrees of density. This conclusion is corroborated by the idea put forward by children on the question of weight (see *Causalité Physique*). Children of 7 to 10 years always imagine that a body is heavier than another of the same mass because it is more " filled up " or " packed."

From this notion to a rudimentary atomism is a short step and the questions help the child to make this step in seeking an explanation as to how stones are made (see the case of Weng) or in asking what would happen if the little pieces of stone were broken up (see the case of Bouv).

Here is a still clearer case, and also a recollection of childhood by an adult :—

MART (11½) : Mart was contrasting a smooth close-grained pebble and a cork. " It's funny, the cork is big and light and the stone is small and heavy, why is that ? —*It is because of what is inside the stone, there are lots of little things, of sand, it is packed tight and there are lots of little stones in it, but the cork has got little holes in it."* After that, a stone and some plasticine of the same size were compared, and Mart said that the stone was heavier because it was bigger. He was told that they were the same size. " *Yes,*" he replied, " *but look at it quite near, it is not made in the same way.*—What are the differences ? —*The stone has got a little more if you look at it hard.*— More what ?—*More sand, more little bits."*

Mart seems to think that the weight comes from the abundance of corpuscles of which a thing is made.

A young man told us that he remembered among other memories of childhood having tried at about 10 or 11 years old to picture the composition of things like earth, stones, leaves of trees, wood, etc. He decided that it was the little bits of them, spaced and grouped variously which gave rise to all sorts of variety in consistency and in appearance. He remembered particularly that the difference in a large dry leaf and a fine green leaf seemed to explain itself thus.

We can conclude that the child's conception of condensation and rarefaction is a sort of transition from explanation by the transformation of heterogeneous substances (air changing itself into water or clouds, for example) and a true atomism. A point of comparison in history can be made in the system of transition of Empedocles, a consideration of which gives further point to the replies recorded above.

But it must be repeated that before considering these replies as really spontaneous, we must first analyse the very suggestive explanations the children give of the difference of the varying densities of objects.

§ 4. ORIGIN OF THE MOUNTAINS.—The explanations for the formation of mountains will allow us to define the exact relations existing between animism and artificialism in the case of objects which are as evidently inanimate as rocks or the earth.

Two stages were apparent in the collected replies. Whilst natural explanation was the characteristic of the second, on the other hand during the first stage the mountains were held to have been made by man. But, strangely enough, in half of the cases of the first stage, mountains were pictured at the same time as living in that they had grown. Here are some examples of this mixture of animism and artificialism :—

EYN (6) : " How were the mountains made ?—*With stones*—How ?—*A mountain came, God put stones inside.* —Inside what ?—*Inside the earth.*—And then ?—*It grew into* a *big stone.*—It was a little stone before?—*Not so very big."*

ROB (7) : " How were the mountains made ?—*Some dirt was taken from outside and it was put on the mountain and then mountains were made with it.*—Who did that ?—*It takes a lot of men to make mountains, there must have been at least four. They gave them the dirt and then they made themselves all alone.*—But if they wanted to make another mountain ?—*They pull one mountain down and then they could make a prettier one."*

HEN (7) said that the stones were put in the dirt, and then it grew, but he could not say how.

COUR (5) said that " *people had to plant the stones of the Salève,"* and then afterwards it began to get bigger and bigger. " *It was the grass which made them grow."*

OL (6 ; 11) said that the mountains were in the beginning due to God and that they had grown, " *and since then they have always been growing."* " Is the Salève still growing ?—*No, because God did not want it to get any bigger.*—Were they made or did they make themselves ? —*God created them and then they made themselves."*

Origin in manufacture and growth are not, it is clear, contradictory for children. Obviously the child does not suppose that the mountain is really conscious, but yet when he holds that they have been made he still believes that they have helped to a certain degree in the process by growing and by making stones in the earth, etc. It is not on inert matter that man works but on something living. But for man nothing would be made, but with his help certain activities of matter are stimulated.

There are other children of the first stage who do not seem to share these ideas but one may doubt whether this apparent lack of them is not a phase and whether at moments they share such views. Probably it is a simple question of emphasis, sometimes it is put on the act of manufacture, sometimes on the activity of the thing which is made.

COUR (6) : " How did the Salève begin ?—*With big stones.*—Where did they come from ?—*People took them. It was a man, lots of men. It was twelve men.*—What did they do ?—*With stones? They took them. They put them on the mountain. They put one stone then they made it like that, pointed."* "Which was there first, Geneva or the Salève? —*The houses came first and afterwards the stones."*

GILL (7) : " How were the mountains made ?—*They're all of stone.*—How did they begin ?—*It was to make them go all round.* (Geneva is in fact surrounded by mountains.) *Big piles of stones all round.*—What made it like that ?— . . . *It was men who carried them there."*

ROU (7): The Salève was made " *by men.*—Why ?— *It couldn't make itself all alone.*—What is it for ?—*For the moon.*—Why ?—*For it to set behind."*

The following is an example in which the mountain although not manufactured is still conceived as existing for the benefit of man alone :—

DUC (6 ; 10) : Mountains " *made themselves all alone.*— Why are there mountains ?—*So that we can skate."*

We have mentioned elsewhere (*Language and Thought*, p. 173) the interesting question asked by Del at the age of 6½ : " *Is there a little Matterhorn and a big Matterhorn ? —No.—Then why is there a little Salève and a big Salève ?* " This question, in its very form artificialist, shows clearly the spontaneity of the child's tendency to regard mountains as " made for " us and in consequence as made by us. To this question of Del, children of 7 replied as follows (*Language and Thought*, p. 227) : " (There are two Salèves) *because there's one for little children and one for grown-ups."* " *The little one's to climb and so is the big,"* etc.

Finally, after the age of 9 or 10 on an average, a second type is found in course of which the children seek for natural explanations :—

DEN (8) : " *It's the earth that has risen up. It's like a big stone.*—Did men make it ?—*No !* "
BOUT (9½) : " *That's made with earth.*—Did anyone make the mountains ?—*No. They're high with earth."*

The conceptions concerning mountains thus clearly confirm what we saw with regard to earth and stones.

CHAPTER XI

THE MEANING AND ORIGINS OF CHILD ARTIFICIALISM

IT remains to be seen if from the outset there is a common direction along which the different phenomena observed are moving. We shall not hide the difficulties of the problem—the replies collected may have been simply made up, or they may have been due to the teaching (religious or otherwise) the child had happened to receive from its parents or from others, and even if these answers show evidence of a spontaneous trend of mind they may be heterogeneous among themselves. Is there then an artificialism belonging specifically to childhood? Does this artificialism obey laws of development? Can one or more origins be assigned to it? These are the questions now to be examined.

§ I. THE MEANING OF CHILD ARTIFICIALISM.—It does not seem to us possible to explain all the answers classified in the preceding chapters as due to romancing. If we apply our three usual criteria we shall, in fact, find as follows. In the first place, children of the same average age give the same answers. In this respect the explanations of night as due to big black clouds and of the clouds as resulting from the smoke from the roofs, etc., are so many reactions whose generality is always striking. Secondly, the artificialist answers are not limited to one age or a single given stage, but they extend over at least two stages. It is thus possible to see a progressive evolution of beliefs, which clearly shows their partially systematic character and excludes the hypothesis of pure romancing

The third criterion, the arrival at the correct answer, is significant. In fact, the children of the last stage do not attain the correct answer or the natural explanation in one bound but seem rather to grope for it and during these gropings may be seen numerous traces of beliefs of the preceding stages. Thus, amongst the children who believe the Lake of Geneva to have been hollowed out solely by the action of the water, may sometimes still be found the idea that Geneva existed before the lake. To explain how the lake came to be situated beside the town, these children are obliged to turn to an immanent artificialism just as in the eighteenth century God was replaced by " Nature."

These three criteria, taken together, thus lead one to suppose that, speaking broadly, the artificialist answers of the children tested were not due to romancing.

Naturally, this conclusion does not mean that all the answers obtained are to be treated as of equal value. On the one hand, a careful distinction must be drawn between the element common to all the children of a given stage —for example, the idea that the sun was made by men or by God—and the embellishments that such and such a child adds to this conviction under the pressure of the questions—for example, that it was made by someone having lit a match. We have quoted the complete answers because the study of these embellishments brings to light many tendencies which would otherwise be missed, but, as regards the general problem that concerns us here, we may treat these individual elaborations as due to romancing and retain only the statement that is common to all. On the other hand, it is obvious that the value of the general element itself varies according to the age of the children. Thus the attempts at natural explanations made by the elder ones (9–10) may be taken more or less literally—the child who compares the sun to a condensed cloud really means what he is saying and is not exaggerating his idea by the words used. The explanations of the younger children, on the contrary, present a mixture of spontaneous tendencies with romancings evoked by the questions. Thus when a child of 5 states that the sun has been made " by men," the essence of what he means is simply that the sun has been made for us. Such a child believes in consequence that the sun is dependent on us, but generally without the question of origin having ever been clearly present to his mind previous to our questions. We must, therefore, seek what can have been the spontaneous tendency behind the answer.

But this latent artificialism, which we maintain to be, broadly speaking, independent of romancing may perhaps be interpreted as the product of the education imposed on the children either by their parents or by observation of the life of their town. On one hand, the child is taught that a God has created Heaven and Earth, that all things are directed by Him and that He watches us from Heaven where He dwells. There is nothing surprising in the child simply continuing to think along the same line and imagining in detail the manner of this creation and supposing that God secured the help of a band of skilled workmen. On the other hand, the child is impressed by the industry he observes in his town (although Geneva is situated very near the country and all the school children are familiar both with fields and mountains). Lakes and rivers are bordered by quays, their beds are cleaned by dredgers, drain-pipes may be seen running into them from the banks, etc. Thence to conclude that nature depends on human activity may easily be but a short step.

But to this last interpretation may be opposed the fact that nothing compels the child to see in these phenomena only that which favours artificialism. Observation of the clouds might provide the child equally with suggestions favouring a natural explanation (their quantity, their height, the way in which from the town they can be watched forming round the mountains, etc.), instead of leading him to consider only the resemblance between the cloud and the smoke from chimneys. Watching the

rivers and the lake might impress the child with their
size, the way the stones are thrown about, the wild nature
of the banks in the country, rather than exclusively with
the signs of human activity, etc. Such selection seems to
result from an interest in what is artificial, the spontaneity
of which can hardly be doubted.

To regard this artificialist interest as entirely due to
religious education is a hypothesis that cannot be borne
out by analysis. A very pronounced artificialism may, in
fact, be found among deaf-mutes or with children who
are too young to have understood or generalised the
religious teaching they may have received. The ideas of
the deaf-mute d'Estrella on the origin of the stars (Chapter
VIII, Introduction) and his ideas of meteorology (Chapter
IX) have, in fact, been given. Another deaf-mute,
Ballard, also quoted by James (*loc. cit.*), imagined that
thunder was caused by a great giant, etc. Also there are
the questions of children as young as the ages of 2 or 3
asking " who made the world ? ", " who puts the stars in
the sky at night ? " etc. Such questions have obviously
preceded any religious teaching. But, even supposing—
what is far from proved—that all the children between
the ages of 4 and 12 examined had been directly influenced
by the theology of the Book of Genesis, there remain three
reasons for maintaining that the artificialist tendency we
have noted is in part at least spontaneous.

In the first place, we have been struck by the fact that
the majority of children only bring in God against their
will as it were, and not until they can find nothing else
to bring forward. The religious instruction imparted to
children between the ages of 4 and 7 often appears as
something foreign to the child's natural thought, and the
conceptions evoked by this teaching lack both the subtlety
and the intricacy of convictions that make no appeal to a
divine activity.

Secondly, even if we admit that the child's artificialism
is an extension of the theological artificialism imposed by
education, it remains to be explained why the child, as

has been shown, thus extends to everything conceptions wherein the religious significance remains so vague, and still more why this extension obeys laws instead of differing from child to child. Thus why do all the youngest children think that Geneva is older than the lake ? And how shall we explain such a general tendency as that which regards the night as made of black smoke, the sun as a fire produced by the smoke from the roofs, etc. If there was here nothing more than a simple extension of a type of explanation they had been given, it would seem that these conceptions ought to vary from child to child. But such is not the case.

Thirdly, and this is the most important objection to be opposed to the theory under discussion, the child's real religion, at any rate during the first years, is quite definitely anything but the over-elaborated religion with which he is plied. As will be shown in the course of this chapter, our results entirely support the thesis of M. Bovet according to which the child spontaneously attributes to his parents the perfections and attributes which he will later transfer to God if his religious education gives him the opportunity. In the problem that concerns us now, it is, therefore, man who is thought to be omniscient and all-powerful, and it is he who has created all things. As we have seen, even the sun and moon and the sky are attributed to the activity of man and not of God, in at least half the cases. Moreover, when the child speaks of God (or "des Bons Dieux," as several boys said) it is a man they picture. God is " a man who works for his master " (Don), " a man who works to earn his living," a workman " who digs," etc. In short, God is either a man like other men, or else the child is always romancing when he speaks of him, in the same way that he speaks of Father Christmas and the fairies.

In conclusion, it does not seem possible to explain the generality and tenacity of child artificialism solely by the pressure of education. We are, on the contrary, faced by an original tendency, characteristic of child mentality, and penetrating, as we shall attempt to show, deep into the emotional and intellectual life of the child.

But the essential of the problem still remains to be solved. Are the beliefs that have been listed in the preceding pages really " spontaneous convictions," that is to say were they formulated by the child previous to the questions or should they be classed as " liberated convictions," that is to say as beliefs aroused by the examination and thus systematised partly as the result of our questions.

It is here best to adopt the simplest hypothesis. This is that the majority of children had never considered the questions we put to them. Therefore, the belief contained in the child's answer was " liberated " by the examination. Two elements thus contribute to this belief. On one hand is the sum total of the mental habits or tendencies of the child questioned, but, on the other, is a certain systematisation due to the exigencies of the question set and to the child's desire to answer as simply as possible, so that the answers we obtained did not arise specifically and directly from the child's spontaneous artificialism. To liberate this spontaneous artificialism it is necessary to delve beneath the surface and find the true explanations that were certainly not in the child's mind in that form before the examination. However delicate an operation it may prove we shall attempt it.

We must first remember that the child's thought is egocentric and as such intermediate between the autistic and symbolic thought of reverie or dreaming and logical thought. The convictions the child may have are, therefore, generally not communicable or at any rate remain uncommunicated. Also even if nature and its phenomena force children to contract a whole series of mental habits they do not formulate any theory or verbal explanation, in the strict sense of the term, which incidentally makes the relative uniformity we noted all the more striking. Such as it is, the child's thought is much more fertile in images and is, above all, motor much more than conceptual.

It consists in a series of attitudes or motor schemas organised in some degree as mental experiences. But as yet nothing is directly formulable. Thus it is often found in making little physical experiments with the child— as, for example, submerging bodies in order to observe the displacement of water—that laws are often correctly foretold even when the verbal explanation by which the child supports his judgment is not only false but even contradictory with the implicit principles which dictate the judgment (see *Causalité Physique*, § 3). It follows that a systematic type of reply such as was observed during our study of the stages of artificialism, implies a sum total of mental predilections in the child, although these predilections may differ largely from the verbal explanation put forward by the child during the course of the test.

How are these implicit mental predilections to be defined in the case of artificialism. In a word, the child conceives every object, including the natural bodies, as, to use his own terms, "made for" a purpose. Now for a natural object, such as the sun, the lake or the mountain, to be considered as "made for" warmth, for boating, or for climbing implies that it is conceived as made "for man" and consequently closely allied to him. It follows that as soon as the child is asked or asks himself how the sun, the lake or the mountain began, he thinks of men, and his mental predilection, which translated into words would be "the sun, etc., is *made for* man" finds utterance in the formula "the sun, etc., is *made by* man." The transition from "made for" to "made by" is easily to be explained when one remembers that the child, whose whole existence is regulated by his parents, regards everything which is "made for" him as having been "made by" his father or mother. Behind the artificialist formula liberated by the questions, it would seem to be the anthropocentric participation which constitutes the core of spontaneous artificialism, and the presumption is strong that this core is made up purely of feelings or mental predilections. It is this that we hope to prove.

In trying to define the spontaneous tendencies which explain the replies obtained in connection with animism it was found that the child's true animism, namely, that which existed prior to our questions, is purely " purposive " rather than explicit and systematised, except as regards the belief that the sun and the moon follow us. The child behaves as if nature were charged with purpose, as if chance or mechanical necessity did not exist, as if each being tended, by reason of an internal and volitional activity, towards a fixed goal. It follows that when a child is asked if a natural body, such as a cloud or a stream, " knows " that it is moving or " feels " what it is doing, he replies in the affirmative because the transition from purposiveness to consciousness is imperceptible. But such a reply does not render the child's true thought, because he has never asked himself the question and would not have asked it except for our intervention, unless it were at the moment when he was on the point of losing his implicit faith in the purposiveness of things.

The artificialist replies given to our questions on the origin of things justify us in making a very similar analysis. We may go further and say that the mental predilections which reveal the spontaneity of child animism are practically the same as those which likewise reveal the spontaneity of child artificialism. We shall understand then why the child clings so tenaciously to artificialism and by the same token why, at least at the outset, artificialism and animism are complementary.

In fact, the child's purposiveness rests on the implicit postulate that everything in nature has its own *raison d'être* in the form of an office or function that each object is called on to perform according to its own characteristics. In one sense this certainly involves animism, since without awareness things could not succeed in playing their part in the social organisation of the world. But this also involves commands and above all commanders, to serve whom is precisely the *raison d'être* of the subordinate bodies. And it is obviously man who is thus felt to be the chief and the *raison d'être* of things. The idea of doubting such a principle so seldom occurs to children that it is never explicitly enunciated—it being granted that a principle is never enunciated until the mind has been faced by a problem, that is to say before the fundamentals of the principle have been directly or indirectly put in doubt. Animism and artificialism constitute, then, two attitudes of mind which are complementary to each other. From this standpoint let us reconsider the three groups of phenomena which seemed to testify to the spontaneity of the child's animistic attitude, namely, finalism, precausality, and the confusion between physical and moral law.

In the first place, the child's finalism argues as much as and even more in favour of the existence of artificialism than of animism. Certainly, when he says that the sun follows us in order " to warm us " he attributes purposiveness to the sun. But an examination of the definitions. in terms of function (Binet et Simon) show that most of them are closely allied to artificialism. Binet, as is well known, has shown that if children of 6 to 8 years are asked " what is a fork " or a " mummy," they reply " it is for eating with " or " it is for taking care of us," etc. The universality of the definition in terms of function has been confirmed by all who have checked the value of Binet's and Simon's tests. Yet these definitions beginning with the words " it is for . . ." (" c'est pour ") cover the whole face of nature and do not apply only to the objects and persons in the child's immediate vicinity (*Judgment and Reasoning*, Chapter IV, § 2). The same thing is found when one is careful not to ask for a series of definitions (which encourages perseveration) but when one asks point-blank in the course of an interrogation : " What is a mountain ? " or " What is a lake ? " A mountain " is for climbing up " or " for skating," etc. A lake is " for going on in a boat " or " for fishes " (in other words " for anglers "). The sun is " for warming us " ; the night " for sleeping " ; the moon " for giving us light " ; a countryside "for travelling in"; clouds "for making it rain" or "for God to live in"; the rain "for watering flowers," etc. That such a viewpoint, not only finalistic but utilitarian and anthropocentric, should necessarily be allied with artificialism, in other words that the definition "it is for . . ." should lead naturally to the explanation "it is *made* for . . ." seems quite evident.

In the second place, we have seen that the pre-causality evidenced by the questions and above all by the " whys " of children between 3 and 7 forms one of the closest bonds between animism and the rest of child thought. In fact, precausality supposes such a lack of differentiation between the psychical and the physical that the true cause of a phenomenon is never to be sought in the " how " of its physical realisation, but in the purpose which underlies it. But these purposes belong as much to an artificialist order as to an animist order. To put it more clearly the child begins by seeking purposes everywhere and it is only secondarily that he is concerned with classing them as purposes of the things themselves (animism) and purposes of the makers of the things (artificialism). Thus when Del (*Language and Thought*, Chapter V) asks " Who makes it run ? " when speaking of a marble on a sloping surface, he is thinking of the purpose in the marble for he adds " does it know you are there ? "—Here precausality tends towards animism. But when Del asks why there are two Salèves and not two Matterhorns, or when he asks why the Lake of Geneva goes only as far as Lausanne and not up to Berne, or when a child of 5 quoted by Stanley Hall[1] asks " Why is there a moon ? " and " why isn't it as bright as the sun," etc., etc., it is of the purpose of the makers of mountains, lakes and planets that the child is thinking, or at least it is of men's decisions, which evidently implies that men count for something in the creation of things.

Finally, in connection with animism, we laid stress on

---

[1] *Pedag. Semin.*, 1903, Vol. X. "Curiosity and Interest."

a phenomenon which we shall often come across again in studying the explanations given by children as to the causes of movement (see *Causalité Physique*), that is to say the lack of differentiation between the idea of the physical law and that of the moral law. Thus the regular reappearance of the sun and moon is due to the fact that they " have to " warm us or give us light, etc. Now it is quite clear that such a lack of differentiation bears witness to a tendency of mind which is as much artificialist as animistic. In fact, for children the moral law presupposes commanders, that is to say men who give orders, as much as bodies which obey. Certainly the sun must have some degree of awareness in order to be able to obey but also it must have someone whom to obey. This someone the child may well have never explicitly defined in its thought, yet it goes without saying that it is man, since man is the *raison d'être* of everything.

To conclude, if artificialism evidently does not exist in the spontaneous thought of the child in such a systematic and explicit form as it has necessarily assumed in the course of our interrogations, it exists none the less in the form of an original tendency of mind intimately connected with finalism and child precausality. This in itself is sufficient to justify our study of artificialism.

§ 2. THE RELATIONS OF ARTIFICIALISM WITH THE PROBLEM OF THE BIRTH OF BABIES.—At any rate in the earlier stages, the child seems to experience no difficulty in conceiving beings as, at the same time, living and artificially made. The planets are living, they grow, they are born, and yet they have been made by man. Similarly mountains, stones, even seeds grow and yet have been artificially made. What is the reason for this combination of animism and artificialism ? To solve this problem it would be well to know children's ideas on the birth of babies. But it goes without saying that there are grave moral and pedagogic reasons for not pursuing such an investigation directly. Since we cannot experiment here, we must rest content with what can be found in children's talk which has been published or which we have gathered, and also with such recollections of childhood as bear on this point. We shall find enough in these sources to define broadly the ideas of children on the birth of babies, and these ideas will enable us to understand the true relations between animism and artificialism.

Two types of children's questions are to be distinguished relating to birth, but it is not certain that these two types characterise two stages. Questions of the first type do not touch on the " how " of birth. There is no question of causality, strictly speaking. The baby is assumed to have existed prior to its birth and the child simply asks *where* it was before that event and how the parents have contrived to introduce it into the family circle. The relation between parents and children is a simple bond and not one of cause and effect : the baby is held to belong to the parents and its arrival is considered as having been wished and arranged by the parents, but no question is raised as to how the baby has been able to come into existence. Questions of the second type, on the contrary, show that the child wonders how babies are made and is spontaneously led to consider the parents as the cause of its creation.

Here are some examples of the first type taken from questions collected by Stanley Hall and his students :—

" *Mamma, where did you find me ?* " (F. 3 ; 6). " *Where was I when you were a little girl ?* " (F. 5). " *Where was I when you were at school ?* " (G. 7). " *Where was I before I was born ?* " (G. 7). " *Where does the doctor find children ?* " (G. 7).[1]

The first of these questions is typical, the baby being clearly conceived as pre-existing the activity of the parents. The last two are less conclusive for when the child asks " where ? " it may well be that he was thinking of the location in the bodies of his parents.

---

[1] *Pedag. Semin.*, 1903, Vol. X, p. 338.

Rasmussen [1] notes on his daughter S. (3 ; 8): " *Mamma, where did I come from ?* " and later " *Where do people get all these children from ?* " Little R. (at 4 ; 10, that is to say 9 months after having asked questions of the second type as we shall shortly see) asked : " *Where is the baby now that a lady is going to have next summer ?* " Mme Rasmussen then replied : " It is inside her." To this the child retorted : " *Has she eaten it then ?* " which certainly seems to indicate the child's idea that the baby existed independently of the parents.

To this type of questions must also be joined those beliefs that have often been noted in children according to which the dead become little and are born again as babies.

" *Do people turn back into babies when they get quite old ?* " (Sully, *loc.cit.*, p. 105–107).

Del (6 ; 6) : " *When I die shall I also grow quite small* (that is to say like a dead caterpillar that he had seen shrivelled up) ? " (*Language and Thought*, p. 177).

Zal (5), when his uncle's death was announced to him : " *Will he grow up again ?* "

S. (5 ; 4) : " *When you die, do you grow up again ?* " (Cramaussel).[2] And then subsequently : " *You never become little,* " and " *when you die you become . . . nothing.* "[3] The latter negations show how strong the affirmations must have been which implicitly preceded them.

And Mme Klein's child : *And then I shall die and you as well, Mamma, . . . and then we shall come back again.* "[4]

It is these questions of the first type which provoke the ridiculous fables told by certain parents, according to which babies are sent by angels, storks, etc. :—

" *Where has the baby come from. Has God let the baby fall down from the sky ?* (G. 5 years) : " *How did God send the baby ? Did he send an angel with it ?—If you hadn't been at home would it have taken it away again ?* " (F. 7 years) : " *Who is Dame Nature ? Did you know she was going to bring you a baby,* " etc.[5]

[1] Rasmussen, *Psychol. de l'enfant. L'enfant entre quatre et sept ans.*
[2] Cramaussel, *Le premier éveil intellectual de l'enfant,* 1903, p. 165.
[3] *Ibid.,* p. 167.
[4] Mme Klein, *Imago,* 1921, Vol. VII, p. 268.
[5] *Pedag. Semin.,* Vol. X (article quoted).

Now, one of two things must be true. Either the children do not believe these stories, which happens more often than would seem. Or else they partially believe in them and try to find out how the parents were able to make the baby come, starting from the implicit idea that it was the parents who arranged its coming. This leads to the question of the second type, to be examined next.

From the point of view of artificialism, how are we to explain the questions of the first type ? It would seem at first that artificialism is completely excluded. The child does not ask how babies are made but where they come from ? Babies pre-exist. This points to a stage anterior to the need of explanation and, therefore, anterior to all artificialism. But such a way of interpreting the facts is obviously too simple. Behind what the child asks must be sought what he does not express because it seems evident to him ; it is the parents who make the baby come, that is to say who arrange its arrival, whatever may be the manner of the arrival. There is as yet no process of making involved but merely a connection which the child feels directly without having any need to state it. There is thus a sort of pre-artificialism comparable to the primitive artificialism we have often found with the youngest children—the sun, etc., has been connected with men from the beginning without having actually been made by men.

On the other hand, questions of the second type reveal the desire to understand the nature of the bond between parents and children, the how of birth. Now an interesting point is that birth is conceived by the child as being an artificial process of production and, at the same time, a process bearing on matter endowed with life, and either, on the one hand, independent of the parents or, on the other, the fruit of the bodies of the parents themselves. In illustration of the first case the following examples show birth identified with artificial production :—

One of Rasmussen's daughters, R., asked, at 4 years and 1 month : *" How are ladies made ? "* Mme Rasmussen replied by asking the child why she asked the question. "*Because there is meat on ladies.*—What ladies? —*You and other ones.*" And then the child added, "*I think it's a meatmaker who makes them, don't you?*" At 4 years 10 months she asks again, "*How are people made?*" [1]

Mlle Audemars related the following spontaneous remarks. Renée (7) had just had a little sister. She was making plasticine figures and pausing, asked: "Mademoiselle, what part of my little sister did they make first? The head?" She was asked: "How do you think a little baby is made, Renée? Hasn't your mother told you?—*No, but I know. Mummy still had some flesh over from when I was born. To make my little sister, she modelled it with her fingers and kept it hidden for a long while.*"

Sully [2] has quoted the remarks: "*Mummy where did Tommy* (himself) *come from?*" To which Tommy replied for himself: "*Mummy bought him in a shop.*"

ZAL (5), whose comment on his uncle's death was quoted above, added: "*Do we grow ourselves or are we built?*" "Grow" ("*pousser*") here obviously means not get bigger (*croître*) but to come quite alone. The child asks if babies come by themselves (if they grow again like the dead uncle) or if their parents make them. In the latter case birth is considered as a process of production.

Cramaussel's daughter, S., declared at 5 years 7 months, when she was told that God made the babies: "*He uses goat's blood for it, then.*" [3]

A little girl asked where babies came from and added: "*I know already, I should go to a butcher and get lots of meat and shape it.*"

These remarks make it clear how animism and artificialism in the child's conceptions come to be complementary and not contradictory. The idea of manufacturing living material presents no difficulty since babies themselves are manufactured. And as we shall see presently, questions about birth are often the starting-point for questions on the origin of things in general. From its very roots,

[1] Rasmussen, *op. cit.*, pp. 48-51.
[2] *Loc. cit.*, p. 109.
[3] Cramaussel, *op. cit.*, p. 130.

then, artificialism assumes the ideas of life and of artificial production to be complementary to each other.

On the other hand, children come very early to grasp the conception that the material out of which parents make children is the fruit of their own bodies :—

Children's beliefs have often been quoted according to which babies come from their parents' blood, from their mouths, from their stomachs, or from their navels.[1]

A little girl of 4½ asserted that if she were to fall down, she would break up into two little girls and so on.[2]

Clan, whose recollections have already been quoted (Chapter IV, § 2) believed for several years that a son simply came out of his father's penis for, as he said, he had heard tell that fathers continued in their sons (" les fi s sont le prolongement des pères ").

We have found ourselves, in those recollections of childhood we have been able to collect, the ideas, well known to psycho-analysis, that the baby came out of the anus and is made from excretum, or that it is in the urine, or again that birth is due to a special food that mothers consume for that purpose. Mlle Audemars has called our attention to the following observations : Dol (7½) asked : " *What do mummies eat to be able to make babies ?* " To which Ray (7) replied : " *They must eat lots of meat and lots of milk.* "

The interesting point is, that where the child knows quite well—from having been told—that the baby comes out of the mother's body, it continues to wonder as to the manner in which each particular limb was made as if there were a separate and special process for each organ. Thus Mme Klein's child asked : " *But where does its little head come from ?* " " *Where do its little legs come from ?* " " *Where does its little stomach come from ?* " etc. Another child, who had been told that a baby comes from its mother's stomach, asked : " *But how can she put her hands in her stomach to make it ?* "

In order to understand how these spontaneous inquiries by children into the problem of birth can have

[1] Spielrein, *Zentralbl. f. Psychoanal.*, Vol. III, 1912, pp. 66-68.
[2] Spielrein, *Intern. Zeitschr. f. Psychoanal.*, VI, 1920, p 156

a bearing on the development of artificialism we must now try to determine broadly the chronology of questions relating to the origin of things. As a matter of fact, the spontaneous curiosity of children plays on the origins of all things, and this point is fundamentally important, since, in itself, it justifies the researches described in the last three chapters. The most superficial examination of children's questions between 3 and 7 years shows that the child asks how the planets, the sky, clouds, wind, mountains, rivers and ocean, raw matter, earth, the universe, even how God himself, commenced. The most metaphysical questions, such as that of the primal cause, are raised at the ages of 6 or 7. Rasmussen's little girl, R., was told at 7 years, that God made the first man. " *Well,*" she replied, " *who made God ?* " etc. The important thing is to find out whether the question on origins in general precedes that on birth, and thus conditions its form, or whether the inverse is the case.

Facts seem to furnish an unambiguous reply. The succession of interests seems to be as follows : first an interest in birth, then in the origin of the race, and at last in the origin of things in general. Here are four groups of facts conforming to this classification :—

Ballard, one of the deaf-mutes quoted by James (Chapters VIII and IX), asked at about the age of 5 how children were born. When he had acquired a rough idea of the truth he began to wonder how the first man had come into being. Thence his interest turned to the birth of the first animal, the advent of the first plant, and finally (towards 8 or 9) to the origin of the sun, the moon, the earth, etc.

Bohn [1] noted in his son, questions asked in this order. At 2 ; 3 : " *Where do eggs come from ?* " Having been told, he asked : " *Well, what do mummies lay ?* " At 2 ; 6 : " *Papa, were there people before us ?—Yes.—How did they come there ?*—They were born just like us.—*Was the earth there before there were people on it ?*—Yes.—*How did it get here if there were no people to make it ?*" At 3 ; 7 : " *Who made the earth ?* " At 4 ; 5 : " *Was there a mummy before*

---

[1] *Pedag. Semin.*, 1916.

the first mummy?" At 4 ; 9 : " *How did the first man get here without having a mummy?"* Then finally at 4 ; 9 : " *How was water made?"* and " *What are rocks made of?"*

Rasmussen's daughters seem to have followed the same sequence. R., having asked how ladies were made, asked a month later, " *Who made the birds?"*—a question of an artificialist character all the more interesting at this age because no one had spoken to her of religion. At 3 ; 8, S. asked how babies were born, at 4½, how the first man had begun, and a little later where the first horse came from. Her own reply was, " *I think it must have been bought,"* which clearly shows that she thought it had been made artificially.

But the clearest example is furnished by Mme Klein. At 4¾ her child had begun to concern himself about birth. The first question was phrased thus : " *Where was I when I had not yet come on the earth?"* Then came the question: " *How is a man made?"* (" *Wie wird ein Mensch?"*) which was repeated often. Following the question : " *Mummy, how did you come on the earth?"* The child was given an explanation of childbirth, but several days later, he asked again : " *How do you grow big?"* " *Where does its little head and its litttle stomach come from?"* etc. And then after these, came another series of questions : " *How do trees grow?"* " *How do flowers grow?"* " *How are streams made? and rivers? and the dust?"* " *How do boats come on the Danube?"* He also asked where raw materials came from and above all, " *Where does glass come from?"*

We can assume then, that in all probability it is curiosity concerning birth which is the starting-point of questions of origin, so numerous between 4 and 7 years, and in consequence the source of child artificialism. It is true that there will be children who ask questions about origins before they ask them about birth but even here the question arises whether it is not an interest in birth which, thwarted and projected, is not at the root of these questions about origins.

What is to be observed in any case—and the point must be stressed so that the relation of the problem of birth to artificialism stands out more clearly—is an evolution of myths relating to the origin of man in the sense of an artificialism increasingly immanent, that is to say, attributed to nature itself.

In fact, shortly after having occupied himself with the question of birth, the child asks himself almost infallibly what can have been the manner of the original appearance of man on the earth. The younger ones, between 4 and 5, respond with a purely artificialist solution, which involves explaining man by man himself in a manner which actually only shelves the problem. That is Marsal's explanation, a defective who will be quoted in the next section. He explains everything by assuming a pair of ancestors who have created everything. But amongst children of 7 to 9, very interesting solutions are to be found, according to which man is descended from animals or plants and these latter from nature herself. Nature becomes the principle of artificial production in conformity with the immanent artificialism which we have seen in children of 9 to 10 years. Here are two clear examples :—

Ballard, the deaf-mute quoted above, finished by convincing himself that the first man must have been born from an old tree-trunk. Afterwards the notion seemed to him to be stupid but he could not think of anything better to replace it.

Vo (9), who was asked how Switzerland began, either did not understand the question or confused the origins of Switzerland with those of humanity and replied thus : " *Some people came*—Where from ?—*I don't know. There were bubbles in the water, with a little worm underneath. Then it got big and came out of the water and fed and grew arms and teeth and feet and a head and it turned into a baby.* —Where did the bubble come from ?—*From the water. The worm came out of the water and the bubble broke and the worm came out.*—What was there at the bottom of the water ?—*The bubble which came out of the ground.*—And what happened to the baby ?—*He got big and had babies. By the time he died the babies had children. Later on some of them became French, some German, some Savoyards. . . .*"

The interest of this myth is clear enough even if it is a piece of romancing. The relation of its content with the Freudian symbols of dreams of birth is evident. It is well enough known how frequently water is associated in dream thought with the idea of birth. And again eggs (frogs' eggs, etc.) and bubbles, being the symbols of eggs, are frequently associated with the same motive. Finally, the image of a worm often appears in dream symbolism as associated with the idea of babies, etc. If once the principle of the symbolism of subconscious thought is admitted, even reducing assumptions to their minimum, Vo's myth cannot be regarded as anything but the symbolical transposition of the idea of birth. In other words, the water would stand for the urine in which children often believe babies are born (and we have seen what a large number of children tend to ascribe lakes and oceans to human activity on these lines), the bubble would represent an egg, the worm a baby coming out of the body. All this urges Vo to believe that nature has made man. If the principle of symbolism is not admitted it is none the less clear that Vo has simply transferred to nature what some years earlier he would have attributed to man alone. In either case we see how nature becomes the depositary of the productive activity of man.

To conclude, children's ideas on the birth of babies or on the origins of man follow the same laws as their ideas on nature in general, namely, artificialism as the starting-point and natural explanation accompanied by traces of immanent artificialism in the superior stages. But it seems that the questions they ask about birth are the source of those on general origin and not the inverse. From this it appears that in the ideas of children on birth lies the explanation of the basic interdependence of artificialism and animism. A baby being considered as at the same time artificially made and living, the child has the tendency to consider all things as possessing the same characteristics.

§ 3. THE STAGES OF SPONTANEOUS ARTIFICIALISM AND THEIR RELATIONS WITH THE DEVELOPMENT OF ANIMISM.— We are now within reach of discovering on broad lines the relations between animism and artificialism. To this end, let us distinguish the four periods in the development of artificialism and try to define, in connection with each, what is the corresponding development in animism.

The first period is that during which the child has not yet raised the question of the origin—in other words of the manufacture—of things.   The only questions about origin are those asked in the form " Where does so-and-so come from ? " and which have a spatial rather than a causal end in view.   If those questions about birth of the first type constitute a stage at all (those which consist in asking *where* the baby is before birth) it is here that this first stage should be placed.   During this period there is, if one may use the term, *diffuse artificialism*.   That means that nature is conceived as being controlled by men or at least as centring around them.   But the child does not try to define the manner of this activity and cannot give any reply to questions about origin, and thus this period is anterior to the first stages which we distinguished in analysing the manifestations of artificialism. During this period magic, animism, and artificialism are completely merged.   The world is a society of living beings controlled and directed by man.   The self and the external world are not clearly delimited.   Every action is both physical and psychical.   The only reality then is a complex of purposive actions which presuppose active beings and in this sense there is animism.   But these actions are either distantly or closely controlled by man, and in this sense, there is an artificialism at least diffuse. Moreover, this artificialism can just as well be magical as direct, from the fact that man's will acts as well at a distance as otherwise.

Take as an example of this stage Roy's first replies (those reported in § 1 of Chapter VIII)—only a part of them, it is true, for he already defines the origins of the sun (a fact which could place them just as well in the succeeding stage).   The sun, Roy says, began to exist and got bigger " *because we began to exist* " and " *because we got bigger.*"   From his point of view, then, there is spontaneous life in things (animism) but there is also the action of man on things. Only this artificialism is not spontaneously accompanied by a myth about origins and, further, it contains no magic element. Most children do not get past this period as far as the majority of natural bodies is concerned, but as soon as they try to define the origins of any particular body they thereby pass into the second period.

Or again, as examples of this first period may be taken the most primitive of those cases where it is believed that the sun, the moon and the clouds follow us. In the one case, these heavenly bodies follow us voluntarily (animism). In the other, their sole function is to follow us and look after us by giving us light and warmth—they are " made for us " (artificialism). And finally, it is we who make them move (magic).

In short, during this first period the child projects into all things the same relation which it feels to subsist between himself and his parents. On the one hand, he feels himself free and aware of his self. On the other, he knows himself to be dependent on his parents and he conceives them as being the cause of all that he possesses. Finally, he feels between himself and them a mass of participations even when he is separated from them.

The second period, which we shall call that of *mythological artificialism*, appears as soon as the child asks himself questions about the origins of things or can reply to questions which he may be asked on this subject. From this moment, the artificialism which hitherto has been diffuse becomes more sharply defined in a number of myths such as those we have recounted. Thus the sun is no longer conceived as being simply dependent on men, but as having been made by men out of a stone or a match. Between these myths (usually " liberated " but sometimes spontaneous, as the study of children's questions proves), and the diffuse artificialism of the first period, there are at the roots—other things being equal—the same relations as those that M. Lévy-Bruhl has stressed as existing between the first stage of primitive mentality, where participations are simply felt and lived, and a second stage where participations begin to be formulated and thus give rise to myths about origins.

It is to this period of mythological artificialism that the first stage distinguished in the earlier chapters must be assigned, that is, the stage during which there is integral artificialism and where the sun, the sky, the night, mountains, rivers, etc., are directly manufactured by men. During this period animism and artificialism are still completely complementary, things are manufactured and living at one and the same time. Their manufacture is comparable to the birth of babies, which are conceived as having been to some extent moulded with the hands, even when the child knows that the material of which they are composed comes from the parents themselves.

This resemblance between manufacture and birth is the more clearly marked during this period in that certain natural bodies are conceived as coming out of man. These notions are probably much more common than the children have admitted. In any case, we have noted that the wind has been identified with human breathing, fog with exhalation, rivers and the sea with spittle or urine, etc. If one thinks of the symbolical contents possible in autistic conceptions, such as the highly probable associations between water and urine and birth, between the earth and birth (children tend quite spontaneously to connect death with birth—dead people " grow again ") or even between the sky, clouds and birth, it will be seen to what extent the external world can be assimilated in children's latent tendencies to a collection of living bodies bound up with human life. Whatever these hypotheses may be worth, there remains a whole body of fact, verifiable by direct observation, which shows that during this period of mythological artificialism things appear to the child to be at the same time living and manufactured. Artificialism and animism still imply each other without let or hindrance.

We shall call the next period that of *technical artificial-*

ism. It corresponds broadly with the second of the stages distinguished in the preceding chapters (when there are three stages), that is to say conditioned (or mitigated) artificialism (a mixture of natural and artificialist explanations). In other words, this second period extends from the ages of 7–8 to 9–10 on the average. Now, as we shall see later (*Causalité Physique*) this is the age which marks the moment where the child's interest begins to turn towards the details of machines and the proceedings of human technique. It is, for example, at about 8 years on the average that boys at Geneva no less than at Paris are able to give from memory the correct explanation of the mechanism of a bicycle. Generally speaking, the child becomes capable of understanding a simple mechanical operation (a steam-engine, etc.). Ideas about crafts and the working-up of raw material become clearer. Such facts, of course, react on artificialism. Hitherto, without his asking " how ? ", the child has conceived all nature as being made by man, or even more, he has never thought of doubting the comprehensive scope of human technique. A machine seemed to him a box of magic out of which everything could be produced from nothing. Henceforth, on the contrary, the " how " of production becomes a problem for him. To state this " how " is to state the difficulties and to renounce belief in human omnipotence ; in short, it is to learn to know reality and its laws. Thenceforth the reaction of these new interests on artificialism will be thus. The child will continue to attribute to man the general disposition of things whilst limiting his activity to operations which are technically realisable. For the rest, it is things which, set in motion by men have perfected nature by natural processes. At this point artificialism is on the wane ; it is supported, in fact, by the laws of nature. This is the mitigated artificialism which we call " technical artificialism." For example, the child no longer asserts that everything connected with the circulation of water is man's handiwork. He will say that man fashioned watercourses and the beds of lakes, but that water falls from the clouds by a natural process. The planets are no longer the exclusive work of man—they result, in the child's view, from the combustion and condensation of smoke clouds, the smoke itself having come from chimneys, etc. The explanation, it will be seen, ceases to mythological. It becomes defined in two senses, it demands of human technique only that which the latter could reasonably be expected to produce and it assigns to natural processes the task of perfecting what man has inaugurated.

As to the relations between technical artificialism and animism, in comparison with those of the preceding periods they show a retrogressive movement—artificialism and animism become contradictory. In point of fact, if artificialism weakens it is because the resistance of material things is in part recognised. For the purely moral laws which, from the child's point of view, have hitherto ruled nature, there is gradually substituted a physical determinism. One may definitely assert that during this period children no longer attribute life to everything but they distinguish imparted movement from inherent movement and attribute life and consciousness only to those bodies animate with inherent movement (the planets, the wind, etc.). As a consequence, the manufactured bodies cease to be regarded as living, and living bodies cease to be regarded as manufactured. From this time on, children assert explicitly that such and such an object cannot know or feel anything " because it has been made."

Finally, towards the ages of 9–10 there appears a fourth period of *immanent artificialism*. This period corresponds to the third of the stages which we distinguished in the preceding chapters (where the explanations offered by children in respect of a given phenomenon were classified in three stages), that is to say in the stage where the idea that nature is made by man disappears entirely. But as we often emphasised in connection with the details of explanations given by children, artificialism is only eclipsed then under its human or theological form to be transferred simply to nature itself. In other words, nature inherits the attributes of man and manufactures in the style of the craftsman or artist. The facts, it will be remembered are as follows. It is at first finalism which persistently outlives the artificialism of the later stages. Thus the sun, even when it is conceived of as being entirely independent of human manufacture, still is held to have been " made for " the purpose of giving us warmth, light, etc. The clouds, though due to natural evaporation, continue to be " made for " the purpose of bringing us rain, etc. All nature is imbued with purpose. Next comes the idea of the generation of bodies which is comparable to birth—the stars come out of the sun and go back into it sometimes, lightning condenses into planets or comes out of the planets, etc. Then finally comes the idea of material force, that is, of spontaneous activity attributed to each thing of itself. The word " make " as employed by the child on every occasion is, in this respect, very significant. Nature itself thus becomes the depositary of the artificialism of the later stages. Due allowances made, it is the artificialism which M. Brunschwig has so admirably treated in Aristotle's physics.

Naturally, the ideas of finality, of material force and many others, current in this period, date from much earlier, and it is from the very beginning of its development that the child endows things with human activity. That is precisely what animism consists of, and in one sense, one may, even in the earliest periods, call animism an immanent artificialism. But the period now under discussion which begins at about the ages of 9–10 is marked by the junction of two very distinct currents, one of which comes from the animism and the other from the artificialism of the preceding periods. Thus certain characteristics attributed henceforth to material bodies are of animistic origin, such as the consciousness and the life, with which about one-third of the children of this fourth period still endow the planets. Other characteristics are of artificialist origin as, for example, the idea of the generation of material bodies by means of each other, which seems to come from the idea of manufacture (all artificial production during the second stage being considered as concerned with living matter). Finally, most characteristics have an origin both animistic and artificialist, such as the ideas of material force, integral finalism, etc.

It is obvious that what has just been said of the third and fourth periods concerns only the child's physics. In the measure that he has received religious instruction, he differentiates between physical and theological factors during these periods, and the human or transcendent artificialism of the first two periods comes to be transferred to God himself. In this case, the creation of the world will continue to be interpreted in terms of an integral artificialism whilst the detail of the phenomena will be interpreted in terms of natural processes and of an artificialism increasingly immanent.

§ 4. THE ORIGINS OF ARTIFICIALISM.—It would be fantastic to try to assign a sole originating cause to child artificialism. A phenomenon so complex can only be the product of many factors. We shall distinguish here, as we have done in the cases of animism and magic, two sorts of causes, those of an individual nature, that is those bound up with the consciousness which the child derives from his own activity, and those of a social nature, that is those bound up with the relations felt by the child to exist between him and his environment and particularly between him and his parents. But whereas individual causes appeared to preponderate in the cases of animism and magic, in the case of artificialism it is the social causes which carry most weight.

Social causes are two in number, namely, the bond of material dependence which the child recognises as existing between himself and his parents and the spontaneous veneration in which he holds them.

Under the first head we can be brief. From the outset

of his conscious life, the child is immediately dependent on his parents' activity for food, comfort, shelter and clothing which is all organised from above for him in accordance with his requirements. The most natural idea for him, the idea he cannot escape from without doing violence to his habits is that all nature centres round him and has been organised by his parents or by human beings in general. " Diffuse artificialism " can be considered then as the immediate product of the feeling of material dependence which the child bears towards his parents. As to mythological artificialism it may be presumed, as we have already shown, that it is the problem of birth which stimulates its appearance. But the problem of birth is once more the problem of the parental function. The child feels himself to belong to his parents, he knows that they determined his arrival. Why and how ? The trend of this interest plays a considerable part in the artificialist solutions which the child proffers.

The second point, namely, the deification of parents will also not detain us long. M. Bovet in a series of remarkable studies[1] has deduced from child psychology a whole theory of the origin of religion which is of supreme interest in this connection.

Psychoanalysts have shown that between the different manifestations of love—filial, parental, and sexual love, etc., there is not heterogeneity but identity of origin. Flournoy, inspired by this view, has tried to prove, particularly in his *Mystique moderne*,[2] that religious emotion is nothing other than sublimated sexual emotion. M. Bovet, trying to widen the field of survey by studying not only mysticism but religion in all its extension has been led to reverse the terms of the problems. If in fact there is a relationship between sexual love, mystic love,

---

[1] P. Bovet, "Le sentiment religieux," *Rev. de Théol. et de Phil.* (Lausanne), 1919, pp. 157-175. "Le sentiment filial et la religion," *Ibid.*, 1920, pp. 141-153. And principally *Le sentiment religieux et la psychologie de l'enfant*, Neuchâtel and Paris (Delachaux et Niestlé), 1925, p. 173.

[2] Th. Flournoy, "Une mystique moderne," *Arch. de Psych.*, 1915 (Vol. XV).

and the love of a child for its mother, must one regard, as Freud does, filial love as sexual and incestuous, or are the diverse forms of love to be regarded as differentiations of one primitive filial love ? This is not only a question of terms. In religious psychology, the line of demarcation is very clear. Sublimated sexual love, it is true, does not cover the whole of religious emotion. But on the other hand, the transference and the sublimation of the primitive filial sentiment furnishes the key to the problem. The essence of religious emotion is, in fact, a mingling *sui generis* of love and of fear which one can call respect. Now this respect is not to be explained except by the relations of the child with its parents. It is the filial sentiment itself.

Here are the facts. The child in extreme youth is driven to endow its parents with all of those attributes which theological doctrines assign to their divinities— sanctity, supreme power, omniscience, eternity, and even ubiquity. We must scrutinise each of these points for they lead straight to the very core of artificialism.

It is a common observation that babies attribute to their parents complete virtue. As M. Bovet has remarked, the proof of this lies in the gravity of the crisis provoked by the discovery of a fault and particularly of an injustice in the parents. The case may be recalled, which we quoted from amongst some recollections of childhood, of the child who, accused and punished in error, ended by convincing himself that he was guilty of the fault with which he was charged.

The supreme power of the parent is still more essential to the point of view with which we are dealing. There are many instances on record of children attributing extraordinary powers to their parents. A little girl asked her aunt to make it rain.[1] M. Bovet quotes Hebbel's recollections of childhood. The child, who thought its parents all-powerful, was staggered to find them one day lamenting over the sight of their fruit-trees ravaged by

[1] Spielrein, *Arch. de Psych.*, Vol. XVIII, p. 307.

a storm. There was then a limit to his father's power !
Spontaneous conduct such as this can be instanced indefinitely and our own data confirm in the clearest manner
M. Bovet's thesis. Not only is it evident that the omnipotence, with which the youngest of the children we have
examined endow mankind in general, must be derived
from the unlimited powers which they attribute to their
parents, but furthermore we have often come across
precise evidence in the shape of facts bearing directly on
the point. We have frequently asked children if their
fathers could have made the sun, the Salève, the lake, the
earth, or the sky. They do not hesitate to agree. Here
is a myth which is very significant, in which the omnipotence of the parents is, it is true, transferred to a
symbolic plane but nevertheless remains quite clearly
defined :—

Marsal (20) is a defective who, it will be remembered,
told us not without some romancing, that the sun had
been thrown up into the air, like a balloon, by his ancestors.
We asked him what these ancestors were : " *I think there
must have been some one to make them.*—And what about
God ?—*Well, to tell the truth I don't much believe in God.
To my mind there must have been something that started the
human reign.*—How did it come about ?—*God couldn't
have taken little bits and made a man. The two sexes must
have come together. There was an old man, not tremendously
old, but old all the same, and he had a woman with him who
was about the same age.*" Marsal had begun to adopt a
serious air. We asked him to describe this woman. He
said : " *Her face is rather like my mother's. I like my
mother more than anything in the whole world.*" As to the
old man he naturally is like his father, without a beard,
with the same features and the same eyes. He is simply
a little younger. These are the ancestors who, according
to Marsal, built the earth and made the sun come forth
from volcanoes.

Such a myth evidently symbolises what little children
are limited to feeling within them, namely, that the world
was made by their parents.

As to the omniscience that the child attributes to his

parents, it is revealed clearly enough by the crisis provoked when he finds his parents out in ignorance or error.
Here as usual the child's convictions are implicit, not
formulated and even informulable, and it is only when the
conviction decays that it is seen to have existed. A very
clear fact related by M. Bovet is the recollection of Edmund
Gosse of first hearing his father say something which was
not quite true. The passage which is of the greatest
interest should be read in its full context.[1] Here we
shall only quote the following: "Here was the appal-
ling discovery, never suspected before, that my Father
was not as God, and did not know everything. The
shock was not caused by any suspicion that he was not
telling the truth but by the awful proof that he was
not as I had supposed omniscient."

We have already remarked the following case : Del, at
6½ (see *Language and Thought*, Chapter V) asks questions
in a way which implies that there is an answer to everything and that the adult knows the answer. "*Why do
you ever make mistakes ?*" he once asked his teacher ?
At 7 ; 2, Dell asks fewer questions about fortuitous occurrences as if he had given up trying to justify everything.
We put to him then his own questions of the year before
and he found them absurd and insoluble. "*If Papa does
not know everything how can I*," he once said. In the
interval Del had passed through a crisis of scepticism in
regard to adult knowledge, a crisis such as M. Bovet has
described and which is of great importance in the child's
thought. In fact, at the time when Del believed in adult
omniscience, he considered the world as a harmoniously
regulated whole from where chance was excluded, whereas
during the period of scepticism of which we are now
speaking he renounces the idea that everything is to be
justified and is ready to admit chance and natural causes.

Parents are also held by younger children to be independent of time. Children have asserted to us that
when their daddies came into the world, the lake was not

[1] Edmund Gosse, *Father and Son.* Chapter II.

yet hollowed out and the Salève was not yet built. Marsal's myth has just shown how children tend to conceive their parents as being anterior to the origin of things.

Finally, in connection with ubiquity every one can recall the feeling of being followed and watched which guilty children experience. The happy child also believes himself constantly to be known, understood and accompanied. Adult omniscience expands into omnipresence.

Such then seems to be the starting-point of the filial emotion—that parents are gods. M. Bovet has very justly remarked in this connection how the notion of God, when imposed in the early stages of education, is useless and embarrassing. Insistence on divine perfection means setting up in God a rival to the parents, and M. Bovet has quoted some very curious facts to illustrate this point. If, on the other hand, such insistence is not made and the child is left to his spontaneous conceptions he finds nothing very sacred about God. He is just a man like anyone else, who lives in the clouds or in the sky, but who, with this exception, is no different from the rest. "A person who works for his master." "A man who earns wages," these are of the type of definition that working-class children of about 7–8 give of God. The child's remark has been quoted who, watching some navvies at work, hailed them as "Gods" ("des Bons Dieux"). A great number of children have also told us that there were many Gods, the word for them being generic, just as are the words "sun" and "moon" for children who believe in the existence of numberless suns. In short every time that children have introduced God into their answers, it has been romancing (as if God were a fairy or a Father Christmas), or otherwise, has been to assign to God an activity which is, in truth, human. Certain children, for example, have hesitated in attributing the lake to God or to men, saying : "I don't know if it was God or some men who did it."

Then comes the crisis. There is necessarily a limit to this deification of the parents. M. Bovet says : "For a

long while the existence of this rationalistic and philosophical period round about the sixth year has been
affirmed ; it is generally put forward as an *awakening* of
intellectual curiosity ; we believe it should be regarded
rather as a *crisis*, intellectual and moral at the same time,
similar in many ways to that of adolescence." [1] The consequences of such a phenomenon are evident. The feelings
experienced by the child up till now towards his parents
must be directed elsewhere, and it is at this period that
they are transferred to the God with which his education
has provided him. It has been said that the child
" divinifies " his parents. M. Bovet retorts with reason
that it can better be said, that he " paternalises " God,
at the moment when he ceases to regard his parents as
perfect. From the point of view of which we are treating,
the powers ceded to parents come to be progressively
attributed to more men or to older men and ultimately
to " early man." Or finally, in certain cases, the crisis
proceeds to such lengths that it is artificialism *en bloc*
which is called in question. However, in general, a more
or less attenuated artificialism survives for some years
after the crisis at the age of 6 to 7.

To conclude, it is clear enough how far the filial sentiment may be the source of artificialism. The parents
being gods, it is obvious that from the child's point of
view, the world is due to their activity or to that of men
in general. It will be clear also why we have not distinguished in detail between human and divine or theological artificialism. They are certainly not to be distinguished at any rate until about 7 or 8 years. Either
God is a person or men are gods, or else God is the chief
of men, but it is by the transference of the filial sentiment.
Above all it is clear how original child artificialism is,
both in its origin and in its manifestations. It would
be in consequence an error to attribute it to religious
education imposed from above and badly assimilated
by the child.

[1] Bovet, *loc. cit.*, 1919, pp. 170-1.

If we pass now to the individual factors which have produced or encouraged artificialism, we find facts which are much more prosaic. But as psychoanalytic studies have shown, children's thoughts are moulded by narcissist interests—even by "auto-erotic" interests, as Freud terms those which attach themselves to all organic functions—as much as by parental complexes. The individual factors of artificialism will then be two in number, namely, the feeling of the child that he is a cause, on the one hand, thanks to his organism, on the other, thanks to his manual activity in general.

The first point is more important than it may seem, but being bound up with all sorts of taboos and repressions we only found faint traces of it in our interrogations. It has been shown how interested the younger children are in their digestive processes and in micturition, and we have seen clear traces of thoughts about micturition in the beliefs relating to the origin of rivers. Having studied the notions of children on the air and the wind (see *Causalité Physique*, Chapter I), it would be hard to doubt that respiration (in the shape of the production of wind) and even wind in the intestines plays a part in forming the child's conception of the world.

The second point is all important. The child's thought is in close connection with his muscular activity. Stanley Hall [1] has shown very clearly the extent to which children's curiosity is related to manual experiments and to the destruction of objects. The observations of Mlles Audemars and Lafendel at the Maison des Petits at the Institute of Jean-Jacques Rousseau have shown how far manual work is essential to the child's mental development. These excellent teachers have come to distinguish three stages in the child's mental development in connection with the relations between thought and manual activity. During the first stage (3–4) the child's thought is "stemmed by action." This is the stage of manipulation. During the second (5–7) "there is henceforth an alliance

[1] *Pedag. Sem.*, Vol. X, 1903.

between motor and mental activity," "action provokes thoughts." During the third stage (after 7 or 8) "work becomes orderly, movement is controlled by thought, because thought precedes action." [1] The full significance of these statements comes out when it is remembered to what an extent at the Maison des Petits, the groundwork of arithmetic and of the whole intellectual life of the child is spontaneously derived from manipulation and from the spontaneous adaptation to the exigencies of manual games. That is to say that thought, directly it becomes conscious of itself, is connected with making things. Mach, Rignano and Goblot have defined reasoning as a " mental experience," or a construction in thought. With regard to the child it is almost a " manufacture of thought " of which we should speak.

Finally, to be complete we must mention a factor accessory to artificialism, namely, language. It is evident that the verbs " to make," " to form," etc., that we apply to nature are pregnant with artificialism. But it is also evident that language is not enough to explain child artificialism, here, as usual, there is simply convergence between the regressive tendencies of language and child mentality. Moreover, as always, the child is original ; it is not so much the word " to do " (faire) as the words " to get done " (faire faire) that he most often uses ("le vent fait faire avancer les nuages," "le soleil fait faire pousser les fleurs," etc.). This expression "faire faire " has a significance that is both animistic and artificialist, it implies an external motor force and an internal principle of realisation.

§ 5. THE ORIGINS OF IDENTIFICATION AND THE CAUSES OF THE DECLINE OF ARTIFICIALISM AND ANIMISM.—It cannot be actually as the result of experience that the child comes to abandon his animism and his artificialism. No direct experience can prove to a mind inclined towards animism that the sun and the clouds are neither alive

[1] M. Audemars and L. Lafendel, *La Maison des Petits de l'Institut J.-J. Rousseau*, Neuchâtel and Paris (Delachaux and Niestlé), 1923.

nor conscious. Neither can adult teaching undeceive the child, since the child does not speak of his animism enough to make the adult expressly seek to supplant it, and also, the child animist incorporates into his own mentality even the best lessons, whatever their subject. As to artificialism, it rests on tendencies of mind that no observation of things will eclipse until precisely such time as the child is ready to abandon all its preconceptions.

The direct pressure of reality on the child's mind cannot, therefore, explain the decline of animism and artificialism, so much as a change in the general trend of its mind. To what must this change be ascribed? The answer varies according as attention is directed to the social or to the individual factors of animism and artificialism.

As regards the social factors, the crisis M. Bovet describes in which the child realises first that his parents, and then that men in general are not all-powerful and do not rule the world is enough to account for the decline of transcendent artificialism. This crisis has evidently a reaction on animism, in leading the child to regard things as much less preoccupied with our doings than they at first seem.

As regards the individual factors, that is to say the factors in this continual assimilation of the world to the self, which causes the child to treat all things as personal, as like ourselves and as gyrating around us, it seems that the progressive decrease in the child's egocentricity is enough to explain how he gradually comes to assume an objective standpoint in regard to things and consequently to abandon the ideas of participation on which animism and artificialism are nourished. Now, the decrease in egocentricity which becomes very marked after the ages of 7 or 8 is due as has been shown elsewhere (*Language and Thought*, Chapters I–III) to the manner in which child thought becomes progressively socialised.

Liberation from the bond that ties him exclusively to his parents and the freeing of his own point of view or self seem thus to be the two principal factors that explain the progressive decline of animism and of artificialism. How next is the progressive evolution of artificialist causality into the higher forms of causality to be explained?

These higher forms, which the child attains spontaneously, are, as has been shown, causality by identification of substance, the form modelled on the notions of condensation and rarefaction, and a certain primitive atomism or synthesis of elements.

The attempt to see identity is very clear in the stages above the ages of 7 or 8. The sun and the moon are identified with the clouds or the air. From the air arise steam and water on the one hand, and fire on the other. Lightning is occasioned by the transformation of the clouds of smoke into fire. Earth and rock are conceived as two aspects of the same substance, etc. But these transformations imply condensations and rarefactions. The sun is made of air or of wind that has been " squeezed," rock is compressed earth and earth is rock broken up into particles and dust. Finally, these condensations and rarefactions suppose the existence of particles or elements and this is clearly shown by children of the age of 11 or 12.

It would certainly seem, therefore, that, as M. E. Meyerson would have it, the first positive form of causality is identification. Only, identification involves a past. It cannot arise all at once and the identifications made by intelligence during the different periods of its development have neither the same value nor form. What was identified by the pre-Socratics we to-day distinguish and what we identify appeared heterogeneous to the pre-Socratics. What then is the genesis of identification in the child? As far as we have been able to observe the genetic progression appears to be as follows.

The child starts by establishing *dynamic participations* between things—the clouds and the rain are attracted to one another; cold, frost and snow are attracted to one another; the wind and the clouds act on one another;

the clouds act on the sun, driving it or chasing it or attracting it, etc. At the stage when all things are man-made and alive, these participations merely imply series of actions at a distance half psychical, half physical, without any real community of being. Certain of these dynamic participations, however, are already continued into participations of substance, that is to say that bodies separated in space are sometimes conceived by the child as directly resulting one from the other (see Chapter IV, § 2, the examples of the air and the shadow).

According as man ceases to be a god in the child's eyes and as nature appears less to gravitate around us and our interests, the child seeks to explain things by means of themselves. Participations between things and ourselves have so far given rise to myths concerning the manufacture of things by man. Henceforth, and according as things become detached from man, participations between the things themselves give rise to myths of *generation*. The sun is the offspring of the clouds, the lightning and the stars are produced by the sun, the wind has collected together to form a cloud, etc. We say generation and not yet strictly identification, since things are still regarded as alive and conscious and because the child does not at first state the nature of the transformation. These myths are entirely comparable to the myth of Vo (§ 2) according to which man has been produced by a worm that has come out of a bubble from the bottom of the water.

From generation to identification strictly speaking, there is only the difference which separates dynamistic from mechanistic thought ; according as things are deprived of life and spontaneous force, the transformation of the clouds into the sun and moon, or of the wind into cloud, becomes mechanistic and the child then turns to the form modelled on notions of *condensation* and of atomistic *composition*. But to explain how children arrive at the necessity of mechanical explanation we must know how they explain natural movements. This involves a detailed study of child physics and the analysis of the explanations children give not only concerning the origin of things but concerning the detail of phenomena and the way in which transformations and movements take place. This will be attempted in the sequel to this work *La Causalité physique chez l'enfant.*

APPENDIX

Note on the relations between belief in efficacy and magic, in connection with §§ 2 and 3 of Chapter IV

In order to dispel all ambiguity we think it useful to say in a few words why we have taken the liberty of using in child psychology the term " magic," which is customarily restricted to a purely sociological use.

In the course of discussions on this subject with I. Meyerson (see p. 157), a difference has arisen between us. I. Meyerson, amongst others, has pointed out that the idea of magic implies actions and beliefs having a collective aspect. This involves in the first case a question of fact, which is, that in all the examples described the magic fits into a social setting. But this is not a chance, a mere fact of circumstance. Reflection would seem to suggest that the content and the form of magical phenomena are bound up closely enough with social actions and with communication between individuals ; its symbolical and formal character, its grammar and its syntax imply an adaptation, and more often a long adaptation, to the sum total of the rites and habits of the group—the language of magic, that is, has a history. The actual form of a spell can show traces of its character. The nature of a conviction must be influenced by the belief that it affects the life of the entire group. These " reverberations " give it not only increased strength but the character of an action with a definite and productive end. A protective conviction which is effective is a different thing from a belief in an evil spell which fails.

Thus, on the one hand, the case of spells or charms

does not exhaust the whole of magic, even from the point of view of pure psychology; on the other hand, it is doubtful whether the nature, and above all the degree, of the belief in spells is the same in the collective cases of adults as in the individual cases of children.

In the cases of children themselves, it is perhaps possible to make certain distinctions :—

(1) In some cases appeal is made to an external power, much more than to a genuine action exerted on the world. In these cases it may be doubted if the question of a spell really arises or if it is a question of oscillations in psychological tension and of attempts to raise this tension by means of processes such as those so well treated by P. Janet.

(2) In other cases there has been personal " experience " accompanied with success and application to a second event appearing in similar conditions. This may be regarded as a form of causal sequence or motive, more nearly approaching a spell than the former, but distinguished, however, by two characteristics. On the one hand, there is certainly present sequence and succession—I. Meyerson, holding that cases of supposed causality and, above all, of magic spells suppose some kind of simultaneity between the event and the gesture or rite necessary to bring it about ; as he has pointed out elsewhere, the " cause " is in this case an aspect or part of the event. On the other hand, the belief the child places in this sort of action is weak and not continuous, in opposition to the strength and continuity of the belief in magical spells.

(3) Finally, there are the cases where at the basis of the child's belief, lies a " social " belief (that is, a general belief or one that the child believes to be general or widespread). For the child, to be

general means equally to be necessary ; to have a quality of inevitability. According to I. Meyerson, only the combination of a child's wish with a belief of this type can give rise to cases which may legitimately be compared to cases of magic spells. And here a distinction must be made between the beliefs the child has acquired from the adult social world and those of strictly childish origin.

This last case would be according to I. Meyerson the most favourable. He would suppose a society of children with its own beliefs, rites or rite-games, rites of initiation and of membership, rites of progression and of creation, rites of exclusion and penalties, language and symbolism —all corresponding to the desires and fears of children as distinct from those of adults. The Boy Scouts with their own special games, songs and symbolism, prove, in his opinion, that it is possible in societies where there is a firmer solidarity than in ours, to find groups of children organised in this way. Such a study would certainly be profitable. It would alone make it possible to see both the original nature of magical causality to the child and the nature of the phenomenon of magic apart from its efficacy. Like every research of social psychology it would naturally have to embrace the study of the phenomenon in its period of full sway, in full social activity ; the study of the acquisition of its beliefs by the individual child ; the study of their variations under the action of social factors and individual experience, and the study of the loss of its beliefs.

The general significance of all these remarks is that to create an atmosphere of magic there must have been a long period of conformity to it.

For our part we fully realise that in all adult society, magic is an eminently social reality and that belief in magical efficacy, therefore, possesses an intensity and a continuity that make it incomparable with the weak and extremely discontinuous beliefs of children. We are also convinced, like I. Meyerson, that in the functioning of any social institution, it is hopeless to try to separate the social from the individual factor ; the social process and its reverberations in individual minds are one and the same thing, or, more exactly they form two aspects of the same reality. We have thus chosen our vocabulary without any intention of identifying individual childish beliefs with primitive social beliefs or of opposing a social psychology to sociological research after the manner of G. Tarde.

We have simply made the following working hypothesis. It has seemed to us that amongst the very numerous and complex characteristics of magic described by sociologists, the belief in efficacy at a distance was the hardest to explain psychologically by studying it in relation to social life instead of isolated by itself. We have, therefore, assumed, solely as a working hypothesis, that there was continuity between the purely individual idea of efficacy and the idea implied in the social beliefs of a magical type. This does not in the least suggest that the social beliefs have not—precisely because they are social—an infinitely greater power of coercion and crystallisation. It means simply that they are made possible by means of an individual psychological substructure.

From this psychological point of view we thus define " magical " phenomenon by the idea of efficacy at a distance and we distinguish two types :—

(1) Individual child magic, in which the belief is weak and probably discontinuous ; and
(2) Magic strictly speaking, or collective magic, characterised by various qualities *sui generis*, amongst them being a much more intense and systematic belief.

It is precisely because of this attempt to seek continuity in the development of the idea of efficacy that the beliefs quoted in § 2 of Chapter IV were all strictly individual child beliefs, that is to say, that they had escaped adult influence and broadly speaking were not due to communication between child and child.

Evidently it would be desirable to supplement our study of the notion of efficacy at a distance by a complete research into the constitution of the child's social magical beliefs. It is here, according to I. Meyerson, that the psychological analysis of what is strictly speaking magic should begin. In our opinion, on the contrary, such a research should be made in conjunction with a study of individual beliefs in efficacy.

In the absence of such work on the children of savages or on societies of civilised children, we may suppose, according to the material collected in connection with § 2, Chapter IV, that with children this social magic consists above all in a consolidation of the belief in efficacy, a consolidation that naturally becomes all the firmer according as the child succeeds in absorbing adult social beliefs or practices.

The following is an example : The young man who told us his personal procedure when playing marbles (p. 142) recalls the following collective fact. He and his friends had the habit, although Protestants, of making the sign of the cross on the marbles they were about to play with to make them go well. In so far as the memory is exact, this custom arose simply from an act of imitation, and ended by the progressive formation of a rite according to which each player adapted himself to the idea that it must be efficacious. The same young man has the impression that such practices were much richer and more complicated ; but he can only recall this detail.

A particular case such as this obviously proves nothing. We shall, therefore, leave the question open, whilst stating that the designation of " magic " to denote the individual beliefs described, is simply intended to permit the idea of a continuity between the notion of efficacy implied in these beliefs and the notions implied by the strictly social magical rites. Apart from this question of terminology and the working hypothesis involved, we are entirely in agreement with Meyerson's criticism.   In particular we agree firmly with him as to the necessity of distinguishing what are, strictly speaking, beliefs in efficacy (whether individual, like those characterising the cases quoted in § 2 of Chapter IV, or social), from the simple means of protection intended to relieve the psychological tension, and from the forms of causality dependent purely on phenomena that lie at the basis of sequence or succession.

INDEX OF NAMES

GENERAL INDEX